Linguistics

Reference Sources in the Humanities Series

James Rettig, Series Editor

The Performing Arts: A Guide to the Reference Literature. By Linda Keir Simons

American Popular Culture: A Guide to the Reference Literature. By Frank W. Hoffman

Philosophy: A Guide to the Reference Literature. Second Edition. By Hans E. Bynagle

Journalism: A Guide to the Reference Literature. Second Edition. By Jo A. Cates

Children's Literature: A Guide to Information Sources. By Margaret W. Denman-West

Reference Works in British and American Literature. Second Edition. By James K. Bracken

Reference Guide to Mystery and Detective Fiction. By Richard Bleiler

Linguistics: A Guide to the Reference Literature. Second Edition. By Anna L. DeMiller

Linguistics

A Guide to the Reference Literature

Second Edition

Anna L. DeMiller

2000
Libraries Unlimited, Inc.
Englewood, Colorado

LIBRARIES UNLIMITED, INC.
P.O. Box 6633
Englewood, CO 80155-6633
1-800-237-6124
www.lu.com

Library of Congress Cataloging-in-Publication Data

DeMiller, Anna L.
     Linguistics : a guide to the reference literature / Anna L.
DeMiller. -- 2nd ed.
              p.   cm. -- (Reference sources in the humanities series)
     Includes indexes.
     ISBN 1-56308-619-0 (cloth)
     1. Reference books--Linguistics Bibliography. 2. Reference
books--Language and languages Bibliography. I. Title. II. Series.
Z7001.D45 1999
[P121]
016.41--dc21   99-16318
                                                                          CIP

Contents

Part 3
LANGUAGES

Preface to Reference Sources in the Humanities Series

Every discipline continuously renews its reference literature to record new theories, revised theses, discoveries, deaths, and developments in the application of theory. New editions of standard works and new titles appear from time to time, while serials bibliographies index each year's outpouring of journal articles, monographs, and Festschriften. Furthermore, new media appear and new forms of reference tools develop to make optimal use of each new medium's strengths, opportunities, and features. This series, Reference Sources in the Humanities, takes as its purpose the identification, description, and organization of the reference literature of the humanities disciplines. This series, emphasizing the Anglo-American reference literature of recent decades, has been planned to meet the needs of undergraduates, graduate students, professors exploring adjunct disciplines, librarians building and using reference collections, and intellectually curious adults interested in a systematic, self-guided study of the humanities. It emphasizes print resources—vital both to current and retrospective understanding of the reference literature of each of the humanities—but it also includes the most recent electronic sources.

Like bibliographic guides to the literature of any discipline, guides in this series are intended to serve various users in different ways. Students being initiated into the ways of a discipline can use these guides to learn the structure of the discipline's secondary literature, to find sources that will enable them to find definitions of specialized terms, to identify significant historical figures, and to gain an overview of a topic. Specialists may use them to refresh their memories about once-familiar sources and to advise their students on approaches to problems. Librarians will use them to build and evaluate reference collections and to answer patron questions.

The Reference Sources in the Humanities Series is designed to serve all of these users and purposes. Each title in the series is organized principally by reference genre, including types specific to each discipline. As electronic reference works have evolved, they have blended the boundaries between and among genre. These have been placed in appropriate chapters, sometimes integrated with print resources, other times set apart because of their unique characteristics. This organization will facilitate their efficient use by reference librarians, a group trained to think in terms of reference genre (e.g., encyclopedias, dictionaries, indexes and abstracts, biographical directories, bibliographies) within subject categories, when they seek a particular type of reference work in one of the humanities disciplines. Because no discipline's reference literature can completely convey its most recent discoveries, each title also includes information on key journals, associations, and research centers—the sources from which much of any discipline's new knowledge emanates and the means by which that knowledge is disseminated. While each of these guides describes the reference literature of its discipline as that literature presently exists, each also contributes to that literature's renewal and growth.

James Rettig, Series Editor

Introduction to the
Second Edition

While the serious study of language has been going on for well over 2,000 years, linguistics as an academic discipline is a recent twentieth century phenomena. It developed out of the comparative philology of the nineteenth century and has long been closely allied to other disciplines, particularly anthropology, philosophy, psychology, sociology, literature, and most recently, to mathematics and computer science.

In Europe, Ferdinand de Saussure, whose early interest was in philology, wrote *Cours de linguistique generale* (Course in General Linguistics). Published posthumously in 1916, it is regarded by many as the foundation of modern linguistics. His work shifted the emphasis from the examination of written records and their analysis and interpretation to the study of the principles governing the structure of living languages.

While Saussure's ideas were being developed in Europe by such groups as the Linguistic Circle of Prague, Franz Boas and other American anthropologists were busy with descriptive studies of living American Indian languages. Works by both Boas and Edward Sapir were influential in the early development of linguistics in America. The publication of Leonard Bloomfield's *Language* in 1933 was another major step in this development. The structuralist and behaviorist views in this work influenced and dominated research and thinking for more than two decades.

The publication in 1957 of Noam Chomsky's *Syntactic Structures* signaled a radical change in approaches to the study of language. Chomsky's concept of generative grammar, later developed into transformational grammar, has seen various reformulations and been challenged in the ensuing years by proposals for alternative models. Controversy in the field subsequently reached a fever pitch at times, so much so that Randy Harris even wrote a book called *The Linguistics Wars* (New York: Oxford University Press, 1993). It was during the 1960s that the university teaching of linguistics emerged. (For additional information on the development of linguistics, refer to *The Cambridge Encyclopedia of Language*, entry 18, from which some of the above details were drawn).

This guide begins coverage of the reference literature with the year 1957, a clear turning point for linguistics. The first edition, published in 1991 with 708 entries, included, with only a few exceptions, material published or reprinted from 1957 through 1989. The second edition with 1039 entries extends coverage through 1998. A few works published early in 1999 have also been added and most of the Web sites cited were last checked in early 1999. This new edition has about 500 new entries (also counting new editions and additional volumes for works previously cited). About 50 of these new entries are for Web sites, and many other entries are enriched with URLs and e-mail addresses. To make room for new works, older citations were pruned if supplanted by later works, or if, in the case particularly of bibliographies, their content could be largely retrieved by simple database searches. Entries for printed indexes and abstracts were combined with their electronic versions into a single entry.

There is reason for the addition of so many new works in the second edition. A multitude of major and minor reference works, not only for linguistics itself but also its allied fields, have been published in the intervening years. Moreover, during this period the Internet has become a more important means of easy communication, and sites then in their infancy are now complex, rich sources of information. There have been other changes as well. Within applied linguistics, the field of translation studies, along with mathematical and computational linguistics have come into their own as disciplines. An impetus for the maturation of translation studies has been the need for understanding others in a shrinking world. This is exemplified by the creation of the European Union, which has spurred research and publication in Europe. Computational linguistics has increasingly defined itself as a separate field in tandem with developments in computing speed and storage capacity. The Web itself is now the repository of large data banks of language corpora, much of it tagged and indexed.

As the field has grown, so has its range and number of reference works. The focus of this work is on bibliographic and information sources rather than general scholarship in the field. Library users—whether undergraduates, graduate students, professors, or researchers (in linguistics or related fields)—should find this book helpful, as will librarians interested in developing collections or providing reference assistance. Since this book's largest audience is Anglo-American, the emphasis is on materials in the English language. However, because so much important research has been published in other languages, it includes selected works in other languages, particularly French and German (which this author reads), and Russian (with which the author has some familiarity). Part 3, dealing with individual languages and families, lists some works in languages other than the above, mainly other Romance languages, since in some cases the best works about a language are in that language itself. In order to provide accurate annotations about works in these languages, other reviewing or reference sources were consulted. All bibliographic information for Russian language entries has been transliterated using the conversion tables found in the user's guide to the *Transliterated Dictionary of the Russian Language: An Abridged Dictionary Consisting of Russian-to-English and English-to-Russian Sections*, edited by Eugene Garfield (Philadelphia: ISI Press, 1979).

With regard to publications cited, only monograph and serial titles are listed except for chapters 4, 10, and 11; chapters, parts of books, and issues of or articles in journals are generally excluded. There are citations to a few critical microfilm or mimeograph items. Web sites are not stable in the same way print or microfilm are, nor can the credit for authorship always be as certain, so a number of additional considerations—although none absolute—were used to guide decisions for inclusion: stability over a period of a year or more which often means group or organization-sponsored rather than an individual effort; maintained and kept up-to-date; scholarly rather than popular; non-commercial; and in English.

A number of the decisions to exclude certain materials were made in order to keep this work to a reasonable length. Certain types of bibliographies are not included: the numerous local language bibliographies published by the Summer Institute of Linguistics (see entry 130 for a bibliography of these publications); the many older documents found in ERIC (which J. G. Drazan has gathered together in *An Annotated Bibliography of ERIC Bibliographies 1966-1980* (Greenwood Press, 1982); those bibliographies reproduced and distributed by the Indiana University Linguistics Club through 1991 (see entry 113); and bibliographies that are essentially compilations from database searches with no added-value.

Part 1 on general linguistics encompasses the traditional areas of general or theoretical linguistics: historical and comparative linguistics, morphology, phonetics, phonology, semantics, and syntax. It does not include speech and hearing, language disabilities, non-verbal communication, sign language, or poetics and stylistics. Part 1 has chapters listing some types of reference sources not found in Part 2 and Part 3; these are professional associations and societies, research resources, and core periodicals.

Part 2 deals with some areas closely allied to linguistics: applied linguistics, mathematical and computational linguistics, psycholinguistics, semiotics, and sociolinguistics. Applied linguistics is the largest chapter in this part even with the exclusion of most materials for the teaching of a particular language or languages, although language teaching in general is covered as is English as a second or foreign language.

Part 3 on languages encompasses works covering many languages as well as those devoted to an individual language or a particular language group (branch, family, etc.). Language study is sometimes thought of as empirical, or practical and applied, compared to linguistic study which is theoretical, or abstract. The reality is that different linguists work at greater or lesser degrees of abstractness. Worthwhile studies of languages can be found all along the continuum. This reference work emphasizes language study at the theoretical end of the scale.

Materials on languages are organized in a hierarchical structure; however, the outline of Part 3 should not be construed as a genetic classification of languages or as reflecting the most recent research. It is simply a practical one, enabling this author to organize material in the most logical manner possible given the nature of the reference material itself and trying to accommodate changes in language classification and nomen-clature over the years. There are a number of works that were difficult to assign to a particular chapter or section. Especially problematic were reference works covering large geographic areas and/or encompassing many types of languages, such as a linguistic survey of India or a bibliog-raphy of Southeast Asia. The subject index should enable the reader to locate this type of material. Language Internet sites have been consolidated into chapter 19. Most of these are meta-sites that gather together the best of the Web and should facilitate the search for Web sites of any particular language, group of languages, or language family.

To effectively research a language, group, or family of languages, the reader should be aware that while works are listed at the lowest possible level of the hierarchy, there may be pertinent materials at higher levels. For example, a reader looking for works concerning the English language should consult the most specific section first (i.e., the English section), move on to the Germanic and Indo-European sections, then finally consult the general and multi-language works in chapter 19. Some languages have very little reference material published (within the scope of this work), so materials has been consolidated under a language group or even language family. For example, the Afro-Asiatic language family includes the Semitic and Berber branches; because there are no more than a handful of entries in this book for the entire family, these are all consolidated under the Afro-Asiatic heading.

A large number of reference works could have gone into Part 3. It was necessary to be selective in choosing only the major language atlases and works dealing with the genetic classification of languages. In regard to surveys and handbooks only those having ready-reference value could be included. In the case of dictionaries and grammars, bibliographies of these types of works are listed rather than the individual titles. In general, coverage is more comprehensive for a language than for its dialects, for works that deal with many languages, and for less commonly studied languages.

For historical linguists, old serial literature, wherever published, is very important. Since indexing and abstracting services generally begin coverage only with more recent serial literature and frequently do not cover such materials as anthologies, dissertations, chapters, and Fest-schriften, coverage of older bibliographies and ones with such types of materials is quite liberal.

In addition to the usual information of author (editor, compiler), title, imprint, pagination, and volumes, a monographic citation includes other information about the character of the work such as indexes, illustrations, bibliographies, and maps. It also provides, when such information is available, LC card number, ISBN, and ED number. Evaluative annotations describe the work, how it is organized, and point out the strengths and weaknesses of certain features. Comparisons to other works are made in order to suggest alternative, more up-to-date, or more effective sources for similar information. References to other entries are made to tie previous and successive works together. With only a handful of exceptions, the author personally examined all materials cited here. In the case of reprints, either the reprint or the original was seen, usually not both.

I am grateful to a number of people who facilitated the writing of this guide. Many thanks to my editor, James Rettig, for his patience and good advice. Kudos go to the entire interlibrary loan staff at Colorado State University Libraries whom I relied heavily upon for obtaining materials. They not only processed hundreds of items for me, but did it with smiles despite an already heavy work load in the aftermath of the "Fort Collins Flood of '97." Of course, this guide could not have been written without access to other library collections and the assistance of their staffs. I would particularly like to thank those where I did most of my on-site research: the University of Colorado at Boulder, Stanford University, and the University of California at Berkeley.

Key to Abbreviations

Aufl. (Ger.) Auflage — edition
augm. (Fr.) augmenté — enlarged
Ausg. (Ger.) Ausgabe — printing, edition
Bd. (Ger.) Band — volume
bearb. (Ger.) bearbeitet — compiled, edited
Beitr. (Ger.) Beiträger — contributor
bibliog. — bibliography
bk — book
ca. — circa, about
Ch. (Russ.) chast' — part
comp(s). — compiler(s)
Dept. — Department
distr. — distributor
ed(s). — editor(s); edition
éd. (Fr.) édition — edition
ED — ERIC [Educational Resources Information Center] document
enl. — enlarged
erw. (Ger.) erweiterte — enlarged
fasc. (Fr.) fascicule — fascicle, part, number
filmog. — filmography
Fr. — French
G. (Russ) God — year
Ger. — German
glav. red. (Russ.) glavnyi redaktor — chief editor
Gos. (Russ.) Gosudarstvo — state
Hft. (Ger.) Heft — part, number
hrsg. (Ger.) herausgegeben — published, edited
Hrsg. (Ger.) Herausgeber — editor(s)
illus. — illustrations, illustrated
index — index(es), indexed
ISBN — International Standard Book Number
ISSN — International Standard Serial Number
It. — Italian
Izd. (Russ.) izdatel' — publisher; izdanie: edition
Jahrg. (Ger.) Jahrgang — annual publication
Jr. — Junior
LC — Library of Congress
Lfg. (Ger.) Lieferung — number, part

Neuaus. (Ger.) Neuausgabe	new edition
neubearb. (Ger.) neubearbeitet	revised
Neubearb. (Ger.) Neubearbeitung	revision
no. (Fr.) numero	number
No.	number
nouv. (Fr.) nouveau, nouvelle	new
Nr. (Ger.) Nummer	number
otv. (Russ.) otvetstvennyi	chief
port(s).	portrait(s)
p.	page, pages
Pt.	part
red. (Russ.) redaktor	editor
ref. (Fr.) refondue	reorganized
rev.	revised
riv. (It.) riveduto	revised
Russ.	Russian
sost. (Russ.) sostavitel'	compiler
t. (Fr.) tome	volume
T. (Ger.): Teil	part
u. (Ger.) und	and
überarb. (Ger.) überarbeiten	revised
übers. (Ger.) übersetzt	translated
URL	uniform resource locator
v.	volume(s)
veränd. (Ger.) verändert	revised
verb. (Ger.) verbesserte	improved
Vol.	volume
vollst. (Ger.) vollständig	completely
vstup. (Russ.) vstupitel'noi	introductory
vyp. (Russ.) vypusk	issue

Part 1
GENERAL LINGUISTICS

1

Dictionaries, Encyclopedias, Guides, and Surveys

The terms "dictionary" and "encyclopedia" have been broadly interpreted in this chapter to survey a range of reference sources variously calling themselves dictionaries, lexicons, indexes of terms, glossaries, encyclopedias, surveys, guides, and handbooks. The use of one of these words in a title, however, can be deceptive as, for example, some of the entries below call themselves dictionaries, but in reality provide no definitions, just indexes of terms. Some are hybrids, such as the encyclopedic dictionaries or the dictionaries that provide definitions, but also have indexes of terms for other languages.

Works listed here range from comprehensive to narrow in scope and from highly technical to very basic. Dictionaries of just traditional grammatical terms are excluded. Monolingual reference sources may be included if in English, German, or French. Bilingual and multilingual dictionaries may be included if in one or more of the above three languages. To point the user to the best of a wide choice of dictionaries, coverage is selective and annotations point out differences among similar works.

1. Abraham, Werner. **Terminologie zur neueren Linguistik.** 2. völlig neu bearb. u. erw. Aufl. Tübingen: Max Niemeyer, 1988. 2v. 1059p. index. illus. bibliog. (Germanistische Arbeitshefte: Ergänzungsreihe, 1; ISSN 0344-6700). ISBN 3-484-10605-0.

The second edition of this already excellent dictionary for contemporary linguistics has now been considerably enlarged and brought up to date. Volume 1 is A-L; volume 2 is M-Z. Entries vary in length from a few lines to a few pages though some are as long as six pages. Head terms are alphabetically arranged with English translations of the terms often given. Many definitions are drawn from original sources, most in German, but a considerable number in English as well. When a work is quoted the author's last name, date of publication, and the page numbers are given at the end of the entry. Some entries also provide references for further study. A bibliography at the beginning of volume 1 cumulates both kinds of references. Abraham has been generous in providing illustrations and cross-references throughout. The good use of space on a page and different sizes and kinds of typefaces make this dictionary a pleasure to use. For the convenience of the English language user there is an English-German index of terms. (See entry 34 for a similar German dictionary of linguistics).

2. Althaus, Hans Peter, Helmut Henne, and Herbert Ernst Wiegand, Hrsg. **Lexikon der germanistischen Linguistik**. 2. vollst. neu bearb. u. erw. Aufl. Tübingen: Max Niemeyer, 1980. 4v. 870p. index. illus. bibliog. LC 80-494571. ISBN 3-484-10396-5 (v.1-4).

Some 103 articles written by scholars in the field of German linguistics are gathered in these 4 volumes. Each article is signed by its contributor and placed under eleven different headings, covering such aspects, for example, as social, individual, ethnic and political, historical, contrastive, and literary. Each article has a substantial bibliography and many are illustrated with drawings, graphs, and diagrams. The emphasis throughout is on German scholarship and linguistics. Nevertheless, it provides a comprehensive survey of the various subfields of general linguistics. An extensive index of terms appears on pages 843-870. This is a thorough, scholarly work.

3.   Ambrose-Grillet, Jeanne. **Glossary of Transformational Grammar**. Rowley, MA: Newbury House, 1978. 166p. index. illus. bibliog. LC 78-1819. ISBN 0-88377-099-7.

The basis for this book is Noam Chomsky's work on transformational grammar. Terms are arranged in alphabetical order and defined using quotations or paraphrases from Chomsky's own texts. References indicate the source and page number of the texts, all of which are listed in a bibliography following the glossary.

The definitions here are written at an introductory level, easily understood by students with a limited linguistics background. This compares to the more technical definitions and greater number of quoted linguists in Palmatier's glossary (see entry 47). However, the latter only covers developments in transformational grammar through 1965 while this glossary carries on through to include Chomsky's *Reflections on Language* and *The Logical Structure of Linguistic Theory*, both published in 1975.

A nice feature of this work is an appendix illustrating and explaining how some basic transformations work, such as dative movement (optional), question transformation (obligatory), tag formation (optional), and WH-movement. In addition to the bibliography of texts there is another bibliography that brings together references on various controversial issues.

4.   Arab League Educational, Cultural, and Scientific Organization. **Unified Dictionary of Linguistic Terms (English-French-Arabic)**. Tunis: The League, 1989. 206p. 66p.(Arabic).

This dictionary will be of primary use to translators and students. The main part of the dictionary is an alphabetized and numbered list of 3,059 terms in English with their Arabic and French equivalents. While it covers more terms than Hanna's dictionary (see entry 28), including terms from related fields, and also provides French equivalents, it provides neither definitions nor examples which are often necessary to determine correct usage. However, it does provide a starting point for users who can then take an equivalent term and look it up in the appropriate dictionary. The main list of terms is followed by an index of French terms keyed to the English entry numbers. There is also an index of Arabic terms keyed to these same entries. (See also entries 6 and 7).

5.   Asher, R. E., ed.-in-chief, and J. M. Y. Simpson, coordinating ed. **The Encyclopedia of Language and Linguistics**. Oxford: Pergamon Press, 1994. 10v. 5644p. index. illus. bibliog. maps. LC 93-37778. ISBN 0-08-035943-4 (set).

The Encyclopedia of Language and Linguistics (ELL) is the most comprehensive of any of the multi-volume or single-volume encyclopedias published in

English. Given the size of the ELL, the only possible comparable work is the 4-volume *International Encyclopedia of Linguistics* (see entry 13) which despite the absence of the word "languages" in its title, provides excellent treatment of such. Both of these multi-volume works are targeted to the same audience so they overlap substantially, but the ELL has a broader scope as described below.

In the Introduction Asher states that he intends the ELL to be authoritative, up-to-date, comprehensive, and international in scope (p. xiii). Asher and Simpson together with members of the Honorary Editorial Advisory Board, the 34 subject editors of the Executive Editorial Board, and the more than a thousand authors representing 75 countries have, despite a few minor blemishes described below, admirably succeeded in fulfilling these goals. Their targeted audience is students and teachers in linguistics, but the encyclopedia invites and deserves a much wider readership given its wide coverage of topics beyond the core areas of linguistics to include related disciplines, interdisciplinary fields (the so-called hyphenated linguistics fields such as anthropological linguistics, sociolinguistics, and psycholinguistics), and areas of study concerned with broader issues of language and communication in society (such as law, language education, literature, politics, media, and religious languages).

The set consists of 10 volumes. The first 9 volumes contain the more than 2,000 articles totaling just over 5,000 pages. Volume 1 has the usual prefatory materials plus names of the members on the two editorial boards accompanied by short biographies, and an Alphabetical list of Articles. Articles grouped by subject into 32 sections are of three types: topical, biographical, and language. Entries vary in quality as might be expected in such a lengthy work with so many contributors. If length can be considered an indication of a topic's importance, then some articles are longer than one might expect, others shorter. For example, the article on Film is 16 pages long while the entry for Language is only 4 pages long. It is not always clear why certain topics rate a separate article, yet others do not; there is an article for Catalan (not widely spoken), but not for Cantonese (a major language), and an article for the Neolinguistic School, but not the Neogrammarian School, though information on this school can be found distributed among other articles. The biographical entries for individual scholars are mostly for those dead, but exceptions are made for a few living linguists nearing retirement. Omission of living linguists is partially offset by short biographies accompanying the names of members of the two editorial boards listed in volume 1; for example, this is where one finds particulars on Noam Chomsky. Articles contain numerous examples, illustrations, cross-references within and at the end of articles, bibliographies, and all but a very few short articles (written by one of 3 contributors) are signed.

Volume 10 of the set is a treasure trove of aids and indexes. There is a Glossary of about 3,000 entries with definitions, each accompanied by a label to show in what area of study used and with cross-references to other entries in the Glossary. A list of Languages of the World, based on the 12th edition of Grimes *Ethnologue* (see entry 572) and not meant to be exhaustive, is a handy reference to the names of varieties of language and their alternative names, an indication if a language name is felt to be offensive and should not be used, genetic affiliation, country(s) in which most widely spoken, and the estimated numbers of speakers. A List of Major Language and Linguistics Journals concentrates on those titles published in English and, while not meant to be comprehensive, nonetheless omits some core journals: *Forum Linguisticum*, *Language Sciences*, and the major

Russian linguistics journal, *Voprosy yazykoznaniya*. There is the obligatory List of Abbreviations used and a List of Logical Symbols Used as well as a section on Transcriptional Conventions and the IPA Alphabet. A Classified List of Entries complements the alphabetical list of entries repeated at the beginning of each of the first 9 volumes. This is followed by a List of Contributors together with the titles of articles they have authored and a Name Index of both persons mentioned in articles and those cited in bibliographies of articles. Some inconsistencies have crept into the names listed, for example Peirce, C. S. is also erroneously listed as Pierce, C. S. and Zholkovskii, A. K. can also be found under Żolkovsky, A. K. To cap off this final volume is an outstanding, comprehensive Subject Index which contains cross-references to foreign language terms and terms of related interest. Elsevier offers online searchable indexes for ELL. The Web home page for this *ELL Electronic Index* is either http://www.elsevier.nl/locate/ellei, or http://www.elsevier.com/locate/ellei. Free registration is required.

6.   Bakalla, Muhammad H., et al. **A Dictionary of Modern Linguistic Terms: English-Arabic & Arabic-English**. Compiled by A Committee of Arab Linguists. Beirut: Librairie du Liban, 1983. 103p. (English); 115p. (Arabic). bibliog.

The members of the Committee of Arab Linguists when compiling this dictionary were either working at or for the Arabic Language Institute of the University of Riyadh. They were attempting to put together a standardized English-Arabic vocabulary of linguistic terminology for translators and students. The first 103 pages make up an English-Arabic section. It is followed by 115 pages of Arabic-English terms. Each section has its own title page and is preceded by an introduction in the relevant language. In the latter section is a short bibliography of Arabic works. No definitions are given. Unlike so many books printed in Arabic script, the type here is clear and easy to read. Like Bakalla's bibliography of Arabic linguistics (see entry 1004) this is a well-executed, reliable work.

7.   Baraké, Bassam. **Dictionnaire de linguistique; français-Arabe: avec un index alphabétique des termes arabes**. 1ère éd. Tripoli, Liban: Jarrouss, 1985. 298p. index. bibliog. LC 86-961659.

There are no definitions provided here, only a listing of general linguistic terms in French with their Arabic equivalents and an index of Arabic terms referring back to the French terms. There is a good bibliography of dictionaries and general language books mainly in French.

8.   Baranov, A. N., and D. O. Dobrovol'skii, eds. **Anglo-russkii slovar' po lingvistike i semiotike: okolo 8,000 terminov**. Tom I. Moskva: Pomovskii i partnery, 1996. 642p. bibliog. ISBN 5-87232-028-0.

This is an English-Russian dictionary of linguistics and semiotics with 8,000 terms from A-Z. The user will find English terms followed by the equivalent Russian terms and very brief definitions in Russian. The definitions, synonyms, cross-references, and see and see also references are variously indicated by arrows and other symbols. This dictionary would be a valuable tool for a translator, less useful for a student seeking definitions. Another volume to follow will have terms arranged from Russian to English.

9. Baranov, Anatolii Nikolaevich, and Dmitrii Olegovich Dobrovol'skii. **Nemetsko-russkii i russko-nemetskii slovar' lingvisticheskikh terminov (s angliiskimi ekvivalentami): okolo 5500 nemetskikh i 5500 russkikh terminov/Linguistisches Wörterbuch Deutsch-Russisch und Russisch-Deutsch (mit Englischen Äquivalenten): Mit etwa 5500 deutschen und 5500 russischen Termini.** Moskva: Pomovskii & Partnery, 1993. 2v. 769p. bibliog. ISBN 5-87232-022-1.

Introductory and explanatory materials of this general linguistics dictionary are in both Russian and German. Volume 1 lists approximately 5,500 German terms with definitions in Russian. Volume 2 has a number of parts: an alphabetical listing of Russian terms with their German and English equivalents, a list of terms in English followed by German and Russian equivalents, and finally a German thematic index and a Russian thematic index. The thematic indexes list a general or collective term such as "Adjektiv" and then proceed to list all the related and more specific terms such as "Adjektivadverb," "Deadjektivum," "adjektivishe Deklination." These lists and indexes should be useful to both researchers and translators. However, they may not find newly coined terms in the field as the most recent English dictionary listed in the source bibliography is dated 1980, for German the most recent is 1988, while the most current Russian one is 1989.

10. Barberis, Jeanne Marie, Jacques Brès, Françoise Gardès-Madray, Robert Lafont, and Paul Siblot. **Concepts de la praxématique; Bibliographie indicative.** Montpellier: Université Paul Valéry, Groupe de recherche en linguistique praxématique, 1989. 114p. illus. bibliog. (Langue et praxis). ISBN 2-905397-32-2.

Pragmatics is one of the youngest subdisciplines of linguistics. It studies language in a human context of use, or put in a different way, it studies the influences on a person's choice of language. In this dictionary, the authors define and explain terms as they are used in its study. Definitions sometimes accompanied by illustrations are often more than a page in length. Following the dictionary part of this work, there is a separately titled bibliography, *Bibliographie indicative de la praxematique*, of articles and books published for the 20-year period from 1970 through 1989.

11. Bartschat, Brigitte, et al. **Lexikon sprachwissenschaftlicher Termini.** Herausgegeben von Rudi Conrad. 1. Aufl. Leipzig: Bibliographisches Institut, 1985. 281p. illus. LC 86-118518.

The *Lexikon* is essentially an updated version of the authors' *Kleines Wörterbuch sprachwissenschaftlicher Termini* (1975) even though it has a different title and is not billed as a revised edition. Its scope covers the whole range of linguistic sciences from grammar and historical and comparative linguistics to trends in modern linguistics such as generative transformational grammar and sociolinguistics. Most entries vary in length from one line to a paragraph. Good use is made of "see" and "see also" references. Words used in the definitions that are entries themselves are so marked. Updating is accomplished mainly through the addition of some new entries for a total of more than 3,000 entries. The dictionary by Ulrich (see entry 68) is similar, but has fewer entries.

12. Boone, Annie, and André Joly. **Dictionnaire terminologique de la systématique du langage**. Paris: L'Harmattan, 1996. 448p. illus. bibliog. port. (Sémantiques). ISBN 2-7384-4104-1.

This is a dictionary which analyzes the terms and concepts found in Gustave Guillaume's work which spanned the first half of the 20th century, his first work having been published in 1911 before Saussure's *Cours de linguistique générale* and his last article appearing in 1958 just after Chomsky's *Syntactic Structures*. Guillaume was a student and disciple of Antoine Meillet, a famous French comparativist who had an enormous influence on French linguistics. After Meillet's death, Guillaume became a lecturer at the École des hautes Études where for the next 22 years he further developed his cognitive approach to language, a study which he called the psychomécanique du langage (psychomechanics of language). Followers of Guillaume began publication of his lecture notes, which he had left in draft form on his death in 1960, as *Leçons de linguistique*. A volume of excerpts from his works, *Principes de linguistique théorique* was published in 1973 and translated into English in 1984 as *Fundamentals for a Science of Language*. In the dictionary are some 400 terms important to Guillaume's work accompanied by articles ranging in length from half a page to more than 5 pages with examples and illustrations. References at the end of each article are keyed to the titles and the page numbers in Guillaume's works.

13. Bright, William. **International Encyclopedia of Linguistics**. New York: Oxford University Press, 1992. 4v. 429p.(v.1). 440p.(v.2). 456p.(v.3). 482p.(v.4). index. illus. bibliog. maps. LC 91-7349. ISBN 0-19-505196-3 (set).

The primary audience for Bright's *International Encyclopedia of Linguistics* (IEL) is students and professional scholars in linguistics and adjacent fields. Most articles presume a reader is already grounded in the fundamentals. The IEL is a broad, comprehensive work covering the full range of linguistics, including descriptive, historical, comparative, typological, functionalist, and formalist specialities. Its 750 articles written and signed by a slate of some four hundred authors from around the word also cover interrelations both within linguistics (for example, syntax and semantics) and with other areas of the social and behavioral sciences (for example, sociolinguistics and psycholinguistics) as well as interdisciplinary studies (for example language and philosophy) and applied linguistics, especially language education (vol. 1, p. ix). In a field notorious for arguments and quarrels, Bright and his 25 topic editors are to be especially commended for having authors inform readers of alternate viewpoints on matters of theory and methodology without allowing them to lapse into debate and dogmatism. In addition to articles on the aforementioned topics, there are language articles. There are signed articles for specific languages as well as brief entries for groups of languages, the latter accompanied by language lists prepared by Joseph and Barbara Grimes. The entry "Languages of the World" provides an overall guide to these language articles and to the genetic classification of world languages. Entries range from ten lines to ten pages with an average length of two to four pages. Both topical and language entries are liberally cross-referenced and illustrated with examples and a variety of graphic aids (maps, charts, diagrams, tables, and outlines) and conclude with bibliographies of works cited.

Volume 4 has a number of useful features. To locate information on the topics covered in the IEL there is both a synoptic outline of the alphabetically arranged entries under some 18 headings and an extensive index. The index is not just topical, but includes names of languages and persons (contributors, cited authors, and persons either discussed within entries or those with their own biographical entry as in the case of famous deceased linguists such as Roman Jakobson). There is a glossary of about 1,800 words prepared by David Crystal. This scholarly, authoritative encyclopedia complements and overlaps with the ten-volume work by Asher (see entry 5) which is in some respects more up-to-date.

14.   Bussmann, Hadumod. **Lexikon der Sprachwissenschaft**. 2. völlig neu bearb. Aufl. Stuttgart: Alfred Kröner, 1990. 904p. illus. maps. (Kröners Taschenausgabe, Bd. 452). ISBN 3-520-45202-2.

See entry 15 below for the English version of this dictionary and a description of its contents. This German edition has, in addition, a list of English terms with their German equivalents as well as 12 language maps showing world-wide distribution of various languages, dialects, and language families.

15.   Bussmann, Hadumod. **Routledge Dictionary of Language and Linguistics**. Translated and edited by Gregory P. Trauth and Kerstin Kazzazi. New York: Routledge, 1996. 530p. illus. ISBN 0-415-02225-8.

This is an English translation based on the 1990 second revised edition (see entry 14) of a German work first published in 1983. However, it is much more than a translation of the original as some 70 European and North American linguists worked to adapt it to English. In the process they eliminated terminology specific to German linguistics and made additions and revisions to the texts, bibliographies, and examples. In some cases they added entirely new articles.

As Bussmann states in her Preface (pages vii-ix), the dictionary aims to be comprehensive. It covers all areas of linguistics, is not restricted to specific theories, and encompasses descriptive and historical, comparative and typological linguistics, as well as the applied subdisciplines. It covers basic terminology for the traditional core areas as well as allied and interdisciplinary fields. In addition it provides descriptions of individual languages and language families with such information as to their classification, number of native speakers, dialects, and countries or areas where spoken or used. The alphabetically arranged entries emphasize analysis, feature extensive cross-references, and offer detailed bibliographies. In the case of language entries, bibliographies include sources for history, grammar, etymology, and dictionaries. Thus the main audience for this dictionary is professional scholars in linguistics and allied fields. A somewhat comparable dictionary of linguistics in English, though targeted more for students and specialists in allied areas and lacking coverage of languages, is Crystal's dictionary of linguistics and phonetics (see entry 19). In regard to terminology it appears that Crystal covers more ground with 1,400 main entry terms, but treating a total of some 4,000 items by various strategies, compared to the 2,500 entries in Bussmann. However, scholarly users should take note that Crystal has eliminated in the recent fourth edition the bibliographical references accompanying entries which Bussman has and are so useful to anyone desiring to do further research.

Students may still profitably use this dictionary, but for terminology they might also want to consult more accessible works designed especially with them in mind, such as Crystal's dictionary of linguistics and phonetics mentioned above, Trask's dictionary of language and linguistics for students, or Matthews' concise dictionary (see entries 19, 67, and 39 respectively). Another choice for students might be Crystal's encyclopedic dictionary of language and languages (see entry 20) written for a general audience which has longer definitions and is written in a clear, straightforward style.

16.   Chinese-English Translation Assistance Group, ed. **Chinese-English Glossary of Linguistic Terms**. 1st ed. Kensington, MD: Dunwoody Press, 1986. 126p. index. LC 86-71174. ISBN 0-931745-21-7.

This is one in the series of Chinese-English glossaries for general, scientific, and technical terms put out by the Chinese-English Translation Assistance Group. Traditional Chinese characters are arranged according to the Kangxi radical system. The characters are followed by Pinyin romanization and expanded Standard Telegraphic Code numbers for the characters. An English equivalent follows. The over 6,500 entries cover a broad interpretation of general linguistics. Names for groups and families of languages and individual languages are also included. The entry index at the back merely shows the beginning character of the first term on each page. See Donner's *Preliminary Glossary* (entry 21) for English to Chinese equivalents.

17.   Collinge, N. E., ed. **An Encyclopaedia of Language**. London: Routledge, 1990. 1011p. index. illus. LC 89-6203. ISBN 0-415-02064-6.

The 26 essays in this one-volume encyclopedia are thematically arranged in three parts. Part A, "The Inner Nature of Language," covers such topics as phonetics, phonology, grammar, and semantics. Part B, "The Larger Province of Language," focuses on allied areas such as psycholinguistics, neurolinguistics, sociolinguistics, and language in education, while part C, "Special Aspects of Language," explores such topics as lexicography, special languages, and who speaks what languages of the world. The essays, signed by some 28 contributors, mainly noted British linguists and other experts, are accompanied by substantial bibliographies and recommendations for further reading. An index of topics and technical terms and an index of names round out this sourcebook written for an educated general audience. This work is a counterpart to Malmkjaer's linguistic encyclopedia, also from Routledge, but published a year earlier (see entry 37). Collinge's work is a fine reference work surveying the study of language. However, it suffers in comparison to the *Cambridge Encyclopedia of Language*, another one-volume encyclopedia (see entry 18) with the same audience but which has a wider scope, greater level of detail particularly in regard to individual languages and language families, and has more access points. In addition, the Cambridge encyclopedia contains a separate glossary.

18.   Crystal, David. **The Cambridge Encyclopedia of Language**. 2nd ed. Cambridge: Cambridge University Press, 1997. 480p. index. illus.(some col.) bibliog. ports. maps (some col.). ISBN 0-521-55050-5.

Crystal, a well-known and respected linguist, author, and editor has revised and improved in this second edition what was already a fascinating, readable work. A wealth of pictures, examples, diagrams, illustrations, maps, and figures not only enhance the text, but also entice the reader to just browse. It is packed with interesting, sometimes odd, facts about language that catch the readers' attention and keep them reading. Though Crystal and his international team of contributors write from a linguistic point of view, the encyclopedia is not meant to be an introduction to linguistics.

Eleven parts with such titles as "Language and identity," "The structure of language," "Child language acquisition," "The languages of the world," and "Language and communication," are further broken down into 65 thematic sections. Each section is complete in itself with cross-references to related sections. Valuable indexes included in eight appendixes provide unusually good access to the text and present further detailed information. These are: a glossary of specialized language terms with brief definitions together with the page(s) in the text where related subject matter can be found, but, regrettably, without a guide to pronouncing some of the less common terms; special symbols and abbreviations; table of the world's languages, noting which language family each belongs to, where it is spoken, and how many speakers it has; notes for further reading; bibliography for all works cited in the body of the text; index of languages, families, dialects, and scripts; index of authors and personalities; and, an index of topics.

This second edition has benefited from the various encyclopedia projects, publication of language statistics, and the 1990s census data published during the ten year period after the first edition appeared in 1987. Crystal has revised socio-political material to reflect the myriad of changes. He has also added text for three topics in which substantial change/progress has been made: speech synthesis and recognition, the world's endangered languages, and natural language processing. In addition he has revised the typography section and noted proposals for changes in the classification of some language families. With the benefit of a four-color printing scheme over a two-color shading in the first edition, many illustrations are new and all maps have been redrawn. The one-volume English language thematic encyclopedias of language/linguistics by Collinge and Malmkjaer meant for the educated general user, which moreover do not cover individual languages per se, pale in comparison to this very readable, lavishly illustrated and indexed work (see entries 17 and 37).

19.   Crystal, David. **A Dictionary of Linguistics and Phonetics**. 4th ed. New York: Blackwell, 1997. 426p. illus. (The Language Library). ISBN 0-631-20096-7.

This fourth edition of Crystal's dictionary, based on his earlier *A First Dictionary of Linguistics and Phonetics* (1980) and the subsequent revised and expanded editions in 1985 and 1991, has become a standard reference work for students of linguistics and phonetics and those researchers working in related fields such as foreign language teaching, speech therapy, psychology, sociology, literary criticism, and philosophy. It had few real competitors when first published, but now competes with an ever-growing number of dictionaries and encyclopedias written in English. Other dictionaries designed for the same audience are Trask's student dictionary and Matthews' concise dictionary (see entries 39 and 67); in addition to terminology both cover prominent languages and language families which this dictionary does not. For language coverage see Crystal's *Encyclopedic Dictionary of Language and Languages* (entry 20) and especially the multi-volume encyclopedias by Asher and Bright (see entries 5 and 13).

To this new edition Crystal has added well over 600 new terms and senses for recent developments in syntax, non-linear phonology, contemporary semantics, speech recognition and synthesis, and acoustics terminology. The latter, along with core terms of traditional grammar, were areas excluded from coverage in the first edition, but have gradually crept in with subsequent editions. In light of the proliferation of newly coined terms in linguistics, Crystal prudently refrained from adding them unless he verified usage in more than one source. Despite this caution, Crystal now treats an estimated 4,000 items either as main entries or within entries either shown in boldface or as special senses generally shown by phrases in inverted commas. He has also made changes within entries themselves in light of new theoretical developments and significantly increased the number of cross-references. The entries go beyond that of strict dictionary definitions by adding ample illustrations, examples, and descriptions; further-more, like an encyclopedia, they often contain discursive material about the historical context of terms. One valuable feature of previous editions, bibliog-raphies at the end of entries for follow-up reading, has been discontinued; it has proven too much of a burden to keep up in light of the expanding vocabulary of this field.

20.   Crystal, David. **An Encyclopedic Dictionary of Language and Lan-guages**. Oxford: Blackwell, 1992. 428p. illus. LC 92-34195. ISBN 0-631-17652-7.

Crystal admirably succeeds in his intent to put together a convenient ready-reference, "one-stop source," for questions people routinely ask about language and languages (p. i). He focuses on popular, practical (applied), and relevant topics to do with language yet provides the reader with basic linguistic terminology. The many linguistic and language dictionaries now available are often too specialized for these types of questions or provide too concise a definition. Included among the more concise works is Crystal's *A Dictionary of Linguistics and Phonetics* (see entry 19) and the more recently published student's dictionary by Trask (see entry 67) while Bussmann's *Routledge Dictionary of Language and Linguistics* (see entry 15) is intended for the scholar and specialist. Encyclopedias, on the other hand, such as Crystal's own *Cambridge Encyclopedia of Language* (see entry 18) and other 1-volume works by Collinge and Malmkjaer (see entries 17 and 37), may exclude terminology; moreover these are usually organized thematically with information on a particular term scattered throughout.

One of the strengths of Crystal's encyclopedic dictionary is its strong coverage of languages. There are entries for languages themselves as well as for countries. Under a language entry one can find out such things as its origin and relationship to other language families and groups, estimated number of speakers, and where it is spoken, or in the case of an extinct language, where it was spoken, or in the rarer instance of an artificial language, who devised it and when. Under a country entry one will find a listing of all the languages spoken there, including lingua francas, dialects, and official languages as well as their relative importance. Also among the nearly 2,750 entries are names of individuals and organizations. Entries are in letter-by-letter alphabetical arrangement including the numerous abbreviations and acronyms which carry cross-references to the full wording. These and other cross-references abound, enabling users to readily pursue items of related interest. Pronunciation is given only for headwords which might stymie the general reader. Illustrations and wry cartoons enliven the text.

21.   Donner, Frederick W., Jr., comp. **A Preliminary Glossary of Chinese Linguistic Terminology**. San Francisco: Chinese Materials Center, 1977. 117p. bibliog. (Chinese Materials and Research Aids Service Center. Occasional Series, No.38).

The intended user of this dictionary is the student of linguistics. The first part is a list of basic general linguistics terms in English with their Chinese equivalents. The second part is Chinese arranged in order of stroke count with the English equivalents. A short bibliography of items in both languages follows. For a more comprehensive Chinese-English glossary see entry 16.

22.   Dubois, Jean, et al. **Dictionnaire de linguistique et des sciences du langage**. Paris: Larousse, 1994. 514p. illus. bibliog. ISBN 2-03-340334-3.

Of the French linguistic dictionaries this one is probably the best. It covers a broad range of linguistic topics and is current to its date of publication. Though it is not limited to any particular approach or school of thought it does reflect the European tradition. In the preface the authors explain that this is really an encyclopedic dictionary. Long and short entries are arranged in one alphabetic sequence. Some 128 long entries, such as "générative (grammaire)," "signe," "structuralisme," and "transformation," constitute the encyclopedic part of the book and provide the foundation and key concepts. By identifying with an asterisk the specific terms in the text of the long articles the user is referred to definitions found in the short entries. Similarly, the use of asterisks in the short definitions can lead the reader back to the long articles and to other related terms. There are frequent citations in all the entries to works by specific linguists which are listed in an extensive bibliography of more than 50 pages. Diagrams and tables, including one of the International Phonetic Alphabet revised to 1989, are scattered throughout.

23.   Ducrot, Oswald. **Nouveau dictionnaire encyclopédique des sciences du langage**. Avec la collaboration de Marielle Abrioux, Dominique Bassano, Georges Boulakia, Michel de Fornel, Philippe Roussin, et Tzvetan Todorov. Paris: Éditions du Seuil, 1995. 668p. index. ISBN 2-02-014437-9.

In light of developments in linguistics in the more than twenty years since the first edition was published in 1972, the editors have completely revised and updated their encyclopedia. The second edition was the basis of a 1979 translation into English. See the description of this translation (entry 24 below) for details on organization and indexing which have remained unchanged. The number of terms defined, however, has increased in this new edition from about 800 to more than 1,100.

24.   Ducrot, Oswald, and Tzvetan Todorov. **Encyclopedic Dictionary of the Sciences of Language**. Translated by Catherine Porter. Baltimore: Johns Hopkins University Press, 1979. 380p. index. LC 78-23901. ISBN 0-8018-2155-X.

While this translation is based on the second edition of the *Dictionnaire encyclopédique des sciences du langage* (Paris: Éditions du Seuil, 1973), the bibliographical material has been updated, the articles on generative grammar and on time and modality in particular have been significantly revised, and English-language publications have been substituted for the French wherever possible.

The material is organized into four main sections: schools, fields, methodological concepts, and descriptive concepts. Each section is further subdivided so that, for example, under fields one can find articles on sociolinguistics, psycholinguistics, poetics, philosophy of language, and so on. In all there are about fifty such articles, each focusing on a well-defined topic and constituting a whole. Many references are provided within and at the end of each article. Also, within these articles about eight hundred terms are defined. There is an index of these terms at the end of the book. Moreover, in the text when a term or topic is alluded to that is discussed elsewhere, a number in brackets indicates the page on which this term or idea is explained. An index of authors refers the reader to the place in the text where they are discussed.

This work can be read as an encyclopedia or used as a dictionary. The authors have intentionally minimized their use of technical language so that the work is useful to beginners as well as specialists.

25.   Engler, Rudolf. **Lexique de la terminologie saussurienne**. Utrecht/Anvers: Spectrum, 1968. 53p. (Comité international permanent des linguistes (C.I.P.L.); Publication de la commission de terminologie). LC 73-358126.)

Ferdinand de Saussure, a Genevan linguist, was a pioneer of modern linguistics at the beginning of the 20th century. This dictionary is the best one for Saussurian terminology. It includes quotes from two works, both published after his death, the *Recueil des publications scientifiques 1879-1912* (Genève, 1922) and the *Cours de linguistique générale* (édition critique, Wiesbaden, 1967). The latter, the *CLG*, was originally published in 1916 and is in fact a reconstruction of his lecture notes and other materials by two of his former students. Quotes used in this dictionary are meticulously documented in the original sources which include the above mentioned publications as well as half a dozen others. Full bibliographic information is given for all these at the beginning of the dictionary in a one-page list of abbreviations. A table at the end gives equivalents for the terms from the *CLG* in Italian, Spanish, German, English, Polish, and Russian.

26.   Gröschel, Bernhard, and Elena Parwanowa. **Russisch-deutsches Wörterbuch der linguistischen Terminologie**. Münster: Institut für Allgemeine Sprachwissenschaft der Westfälischen Wilhelms-Universität, 1985. 2v. 935p. (Studium Sprachwissenschaft, Beiheft 3). LC 86-153507. ISBN 3-89083-103-4.

An extensive introduction of 99 pages provides a valuable discussion (in German) of the history and development of both Russian and German linguistic lexicography. A fold-out sheet inserted between pages xxii and xxiii compares in a matrix 27 linguistic dictionaries (Russian, multi-lingual with Russian as one of the languages, or at least including Russian terms) with respect to: type (dictionary, word list, thesaurus, or monograph), dictionary or encyclopedic orientation, alphabetic or systematic arrangement, explication throughout, language(s) included, scope of topics covered, methods (traditional, structuralist, or post-structuralist), and number of entries. The introduction contains a bibliography of about 125 linguistic dictionaires used in this dictionary's preparation. According to the authors, a dictionary by N.N. Durnovo (1924) marks the beginning of contributions to Russian terms; a work by Walther Hofstaetter (1930) is the oldest contribution to German.

The main part of this dictionary consists of an alphabetical list of 16,520 Russian words along with their numbered German equivalents. No definitions are given. Volume 1 contains A-P while volume 2 contains R-YA. Terms from both general/theoretical and applied linguistics are covered, plus a wide scope of allied disciplines. The second volume has a list of German terms in alphabetical order where the user is referred, by entry number, back to the Russian term in the main part of the dictionary.

27.   Hamp, Eric P. **A Glossary of American Technical Linguistic Usage, 1925-1950**. 3rd ed. Utrecht/Antwerp: Spectrum Publishers, 1966. 68p. bibliog. (Permanent International Committee of Linguists (C.I.P.L.); Publication of the Committee for Terminology).

Though this is a third edition, it is essentially a reprinting of the second edition (1963) which itself was only a slightly revised version of the first (1957). A new preface does list additional sources which have appeared since preparation of the original edition and would augment the present work, if included. This list is limited to works which continue the theoretical tradition of the original glossary; it does not include titles from the transformational-generative literature. Only terminology which has distinctly American characteristics is included. This accounts for a beginning publication date of 1925 for source material. That was a watershed year since the journal *Language* published by the Linguistic Society of America began publication then. Edward Sapir's book, *Language,* published in 1921 is the only exception to the 1925 date, being included since Sapir had such a great influence on later scholarship through his pupils. The 1930's saw the establishment of "basic distinctive 'American' terminology now in widespread use in this country for linguistics as a whole and for the subfield of phonology."(p.5-6). The 1940s saw further development in phonology as well as parallel developments for morphology.

Utilizing quotations from some 113 sources listed at the beginning of the book, Hamp attempts to show the meanings of technical terms in both diachronic and synchronic senses. He excludes terms from neighboring disciplines such as logic, anthropology, sociology, psychology, mathematics, philosophy, and even semantics, as well as terms for particular form classes or categories of individual languages.

28.   Hanna, Sami A., Karim Zaki Husam Al-Din, and Naguib Greis. **Dictionary of Modern Linguistics, English-Arabic**. Beirut, Lebanon: Librairie du Liban Publishers, 1997. 156p. index. illus. bibliog.

The authors, professors at Portland State University and Cairo University, designed this dictionary for Arab students and scholars without an extensive background in linguistics (p. ix). It includes significant terms in both theoretical and applied linguistics, history of linguistics, and allied fields. The main part of the dictionary consists of head words in English with their Arabic equivalent(s) and a definition in Arabic with examples provided mainly from the Arabic language. There is a brief introduction in English; in Arabic there is a slightly longer introduction and a separate short history of linguistics. The bibliography of sources cites many of the more recently published encyclopedias and dictionaries in English (see entries 5, 13, 20, and 37) as well as classical works by Bloomfield, Saussure, and other works published in the intervening years, but just one work in Arabic. The dictionary concludes with an index of Arabic terms keyed to the English head words.

29. Holmes, Philip. **Linguistic Terms: A Handbook for Students of the Nordic Languages**. 2nd ed. Hull: Dept. of Scandinavian Studies, University of Hull, 1984. 70p. index. illus. bibliog. (Linguistic Terms, No. 1). ISBN 08598-534-4.

The author has targeted this book at students of the Scandinavian languages and the problems they encounter in approaching the terminology and concepts of linguistic description and analysis. The aim is practical rather than theoretical. In the course of providing an introduction to basic linguistics as applied to the Scandinavian languages some 450 linguistic terms are explained. Many examples are used, mainly from Swedish, but also Danish, Norwegian, and other European languages. There are English-Swedish and Swedish-English indexes to terms, plus a list of some Danish-based terms used by Danish linguists in preference to the more common Latin-based terminology.

30. International Phonetic Association. **The Principles of the International Phonetic Association; Being a Description of the International Phonetic Alphabet and the Manner of Using It, Illustrated by Texts in 51 Languages**. London: International Phonetic Association, 1949. 53p. illus. LC 52-17468. ISBN 0-9503231-0-1(1984 reprint).

The International Phonetic Association (IPA) was founded in 1886, as the Phonetic Teachers' Association, by a group of leading phoneticians from Germany, France, Britain, and Denmark. The set of phonetic symbols described here was first published by them in 1888 along with detailed recommendations for usage; it has been reprinted and revised many times since then. The latest revision in 1993 (updated 1996) can be found on the IPA Web site at http://www.arts.gla.ac.uk/IPA/ipachart.html (see also entry 49). The original IPA alphabet contained quite a few of the special letters used today, but was imperfect in various respects. It has subsequently been worked on, improving signs that proved unsatisfactory, and extending the alphabet to cover languages for which it did not originally provide.

The *Principles* contains numerous figures of vowels and a 1-page chart setting out the principal consonant letters and the chief vowel letters. One example from a language is given for each symbol in the chart. Following this are remarks on other letters (such as palatals and velarized consonants), digraphs, diacritical marks, length, stress, and tones. Examples are given in 53 languages (or varieties of a language) of "broad" and "narrow" transcription.

The IPA Web site with the latest revisions to the alphabet displays charts showing: consonants (pulmonic), consonants (non-pulmonic), diacritics, other symbols, suprasegmentals, tones and word accents, and vowels. A *Handbook of the International Phonetic Association: A Guide to the Use of the International Phonetic Alphabet* is scheduled for publication by Cambridge University Press mid-1999. This will be a 200-page handbook with 3 parts. Part 1 will contain 10 chapters on the principles of the IPA. Part 2 will show 29 language illustrations of the use of IPA principles. Part 3 with 4 appendixes will include complete tables of computer coding conventions for IPA symbols and extended IPA symbols. There will be charts of the International Phonetic Alphabet, IPA numbers, and extended IPA characters.

31. Jedlička, Alois, ed. **Slovník slovanské lingvistické terminolo-gie/Slovar' slavyanskoi lingvisticheskoi terminologii/Dictionary of Slavonic Linguistic Terminology**. Hamburg: Helmut Buske, 1977-1979. 2v. 553p.(v.1); 483p.(v.2). ISBN 3-87118-270-2(set); ISBN 3-87118-271-0(v.1); ISBN 3-87118-272-9(v.2).

The decision to compile this dictionary was made by the 1960 Prague session of the International Committee for Linguistic Terminology (ICLT). It eventually became an international project with work contributed by linguists from many different countries. It is a complete register of generally used Slavonic linguistic terms. The principle concept-terms are in Czech with equivalents in other Slavonic languages and three Western European languages. Sometimes, however, non-Czech terms are used as principle concept-terms. This usually occurs when a term is characteristic of a phenomena in a certain language, or when used only in a single language, but merits adoption in the terminology of the remaining languages.

Volume 1 consists of 2,266 concept-terms organized into a 9-part systematic classification system: universal notions (i.e., general linguistics), the phonic aspect of language, the graphical aspect of language, lexicon, parts of speech, the structure of the word, syntax, style, and finally new trends, methods, and schools of linguistic thought. Source terms and their equivalents are arranged so that they are all printed on two opposite pages. The upper left-hand side contains terms for Czech, Slovak, Polish, and Upper Sorbian and Lower Sorbian; the upper right-hand side lists terms for Russian, Ukrainian and White Russian; the lower left-hand side consists of terms for Bulgarian, Macedonian, Serbo-Croat and Croat-Serbian as well as Slovene; the lower right-hand gives the equivalents in English, French, and German. Definitions are not provided, explication being given only in special cases usually involving terms specific to a given language or a given linguistic tradition.

Volume 2 contains alphabetical indexes in all fourteen languages of all the terms in volume 1. In both volumes the introductory materials and the tables of contents (the latter found on the last page of each volume) are in Czech, Russian, and English. The dictionary is useful for delineating the range of meaning of particular terms and the circumstances in which they are used in particular languages. Translators should find it particularly helpful.

32. Knobloch, Johann, Hrsg. **Sprachwissenschaftliches Wörterbuch**. Heidelberg: Carl Winter, 1961-1991. Bd.1(Lfg.1-11), Bd.2(Lfg.1-2). (Indoger-manische Bibliothek. II. Reihe. Wörterbücher). ISBN 3-533-00664-6 (Bd.1); ISBN 3-533-04075-5 (Bd.2). (In progress).

Volume 1 with entries A-E was completed in 1986; Volume 2 with several parts published in 1988 and 1991 continues this ongoing work with entries for F-Frianlisch. It is a very thorough, scholarly dictionary of general and compara-tive linguistics, quite useful for older terms. Entries are arranged alphabetically and vary in length from several lines to several pages, most being one or two paragraphs long. Users are referred from terms in English, French, Latin, Italian, and Russian to the German entries. An asterisk marks words in the definitions which are themselves entries. Brackets around a reference indicate the first use of a term. Parentheses around a reference indicate the source from which exam-ples are drawn; the emphasis is on German scholarship here. At the rate this dictionary is being produced we will be well into the 21st century before it is complete.

33.   Koerner, E. F. K., and Asher, R. E., eds. **Concise History of the Language Sciences from the Sumerians to the Cognitivists**. New York: Pergamon, 1995. index. illus. bibliog. LC 95-35131. ISBN 0-08-042580-1.

This survey of the history of linguistics is drawn from articles which originally appeared in the 10-volume encyclopedia of language and linguistics (see entry 5) for which Koerner was the subject editor for the history of linguistics and Asher the editor-in-chief. Some articles have been revised and updated; the chapter on the Hebrew grammatical tradition is newly written (p.xii). While the survey goes beyond the scope of previous works in the field which tended to focus on major periods of the history of Western linguistics—with perhaps some small account of the work of Indian grammarians and that of Arabic linguists—a complete history of linguistics through the ages is beyond the reach of a single volume work. Thus, the editors have concentrated on traditions judged to have the greatest international impact.

The 64 chapters are arranged in 11 sections. The first section contains several chapters written by Koerner, one on the history of linguistics, the other on the historiography of linguistics. Sections 2-10 are devoted to periods ranging from Antiquity, through the Middle Ages, the Renaissance, 17th and 18th century Europe, the 19th century, and finally the 20th century. Geographic coverage is greater for the earlier time periods. Section 11 is devoted to coverage of applied areas, such as machine translation and phonetics. An international slate of authoritative scholars is responsible for the chapters accompanied by examples, illustrations, and thorough bibliographies. A final section contains indexes for subjects and biographical names as well as a list of contributors together with their affiliations and the titles of articles which they have written.

34.   Lewandowski, Theodor. **Linguistisches Wörterbuch**. 6. Aufl. Heidelberg: Quelle & Meyer, 1994. 3v. 1287p. (Uni-Taschenbücher, 1518). ISBN 3-494-02173-2 (set).

The 6th edition of this standard German dictionary of linguistics is basically a reprint of the 5th revised edition published in 1990. Volume 1 contains A-H, volume 2 covers I-R, and volume 3 completes the set with S-Z. It covers most schools of linguistic thought as well as selected terminology from allied fields such as psycholinguistics, sociolinguistics, and applied linguistics. Sometimes the equivalent term in one or more languages such as English, French, Russian, or others follows the German entry word. The definitions include many examples of usage. Words used in the definitions which are themselves entries in the dictionary are so indicated. Significant entries are accompanied by bibliographies, quite extensive in some cases, with most of the references in the bibliographies to German language materials; but a number are in English and other languages.

In comparison to Abraham's dictionary (see entry 1), a similar scholarly German dictionary of linguistics last revised in 1988, Lewandowski's is somewhat more up-to-date, often has longer definitions, includes more examples, and has longer bibliographies. Abraham on the other hand includes an English-German list of technical terms which is helpful to the English language user.

35. **La Linguistique**. Paris: Le Livre de Poche, 1978. 208p. index. illus. bibliog. (Encyclopédie du monde actuel). ISBN 2-2530-2073-7.

A lot of information is packed in this small French pocket encyclopedia. Some thirty alphabetically arranged articles are all two pages in length. They cover such topics as language acquisition, diglossia, functionalism, generative grammar, morpheme, prosody, and sign. About a quarter of the articles cover individual linguists, including Antoine Culioli, Gustave Guillaume, William Labov, André Martinet, Edward Sapir, and Ferdinand de Saussure. There is an index of terms, names, and languages cited in the text. The chief use of this encyclopedia would be to obtain introductory background information.

36. MacKay, Ian. **Phonetics and Speech Science: A Bilingual Dictionary/Dictionnaire bilingue de la phonétique et des sciences de la parole**. New York: Peter lang, 1989. 249p. bibliog. (American University Studies. Series XIII: Linguistics, Vol. 10; ISSN 0740-4557). ISBN 0-8204-1036-5.

Introductory and explanatory materials of this work are in both English and French. MacKay's purpose is not to define words, but to provide a comprehensive lexicon of equivalent terms for the two languages. The author lists terms from general phonetics, acoustic phonetics, and physiological phonetics as well as major terms from phonology, speech pathology, audiology, and writing (p. xvii). Part I lists English terms with their French equivalents; Part II translates French terms into their English equivalents. MacKay gives both English and British spellings and provides synonyms and cross-references when appropriate. In instances where there is no exact equivalent term, he helpfully provides explanations. Usage notes are also used to clarify particularly problematic terms.

37. Malmkjaer, Kirsten, ed. **The Linguistics Encyclopedia**. North American consultant editor, James M. Anderson. London: Routledge, 1991. 575p. index. illus. bibliog. LC 90-38466. ISBN 0-415-02942-2.

Malmkjaer along with 26 primarily British, but also American, Canadian, Australian, and other scholars have contributed to the more than 80 articles in this encyclopedia designed to serve the needs of students and teachers in linguistics and language study at all levels and professionals in related fields of interest. A list of subjects preceding the articles provides the reader with an overview of the topics covered along with numerous cross-references. The articles are alphabetically arranged from acoustic phonetics to writing systems and explore traditional areas of the field as well as current areas of research and allied areas, but with a clear focus on theoretical aspects of modern linguistics. Information on some 60 linguists can be found in entries relating to their specialities or their schools of thought. There is no detailed coverage of languages (but Routledge has published a two-volume companion work for this purpose, Campbell's compendium of the world's languages, see entry 555). The signed articles are accompanied by lists for further readings. They feature extensive cross-referencing and are illustrated using diagrams, tables, and figures. At the end of the volume there is both a cumulative bibliography listing cited references from all the articles and a well-designed index of key terms and topics that appear as main headings or are highlighted within the text. There is no separate glossary. Several multi-volume English language encyclopedias with more extensive coverage and containing information on languages and language families have been published since this encyclopedia first appeared (see entries 5 and 13).

38.   Marciszewski, Witold, ed. **Dictionary of Logic as Applied in the Study of Language: Concepts, Methods, Theories**. The Hague: Martinus Nijhoff, 1981. 436p. index. bibliog. (Nijhoff International Philosophy Series, Vol.9). LC 81-3971. ISBN 90-247-2123-7.

While useful to philosophers, this dictionary was designed particularly for specialists in the field of "the study of language," that is, those from the areas of linguistics, information science, philosophy of language, and semiotics. The main part of the dictionary consists of 72 alphabetically arranged articles on such topics as: name; questions; sentence; syntax, logical; semantics, logical; pragmatics, logical; and grammar formal. Each article is written and signed by one of fifteen contributors, all but two of whom are from universities or scholarly institutions in Poland. Appended to each article is a list of references. A few of these references are repeated in a bibliography at the end of the dictionary, but for the most part this general bibliography consists of further works such as classical contributions to mathematical logic and its applications, textbooks, and collections. When a term is defined within an article it is italicized. These italicized terms plus other key concepts can be found in a subject index and glossary.

39.   Matthews, P. H. **The Concise Oxford Dictionary of Linguistics**. Oxford: Oxford University Press, 1997. 410p. illus. (Oxford Paperback Reference). LC 97-12848. ISBN 0-19-280008-6.

Matthews, a well-respected scholar, writer and Professor of Linguistics at Cambridge University, is responsible for this authoritative dictionary useful for both students and the general reader. It compares favorably with Trask's student dictionary (see entry 67). Coverage is thorough for core linguistics terms and ideas, less thorough for applied linguistics and allied areas, and not at all for computational linguistics which Matthews sees as a field of study belonging more to computer science than linguistics and the study of language. There are entries for all major languages and families of languages as well as for both historical and contemporary personages important to the field. Clear, concise definitions written in accessible language range in length from a sentence to several paragraphs. Numerous cross-references are provided and words used in definitions which are entries themselves are identified by an asterisk. Examples abound and simple black and white illustrations accompany a few entries. Matthews supplies pronunciations only for obscure terms.

40.   Mel'čuk, Igor A. **Towards a Language of Linguistics: A System of Formal Notions for Theoretical Morphology**. Revised and edited by Ph. Luelsdorff. München: Wilhelm Fink, 1982. 160p. index. illus. bibliog. (Internationale Bibliothek für allgemeine Linguistik=International Library of General Linguistics, Bd.44). ISBN 3-7705-1965-5(paper).

The author has written this book in order to provide "a fragment of a concept system for theoretical morphology." (p.22). He sees in the field extreme fuzziness of linguistic concepts and sloppiness with terms, even going so far as to say that linguistics lacks a consensus on what a rigorous definition means. The majority of linguistic terms vary in meaning among the different schools and can even vary within the work of one linguist. Moreover, closely related and even identical notions can be denoted quite differently. There are works which use well-defined, rigorous definitions, but he does not see these attempts as fitting into a general framework. Many dictionaries of linguistic terms have been published, but since they are descriptive, not prescriptive, they have been of little help in solving this problem. They merely reflect usage, when in fact it is the usage itself that needs to be revised and corrected.

After setting some preliminary ground rules for the definitions, the author provides on pages 37-40 the following: a list of the fifty notions in the order of their introduction, some of which are "segmental," "suprasegmental," "root," "affix," "infix," "morpheme," "megamorph," and "submorph"; a diagram showing the interrelations among all the notions; and a list of such things as symbols and abbreviations. The definitions of the notions themselves are succinct, usually only a sentence or two, while comments on the definitions can be extensive, sometimes as long as several pages. Notes to the text and references are gathered at the end of the book. There are also two indexes. One is for subjects and terms. The other is a selection of linguistic forms quoted in the text judged by the author to be representative of certain linguistic phenomena.

41. Mounin, Georges. **Dictionnaire de la linguistique**. Paris: Presses universitaires de France, 1974. 340p. bibliog. LC 75-501409.

Many of the entries in this dictionary are signed with the initials of one of the 19 people who collaborated with Mounin. The terms, in bold type, are set off by themselves on the outer margins of each page, making it easy to find the desired entry. Definitions for the majority of items are one or two paragraphs long. Each is generally preceded by an indication of the area or branch of linguistics toward which the definition is oriented such as: semantics, phonology, generative grammar, applied linguistics, prosody, and rhetoric. When a term is used in a definition that is defined elsewhere in the dictionary it is marked with an asterisk. Some examples are given and references are made in the definitions to linguistic literary studies, but these references are not gathered together in a single bibliography. There is a list of references, but that is a list of sources from which the entries were drawn. Preceding the entries is a table of five alphabets: International Phonetic Alphabet, the alphabet of the romanists (Straka), the "machine à écrire" alphabet, the alphabet of the arabists, and the alphabet of the sanskritists.

42. Newmeyer, Frederick J., ed. **Linguistics: The Cambridge Survey**. Cambridge: Cambridge University Press, 1988. 4v.

43. Volume I: **Linguistic Theory: Foundations**. 500p. index. LC 87-24915. ISBN 0-521-30832-1.

44. Volume II: **Linguistic Theory: Extensions and Implications**. 320p. index. LC 87-18386. ISBN 0-521-30833-X.

45. Volume III: **Language: Psychological and Biological Aspects**. 350p. index. LC 87-25671. ISBN 0-521-30835-6.

46. Volume IV: **Language: The Socio-cultural Context**. 294p. index. LC 87-23876. ISBN 0-521-30834-8.

Newmeyer, the nine members of the editorial board, and the various other contributors responsible for individual chapters in this survey are all top scholars and researchers, well-known in their areas of expertise. In the words of its editor, this work comprised of 60 relatively short chapters and published in four volumes is "a comprehensive introduction to research results and current work in all branches of the field of linguistics, from syntactic theory to ethnography of speaking, from signed language to the mental lexicon" (vol. 1, p. vii). It provides overviews of the various subdivisions of the field (with the exception of four topics originally planned for, but not included: linguistics and artificial intelligence, linguistics in literary analysis, language and education, and linguistics and semiotics). There is some overlap between chapters, both within and across volumes, but for the most part these overlapping chapters deal with different aspects of a topic or present differing viewpoints. For example, several chapters in volume 2 debate differing positions on creole languages, while a chapter in volume 4 approaches pidgins and creoles from a sociolinguistic standpoint. A special feature of volume 1 is an appendix in which R. H. Robins provides the reader with a history of linguistics. Each volume in the set has indexes for names and subjects and conveniently lists the contents of the other three volumes. Beginning students of linguistics as well as more advanced students and specialists will find much of interest to them in this excellent overview of the field and allied areas even though there have been new developments in many areas since it was written.

47.   Palmatier, Robert Allen. **A Glossary for English Transformational Grammar**. New York: Appleton-Century-Crofts, 1972. 207p. bibliog. LC 79-187737. ISBN 0-390-69109-7.

The time span covered by the terms in this glossary is the fourteen-year period from 1956 through the 1960s. (For coverage through 1975 see entry 3). The terms were derived from the author's survey of some 72 works in English relating to transformational grammar in general or to English transformational grammar in particular. Each definition is referenced by page numbers from one or more of these works. The works are listed in a separate bibliography at the end. Technical terms from traditional grammar or structural linguistics are not included here unless their use is maintained in transformational theory. Palmatier clearly labels all definitions in regard to their bias: toward first-generation transformational grammar, reflecting the model in Chomsky's *Syntactic Structures* (1957); toward second-generation transformational grammar, reflecting the model in Chomsky's *Aspects of the Theory of Syntax* (1965); toward semantic-based transformational grammar, reflecting the neotransformational studies of case grammar and generative semantics; or, toward more than one of these models.

48.   Phelizon, Jean-François. **Vocabulaire de la linguistique**. Paris: Roudil, 1976. 280p. illus. bibliog. (Les Études par l'example). LC 77-46289.

Through its definitions of about 1,200 linguistic terms, the glossary covers all areas of linguistics, but is not exhaustive. Intended mainly as a tool for students, its definitions tend to be brief, almost cryptic in some cases, with frequent quotations from original sources. The sources range in date from 1821 to 1973 and include works from mostly French scholars, although some are from other Western Europeans and Americans. The latter include Chomsky, Greenberg, Hockett, and Katz. The Greek or Latin word from which a term is derived is sometimes given. Appendixes include the following: symbols currently used in linguistics, principal diacritic signs of the Latin alphabets, principal signs of the International Phonctic Alphabet, a list of the languages of the world organized by groups within families, and a bibliography of sources.

49.   Pullum, Geoffrey K., and William A. Ladusaw. **Phonetic Symbol Guide**. 2nd ed. Chicago: University of Chicago Press, 1996. 320p. index. illus. bibliog. LC 95-42773. ISBN 0-226-68535-7.

This edition is a fully updated revision of Pullum's guide first published in 1986 and is intended to be comprehensive for both current and historical phonetic transcription practice (p. vii). In 1989 a convention was held for the purpose of making recommendations for specific revisions to the International Phonetic Association's phonetic alphabet (both the association and the alphabet are commonly referred to as IPA, with context determining which is being referred to). Some radical changes were recommended in 1989, and as discussion continued, further changes were approved by the IPA council in 1993. Pullum and Ladusaw have incorporated both the 1989 and 1993 changes for a total of some 61 new symbol entries (conveniently listed all in one place on pages xxxvi -xxxvii).

Character entries are arranged dictionary style according to the shape of the symbol. A user can thus look up an unfamiliar phonetic or phonological symbol by its shape to determine its meaning. This system works well for the most part with cross-references inserted at points where there might be confusion. There are two types of character entries: major and minor. Major entries are for symbols officially approved by the International Phonetic Association (IPA) as of the last revision in 1993. They are easily recognized as they always begin a new page and have a large illustrative character in a double-edged box. Thus, the set of entries with the double-edged boxes constitutes a complete guide to the IPA. Minor entries are interspersed among the major entries and are for characters in a variety of different categories: characters less widely used, widely used but not IPA-approved, or for those which are composites of characters and diacritics. In both major and minor entries, symbols may be followed by sections labeled: IPA Usage, American Usage, Other Uses, Comments, and Source. Following the character entries is a section for diacritic entries. Here again, any diacritic with a current official IPA value is surrounded by a double-edged box.

There are a number of other useful features in the book. A glossary giving short, basic definitions for technical terms used in the guide is followed by a lengthy list of references. Next come useful charts for cardinal vowels, IPA symbols for unrounded and rounded vowels, Bloch and Trager's vowel symbols, American usage vowel symbols, the Chomsky/Halle vowel system, American usage consonant symbols, IPA consonant symbols, IPA suprasegmental symbols, and IPA diacritics. Indexes for language, subject, and symbol name complete this reference work. It is an indispensable resource for linguists, phoneticians and others working with languages. (See also entry 30).

50.   Sebeok, Thomas Albert, ed. **Current Trends in Linguistics**. The Hague: Mouton, 1963-1976. 14v. in 21. LC 64-3663.

As originally conceived, this series was to "assess the current state of linguistic activity in all fields and all countries" (Vol. 1, p.v). The fundamental organizing principle was geopolitical, i.e., orientation towards a particular area, except for volumes 3 and 11-13 which have a theoretical orientation instead. Though Sebeok was the general editor of the entire series, each volume also had its own editorial board. Contributors from all over the world were enlisted to write chapters in their areas of expertise. All but a handful of articles were either written in English originally, or translated into English before publication. As expected in a work of this size not all the volumes turned out as originally planned. Often a planned article or two is missing from the final work. In Sebeok's introductions, with which he begins most volumes, he points out these omissions. In successive volumes after the first, he also cites reviews of previous volumes in the series.

In the descriptions of the contents of the volumes below readers should assume that each of the first thirteen volumes has biographical notes on its editors and contributors. Also, they should assume that those volumes devoted to studies of particular areas have an index of languages and an index of names for the authors and coauthors of the bibliographies accompanying the chapters. The theoretical volumes, on the other hand, while having biographical notes and indexes of names, vary in having other features. These are noted below.

51.   **Volume 1: Soviet and East European Linguistics**. 1963. 606p. index.

The first part of this volume, taking up nearly three-fourths of the book, deals with selected topics in Soviet linguistics. Besides articles on general and applied linguistics, there are nine others dealing with languages, language families, and geographic groupings such as Indo-European, Belorussian and Ukrainian, Latvian, Lithuanian, Altaic, and Semitic. Only five articles make up the last section on linguistics in East Europe. They are organized around the countries of Bulgaria, Czechoslovakia, Hungary, Poland, and Yugoslavia.

52.   **Volume 2: Linguistics in East Asia and South East Asia**. 1967. 979p. index.

More than twenty essays by various contributors make up this volume. Seven are on China, eight on Japan. One of the essays on China is an extensive bibliography of Chinese linguistics by William S.-Y. Wang. There is one article each on Korea, Mongolia, Tibet, Burma, Thailand and Laos, Vietnam, Indonesia and Malaysia, and Cambodia. An additional feature of this volume is a comparative table of transcription for Chinese. It compares the Pinyin, Yale, Wade-Giles, Zhuyin Zimu, and Gwoyen Romatzyh (tonal spelling) systems.

53.   **Volume 3: Theoretical Foundations**. 1966. 537p. index.

The seven chapters appearing here are consolidated and expanded versions of talks delivered over a period of a week as part of the Trends in Linguistics Lecture Series at the 1964 Linguistic Institute of the Linguistic Society of America, held at Indiana University (p.vi). The contributors are well-known linguists: Noam Chomsky, Joseph H. Greenberg, Mary R. Haas, Charles F. Hockett, Yakov Malkiel, Kenneth L. Pike, and Uriel Weinreich. Appendix I and II also contain lectures by Robert Godel and Edward Stankiewicz. The important currents in linguistic theory covered in this volume were not meant to be exhaustive of the topic. Indeed, later volumes, volumes 11-13, in the series go on to deal with other theoretical issues.

54.   **Volume 4: Ibero-American and Caribbean Linguistics**. 1968. 659p. index.

Part I of this book contains seven essays on general and Ibero-American linguistics, covering such topics as Hispanic phonology, lexicography, dialectology, and philology as well as Brazilian linguistics. Part II covers the non-Ibero-American languages. A third part goes on to deal with applied linguistics in the area while the final part deals with sources and resources of the region in two articles, one on the organization of linguistic activities (institutions, professional organizations, and journals), the other on the present state of linguistics.

55.   **Volume 5: Linguistics in South Asia**. 1969. 814p. index.

This volume begins with articles covering Indo-Aryan languages, Dravidian languages, and other language families such as Munda, non-Munda Austroasiatic, Tibeto-Burman, and Iranian. Part 2 covers a diversity of topics relating to this area of the world, for example, Pāṇini, sociolinguistics in South Asia, semantics of kinship in South India and Ceylon, linguistic studies in Pakistan, and two chapters on linguistics in Ceylon.

56.   **Volume 6: Linguistics in South West Asia and North Africa**. 1970. 802p. index.

Sections on three language families begin this volume: Indo-European (Iranian and Armenian), Altaic (Turkish and Mongolian), and Afroasiatic (Semitic, Egyptian, Coptic, Cushtic, and the Berber languages). The final section deals with a number of regional language issues and observations on the study and teaching of language in the area.

57.   **Volume 7: Linguistics in Sub-Saharan Africa**. 1971. 972p. index.

In addition to articles dealing with specific languages or families (Arabic, Mande, Gur, Kwa, and Chadic) there are articles on click languages, pidgins and creoles, and even one on surrogate languages of Africa.

58.   **Volume 8: Linguistics in Oceania**. 1971. 2v. 1381p. index.

This volume appears in two physically separate parts. The first covers indigenous languages of the area with 13 articles on Austronesian, several on Papuan, three on Australian, and a final article by Joseph H. Greenberg on the Indo-Pacific hypothesis.

The second part concerns itself with selected topics such as intrusive languages, languages in contact, sociolinguistic problems, and pre-contact writing in Oceania. Geoffrey N. O'Grady and Charles A. Zisa round out the two volumes with a checklist of Oceanic language and dialect names.

59.   **Volume 9: Linguistics in Western Europe**. 1972. 2v. and index of names. 1926p. index.

The first tome of this ninth volume is concerned with fields of linguistics in Western Europe. There are articles covering various areas of general linguistics, for example, comparative, phonology and phonetics, descriptive, general diachronic, and semantics. It also has articles dealing with aspects of applied linguistics.

Articles in the second tome deal with the study of selected languages or families of the area plus articles with a broader frame of reference such as comparative Romance linguistics, Latin and the languages of ancient Italy, and the Scandinavian languages.

In addition to the usual biographical notes and index of languages, the appendixes include two articles. One by R.R.K. Hartmann surveys, country by country, organizations devoted to

linguistic research and teaching. The other written by Curtis Blaylock surveys periodical publications devoted to Western European languages and published in Western Europe. A physically separate index of names goes along with this two-volume set.

60.   **Volume 10: Linguistics in North America**. 1973. 2v. 1624p. index.

Volume 1 of this ninth volume has articles on the major languages of North America: English, French, and Spanish. It also has several chapters on other immigrant languages and a number of articles dealing with general topics in the study of native languages. In an exception to the basic editorial policy of the entire series that requires all contributions to appear in English Sebeok has kept in the original French the four articles written by Canadians. This is in recognition of the sensitive bilingual situation in Canada.

The second volume contains chapters on the geographic groupings of North American native languages: Eskimo-Aleut, Na-Dene, the Northwest, California, Mexico, the Southwest and Great Basin, and East Central (Algonquian, Siouan, Iroquoian, and Caddoan). Further, there is a checklist by Herbert J. Landau of tribes and languages of North America and maps by William Sorsby of tribal groups of North and Central America.

Completing the volume is a directory of current resources in linguistics within the United States. As expected, it is now woefully out-of-date.

61.   **Volume 11: Diachronic, Areal, and Typological Linguistics**. 1973. 604p. index.

The organization of this book is unique. The Editorial Board decided to divide it into two sections. The first section was to consist of a series of chapters devoted to a variety of methodological issues, each to be followed in the next section by a case study exemplifying that particular mode of inquiry. Thus, a reader can read all the methodological chapters first, then all the case studies, or, alternatively read the methodological chapters one at a time, then the corresponding case study. The organization did not work out exactly as planned since there are two case studies for the one methodological statement of lexicostatistic theory and no methodological chapter corresponding to a case study of the Altaic languages. A history of language classification by R.H. Robins introduces the volume while an index of languages and writing systems completes it.

62.   **Volume 12: Linguistics and Adjacent Arts and Sciences**. 1974. 4v. 3037p. index.

According to Sebeok, this set of four volumes was designed to counteract the previous volumes of this series which seemingly reinforced the tendency of linguistics to become highly specialized. Citing Edward Sapir as far back as 1927, he makes a plea in his introduction for the linguistic community to be receptive to external ideas and to assimilate knowledge from other segments of the arts and the sciences to keep from "lapsing into stale dogmatism" (p.vi).

The set is divided into numerous parts roughly according to disciplines. Each part is comprised of from one to as many as eleven chapters on such areas of study as: linguistics and philosophy, semiotics, linguistics and the verbal arts, linguistics and psychology, and even range to bio-medicine and computer applications.

The last volume contains indexes for topics, names, and languages.

63.   **Volume 13: Historiography of Linguistics**. 1975. 2v. 1518p. index.

All of the first volume and over half of the second in this set are devoted to studies of the Western tradition. There are chapters covering India; classical antiquity; the Middle Ages; the seventeenth, eighteenth, and nineteenth centuries; European and American structuralism; and finally an annotated bibliography by Robert Austerlitz on the history of phonetics. In the second half of volume 2 are areal studies, such as articles on the Far East, linguistics among the Arabs, the Hebrew tradition, native North America, and native Ibero-America. Edward Stankiewicz contributes a selected bibliography of the history of linguistics from 1945 through the early 1970s. It is followed by an index of names and an index of languages.

64.   **Volume 14: Indexes**. 1976. 952p.

The final volume of this whole series contains the following:

1.   Contents of Volumes 1-13, Including Bibliographical Information
2.   Contents of Volumes 1-13, Alphabetized by Authors' Names
3.   Index of Languages
4.   Subject Index
5.   Index of Names
6.   Biographical Notes of Editors and Contributors

The last four items are essentially compilations of the various indexes and biographies found in the first 13 volumes. Unquestionably they are critical for access to such a voluminous and wide-ranging work.

65.   Trask, Robert Lawrence. **A Dictionary of Grammatical Terms in Linguistics**. London: Routledge, 1993. 335p. illus. bibliog. LC 92-24806. ISBN 0-415-08627-2.

The author, a linguist and instructor affiliated with the University of Sussex, has captured and defined 1,500 terms used in grammatical literature, mainly the descriptive terms used in syntax (sentence structure), but also to some extent those used in morphology (word structure). All but the terminology found in more highly specialized works was included. The terminology of traditional grammar is of course included. In regard to particular theories of grammar, inclusion of terms from Government-Binding Theory is meant to be comprehensive, while that of Generalized Phrase Structure Grammar, Lexical-Functional Grammar, Relational Grammar, and Role-and-Reference Grammar is more limited. Terminology specific to other theories is not covered though every theory of grammar has an entry under its own name. The user will also find terms associated with mathematical and computational linguistics (pp. iix-ix). In addition to definitions, Trask provides examples, pronunciations (typical for the south of England), notes on original sources of terms, and suggestions for further reading. As with his other specialized dictionaries, he is writing mainly for students and teachers of linguistics.

66.   Trask, Robert Lawrence. **A Dictionary of Phonetics and Phonology**. London: Routledge, 1996. 424p. illus. bibliog. LC 95-16583. ISBN 0-415-11260-5.

Even with its focus narrowed to just phonetics and phonology there are still more than 2,000 terms in this dictionary. Most entries are for core vocabulary which has been around for some time as well as terms used in articulatory phonetics, acoustic and perceptual phonetics, and speech science. Trask is thorough in capturing the terminology of classical phonology (the Prague School, Daniel Jones, the American Structuralists), classical generative phonology, and the principal terms from various developments in phonology during the last two decades. Both traditional and recent terms of phonological variation and change, including that of metrics, is well covered. Phonology of English is covered more thoroughly than for other languages. Entries nearly always give pronunciation which is in International Phonetic Alphabet (IPA) notation, albeit for the pronunciation typical of the south of England. Illustrations and examples are used to good advantage; the IPA given is the one revised to 1993. Compared to Crystal's *Dictionary of Linguistics and Phonetics* (see entry 19), definitions are longer and somewhat more technical, many entries have references for further reading, and there is a substantial bibliography appended.

67. Trask, Robert Lawrence. **A Student's Dictionary of Language and Linguistics**. London: Arnold, distr. St. Martin's Press, 1997. 247p. illus. bibliog. ISBN 0-340-65267-5.

Trask aimed this dictionary chiefly at beginning students, but it should be useful to anyone doing reading in the field (p. v). It covers terminology from general linguistics as well as traditional grammar, allied areas (such as sociolinguistics, psycholinguistics, and computational linguistics), language change, and origin and evolution of language. Common everyday terms used in academia and as well as terms related to Internet usage are helpfully defined. In addition there are entries for prominent languages and language families, biographical entries for persons prominent in linguistics and related fields, and entries for organizations. Many common abbreviations appear with cross-references to the spelled out entries. Concise definitions are written in simple, straightforward language with examples, illustrations, and cross-references used to good advantage. Completing the dictionary is an annotated list of suggested readings for further study, conveniently grouped into categories. This is an up-to-date, very useful, clearly understood basic dictionary for linguistics. For the university student and teacher needing more technical definitions, Crystal's dictionary of linguistics and phonetics (see entry 19) or even the scholarly work by Bussmann (see entry 15) would be good choices. For the more general reader there is Crystal's encyclopedic dictionary (see entry 20) which also, compared to this work, covers more languages and language families more thoroughly, provides longer definitions, and guides the user in the pronunciation of less familiar terms.

68. Ulrich, Winfried. **Wörterbuch, linguistische Grundbegriffe**. 3. erneut bearb. u. erw. Aufl. Kiel: Ferdinand Hirt, 1981. 191p. illus. bibliog. (Hirts Stichwortbücher). LC 81-165313. ISBN 3-55480337-5.

The German linguistic dictionary by Bartschat (see entry 11) is similar in scope and format to this one by Ulrich.

69. Urdang, Laurence and Frank R. Abate, eds. **Literary, Rhetorical, and Linguistics Terms Index; An Alphabetically Arranged List of Words and Phrases Used in the English-speaking World in the Analysis of Language and Literature, Selected from Authoritative and Widely Consulted Sources, Presented in a**

Format Designed for Quick Reference, and Including a Descriptive Bibliography of the Sources. Detroit, MI: Gale Research Co., 1983. 305p. index. bibliog. LC 83-1636. ISBN 0-8103-11984.

The purpose of this index is to facilitate access to definitions of the vast and ever increasing terminology of the literary critic, the grammarian, and the linguist. The bibliography preceding the terms index itself lists the 17 "authoritative and widely consulted sources" mentioned in the overly long subtitle of this reference work. Only three linguistic dictionaries are among these sources: the 1979 edition of Ducrot's *Encyclopedic Dictionary of the Sciences of Language* (see entry 24), Crystal's *First Dictionary of Linguistics and Phonetics* (see entry 19), and Pei's *Glossary of Linguistic Terminology* (Anchor Books, 1966).

The index lists over 17,000 words and phrases. Under each word or phrase is a reference to one or more of the sources where a definition of the term can be found; no definitions are given here. Since terms are represented here as they are in the original sources, entries that differ only in minor respects are listed separately. The term "nasalized" is separate from "nasalized" as is "semantic feature" from "semantic features." If one had all three linguistic dictionaries on hand, it would be almost as fast to look up a linguistic term in each one as it would be to locate it here first. For literary and rhetorical terms it would probably be of more use.

70. Vachek, Josef. **Dictionnaire de linguistique de l'École de Prague**. Avec collaboration de Josef Dubský. 3e éd. Utrecht/Anvers: Spectrum Editeurs, 1970. 104p. index. (Comité international permanent des linguistes; Publication de la Commission de terminologie).

Definitions in this dictionary range from one- to twelve-word phrases. Entries nearly always include quotes from original sources. These sources include material published from 1928-1958 by linguists associated with the Linguistic Circle of Prague, collectively known as the Prague School. Havránek, Mathesius, Jakobson, Skalička, and Trnka are among the scholars quoted. English, German, and Czech equivalents for the technical terms are given both within the entries and in separate indexes.

71. Yartseva, V. N., glav. red. **Lingvisticheskii entsiklopedicheskii slovar'**. Moskva: "Sovetskaya Entsiklopediya," 1990. 685p. illus. ISBN 5-85270-031-2.

In addition to the chief editor there are some 13 other associated editors of this scholarly encyclopedia of linguistics. Each of its articles is signed by one of its many contributors and has an appended list of citations for further reference. Articles are written in Russian while citations in the appended lists are in original language of publication. Length of entries ranges from a few lines to several pages for more general topics. For example, the entries for "typology," "historical linguistics," and "mathematical linguistics" warrant more lengthy treatment. Following the entries is an index listing article headings (in bold type) and terms treated within articles along with the appropriate page(s) number(s). An index of languages is keyed to page numbers for article headings (in bold type) and for other articles in which the language is treated. Another index is for persons cited within articles (names in Latin script are transliterated into Cyrillic).

2

Biographical Sources

There are no geographically and chronologically comprehensive reference sources for biographical information on linguists. Various encyclopedias and dictionaries listed earlier in chapter 1 can supplement the sources listed below. Chapter 8, which contains bibliographies of linguists, can be used fruitfully to obtain information about individuals. Some general biographical indexes and sources to consult include: *Biography and Genealogy Master Index* (Gale Research), *Biography Index* (H. W. Wilson), *American Men and Women of Science* (R. R. Bowker), and the various "who's who" type directories issued by various publishers.

72.   Brekle, Herbert Ernst, Edeltraud Dobnig-Jülch, Hans Jürgen Höller, and Helmut Weiss, Hrsg. **Bio-bibliographisches Handbuch zur Sprachwissenschaft des 18. Jahrhunderts: die Grammatiker, Lexikographen und Sprachtheoretiker des deutschsprachigen Raums mit Beschreibungen ihrer Werke.** Tübingen: Max Niemeyer, 1992-1996. 4v. 378p. (v. 1); 438p. (v. 2); 411p.(v. 3); 404p. (v. 4). ISBN 3-484-73020-X (set); ISBN 3-484-73021-8 (v. 1); ISBN 3-484-73022-6 (v. 2); ISBN 3-484-73023-4 (v. 3); ISBN 3-484-73024-2 (v. 4). (In progress).

In the introduction to this authoritative handbook the editors list the many works they have consulted for information for this work in progress. It is a biographical and bibliographical source for those persons living in German-speaking countries whose work in linguistics, lexicography, or grammar was published during the 18th century. The editors list individuals alphabetically and have arranged materials under each name into three sections. The first section gives biographical information, the second pertinent information and an overview of the individual's work, while the third is a comprehensive bibliography of primary and secondary literature. At the end of each volume is an appendix listing persons the editors considered for inclusion, but rejected for not meeting their criteria (linguistic relevance, publication within the time and area selected for the handbook). This work provides information on some generally neglected linguists who made contributions that paved the way for advances in the century following. Band 1 (1992) covers A-Br, Band 2 (1993) Bu-E, Band 3 (1994) F-G, and Band 4 (1996) H-I.

73.   Bronstein, Arthur J., Lawrence J. Raphael and CJ Stevens, eds. **A Biographical Dictionary of the Phonetic Sciences**. New York: Press of Lehman College, 1977. 255p. index. bibliog. LC 77-087592.

Nearly 200 contributors to the field of phonetic science are profiled here. To be included a contributor had to have lived and worked in North America or Western Europe and made a significant contribution to the field by a cut-off date of 1960. The field of phonetic sciences as defined here by the editors encompasses general phonology, general-articulatory phonetics, dialectology, and experimental/acoustic phonetics. A short paragraph detailing such information as birth and death dates, education, positions, and areas of interest begins each entry. A paragraph or so follows listing important publications along with notes on the entrant's other contributions. This may be followed by a special evaluation written and signed by a scholar in the field.

74.   Kürschner, Wilfried, Hrsg. **Linguisten Handbuch: Biographische und bibliographische Daten deutschsprachiger Sprachwissenschaftlerinnen und Sprachwissenschaftler der Gegenwart**. Tübingen: Gunter Narr, 1994. 2v. 1191p. index. ports. ISBN 3-8233-5000-5.

This two-volume bio-bibliographical handbook of linguists contains information on German-speaking linguistics teachers and linguists of the present (Bd.1, A-L; Bd.2, M-Z). Each entry contains brief biographical information along with address (and often a picture), educational background, professional positions, areas of research, and a bibliography. Entries contain numerous abbreviations, but not so many as to detract from its readability. Well-constructed indexes enhance its value to the user. There are indexes of persons by area of research; one is for language under study, the other for subject area. There is also an index of persons by affiliated institution organized first by country and then by city. Inclusion of scholars and teachers is the most thorough for Germany, uneven for countries in the rest of Europe, and less thorough for elsewhere in the world.

75.   Pop, Sever, and Rodica Doina Pop. **Encyclopédie linguistique; membres du premier Congrès international de dialectologie générale (Louvain-Bruxelles, 1960)**. Louvain: Centre international de dialectologie générale, 1960. 237p. (Travaux publiés par le Centre international de dialectologie générale près l'Université catholique de Louvain, fasc. VI). LC 61-1910.

Short biographies accompanied by a portrait of each of the members of the First International Congress of Dialectology are arranged here in alphabetical order. The authors have gathered for each biography such information as date and place of birth, degrees obtained, professors studied under, professional activities and memberships, most important scientific initiatives, honors and awards, and publications. It begins with an entry on Jacques Allières, ends with Eberhard Zwirner and includes in between the two authors of this book and other figures important in the history of dialectology such as Bernard Pottier, Johann Knobloch, Marguerite Durand, and Hans Kurath.

76.   Sebeok, Thomas Albert, ed. **Portraits of Linguists; a Biographical Source Book for the History of Western Linguistics, 1746-1963**. Bloomington: Indiana University Press, 1966. 2v. 580p.(v.1); 605p.(v.2). index. (Indiana University Studies in the History and Theory of Linguistics). LC 64-64663.

In these two volumes biographies of 90 linguists born prior to the beginning of the twentieth century are arranged chronologically by date of birth. Volume 1 begins with a biography of Sir William Jones born in 1746 and volume 2 concludes with Benjamin Lee Whorf born in 1897. None of the linguists are still living. Franklin Edgerton, the last one who lived, died in 1963, thus accounting for that date in the title of this book. Because this is an anthology of previously published biographies, Sebeok explains that some linguists one would expect to find here were omitted because he was not able to turn up a worthy portrait of them. On the other hand, he has included as many as three portraits on others because they were available. Articles ranging in length from four to over forty pages are in English, French, or German, though there is one on Paul Passy reprinted in IPA transcription of English. Volume 2 has an index of names.

3

Indexes, Abstracts, Serial Bibliographies, and Electronic Databases

The major indexes, abstracts, serial bibliographies, and electronic databases (CD-ROM and online) for general, theoretical, and historical linguistics are listed here as well as selected multidisciplinary indexes. More specialized ones can be found throughout later chapters in part 2 on the allied subject areas of anthropological linguistics, applied linguistics, mathematical and computational linguistics, psycholinguistics, and sociolinguistics as well as in the various language chapters of part 3. The electronic databases (CD-ROM, online, and Internet) are those available at many academic and larger public libraries from the producers and distributors listed below.

Information for this chapter was gathered from a variety of sources, including vendor and producer literature, Internet sites, and the following directories: *CD-ROMs in Print* (Westport, CT: Meckler, 1997), *Key Guide to Electronic Resources: Language and Literature* (Medford, NJ: Information Today, 1996), *Information Industry Directory* (Detroit, MI: Gale Research, 1999), and the *Gale Directory of Databases* (Detroit, MI: Gale Research, 1998). Because details of any particular electronic database differ from vendor to vendor, the reader who requires more information should contact directly the producers and distributors listed below:

> Blackwell Publishers Inc.
> 350 Main St.
> Malden, MA 02148
> (781) 388-8200
> subscrip@blackwellpub.com
> http://www.blackwellpub.com
>
> Cambridge Scientific Abstracts (CSA)
> 7200 Wisconsin Ave., Suite 601
> Bethesda, MD 20814
> (301) 961-6700; (800) 843-7751
> service@csa.com
> http://www.csa.com
>
> Dialog Corporation
> 11000 Regency Parkway, Suite 10
> Cary, NC 27511
> (919) 462-8600
> customer@dialog.com
> http://www.dialog.com

EBSCO Publishing
10 Estes St.
Ipswich, MA 01938
(978) 356-6500; (800) 653-2726
ep@epnet.com
http://www.epnet.com

G. K. Hall, c/o Macmillan Publishing
866 Third Ave.
New York, NY 10022
(207) 948-5996; (800) 223-1244, ext. 247
holly_ingraham@prenhall.com

Information Access Company (IAC)
362 Lakeside Dr.
Foster City, CA 94404
(650) 378-5000
info@informationaccess.com
http://www.informationaccess.com

Institut de l'Information Scientifique et
      Technique (INIST)
2, allée du Parc de Brabois
F-54514 Vandoeuvre-lès-Nancy Cedex, France
33 83504619
appel@inist.fr
http://www.inist.fr

Institute for Scientific Information (ISI)
3501 Market Street
Philadelphia, PA 19104
(215) 386-0100; (800) 336-4474 (at the
      prompt press 2)
sales@isinet.com
http://www.isinet.com

National Information Services Corp. (NISC)
Wyman Towers, 3100 St. Paul St.
Baltimore, MD 21218
(410) 243-0797
info@nisc.com
http://www.nisc.com

OCLC, Online Computer Library Center, Inc.
6565 Frantz Rd.
Dublin, OH 43017-3395
(614) 764-6000
oclc@oclc.org
http://www.oclc.org

Ovid Technologies, Inc.
333 Seventh Ave.
New York, NY 10001
(212) 563-3006; (800) 950-2035, ext. 249
sales@ovid.com
http://www.ovid.com

Research Libraries Group (RLG)
1200 Villa St.
Mountain View, CA 94041-1100
(650) 691-2333; (800) 537-7546
bl.ric@rlg.org
http://www.rlg.org

SilverPlatter Information, Inc.
100 River Ridge Dr.
Norwood, MA 02062-5043
(781) 769-2599; (800) 343-0064
customerrelations@silverplatter.com
http://www.silverplatter.com

STN International - CAS
2540 Olentangy River Rd.
Columbus, OH 4320
(614) 447-3731; (800) 753-4227
helpw@cas.org
http://www.fizkarlsruhe.de/stn.html

University Microfilms International (UMI)
300 North Zeeb Rd.
Ann Arbor, MI 48106-1346
(734) 761-4700; (800) 521-0600
info@umi.com
http://www.umi.com

H. W. Wilson Company
950 University Ave.
Bronx, NY 10452-4224
(718) 588-8400; (800) 367-6770
custserv@hwwilson.com
http://www.hwwilson.com

77. **Arts & Humanities Citation Index**. Philadelphia, PA: Institute for Scientific Information, 1975- . semiannual. ISSN 0162-8445.

AHCI indexes more than 1,150 journal titles in the arts and humanities and selectively indexes items from over 7,000 science and social science journals. Among the topics covered are linguistics and philology, language, literature, and philosophy. It has a source index (author and main entry), permuterm subject index, corporate index, and citation index which allows a user to locate current articles citing older publications. It is available back to 1990 on CD-ROM (ISI), back to 1980 online (Dialog), and via the Internet (ISI Web of Science, OCLC FirstSearch).

78.   **Bibliographie linguistique de l'année . . . et complément des années précédentes.** Vol. 1- , 1939/47- . Dordrech, Netherlands: Kluwer Academic, 1949- . annual.

A second title page in English identifies this work as *Linguistic Bibliography for the Year . . . and Supplement for Previous Years.* It is published by the Permanent International Committee of Linguists under the auspices of the International Council of Philosophy and Humanistic Studies. The initial two volumes cover the years 1939 to 1947; subsequent volumes cover a year at a time with only supplementary inclusion of material for previous years. Until the volume for 1976 it was published by Spectrum Publishers in Utrecht, The Netherlands.

This serial index is of primary importance in linguistic research since it provides comprehensive, world-wide coverage of periodical articles, dissertations, and contributions to collected works such as Festschriften and conference proceedings, including substantial reviews of such publications. Though comprehensive, it is not current. The bibliography for 1994 with 23,000 entries was published three years later in November 1997. Another drawback of this bibliography is that it does not have a subject index. A classification scheme detailed in the table of contents partially compensates for this lack.

In very broad terms the bibliography has a section on general linguistics and related disciplines that is followed by various sections devoted to language groups and languages. An author index is included at the end of each volume; writers of book reviews, however, are not included in this index. Many of the entries contain brief notes. These notes consist of a variety of items such as references to reviews, cross-references, short explanatory notes on content not indicated by the title, translation of title into usually French or English, language(s) under study, and references to summaries in other languages.

Because extensive use is made of abbreviations, lists of these are provided at the beginning of each volume. For periodicals the list is alphabetical by abbreviation. There is no reverse list alphabetical by full title. This makes it difficult to determine if *BL* indexes a particular periodical; you have to try and guess the abbreviation first, then go through the list which can be tedious. Starting with the volume covering publications in the years 1993-1994, a CD-ROM version is being planned. More information can be obtained at the publisher's Web site at http://www.wkap.nl/book.htm/0-7923-4710-2 (accessed: March 6, 1999).

79.   **Bibliographie linguistischer Literatur (BLL); Bibliographie zur allgemeinen Linguistik und zur anglistischen, germanistischen und romanistischen Linguistik/Bibliography of Linguistic Literature (BLL): Bibliography of General Linguistics and of English, German, and Romance Linguistics.** Bd. 4- , 1978- . Frankfurt am Main: Vittorio Klostermann, 1979- . annual. ISSN 0172-3960.

The title for Bänden 1-3 of this classified bibliography published for the Stadt- und Universitätsbibliothek Frankfurt, the Frankfurt City and University Library, is *Bibliographie unselbständiger Literatur-Linguistik (BUL-L).* Band 1 covered the years 1971-1975 and only included non-monographic literature with subsequent volumes of both the *BUL-L* and *BLL* becoming annual and picking up supplementary material for previous years. From 1976 on it covers articles in periodicals and essays in collective works, including conference/congress proceedings, dissertations, and Festschriften. The number of periodicals it covers has gradually increased from 123 in Band 1 to about 1,000 in 1998. Coverage is international in scope and quite current with only a one or two year time lag. Complete bibliographic information is provided with a minimum of abbreviation; there are no annotations.

The division on general linguistics includes coverage of the allied areas bio-, ethno-, neuro-, patho-, psycho-, socio-, and pragmalinguistics, as well as computer linguistics, and semiotics. There are also divisions on English, German, and Romance linguistics. Each of these divisions is subdivided into a form section, a systematic section, and a language section (the latter missing of course in the general linguistics division). The systematic section of each division contains all the entries for that division classified under appropriate subject categories. These entries may also qualify for listing again in the form and/or language sections. This whole classification scheme is fully explained in the introduction which, beginning with Band 7, appears in both German and English, as are the headings. With volume 13 literature pertaining exclusively to language teaching is omitted. A cumulative author index and subject and name index complete each annual volume.

This index and the *Bibliographie linguistique/Linguistic Bibliography* (see entry 78) are international in scope. The *BLL* however, is more current and has the advantage of a subject index. On the other hand it does not begin to cover the variety of languages which the *Bibliographie linguistique* does. The *BLLDB* (Bibliography of Linguistic Literature Database) is now available online (STN) from 1971 and is updated every second month; a Web interface is under development.

80. **Dissertation Abstracts International**. Ann Arbor, MI: University Microfilms International, 1938- . monthly. ISSN 0419-4209.

This print index and several related titles cover dissertations back to 1861. *DAI* now includes abstracts for doctoral dissertations accepted at U.S. institutions and an increasing number of European institutions. Since all subject areas are covered, anyone doing a comprehensive literature review should search this index. The *DAI* database goes back to 1861 with abstracts available for most dissertations published from mid-1980 to present and includes master's theses with abstracts from spring 1988. It is available as a CD-ROM (SilverPlatter, UMI), online (Dialog, Ovid), and via the Internet (OCLC FirstSearch, SilverPlatter).

81. **FRANCIS**. [CD-ROM]. Vandoeuvre-les-Nancy Cedex, France: Institut de l'Information Scientifique et Technique (INIST), 1984- . annual updates.

The FRANCIS (French Retrieval Automated Network for Current Information in Social and Human Sciences) bibliographic database was previously sponsored by the French Centre National de la Recherche Scientifique (CNRS), but since 1991 has been the responsibility of INIST. It began as a print publication with comprehensive multilingual and international coverage of the humanities and social sciences literature (books, journals, reports, conference proceedings, dissertations, and other documents). From 1947 through 1968 it contained abstracts. Linguistics was covered by sections that went through successive title changes: 1947-1960, *Bulletin signalétique: Philosophie, sciences humaines*; 1961-1966, *Bulletin signalétique. Sec.21, Sociologie, sciences eu langage*; and 1967-1968, *Bulletin signalétique 24, Sciences du langage*. In 1969 it became a bibliography only and later went through one more title change to become for 1991-1994 *FRANCIS bulletin signalétique. 524. Sciences du langage.*

Coverage of the linguistic literature drawn from the FRANCIS database includes topics such as biology and pathology of language, psycholinguistics, sociolinguistics, ethnolinguistics, historical and descriptive linguistics, linguistics and mathematics, semiotics, and applied linguistics. Because of its wide international, multilingual and multidisciplinary scope covering all time periods, it provides access to materials not available in many other databases. There is extensive indexing and brief abstracts are provided for most citations in French or English. In addition to the CD-ROM (INIST), there is a FRANCIS online database (RLG CitaDel) which also provides coverage from 1984 to the present and has monthly updates.

82. **Humanities Index**. New York: H. W. Wilson Co., 1984- . quarterly. ISSN 0095-5981.

Language and literature as well as philosophy are among the subjects covered by this index of some 400 English-language periodicals. The index, abstracts, and full-text are variously available through the producer and a variety of vendors on CD-ROM, online (Dialog, Ovid), and via the Internet (OCLC FirstSearch, SilverPlatter, Wilson, WilsonWeb).

83. **International Bibliography of the Social Sciences**. 1951- . London: Routledge, 1952- . annual. ISSN 0085-2058.

The print index compiled by the British Library of Political and Economic Science of the London School of Economics and Political Science is published annually in four parts devoted to the fields of anthropology, sociology, economics, and political science. The electronic database combines all four areas; it contains bibliographic information from an international selection of publications, including more than 2,600 journals, 6,000 books, book reviews, and book chapters. Coverage is from both core and specialized materials from over 100 countries in more than 90 languages. Approximately 70% of the citations are in English, but if in another language, the original title is given along with an English translation. It contains a surprising amount of core linguistic material as well as that of allied subject areas such as anthropological linguistics and sociolinguistics. The database is available on CD-ROM and via the Internet from SilverPlatter.

84. **Linguistics Abstracts**. Vol. 1- , No. 1- . Oxford, England: Basil Blackwell, 1985- . quarterly. ISSN 0267-5498.

Under the editorship of David Crystal, the focus of this abstracting service is the theory and practice of general linguistics, not applied linguistics, nor the descriptive or historical study of individual languages or dialects. The signed abstracts are descriptive, not evaluative, and are classified into seventeen thematic categories. At the end of the thematic sections there are liberal cross-references to other sections. Each issue has an author index, subject index, and a list of journals abstracted. The author and subject indexes are cumulated in the fourth issue each year. Many issues also have an introductory survey article written as a personal statement by a linguist about some current trend in the field. Some of the topics covered in the first three volumes have been "Whither Linguistic Theory?" "Computerized Text Processing in Linguistic and Literary Research," and "Linguistic Historiography." Coverage is somewhat limited, indexing approximately 300 journals, compared to more comprehensive indexes such as *LLBA* or *MLA* (see entries 85 and 88), but it does pick up some material not covered by other abstracting services and the time lag is only about a year. As *Linguistics Abstracts Online*, or *LABS*, this database is available on the Web (Blackwell Publishers).

85. **Linguistics and Language Behavior Abstracts**. Vol. 1- , No. 1- . San Diego, CA: Sociological Abstracts, 1967- . quarterly. ISSN 0888-8027.

Until volume 19 was published in 1985 the title of this abstracting index was *Language and Language Behavior Abstracts* (ISSN 0023-8295). It is often referred to by its acronym *LLBA*. Through the years it has had a variety of publishers beginning with Appleton-Century Crofts. At that time it had an author index, an index of journals examined and a table of contents listing 21 subject areas. There was no detailed subject index until cumulative indexes to the first 5 volumes (1967-1971) were published in 1973. Beginning with volume 6 (1972) an annual cumulative index containing an author index, subject index and source publication list is published. A book review index was included only through volume 12 (1978).

In each issue abstracts are classified into about thirty major subject areas. *LLBA* is particularly strong in the areas of applied linguistics, descriptive linguistics, and psycholinguistics. Among other topics it covers are syntax, sociolinguistics, theory of linguistics, interpersonal behavior and communication, semantics, phonetics, phonology, discourse analysis, and poetics. In 1988 subject coverage of literacy and reading was enhanced with the incorporation of *Reading Abstracts* (La Jolla, CA: Essay Press, 1975-1987?). Over 1,500 publications in a wide range of disciplines are regularly scanned for relevant articles. Recently published books in linguistics are also included. Coverage of non-English materials is very good with some thirty languages represented. The titles of these articles are given in the original language along with their English translation. Substantial abstracts are provided for all articles and books with the exception of references from *Dissertation Abstracts International*.

One difficulty in using this otherwise excellent index is that the terms in the subject index are often so broad users have to sift through hundreds of entries under a term to find what they want. Moreover, pages lack headings of any sort. Fortunately it is now an electronic database and can be searched back to 1973 on CD-ROM (NISC, SilverPlatter), via the Internet (CSA, SilverPlatter), and online (Dialog). Updates are quarterly. An *LLBA User's Reference Manual* now in its third edition (1987) includes valuable information on editorial and indexing practices, descriptor terms, and other information. A *Thesaurus of Linguistic Indexing Terms*, 2nd edition (1998) revised and updated the descriptors and hierarchical displays. Both the manual and thesaurus are essential for effective retrieval. A quarterly newsletter, *Note Us*, informs regular users of new developments in *LLBA*.

86. **Linguistics Proceedings Directory**. Available: http://www.cascadilla.com/proceedings.html. (Accessed: March 8, 1999).

Cascadilla Press is compiling an online directory of published proceedings from linguistics conferences. A visitor to this Web site can either browse the alphabetical list or search the directory with keywords. Once a conference proceedings is located, information varies, but may include date and location of conference, editor of proceedings, date published, original publisher, publisher proceedings available from (with contact information), and a link to the table of contents. Information is also supplied on conferences that were not published. At last page update October 5, 1998 there were 22 conferences listed including a number of the COLING, ESCOL, LACUS, NELS, and SALT conferences. This effort is just beginning so there is not yet much depth in terms of years covered, with the exception of a few dating back to the mid-1970s and mid-1980s, but promises to become an important resource as time goes on for hard to find conference papers.

87. **LWPD: Linguistics Working Papers Directory Home Page**. Available: http://www.lingref.com/lwpd/index.html. (Accessed: March 8, 1999).

At this Web site Cascadilla Press is compiling an online directory for linguistics working papers. Each of the 29 working papers series is listed alphabetically and linked to information about the series as well as contact and ordering information. Tables of contents are listed for some volumes. Abstracts for many of the current working papers can be found in Blackwell's *Linguistics Abstracts* (see entry 84). If this Web site continues to grow, it will become an important resource for this type of hard-to-locate material.

88. **MLA International Bibliography of Books and Articles on the Modern Languages and Literatures**. 1921- . New York: Modern Language Association of America, 1922- . annual. ISSN 0024-8215.

The coverage, format, and title of this publication has changed since it first began publication as a supplement to *PMLA* (Publications of the Modern Language Association of America). It continued as a supplement to *PMLA* through the volume for 1968. From 1921-1955 it was entitled *American Bibliography*; it changed to *Annual Bibliography* for the years 1956-1962; and, from 1963 to present it has been the *MLA International Bibliography*. . . . The volumes for 1921-1955 were reprinted as the *MLA American Bibliography* . . . and for 1956-1968 as the *MLA International Bibliography* . . . (New York: Kraus Reprint Corp.).

Linguistics has been included in *MLA*'s coverage since the beginning issue and as its scope and language coverage increased through the years so did its inclusion of linguistic items. As the *American Bibliography* it covered less than a dozen journals plus book sources and was limited to American writers on literatures of various countries. The change to the title of *Annual Bibliography* in 1956 signaled a shift from national to international coverage with articles written in French, German, Spanish, Italian, Portuguese, Scandinavian, and Dutch now being added. By 1962 ten East European languages had been added and the master list of periodicals expanded to about 1,000 sources. This expanded coverage continued with Celtic, Rumanian, Medieval and Neo-Latin, Modern Greek, Oriental, and African languages being included in the volume issued for 1968.

With the 1969 annual issue came a major change in format with a shift to a multi-volume arrangement. The first two volumes contained sections on literature and folklore while the third volume was devoted to linguistics. The annuals issued for 1969-1972 also contained a fourth volume with listings on pedagogy in the modern foreign languages, compiled under the auspices of the American Council on the Teaching of Foreign Languages. The arrangement of entries was a classified one, with the system being outlined in a detailed table of contents for each volume. There was no subject index though each volume did index authors. For a six-year period from 1970-1975 abstracts for some of the entries (marked with an asterisk preceding item numbers) were available in another publication, *MLA Abstracts* (see entry 121). The number of sources for periodical articles continued to expand and in 1979 MLA published a directory of these, the first of what was to become a biennial guide to journals and series in languages and literatures (see entry 237).

Another change in format, and the one still in use, came in 1981 with a 5-volume arrangement and cumulative author (as well as editor and compiler) and subject indexes for the year. Volume 3 continued to be devoted to linguistics. All areas of linguistic study are covered with no restrictions concerning either the place of origin or publication or original language of works. It includes articles from journals, monographs, and collections (such as working papers, Festschriften, conference papers and proceedings) as well as indexes, bibliographies, catalogs, handbooks, dictionaries, and other types of reference works, plus citations to *Dissertation Abstracts International*. Reviews are generally not included unless they survey a number of scholarly works or make an independent contribution to scholarship.

A look at the guide to the classified listings in volume 3 shows headings for topics of general linguistic interest as well as headings for specific languages organized around such groupings as Indo-European languages, Caucasian languages, African, Native American, Sino-Tibetan, and invented languages. There is comprehensive coverage of theoretical and descriptive linguistics and comparative and historical linguistics as well as allied areas such as applied linguistics, psycholinguistics, sociolinguistics, mathematical linguistics, paralinguistics, stylistics, and translation. The inclusion of a subject index since 1981 greatly increases the usefulness of this bibliography. Publication lags about two years. It is more up-to-date in its various electronic formats which begin coverage in 1963 (OCLC FirstSearch, Ovid, SilverPlatter) and has ten updates a year. Additional information can be found on MLA's Web site available at http://www.mla.org/set_pub.htm (accessed: March 11, 1999).

89. Novaya Literatura po Sotsial'nym i Gumanitarnym Naukam: Yazykoznanie. Moskva: RAN INION, 1993- . monthly. ISSN 0134-2762.

The above publication reporting new literature in the social and humanities sciences, linguistics section, was formed by the merger and continuation of two former titles. The first of these titles listed non-Soviet publications and was initially titled *Novaya Inostrannaya Literatura po Yazykoznaniyu* (1953-1975) and then became *Novaya Inostrannaya Literatura po Obshchestvennym Naukam: Yazykoznanie* (1976-1992). The second of these titles covered Soviet works and was initially titled *Novaya Sovetskaya Literatura po Yazykoznaniyu* (1954-1975), became *Novaya Sovetskaya Literatura po Obshchestvennym Naukam: Yazykoznanie* (1976-91), and then finally *Novaya Otechestvenna Literatura po Obshchestvennym Naukam: Yazykoznanie* (1992). This second title was of particular value since it covered Soviet publications not indexed by other bibliographies. Material in the former title was more thoroughly covered elsewhere. This publication and all former titles are known collectively as the *Bibliograficheskii Ukazatel'*, or bibliographic index; each of these monthlies lists current articles and monographs on linguistics and is organized according to the same classified arrangement with the same kinds of indexes.

The current work encompasses all fields of languages and linguistics including general linguistics, sociolinguistics, psycholinguistics, applied linguistics, and languages. The language sections, as expected, are particularly rich for Slavonic languages. Works arranged by author under topics are listed in the language of publication and most have brief annotations in Russian. Each issue has an author index, subject index, and a list of publications consulted. There are no cumulative indexes.

90. **Russian Academy of Sciences Bibliographies**. [online database]. Moskva: INION, 1992- . bimonthly.

RAS cites books, manuscripts, dissertations, plus articles from more than 10,000 periodicals and provides abstracts for about 50% of the citations. It is a unique source of information for materials published in the Commonwealth of Independent States and Eastern Europe and an especially rich source for Slavic studies. Author and title are in original language of publication. Abstracts and keywords are in Russian, but subject headings are in both Russian and English. The file is only available as an RLG CitaDel file and an institution can choose to search *RAS* via Eureka and see all data in Latin transliteration, or via the RLIN interface that presents data in its original Cyrillic script.

91. **Science Citation Index**. Philadelphia, PA: Institute for Scientific Information, 1961- . bimonthly. ISSN 0036-827X.

The print *SCI* indexes more than 3,500 of the world's leading scientific and technical journals. It is an international multidisciplinary file covering every area of the pure and applied sciences. It would be a good index to search for topics in the areas of mathematical and computational linguistics, neurolinguistics, and psycholinguistics. It has a source index (author and main entry), permuterm subject index, corporate index, and citation index which allows a user to locate current articles citing older publications. As a database it is available back to 1980 and with abstracts back to 1991 on CD-ROM (ISI). There is an expanded online version covering some 1,900 additional journals and going back to 1974 (Dialog, STN). It is also available via the Internet (ISI Web of Science).

92. **Social Science Citation Index**. Philadelphia, PA: Institute for Scientific Information, 1972- . triannual. ISSN 0091-3707

The print *SSCI* indexes more than 1,700 social science journals and individually selected relevant items from more than 5,600 scientific and technical journals. It includes many important monographs as well. Every area of the social and behavioral sciences is covered including linguistics, anthropology, sociology, psychology, education, philosophy, area studies, and communications. It has a source index (author and main entry), permuterm subject index, corporate index, and citation index which allows a user to locate current articles citing older publications. It is available back to 1981 and with abstracts back to 1992 on CD-ROM (ISI), available via the Internet (ISI Web of Science), as well as online back to 1972 (Dialog).

4

Internet Meta-Sites

93. **Alternative Site Information**. Available: http://clwww.essex. ac.uk/other_sites/. (Accessed March 19, 1999).

Doug Arnold, CL/MT (Computational Linguistics/Machine Translation) Group, Department of Language and Linguistics at the University of Essex, UK maintains this Web site of linguistics links. Formerly a random lists of links, it was recently organized into 16 categories plus a new additions link and an index. Categories include other meta-sites, mailing lists and newsletters, associations and organizations, online services, publishers, journals, software, languages, jobs/courses/funding bodies, and linguistic fields (computational linguistics and MT, grammar, phonetics/phonology and speech, sociolinguistics, applied linguistics, and corpus linguistics). Occasionally links are annotated. Last updated March 10, 1999.

94. **BUBL Information Service Home Page**. Available: http:// bubl.ac.uk/. (Accessed: March 19, 1999).

BUBL is a national information service for the higher education community in the UK, funded by the JISC (Joint Information Systems Committee). There are eight links on the BUBL home page for: link, search, UK, archive, journals, news, mail, and admin. "BUBL Link" is a catalog of selected Internet resources which can be approached a variety of ways: through grouped subject areas (e.g. general reference, creative arts, humanities), an alphabetical list of subjects, an A-Z list (which is more detailed that the subjects list), a Dewey classification schedule, by countries, and by type of material (e.g. bibliography, dictionaries, directories, proceedings). "BUBL Search" allows a visitor to search either BUBL itself or the Internet. "BUBL Mail" has links to a half dozen of the largest mailing list services and directories. This is a well-organized, rich source of material for linguistics, allied areas, and individual languages and dictionaries, plus directories, publishers, societies and the like.

95. **Home pages related to phonetics and speech sciences**. Available: http://fonsg3.let.uva.nl/Other_pages.html. (Accessed: March 19, 1999).

Speech on the Web is hosted by the Instituut voor Fonetische Wetenschappen (IFA), the Institute of Phonetic Sciences, in Amsterdam. The large collection of links, most with descriptive notes, is divided into eight parts: congresses, meetings, and workshops; links and lists; phonetics and speech (in the Netherlands, Europe, North and South America, and Australia); natural language processing, cognitive science, and AI; computational linguistics; dictionaries; other; and electronic newsletters, journals and publishers.

96.   **The Human-Languages Page**.
See entry 638 in chapter 19.

97.   **Languages and Linguistics**. Available: http://english-www.hss.cmu.edu/langs/. (Accessed: March 19, 1999).
Languages and Linguistics. is a page identifying works or links on language, linguistic theory, and structural linguistics. Since it consists of two pages of alphabetically arranged links without annotation it is difficult to know ahead of time whether one will find say a full-text dictionary or just links to a dictionary or dictionaries. The English Server hosts this site which began as a project run by students in the English Department at Carnegie Mellon University as a means to provide access to community scholarly resources. Lots of full-text here.

98.   **The LINGUIST List**. Available: http://www.linguistlist.org/. (Accessed: March 19, 1999).
Maintaining *The LINGUIST List*, along with LINGUIST, the main worldwide mailing list for linguists, is a collaborative effort by scholars and graduate students at Wayne State University, Eastern Michigan University, University of Arizona, University of Stockholm, and Texas A & M. The LINGUIST site is provided by the Linguistic Data Consortium at the University of Pennsylvania. It is one of the most comprehensive sites for linguistics sources and has lots of links with content. Many links have brief descriptive annotations. It now incorporates the WWW Virtual Library for Linguistics. LINGUIST List can be read in other languages—German, Spanish, French, Italian, and Portuguese. A visitor can search the LINGUIST List Web site as well as the archives of the LINGUIST. New features include a site map and availability of other mailing lists.
The home page is divided into the following major sections: the profession (conferences, linguistic associations, fund sources, jobs, linguistics programs, e-mail address, mailing lists), research and research support (papers, dissertation abstracts, projects, bibliographies, topic-oriented sites and pages, texts), publication (book reviews and announcements, journals and newsletters, journal tables of contents, publishers), pedagogy (classes and syllabi, ESL and EFL), language resources (languages and language families, dictionaries, regional information), computer support (fonts, software, SGML and TEI, MOOs and MUDs, citing online sources), new resources (adding new links to LINGUIST, adding dissertation abstracts), interacting with LINGUIST, LINGUIST policies and information, and LINGUIST sites.

99.   **Linguistic Links**. Available: http://www.ling.rochester.edu/linglinks.html. (Accessed: March 19, 1999).
This set of links is maintained by the Linguistics Department at the University of Rochester. The home page has a list of thirteen links which leads a visitor into a comprehensive, well-maintained site. Covers many topics of both professional and scholarly interest for linguists. Only the mailing lists page is annotated.

100.   **Linguistics Meta-index**. Available: http://www.sultry.arts.usyd.edu.au/links/linguistics.html. (Accessed: March 19, 1999).
A small, personalized site for linguistics and computational linguistics resources maintained by Christopher Manning, Department of Linguistics at the

University of Sydney. He has chosen a few good sites and provides pithy comments. In addition his Web page has several added attractions: a link to the Australian linguistics network (which he also maintains) and links to eleven linguistic theories often buried several levels down on other sites. Last updated March 7, 1999.

101. **Linguistics Resources**. Available: http://www.blackwellpublishers. co.uk/linguist/. (Accessed: March 19, 1999).

Blackwell Publishers hosts this Web site of linguistics resources. Off-line for some months, it is newly organized and updated as of March 9, 1999. The aim of this list is to be useful, not necessarily comprehensive. The main page has a table of contents featuring: stars of the web (six of the top meta-sites); general indices (other meta-sites); theoretical linguistics; computational linguistics; foreign language learning/teaching; foreign language resources; fonts, tools, and software; dictionaries and reference; miscellaneous; university departments; job-related resources; conference-related resources; journals; online corpora; email lists and newsgroups; organizations; current publications in linguistics. The site has obviously been put together with great care and selectivity. Contributing to its aim of being useful is the practice of ordering, within each section where comparisons are made, the links from most-to-least useful and providing evaluative comments.

102. **SIL Home Page**. Available: http://www.sil.org/. (Accessed: March 19, 1999).

The Summer Institute of Linguistics (SIL) maintains a well-organized, comprehensive site for languages and linguistics, including computational linguistics, NLP, translation, and language learning. It is an excellent source for electronic texts and dictionaries, computing resources, and provides online access to a number of SIL publications including searchable versions of *Ethnologue*, the massive catalog of more than 6,700 languages along with its language name and language family indexes, and the *SIL Bibliography* with over 21,000 entries (see entries 130 and 572). Last updated March 4, 1999.

5

Bibliographies of Bibliographies

103. Kukushkina, E. I., and A. G. Stepanova. **Bibliografiya bibliografii po yazykoznaniyu; annotirovannyi sistematicheskii ukazatel' otechestvennykh izdanii**. Red.: E.S. Kubryakova. Moskva: Gos. biblioteka SSSR imeni V.I. Lenina. Otdel spravochno-bibliograficheskoi i informatsionnoi raboty, 1963. 411p. index. LC 64-39779.

All of the 2,112 books and periodical articles cited in this bibliography of bibliographies were published in the USSR from the late 1800s to 1962. Most fields of linguistic study are covered, including applied linguistics. The arrangement is a classified one which is detailed in the table of contents on pages 406-411. There is an index for authors and another for languages.

6

General Bibliographies

104.   Allen, Harold Byron. **Linguistics and English Linguistics**. 2nd ed. Arlington Heights, IL: AHM Pub. Corp., 1977. 184p. (Goldentree Bibliographies in Language and Literature). LC 75-42974. ISBN 0-88295-562-4 (cloth); ISBN 0-88295-558-6 (paper).

The second edition of this bibliography, like the first edition published in 1966, is intended for advanced students of linguistics, English, education, psychology, speech, sociology, and anthropology as well as scholars in other fields doing research in linguistics. Only books and articles published in English from 1922 to 1975 are included among the 3,000 unannotated entries. The year 1922 was chosen for a beginning date because Arthur G. Kennedy's work *A Bibliography of Writings on the English Language from the Beginning of Printing to the End of 1922* (see entry 750) covers material on English up to that date. Other types of excluded material are theses and dissertations; textbooks; ERIC documents; and articles in Festschriften, conference proceedings, and other collections that are already listed as books in the bibliography. For the user's benefit, items of more than ordinary importance are marked with an asterisk and reviews are listed for many of the books.

The table of contents details the classified arrangement. The main sections are bibliographies; dictionaries and grammars; collections: Festschriften; collections: miscellaneous; linguistics; English linguistics; special topics; and, reading and linguistics. Allen also includes an index of authors.

105.   Ashnin, F. D., et al. **Obshchee yazykoznanie; bibliograficheskii ukazatel' literatury, izdannoi v SSSR s 1918 po 1962 g**. Otv. red.: B.A. Serebrennikov. Moskva: Izd. Nauka, 1965. 276p. index.

Here Ashnin has compiled a bibliography of books and articles by Russian authors on general linguistics published from 1918 to 1962. The main section of the book is a classified listing of some 4,348 items. Only a few items have brief notes. The book includes an alphabetical author index, gathering together all of a person's works from various parts of the main section and referring the reader to the main entry for complete bibliographic information. This bibliography is continued for the years 1963-1967 and 1968-1977 by two Malinskaya bibliographies (see entries 119 and 120 respectively).

106.   Debets, N. P., et al. **Bibliograficheskii ukazatel' literatury po yazykoznaniyu izdannoi v SSSR s 1918 po 1957 god. Vypusk 1. Knigi i sborniki na russkom yazyke, izdannye v SSSR 1918-1955**. Otv. red.: S.I. Kotkov. Moskva: Izd. Akad. Nauk SSSR, 1958. 367p. index. LC 59-21021.

Only this first volume of what was to be a 5-volume set was ever published. It covers books, collections, conferences, histories, bibliographies, and dissertations published in the USSR from 1918 to 1955. Only monographs are included in the 1,849 annotated entries. The arrangement is a classified one with an index of names. It has been replaced by subsequent bibliographies such as Ashnin's (see entry 105).

107.   Dingwall, William Orr, comp. **A Bibliography of Linguistic Esoterica: 1970**. Edmonton, Alta./Champaign, IL: Linguistic Research, 1971. 163p. index. (Linguistic Bibliography Series, 1). LC 72-195378.

The author's purpose in compiling this bibliography was to bring to the attention, of students in particular, the vast number of works which are in what he calls a semi-underground literature. In this category of linguistic esoterica he includes unpublished and projected papers, books which may have escaped the reader's notice, research reports, master's theses, doctoral dissertations, clandestine conferences, and even important published collections of former esoterica and books. The bibliography is selective and covers one year only, 1970.

Particularly useful is a list of sources that includes bibliographies, conference and lecture series, working papers, esoteric journals, and some bookstores dealing in linguistic esoterica. The items are alphabetically arranged by author. In addition to fairly complete bibliographic information and author's affiliation (if known), each entry lists at least one and as many as four topics with which a work is concerned. He provides an index of these topics plus an index of languages and language families.

108.   Fox, Samuel E., Woodford A. Beach, and Shulamith Philosoph, eds. **CLS Book of Squibs; Cumulative Index, 1968-1977**. 1st ed. Chicago: Chicago Linguistic Society, University of Chicago, 1977. 174p. LC 77-83905.

As the preface to this book explains, "in linguistic usage, 'squib' has come to be defined as a brief argument for or against a claim, a datum affecting the status of certain claims or posing problems for them, a note pointing out the ramifications of a given position, or a fact which, while evidently true, resists any account." The first half of this book contains some fifty squibs written just for this book. The second half is an index of Chicago Linguistic Society squibs published from 1968-1977. The index is alphabetical by author, preceded by a subject index. All the items in this index except for those published in 1968 and 1969 are included in Gazdar's *Bibliography of Contemporary Linguistic Research* (see entry 109). On the other hand, the *Index to BLS-CLS-NELS* (see entry 132) covers 1968-1976, not 1977, but provides only a language index, not a subject index.

109.   Gazdar, Gerald, Ewan Klein, and Geoffrey K. Pullum, comps. **A Bibliography of Contemporary Linguistic Research**. New York: Garland, 1978. 425p. index. (Garland Reference Library of the Humanities, 119). LC 77-83358. ISBN 0-8240-9852-8.

Books and book reviews are not included in this bibliography. Instead it covers articles and short notes published in scholarly journals, conference proceedings, specialist anthologies, parajournals, various series of working papers, and some dissertations (when the latter manage to enter the literature through indirect means such as the informal publications of the Indiana University Linguistics Club). The compilers regard the sources they have chosen to include as the primary means by which linguists keep abreast of developments in their field. They list some 5,001 items published between 1970 and 1978, primarily in English, but with a few items in French, German, Dutch, Swedish, and a few other European languages. The unannotated entries are listed in alphabetical order by author. Though the focus is on what they regard as the core areas of syntactic, semantic, phonological, and pragmatic theory, some items relating to fringe areas of linguistics do appear. (For additional indexing of parajournals see entries 108 and 132).

The compilers in their introduction state that they intend for this work to complement, not supplant, the *Bibliographie Linguistique* (see entry 78) which aims for total coverage. They provide on the other hand a subject index which the *BL* lacks. There are two indexes in fact, one a language index, the other a subject index. The latter however is difficult to use because of the awkward way in which the subject headings were constructed.

110. Girke, Wolfgang, Helmut Jachnow, and Josef Schrenk. **Handbibliographie zur neueren Linguistik in Osteuropa. Band I: 1963-1965**. München: Wilhelm Fink, 1974. 344p. index.

111. Girke, Wolfgang, Helmut Jachnow, and Josef Schrenk. **Handbibliographie zur slavistischen und allgemeinen Linguistik in Osteuropa. Band II: 1966-1971**. Tübingen: Max Niemeyer, 1980. 727p. index. ISBN 3-484-60155-8.

112. Girke, Wolfgang, and Helmut Jachnow. **Handbibliographie zur slavistischen und allgemeinen Linguistik in Osteuropa: Bulgarien, ČSSR, Jugoslawien, Polen, Rumänien, UdSSR, Ungarn. Band III, 1 and 2: 1972-1977**. Tübingen: Max Niemeyer, 1988. 1127p. index. ISBN 3-484-60272-4.

Despite the title change with Band II, this and subsequent volumes are essentially a continuation of Band I. The new title though perhaps more accurately reflects the emphasis on Slavonic linguistics in these additional volumes while still covering general linguistic study in Eastern Europe. The first volume contains 5,986 entries, the second 18,203 entries, the third 27,344 entries. These numbers reflect the increasing scholarly output during the time period covered.

The unannotated entries include both monographs and the serial literature, mainly in East European languages. Russian titles are transliterated. The classified arrangement varies a bit from volume to volume with from 26 to 31 main categories and numerous subcategories. With each volume the detailed table of contents serves as the subject index. The tables of contents as well as the section headings in the bibliographies themselves are in German, Russian, and English. All volumes have author indexes and extensive listings for the periodicals and other works from which the entries are drawn.

113. Indiana University Linguistics Club. **Bibliography of Works Published by the Indiana University Linguistics Club, 1967-1991/Laterculum operum editorum a Societate Linguistica, Universitatis Indianensis: a.d. mcmlxvii-mcmxci**. Bloomington, IN: Indiana University Linguistics Club Publications, 1991. 24p.

The papers and dissertations reproduced and distributed by the Indiana University Linguistics Club (IULC) from 1967 through 1991 are listed here. The entries are arranged alphabetically by author's last name and consist of author, date, title, and a reference, when applicable, to where the work was published after the IULC discontinued distribution. Though some entries are marked with an asterisk indicating current distribution by the Club, this indication can not be relied upon for ordering as the status of manuscripts changes frequently. Users are advised to consult the IULC current publications list for in print items. A subject or language index would make this simple list more serviceable.

114.   Jokovich, Nancy. **A Bibliography of American Doctoral Dissertations in Linguistics: 1965-1967.** Arlington, VA: ERIC Clearinghouse on Languages and Linguistics, Center for Applied Linguistics, 1975. 56p. index. (CAL-ERIC/CLL Series on Languages and Linguistics, No.28). ED 115119.

115.   Jokovich, Nancy, and Sophia Behrens. **A Bibliography of American Doctoral Dissertations in Linguistics: 1968-1974.** Arlington, VA: ERIC Clearinghouse on Languages and Linguistics, Center for Applied Linguistics, 1977. 153p. index. (CAL-ERIC/CLL Series on Languages and Linguistics, No.53). ED 140615.

These two bibliographies continue one by Rutherford that covers the years 1900-1964 (see entry 124). The format of these two compilations is the same as this earlier work, each entry giving author's name, title, institution, and date. There are no annotations, but a subject and language index is provided. Unlike Rutherford's work, the second bibliography above excludes works on bilingual/bicultural education and the teaching of English as a second language (see entry 408). Together the above works list nearly 3,000 dissertations in linguistics and linguistics-related fields such as anthropology, education, languages and literature, psychology, sociology, and speech.

116.   Korotkina, Bela Mikhailovna. **Mezhdunarodnye kongressy po yazykoznaniyu: Bibliograficheskii ukazatel'. Vyp. 1: Obshchee yazykoznanie.** Izd. 2-e. Leningrad: Biblioteka Akademii nauk SSSR, 1987. 384p. index.

117.   Korotkina, Bela Mikhailovna, and Z. A. Panova. **Mezhdunarodnye kongressy po yazykoznaniyu: Bibliograficheskii ukazatel'. Vyp. 2: Slavyanskie yazyki.** Izd. 2-e. Leningrad: Biblioteka Akademii nauk SSSR, 1983. 356p. index. (In progress).

The first edition of this bibliographic index to international linguistic congresses, published with the same main title and by the same publisher (1973), chronologically lists in one volume 456 congresses for the years 1838 through 1978 along with date and place, and includes a number of indexes. Two volumes of what is to be a 3-volume set for the second edition have been published. It picks up omissions from the first edition beginning in 1906 and continuing through 1986. Volume 2 on Slavic languages was published in 1983 before volume 1 so as to appear at the same time as the 9th International Congress of Slavicists convened in Kiev. The material organized in seven chapters by particular congress or conference is accompanied by a chronology, several abbreviation lists, and indexes for locations and names. Volume 1 which followed in 1987 covers international and national linguist conferences and congresses. Coverage of national conferences, however, is limited to just seven countries (Austria, Finland, West Germany, Holland, Italy, Spain, and the United States). It also details conferences and congresses devoted to specific areas of linguistic research. Indexing in this volume is similar to that in volume 2. Volume 3 will cover languages of Europe.

In addition to listing conferences and congresses with their date and place, each volume of this bibliography provides valuable information as to the publication of materials, programs, reports from and evaluations of particular events, and reviews of published proceedings. Though users will find omissions and numerous errors, both factual and misprint, they should still find these volumes beneficial as there is no other publication providing such information.

118.   Kreuder, Hans-Dieter. **Studienbibliographie Linguistik: Bibliographie zur Sprechwissenschaft von Lothar Berger und Christa M. Heilmann**. 3. erneut überarb. und ergänzte Aufl. Stuttgart: Franz Steiner, 1993. 198p. index. ISBN 3-515-06362-5.

The main part of this bibliography is a classed arrangement consisting of 2,128 entries. Books and articles in the periodical literature written in both German and English are listed. The entries for books have brief, descriptive one sentence annotations. Materials range from introductory, marked with an asterisk, to specialized sources. In addition to general linguistics they cover such allied topics as sociolinguistics, applied linguistics, psycholinguistics, and speech communication. The table of contents functions as a subject index; in addition there is an author index.

119.   Malinskaya, B. A., and M. Ts. Shabat. **Obshchee i prikladnoe yazykoznanie; ukazatel' literatury, izdannoi v SSSR s 1963 po 1967 god**. Otv. red.: R. R. Mdivani and A. A. Reformatskii. Moskva: Izd. Nauka, 1972. 295p. index. LC 73-324705.

This bibliography of 5,824 items on general and applied linguistics published from 1963 through 1967 is a continuation of two titles by Ashnin covering materials by Russian writers published from 1918 through 1962. One of these is on general linguistics and the other is on structural and applied linguistics (see entries 105 and 137 respectively). Like these two previous bibliographies the arrangement is a classified one; the classification scheme appears on pages 293-295. There is also an index of authors and titles. Malinskaya and Shabat in turn continue this bibliography by a title which picks up materials published 1968-1977 (see entry 120).

120.   Malinskaya, B. A., and M. Ts. Shabat. **Obshchee i prikladnoe yazykoznanie; ukazatel' literatury, izdannoi v SSSR v 1968-1977 gg**. Otv. red.: R. R. Mdivani. Moskva: INION AN SSSR, 1981-1986. 13v. index.

Each of the first 12 volumes of this 13-volume set is devoted to a different topic within general and applied linguistics and has its own classified arrangement as well as an author/main entry index. Volume 13 functions as a cumulative subject and name index for the preceding volumes. It also contains outlines of the classified arrangements for the 12 volumes.

Among the topics covered by this set are: general problems of theoretical linguistics, phonology, morphology, grammar, semantics, phraseology, lexicography, stylistics, sociolinguistics, psycholinguistics, and language instruction. An entry provides brief bibliographic information and occasionally a short annotation. Volume 13 contains appendixes. It reprints the tables of contents for volumes 1-12 and has a subject index for the entire set. There is also an index of personalities, that is, linguists and others whose works are discussed in the references cited in the prior volumes.

By listing works published from 1968 through 1977 this set completes a series of bibliographies covering books and articles by Russian writers published from 1918 through 1977 (see entries 105, 119, and 120).

121. Modern Language Association of America. **MLA Abstracts of Articles in Scholarly Journals**, 1970-1975. New York, Modern Language Association, 1972-1977. annual. index. LC 72-624077. ISSN 0272-1783.

Published only for six years, this work provides abstracts for some of the entries in the *MLA International Bibliography* (see entry 88). The arrangement of each annual into three volumes, each with its own classified arrangement, follows that of the bibliography itself with linguistics in volume 3. (For scope and coverage see the description of the bibliography). An asterisk preceding an item number in the bibliography indicates the presence of an abstract in this work. Likewise an asterisk preceding a journal title in the master list of journal acronyms there, indicates journals from which abstracts appear here. Item numbers sensibly correspond between the two works. Unlike the bibliography which has no subject index, all three volumes for each year have a subject index, thus providing partial indexing for the main work. Most of the abstracts which average about a paragraph in length have been written by the authors of the original articles.

122. **Renaissance Linguistics Archive, 1350-1700: A ... Print-out from the Secondary-Sources Data-Base**. Ferrara: Istituto di Studi Rinascimentali, 1987-1990. 3v. 288p. (v.1); 299p. (v.2); 315p. (v.3). index. (In progress).

The Renaissance Linguistics Archive (RLA) aims to be a comprehensive database covering scholarly publications since 1870 which deal with aspects of linguistic thought in the Renaissance from 1350 to 1700. So far, three print-outs of about 1,000 secondary sources each have been published, the first in 1987, the second in 1988, and a third in 1990. The ongoing project is the result of the work by an international team of contributors which began with 29 scholars and now numbers over 50. Mirko Tavoni was editor of the first volume; Pierre Lardet assisted him with volume two, and John Flood with the third volume. The project is being conducted in collaboration with the Henry Sweet Society for the History of Linguistic Ideas (Oxford), the Société d'histoire et d'épistémologie des sciences du langage (Paris), and the Istituto di studi rinascimentali (Ferrara, Italy).

In Part I there is a list of the periodicals and collective works indexed in the bibliography. Part II is the bibliography itself with each entry annotated by subject-authors, key terms, countries and localities, and languages and dialects. Part III then contains the indexes for these four types of annotations. The bibliography is rich in materials written in European languages, but as the editors point out in their introduction to the third print-out, provides somewhat sketchy coverage of English language works. They will address this lack in subsequent volumes.

123.   Rice, Frank A., and Allene Guss, comps. and eds. **Information Sources in Linguistics; a Bibliographical Handbook**. Washington, DC: Center for Applied Linguistics, 1965. 42p. index. ED 130498. LC 65-19794.

This handbook was compiled mainly for the American student of linguistics at the upper undergraduate or graduate level. Thus, most of the materials cited have been published in English with some in French, German, Russian, and a few in other languages. The 537 mostly unannotated entries are arranged by subject in six parts: fields within linguistics, linguistics and related disciplines, applied linguistics, abstracts, classification systems, and manpower. Many types of reference material are represented, including abstracts, bibliographies, textbooks, periodicals, maps, atlases, handbooks, histories and surveys, dictionaries, and directories. There is an author index. As one would expect with a publication date of 1965, it is now out-dated.

124.   Rutherford, Phillip R. **A Bibliography of American Doctoral Dissertations in Linguistics, 1900-1964**. Washington, DC: Center for Applied Linguistics, 1968. 139p. index. ED 016966. LC 68-27431.

Rutherford in making this compilation has attempted to be exhaustive in listing dissertations completed at American universities for the years 1900-1964. The 1,733 entries are listed alphabetically by author and provide title, institution name, and date of completion. The subject/topic index includes the language(s) dealt with in each work. It incorporates all the entries found in a similarly arranged bibliography compiled by Amy E. Shaughnessy, *Dissertations in Linguistics: 1957-64* (Washington, DC: Center for Applied Linguistics, 1965). This bibliography is continued by the two Jokovich bibliographies covering the years 1965-1967 and 1968-1974 (see entries 114 and 115).

125.   Sabourin, Conrad, and Denise Daoust. **Travaux québécois de linguistique: recherches en cours au Québec**. Québec: Gouvernement du Québec, Office de la langue française, 1982. 191p. (Langues et sociétés). LC 83-142834. ISBN 2-551-04743-9.

An errata sheet corrects the subtitle of this book to read *Inventaire des travaux linguistique*. Thus, it is an inventory of works on linguistics in Quebec. Most of the 2,598 unannotated items are dated from the mid-1960s through 1981 with a few works included from the 1950s. It includes books, periodical articles, theses, dissertations, reports put out by educational institutions, and even government reports. Most are in French, but a few other languages such as English and Russian are represented. The entries are arranged alphabetically by author. Quite a few entries are incomplete, sometimes missing parts of the title, having an incomplete date, or giving no pagination. Since the research represented here includes a wide range of topics, some sort of classified arrangement or a subject index would have made it more useful.

126.   Schmitter, Peter. **Bibliographien zur Linguistik; nach Themenkreisen unter Mitwirkung einer Arbeitsgruppe zusammengestellt und versehen mit einem anhang: Zur Technik der Titelaufnahme**. 3. Aufl. Münster: Institut für Allgemeine Sprachwissenschaft der Westfälischen Wilhelms-Universität, 1984. 91p. (Studium Sprachwissenschaft, Bd.2; ISSN 0721-7129). LC 84-200804. ISBN 3-89083-302-0.

Originally compiled for the use of students, this is a handy source of basic linguistic reference material in German and English. A few items are in Russian and other European languages. Almost no new entries have been added for this third edition; the bulk of the coverage is through 1978. Entries are grouped by topic such as morphology, pragmatics, sociolinguistics, bilingualism, etc. There is also a handy section of bibliographies on individual linguists and linguistic schools.

127. Schwarz, Christa. **Ex libris a Guilelmo L. B. de Humboldt legatis: Das Legat Wilhelm von Humboldts an die Königliche Bibliothek in Berlin**. Paderborn: Ferdinand Schöningh, 1993. 80p. index. illus. LC 94-169748. ISBN 3-506-78282-7.

Wilhelm von Humboldt who lived from 1767-1835 was a Prussian statesman and man of letters firmly grounded in classical languages. Among his wide-ranging scholarly pursuits was an interest in language. He studied intensively the characteristics of a number of languages and published material on American Indian languages, the Kawi language of Java, Sanskrit, and others. This book itemizes in three sections the 533 items from his library which are now in the Königliche Bibliothek in Berlin. The first section listing material on general and comparative linguistics and languages is organized into five major geographical areas (Europe, Asia, Africa, the Americas, and Australia and Oceania); containing 456 items, it accounts for the bulk of the collection. While many of the titles are for German language materials, a wide variety of languages are represented. There is an index of names as well as for languages and dialects (as subject of study).

128. Trypućko, Józef. **Dziesięć Lat Y̨ezykoznawstwa Polskiego, 1956-1965. Próba Bibliografii/Ten Years of Polish Linguistics, 1956-1965. A Bibliography**. Stockholm: Almqvist & Wiksell, 1973. 514p. (Acta Universitatis Upsaliensis. Studia Slavica Upsaliensia, 13; ISSN 0562-3030). LC 73-362702. ISBN 91-554-0068-X.

129. Trypućko, Józef. **Pięc Lat Językoznawstwa Polskiego, 1966-1970: Próba Bibliografii/Five Years of Polish Linguistics, 1966-1970: A Bibliography**. Stockholm: Almqvist & Wiksell, 1984. 399p. (Acta Universitatis Upsaliensis. Studia Slavica Upsaliensia, 22; ISSN 0562-3030). LC 85-130153. ISBN 91-554-1611X.

Trypućko includes in his bibliography (1973) all works of Polish and non-Polish authors dealing with linguistics published in Poland as well as works of Polish authors published outside Poland from 1956 through 1965. The majority of entries are for works written in Polish and other Slavonic languages. It is meant to be comprehensive for linguistics proper with the author opting for inclusion over exclusion when dealing with allied subject areas. As expected, the entries for Slavonic languages are more numerous in the sections for language study than for other language groups. The more than 7,500 unannotated entries are arranged according to a subject scheme that proceeds from general to specific topics. The introduction, table of contents, and subject headings are in both Polish and English. There is an author index.

The supplemental bibliography (1984) for publications from 1966 through 1970 covers the same types of material and has the same format. No further volumes will be forthcoming.

130. Wares, Alan Campbell, comp. **Bibliography of the Summer Institute of Linguistics**. Dallas, TX: Summer Institute of Linguistics, 1992. 603p. index. illus. ISBN 0-88312-824-1 (cloth); ISBN 0-88312-821-7 (paper). Available: http://www.sil.org/htbin/silbiblio. (Accessed: March 11, 1999).

The ninth edition of this ever-growing bibliography includes all works by members of the Summer Institute of Linguistics (SIL) as well as works published by the Institute or by any of its branches, regardless of author affiliation, for the years 1935-1991. For the first time it incorporates an updated version of Ware's *Bibliography of the Wycliffe Bible Translators* (Santa Ana, CA: Wycliffe Bible Translators, 1970). With the addition of these entries for Bible translations and related materials the number of entries has risen to nearly 21,000. The bibliography is divided into two parts. Part I lists academic works, such as articles and books on particular languages or groups of languages, bibliographies (143 are now listed in the index), dictionaries, theses, dissertations, and translations. The 8,617 entries are arranged alphabetically by author. Part II gathers together vernacular works arranged first by country, then by language, and finally by author or main entry. It encompasses such works as books designed to teach people to read in their own language; books on agriculture, arithmetic, health and hygiene, social studies, writing; folk tales; school textbooks; and even creative works by native speakers of indigenous languages. The language and subject indexes are only for the academic works in Part I.

A searchable version of the academic works from Part I of the printed bibliography is available on the Web. The site is updated periodically. As of 8/22/97 there were 11,159 entries. Searching is limited to authors' names, words in titles, and codes for country, language, subject, and entry type. Users should take note of the database limitations spelled out on the Web page; because of its limitations, the electronic version does not replace the printed bibliography. There are links to clear, detailed searching instructions.

131. Wawrzyszko, Aleksandra K. **Bibliography of General Linguistics, English & American**. Hamden, CT: Archon Books, 1971. 120p. index. LC 75-150766. ISBN 0-208-01203-6.

The focus of this bibliography is British and American linguistics of the mid- and late 1960s, including monographs, series, and periodicals. Citations to individual periodical articles are not included. The author chose to concentrate on that time period because of the marked expansion in the field of linguistics in number of new journals that appeared as well as published works in pure linguistics, and works linking linguistics with other fields, such as psycholinguistics. It is aimed at all linguists and students of linguistics, especially those beyond the introductory university level.

Part I lists 294 references on general sources and selected special topics, distributed among such form subdivisions as directories, bibliographies, and dictionaries and such subject subdivisions as history of linguistics, phonetics, syntax, sociolinguistics, and study and teaching. Part II lists in alphabetical order 50 linguistic periodicals and series. Careful annotations averaging about a paragraph in length accompany all the entries. Most are descriptive, though there are some evaluative comments too. Others include a helpful note indicating what audience can make the most use of an item. There are two indexes, one for authors, another for periodicals and series.

132. Whistler, Kenneth W., comp. **Index to BLS-CLS-NELS: A Composite Index of the Contents, Authors, Titles and Languages Cited in the Publications of the Berkeley Linguistics Society, The Chicago Linguistic Society & The North Eastern Linguistic Society, 1968-1976**. 70p. Berkeley, CA: Berkeley Linguistics Society, 1977.

Various so-called parajournal publications of these three linguistic societies for the nine-year period 1968-1976 are indexed here. The tables of contents for all the publications are detailed and coded in the first part of the index, with author, title, and page number provided. Author, title, and language indexes follow and refer the user back to the tables of contents by means of these codes.

Though somewhat limited, this is still a useful index since these publications are not picked up by other indexing services. Several cumulative bibliographies do provide partial coverage. Gazdar's bibliography (see entry 109) includes these publications for the years 1970-1978 and the *CLS Book of Squibs* (see entry 108) indexes the years 1968-1977 for just the Chicago Linguistic Society.

133. Yasui, Minoru, comp. **Current Bibliography on Linguistics and English Linguistics, 1960-1978**. rev. and enl. ed. Tokyo: Kaitakusha, 1979. 269p. index. LC 80-462092.

134. Yasui, Minoru, comp. **Current Bibliography on Linguistics and English Linguistics 1978-1982**. Tokyo: Kaitakusha, 1983. 887p. index. LC 83-239592. ISBN 4-7589-0350-6.

The bibliography for 1960-1978 listing over 5,000 items is a revised and enlarged edition of an earlier one covering 1960-1974 (Tokyo: Kaitakusha, 1974). The bibliography for 1978-1982 both supplements and continues these works, listing some 5,200 more items. As the titles indicate, both bibliographies cover the areas of general linguistics and English linguistics. It covers Festschriften, miscellaneous volumes of collected papers, monographs, squibs, book reviews, and periodical literature from selected journals (25 journals were scanned for the 1979 edition and 50 journals were used for the 1983 edition).

The arrangement is a classified one with major fields of study and topics (including languages) arranged in alphabetical order. When an item deals with more than one topic it is listed under all that are relevant. This is particularly important for the latest bibliography as headings for this volume have gotten considerably more specific than in the prior volumes. For example, the previous heading of "phonology" now has some forty specific headings such as "phoneme," phonetic change," "phonological change," "phonological variant," "phonotactics," and so on. None of the items are annotated. An author index completes each compilation.

There is considerable overlap between these bibliographies and other major indexes such as the *Bibliographie Linguistique* and the *MLA Bibliography* (see entries 78 and 88).

7

Topical Bibliographies

135. Angenot, Marc. **L'analyse du discours: Bibliographie de travail**. Montréal: Ciadest, 1992. 90p. index. (Centre interuniversitaire d'analyse du discours et de sociocritique des textes. Cahier de recherche, 11).

The author compiled this highly selective bibliography on discourse analysis for both the researcher and student. The 971 unannotated entries, including some cross-references, provide brief and, in some cases, incomplete bibliographic citations for materials such as books, articles, and conference proceedings written mainly in French, German, and English. Coverage is for the years 1960-1992 with a few earlier published works. A subject index facilitates use.

136. Antilla, Raimo, and Warren A. Brewer. **Analogy: A Basic Bibliography**. Amsterdam: John Benjamins, 1977. 50p. index. (Amsterdam Studies in the Theory and History of Linguistic Science. Series V: Library and Information Sources in Linguistics, Vol. 1; ISSN 0165-7267). LC 78-319562. ISBN 90-272-0991-X.

While the emphasis in this bibliography is on works from the years 1968 to 1976 there are a few earlier ones back to 1816 and half a dozen from 1977 as well. The preface provides an unusually good, succinct introduction to the subject from an historical perspective. This is complemented by the inclusion of a year index showing the continuous flow of studies on this subject even though analogy was dismissed for a period of time by many transformationalists as of little use in matters of linguistic theory. It is a rather short bibliography not meant to be comprehensive. Only those items that would contribute to making this a "useful tool for 'linguistic' research" (p.xi) were covered. Thus the authors have included little from the linguistic subfields of dialectology, language acquisition, and speech pathology. Likewise they chose not to handle analogical argumentation in theology, philosophy, and scientific method or the psychological aspects of analogy.

Works in a variety of languages are represented, not only in English, French, and German, but Finnish, Danish, Italian, and others. Short comments and notes giving information on reviews or reprints accompany many of the citations.

137. Ashnin, F. D., et al. **Strukturnoe i prikladnoe yazykoznanie; bibliograficheskii ukazatel' literatury, izdannoi v SSSR s 1918 po 1962 g.** Otv. red.: A.A. Reformatskii. Moskva: Izd. Nauka, 1965. 194p. index. LC 66-37879.

The subject of this bibliography is structural and applied linguistics. Ashnin lists books and articles for 2,875 items written by Russians and published from 1918 through 1962. The arrangement, type of information included, and index of authors and titles are the same as for his companion bibliography on general linguistics (see entry 105). The classification scheme here is laid out on pages

61

193-194. This book has one additional feature, a two-page listing extracted from the bibliography of books and articles which were the subject of reviews. This bibliography is continued for later years (see entry 119).

138. Beard, Robert, and Bogdan Szymanek, comps. **Bibliography of Morphology, 1960-1985**. Amsterdam: John Benjamins, 1988. 193p. index. (Amsterdam Studies in the Theory and History of Linguistic Science. Series V: Library and Information Sources in Linguistics, Vol. 18; ISSN 0165-7267). LC 87-34172. ISBN 90-272-3742-5.

The focus in this bibliography is on major and selected minor works of contemporary (generative) theoretical morphology and its immediate background; thus it is limited to works written after 1960 (to 1985). Earlier works, no matter how influential, are excluded. In an attempt to provide morphologists seeking language-specific evidence for general hypotheses, the compilers include a sampling of descriptive works on a wide typological variety of some 250 languages. They have gathered published works such as books, articles, working papers, proceedings, and materials distributed by such organizations as the Indiana University Linguistics Club, but excluded dissertations. Works cited are mainly in English, French, German, and Russian, though some crucial works and works by established morphologists in lesser known languages have been added in a few rare instances. The bibliography is arranged alphabetically by author with entries in non-Latin alphabets transliterated. Both a language and subject index are provided; the latter, however, disappoints since entries are indexed under just one heading. Only materials dealing in a substantial way with a particular language are referenced in the language index. Works dealing with English, however, are not indexed in the language index (though they are included in the subject index) as they constitute an overwhelming majority of the entries.

139. **Bibliographie sélective: terminologie et disciplines connexes/Selective Bibliography: Terminology and related fields**. Ottawa: Direction de la terminologie/Terminology Directorate, 1988. 87p. ISBN 0-660-54120-3.

Terminology is a relatively new field, closely related to a number of disciplines dealing with questions of language. This unannotated, selective bibliography gathers recent publications and articles on terminology in more than 20 related subject areas, including: language for special purposes, lexicography, computational linguistics, linguistic planning, semantics, translation, and terminology units. Most of the works cited are dated 1980 or later. Introductory material and headings are in both French and English.

140. Campe, Petra. **Case, Semantic Roles, and Grammatical Relations: A Comprehensive Bibliography**. Amsterdam: John Benjamins, 1994. 645p. index. (Case and Grammatical Relations across Languages, Vol. 1). ISBN 90-272-2811-6.

Work on this bibliography began as part of a Leuven University project on case and thematic relations, itself part of an interuniversity research network begun in 1990, to assist scholars working on the project. The team of researchers was particularly interested in case phenomena in different languages, both Indo- and non-Indo-European. The bibliography is very comprehensive for the domains of case, semantic relations, grammatical relations, valence and transitivity, less so for domains not primarily related to case. The majority of the 6,643 unannotated entries are for books and articles published in the twentieth century with a smattering from the nineteenth century and even earlier. Citations with complete bibliographic information and virtually no abbreviations make it easy to use. A very detailed and well-executed subject index will delight the serious researcher as it provides unusually good access to the alphabetized entries. In addition there is a two-part language index and guide that inventories all the languages or language groups explicitly dealt with in the entries and then places them for the researcher's convenience within the larger framework of language families.

141.   DiCristo, Albert. **Soixante et dix ans de recherches en prosodie: bibliographie alphabétique, thématique et chronologique**. Aix-en-Provence: Éditions de l'Université de Provence, 1975. 351p. (Études phonétiques, 1). LC 76-453285. ISBN 2-8539-9002-8.

DiCristo in compiling this bibliography has interpreted the notion of prosody in its fullest meaning, including works not only on intonation, but also stress, pauses, rhythm, and intensity. Even works on versification were added when they seemed important to prosodic analysis as well as studies on tone and psychoacoustics. The bibliography of 4,390 entries is intended to be exhaustive for the years 1900-1973. The citations to books, serial publications, and dissertations are in a wide variety of languages. There are no annotations. The author states that a second volume indexing the entries by language and subject is to follow this first volume; as yet it has not appeared.

142.   Dingwall, William Orr. **Transformational Generative Grammar, a Bibliography**. Washington, DC: Center for Applied Linguistics, 1965. 82p. index. LC 65-27753.

Books, journal articles, proceedings of congresses, dissertations, and unpublished conference papers on all aspects of transformational generative grammar are covered here. The nearly 1,000 alphabetically arranged entries dating through 1965 are not annotated, but are coded for some 18 different topics with most entries assigned one or two topic codes. It would have been useful to have an index of these topics. There is, however, an index of languages and language families. For a more extensive bibliography covering a slightly longer time period consult Krenn's bibliography (see entry 160).

143.   Dressler, Wolfgang U., and Siegfried J. Schmidt. **Textlinguistik: kommentierte Bibliographie**. München: Fink, 1973. 120p. (Kritische Information, Bd.4). LC 74-301254.

This selective annotated bibliography on discourse analysis includes books, journal articles, dissertations, manuscripts, and works in progress. The entries are alphabetically arranged in three sections: works directly related to discourse analysis, applied discourse analysis, and works (on other subjects) relevant to discourse analysis. Publications in a variety of languages are cited, but unfortunately many contain typographical errors. Nearly 70 items are appended at the end without annotations.

144.   Ehlich, Konrad, Florian Coulmas, and Gabriele Graefen, eds. **A Bibliography on Writing and Written Language**. Compiled by Gabriele Graefen and Carl Werner Wendland in collaboration with George F. Meier and Reinhard Wenk.

Berlin: Mouton de Gruyter, 1996. 3 vols. 2096p. (v.1 and 2); 747p. (v.3). index. (Trends in Linguistics. Studies and Monographs, 89). LC 96-862. ISBN 3-11-010158-0.

The editors' motivation behind this bibliography was to gather those sources which could "contribute in various different ways to a better understanding of what writing is, how writing systems work, and what functions they serve . . . is interdisciplinary by sheer necessity" (p.viii-ix). The 27,500 entries in volumes 1 and 2 span the years 1930 through 1992 with no restrictions on language or country of publication. Though not comprehensive for the specialist in any one field, this wide coverage should facilitate research across a variety of disciplines. Entries are arranged alphabetically by author or editor. Most titles are given in the original language (transliterated) and except for German and French titles are followed by an English translation. Complete bibliographic citations, sometimes with information on reviews, are followed by index abbreviations consisting of 4-letter codes printed in a special typeface. Volume 3 collects in separate index-chapters all items with a particular code; here items are cited simply by author and year with any remaining codes permitting easy reference back to the complete citations in volumes 1 and 2. Some 94 of these codes refer to scripts (African, Cretan, Gothic, Sumerian) and subjects (decipherment; linguistic, semiotic and social aspects of scripts, writing, and reading; transliteration; typography). Both volumes 1 and 3 feature detailed user guides.

145.   Engh, Jan, and Kristian Emil Kristoffersen. **Control: A Bibliography**. 1998. Available: http://www.ub.uio.no/uhf/biblgr/. (Accessed: September 27, 1998).

The authors, Engh and Kristoffersen, based respectively in the Library and Department of Linguistics respectively at the University of Oslo, have done a service to scholars in compiling this bibliography on semantic and syntactic control. The concept is not easily searched for even in databases as "control" in English and its equivalents in other languages is a fairly general word. Results of searches thus require a lot of sifting in order to identify relevant citations. They have supplemented such searches in both widely accessible bibliographical databases and locally available databases with searches of printed bibliographies, queries on the Linguist list, and private bibliographical research. The list (updated at least as recently as June 8, 1998) contains more than 300 citations to books, dissertations, articles from 65 different journals, book chapters, and papers in published proceedings. Most are for publications written in English, but a significant number are in German and a few in other languages such as Polish, Chinese, and Korean. Items are arranged in alphabetical order by author; there are no annotations. The authors intend to post corrected and augmented versions of the bibliography at irregular intervals.

146.   Fetzer, Wilfried. **Bibliographie sprachwissenschaftlicher Wörterbücher: Eine Ergänzung zu Koerner und Hartmann**. Wiesbaden: Vieweg, 1981. (Linguistische Berichte-Papier, Nr. 64).

With this compilation Fetzer updates several earlier annotated bibliographies of glossaries of linguistics by Koerner and Hartmann published in 1972 in *Linguistische Berichte*, Hft. 18 and 21 respectively. Nearly 200 mono-, bi-, and multilingual dictionaries and glossaries in German, English, and other languages are listed together with citations to reviews.

147. Fries, Norbert. **Ambiguität und Vagheit: Einführung und kommentierte Bibliographie.** Tübingen: Max Niemeyer, 1980. 149p. index. (Linguistische Arbeiten, 84; ISSN 0344-6727). LC 80-502698. ISBN 3-484-10376-0.

There are two parts to this book. The first is a lengthy introduction in German while the second beginning on page 86 is the bibliography on ambiguity and vagueness. The 384 items are mainly in English and German with a sprinkling of Russian and French titles. A few have notes, sometimes with quotes and examples from the text of the reference itself. Nearly all have page numbers referring the user back to the book's introduction, or even to another item in the bibliography. The time span covered by the entries stretches from the early 1900s through 1977 with a few dated as late as 1979. There are indexes of terms and names which refer to both the introduction and the bibliography.

148. Gipper, Helmut, and Hans Schwarz. **Bibliographisches Handbuch zur Sprachinhaltsforschung. Teil I. Schrifttum zur Sprachinhaltsforschung in alphabetischer Folge nach Verfassen mit Besprechungen und Inhaltshinweisen.** Hrsg.: Leo Brandt. Köln/Opladen: Westdeutscher, 1962-1985. Bd.I-IV (Lfg.1-32). 4038p. (Wissenschaftliche Abhandlungen der Arbeitsgemeinschaft für Forschung des Landes Nordrhein-Westfalen, Bd.16a). LC 74-227405.

149. Gipper, Helmut, and Hans Schwarz. **Bibliographisches Handbuch zur Sprachinhaltsforschung.** Hrsg.: Leo Brandt. Opladen: Westdeutscher, 1974-1980. Beiheft 1-2. 82p.(v.1); 188p.(v.2). (Wissenschaftliche Abhandlungen der Arbeitsgemeinschaft für Forschung des Landes Nordrhein-Westfalen, Bd.16a). ISBN 3-531-09873-X (v.1); 3-531-09874-8 (v.2).

150. Gipper, Helmut, and Hans Schwarz. **Bibliographisches Handbuch zur Sprachinhaltsforschung. Teil II: Systematischer Teil (Register).** Opladen: Westdeutscher, 1980-1989. 4v.(A-D).

In this comprehensive annotated bibliography on the semantic content of language, very broadly interpreted, there are an impressive 30,744 entries alphabetically arranged by author (Teil I, entry 148). Coverage is international with works cited in many different languages. Citations come from as far back as the late 1800s. As publication progressed from Lfg. 1 in 1962 to Lfg. 32 in 1985 the dates of the works included also progressed so that the last number published included items dated as recent as 1981. Detailed bibliographic information is given for each entry, including reprint dates, different editions, reviews, and content notes. Important works are accompanied by annotations in very fine print, often over a page in length. There are elaborate indexes (Beiheft 1-2 and Teil II, entries 149 and 150) for names, concepts, subjects, and dictionaries.

151. Gordon, W. Terrence. **Semantics: A Bibliography, 1965-1978.** Metuchen, NJ: Scarecrow Press, 1980. 307p. index. LC 79-24719. ISBN 0-8108-1300-9.

152. Gordon, W. Terrence. **Semantics: A Bibliography, 1979-1985.** Metuchen, NJ: Scarecrow Press, 1987. 292p. index. LC 87-16344. ISBN 0-8108-2055-2.

153.   Gordon, W. Terrence. **Semantics: A Bibliography, 1986-1991**. Metuchen, NJ: Scarecrow Press, 1992. 280p. index. LC 92-27597. ISBN 0-8108-2598-8.

The third annotated bibliography in this fine scholarly series on semantics published in 1992 continues two previous bibliographies published in 1980 and 1987. The bibliographies are interdisciplinary for the fields of linguistics, philosophy, psychology, and anthropology. Gordon includes material on semantics rooted in the older European traditions of philology, but excludes works on the history of semantics, semiotics, meaning and style, semantics applied to teaching or to translating, discourse analysis, lexicology, and logical semantics. Entries for books, Festschriften, dissertations, papers in collections, conference papers, and journal articles whether in English, German, French, Italian, Portuguese, and Spanish are numbered sequentially through the series for a grand total of 7,385 works published from 1965 to the end of 1991. In each volume books and surveys of semantics are listed first, then the remaining entries are alphabetically arranged under 21 major topics. Though Gordon intends his book primarily for advanced researchers in semantics, his 30 some page introduction provides an overview of the field of semantics for beginning students or researchers new to this area of study. A glossary follows the introduction; it contains working definitions of terms which appear in the titles and annotations of the bibliography. There is also a lexical index and an author index.

154.   Guimier, Claude. **Prepositions: An Analytical Bibliography**. Amsterdam: John Benjamins, 1981. 244p. index. (Amsterdam Studies in the Theory and History of Linguistic Science. Series V: Library and Information Sources in Linguistics, Vol.8; ISSN 0165-7267). ISBN 90-272-3734-4.

The aim of this bibliography is to gather into a single list books and articles dealing with problems related to prepositions in natural language. In trying to make this as comprehensive as possible all languages are included, though Indo-European languages are better represented than others, and entries can be found dating as far back as the late 1800s and going up through 1979. Most of the 1,700 entries are not annotated, and only reviews are noted for a few. Arrangement is alphabetical by author with an index of languages and subjects.

155.   Hewes, Gordon Winant, comp. **Language Origins: A Bibliography**. 2nd rev. and enl. ed. The Hague: Mouton, 1975. 2v. 890p. index. (Approaches to Semiotics, 44). LC 75-330870. ISBN 90-279-3401-0.

In compiling this bibliography, Hewes has striven for maximum coverage of the topic. He gathered together literature scattered through such diverse disciplines as psychology, anatomy, philosophy, anthropology, speech pathology, animal communication, and, of course, linguistics. Some 11,000 entries include books, journal articles, manuscripts, dissertations, pamphlets, and other ephemera in about 25 languages. The majority of items are in English, French, German, Italian, and Russian in order of descending frequency. It begins by citing early Greek and Roman and Biblical accounts of the origins of language and goes up to 1972.

The arrangement is alphabetical by author and then by date under each name. Some items have brief notes, usually on the contents of a work. On pages 812-890 is a subject index of some 150 topics. For very specific topics such as "iconicity," "whistle language," "sign language of the Australian aborigines," or "music and origins of language" the index works well. It works less well for broad topics where many hundreds of items are listed without further specification. For example, the heading "origin of language theories" has five pages in fine print of just authors names and dates.

156. Hofmann, Thomas R. **Bibliography on the Semantics of Human Language**. Ottawa: University of Ottawa Press, 1974. 118p. (Linguistic Bibliography Series, No. 1). LC 75-305393. ISBN 0-7766-4601-X.

References in this unannotated bibliography are arranged alphabetically by author's last name. The work covers both books and journal articles across the whole range of linguistic semantics with some references from the fields of logic, computer science, philosophy, psycholinguistics, semiotics, cognitive psychology, cognitive anthropology, and artificial intelligence. The introduction states that it is weak in European entries, especially East European. Most of the references are dated from 1950 to 1974 with the majority dated from the last ten years of this period.

Since the bibliography was prepared on a computer that had some limitations in arranging the bibliographic format, the author, title, and imprint information is not arranged in the order that one is accustomed to. However, the usual bibliographic information is included. There are appendixes explaining the format of entries and the journal and other abbreviations used in the citations.

157. Juilland, Alphonse G., and Alexandra Roceric. **The Linguistic Concept of Word. Analytic Bibliography**. The Hague: Mouton, 1972. 118p. index. (Janua Linguarum. Series Minor, 130). LC 75-190145.

There are three parts to this book: an analytical bibliography, an index of subjects, and an index of languages. The focus is on the modern study of "the concept of word in general and about the principles which govern its delimitation in particular languages" (p.5). There are 135 studies, both monographs and journal articles, most published after 1916. Each entry includes full bibliographic information plus listings of topics and languages and language families whose words are discussed, each with numbers referring the reader back to pages in the cited work.

158. Knoop, Ulrich, Manfred Kohrt, and Christoph Küper. **An Index of "Bibliographie zur Transformationsgrammatik" by H. Krenn and K. Müllner**. Heidelberg: Carl Winter, 1971. 116p. (Bibliothek der allgemeinen Sprachwissenschaft. 2.Reihe). ISBN 3-533-02162-9.

There is a description of this index under the entry for the bibliography itself. (See entry 160.)

159. Koerner, E. F. Konrad. **Western Histories of Linguistic Thought: An Annotated Chronological Bibliography 1822-1976**. Amsterdam: John Benjamins, 1978. 113p. index. (Amsterdam Studies in the Theory and History of Linguistic Science. Series III: Studies in the History of Linguistics, Vol. 11; ISSN 0304-0720). LC 80-459699. ISBN 90-272-0891-3; 90-272-0952-9.

Koerner has divided this bibliography of over 400 entries into four parts: 1822-1915; 1916-1961; 1962-1976; and an addendum for 1845-1972. Each of the first three parts is introduced by a short essay discussing developments in the study of history of linguistics for that particular time period and the principles guiding inclusion of items for that part. The author makes no claims for completeness, but has attempted to provide "comprehensive coverage of 'general' accounts of the history of linguistic thought in the western world."(p.v). Only book length or individual publications are included, not articles or parts of collections. In general, monographs dealing exclusively with a particular phase, author, or aspect in the history of linguistics have been omitted.

The starting date of 1822 was picked rather arbitrarily. It was originally chosen so as to have the work cover 150 years, though it ended up actually covering 155. The date of 1916, the start of Part II, marks the publication of Ferdinand de Saussure's influential work, the *Cours de linguistique générale* often said to be the start of modern linguistic study. Part III begins with the year 1962. There was a marked increase in this year and onwards of studies in the history of linguistics. The author attributes this both to Chomsky's presentation at the Ninth International Congress of Linguists that year and to publication of Thomas S. Kuhn's *The Structure of Scientific Revolutions* (University of Chicago Press, 1962) from which historians of linguistics borrowed the concept of "paradigm." The addendum in Part IV merely picks up items missed during compilation of the previous parts.

The organization of entries is chronological. Accompanying the entries are annotations, usually analyzing the contents of the publications, listing reviews of them, and occasionally offering evaluative comments. An index of names facilitates access not only to the authors, but also to editors of books, contributors to a collective volume, reviewers, and translators.

160.   Krenn, Herwig, and Klaus Mullner. **Bibliographie zur Transformationsgrammatik**. Heidelberg: Carl Winter, 1968. 262p. (Sprachwissenschaftliche Studienbucher).

With its 2,459 entries this bibliography on transformational grammar contains two and a half times the number of works in Dingwall's earlier bibliography, the first on this subject (see entry 142). Krenn has made a special attempt to include recent congresses, colloquia, and symposia in addition to monographs, periodical literature, research reports, dissertations, and reviews of some of the more important works. The entries are arranged alphabetically by author. A separately published keyword index prepared by Knoop provides subject access (see entry 158). Though the bibliography itself contains publications in many different languages, the technical terms in the index have all been translated into English.

161.   Krommer-Benz, Magdalena, and Maria Schernthaner. **Infoterm: International Bibliography of Terminological Literature**. Wien: TermNet/International Network for Terminology, 1989. 284p. index. (TermNet bibliographical series, 1). ISBN 3-901010-01-7.

This publication with nearly 4,000 items continues the bibliography of Guy Rondeau and Helmut Felber, the *Bibliographie internationale de la terminologie* (Quebec: GIRSTERM/Infoterm, 1984), updating it and emphasizing publications since 1981. As such it covers literature on terminology science and research and related fields, in addition to which the authors are now adding publications dealing with computerized terminography, previously published in Krommer-Benz's *International Bibliography of Computer-Assisted Terminology* (Paris:

Unesco, 1984). The eventual aim is to collect bibliographic data relating to terminological literature in all countries and to develop a database which can be easily updated and distributed. (Look for information about the database on the Internet at the URL http://www.termnet.at/.) Items in the bibliography are arranged according to a classification scheme with cross-referencing to other relevant categories. In addition, language(s) treated is indicated by a two-letter language code. There is material written in some 28 languages indicated by these same codes; titles for all non-English language entries are translated into English. The authors have been diligent in providing complete, accurate bibliographic information.

162.   Laver, John. **Voice Quality: A Classified Research Bibliography**. Amsterdam: John Benjamins, 1979. 225p. index. (Amsterdam Studies in the Theory and History of Linguistic Science. Series V: Library and Information Sources in Linguistics, Vol.5; ISSN 0165-7267). LC 81-456175. ISBN 90-272-0996-0.

The wide scope of this bibliography is reflected in the hundred topics which form its classification system. It is comprehensive except in the areas of speech pathology and medical-related topics. Books and journal articles in English make up the vast majority of the unannotated entries. Historical coverage is very good with numerous entries from prior centuries, one item even from 1570. Though the author does not state a cut-off date, 1977 seems to be the last year thoroughly covered. Accompanying each entry is at least one and as many as eight alphanumeric codes indicating the subject(s) of the work. The codes correspond to items in the classification key. There is also a topic index.

163.   Mayer, Stefan, and Michael Weber. **Bibliographie zur linguistischen Gesprächsforschung**. Hildesheim: Georg Olms, 1983. 214p. (Germanistische Linguistik, 1-2/81; ISSN 0721-460X). ISBN 3-487-07399-4.

There are three parts to this bibliography on discourse analysis. Part I is an introduction, list of abbreviations, and explanation of the classification system used in the next part. In Part II entries consisting of an author with date are arranged under the numbered headings and subheadings of the classification system. The complete bibliographic citation may then be found in Part III which lists the nearly 1,500 entries alphabetically by author. At the end of each citation a number indicates where this entry can be found in the preceding classification system. Books, dissertations, and serial literature from 1970 to December 1982 are included. Most of the listed works are in German, a lesser number are in English.

164.   Meier, Rolf. **Bibliographie zur Intonation**. Tübingen: Max Niemeyer, 1984. 156p. (Bibliographische Arbeitsmaterialien, 5; ISSN 0176-5418). ISBN 3-484-26005-X.

The classified table of contents serves as the subject access to the contents of this unannotated bibliography on intonation. The author supplements the usual published materials with references to dissertations, working papers, publications of university departments, and laboratory reports. Many of the cited works are written in English, somewhat fewer in German, and even less in French and other languages; coverage of the various languages as subject of study parallels this distribution.

165. Nevis, Joel Ashmore, Brian D. Joseph, Dieter Wanner, and Arnold M. Zwicky. **Clitics: A Comprehensive Bibliography, 1892-1991**. Amsterdam: John Benjamins, 1994. 274p. index. (Amsterdam Studies in the Theory and History of Linguistic Science. Series V: Library and Information Sources in Linguistics, Vol. 22; ISSN 0165-7267). LC 94-27029. ISBN 90-272-3748-4.

The study of clitics suffers from the lack of a clear definition, hampering cross-linguistic application. As the linguists who compiled this bibliography point out in their preface, "clitic" is an umbrella term and not a genuine category in grammatical theory. Thus, some of the entries found in this bibliography may seem to be out of place as the authors have cast a very wide net in their determination to gather work that pertains in some way to the study of clitics and which has until now been obscure, scattered, and sometimes unrecognized. Likewise, there are some omissions despite the word "comprehensive" in the title. Introductory material provides background information on the history of the study of clitic-like elements in languages of the world and a guide to using the bibliography. They include only material published in the years 1892 to 1991, the 100-year period following Jacob Wackernagel's paper which was to first to deal with clitic phenomena. The alphabetized entries are annotated with key word descriptors. Two indexes of these descriptors follow: a language index and an analytical index.

166. Nuyts, Jan, and Jef Verschueren, comps. **A Comprehensive Bibliography of Pragmatics**. Compiled under the auspices of the International Pragmatics Association. Amsterdam: John Benjamins, 1987. 4v. 2197p. index. LC 87-20824. ISBN 90-272-2031-X(set); 90-272-2032-8(v.1); 90-272-2033-6(v.2); 90-272-2034-4(v.3); 90-272-2050-6(v.4).

This work while based on previous bibliographies (see entry 175), attempts to sharpen the focus of pragmatics here. The compilers, dissatisfied with the unfocused Anglo-American tradition in pragmatics and thus the contents of these bibliographies, have decided here to return to Charles Morris' original definition of pragmatics as "the study of the relation of 'signs' to 'interpreters,' encompassing all the functional, psychological, biological, and social phenomena which play a part in the use of language." The authors feel that by returning to this earlier definition of pragmatics and by considering it to be a "perspective" on language, not a "component" of language like phonology or syntax and not in contrast with such disciplines as sociolinguistics, this bibliography would contribute to the search for coherence in this field.

Volume I contains an introduction, list of abbreviations, and indexes for subjects, words, languages, and persons (those persons whose work is the central topic of a publication in the bibliography). The remaining volumes contain the annotated bibliography itself, arranged alphabetically by author's last name, volume II, A-F, volume III, G-M, and volume IV, N-Z.

No attempt was made to include or exclude an item based on a judgment of quality, only on the basis of whether it belonged to what the authors perceived as the pragmatic perspective on language. Thus works from many fields are represented, such as text linguistics, discourse analysis, semiotics, neurolinguistics, speech act theory, artificial intelligence, and many more. The majority of publications are in English, French, German, and Dutch. The cut-off date with few exceptions is 1984. Supplements as well as a computer-readable version are planned.

167. Nyyssönen, Heikki, Elise Kärkkäinen, Arja Piirainen-March, Seija Sipola, and Kauko Timlin, eds. **Bibliography of Discourse Analysis and Text Linguistics**. Oulu: University of Oulu, 1985. 104p. index. (University of Oulu. Publications of the Department of English, 6: ISSN 0358-2760). ISBN 951-42-2018-8.

This is a short, unannotated bibliography of materials the editors collected for a department project so it makes no claims to comprehensiveness. Nonetheless, it should be of use to students and researchers. The entries for books, articles, chapters, and conference proceedings are put into a classified arrangement with seven main headings which the editors point out are rather arbitrary, but convenient for their material. Nearly all the cited works are written in English for the 30-year period 1951 to 1981. There is an index of principal authors.

168. Ostler, Rosemarie. **Theoretical Syntax 1980-1990: An Annotated and Classified Bibliography**. Amsterdam: John Benjamins, 1992. 192p. index. (Amsterdam Studies in the Theory and History of Linguistic Science. Series V: Library and Information Sources in Linguistics, Vol. 21; ISSN 0165-7267). LC 91-42086. ISBN 90-272-3747-6.

Ostler intended her bibliography to serve both practicing scholars and students new to the topic of theoretical syntax and to cover both major trends as well as minor ones of the decade covered. She accomplished both goals in the 914 items of her bibliography despite limiting coverage to English language materials in books and a selected core of 14 journals. The core journals are those she considers to be influential, widely available, and often cited. Short, one- to three-sentence descriptive annotations accompany entries which are organized into ten subject categories. In addition there are indexes for authors, topics, and languages.

169. Petöfi, János S., ed. **Logic and the Formal Theory of Natural Language: Selective Bibliography**. Hamburg: Helmut Buske, 1978. 333p. (Papiere zur Textlinguistik, Bd.10). LC 79-309620. ISBN 3-87118-309-1.

The main purpose of this bibliography according to its preface is "to provide a systematic orientation for 'linguists' interested in the description of natural-language fragments by means of logical methods, or in the construction of an integrated 'logic-oriented' theory for the semiotic (i.e. syntactic-semantic-pragmatic) description of natural languages" (p.v). The bibliography itself which contains references up to 1975 is divided into six chapters. The first two chapters contain general works while chapters 3 through 6 conform to an outline or "Map of Logic" developed by N. Rescher. Various scholars compiled each chapter, or part of chapter, and wrote short introductions to them. The unannotated entries are then arranged alphabetically by author following these introductions. Chapter 7, not part of the bibliography per se, is a paper by the editor concerning some of the basic questions arising from the application of logic to linguistics.

170. Pop, Sever. **Bibliographie des questionnaires linguistiques**. Louvain: Commission d'enquête linguistique, 1955. 168p. index. (Comité international permanent de linguistes. Publications de la Commission d'enquête linguistique, VI). LC 57-2840.

This is the first attempt at a chronological bibliography of questionnaires used in linguistic fieldwork. The term "linguistic questionnaire" has been extended here so as to include a number of other publications, or even just events, which are important in the history of dialectology. The first entry is dated 1394 and the last is 1954. In between are recorded the major pioneering efforts of such people as Georg Wenker (1876) on the *Sprachatlas des Deutschen Reichs*, Edmond Edmont (1897-1901) on the linguistic atlas of France, and Hans Kurath (1931) on the linguistic atlas of the United States and Canada. The chronological listing of entries highlights historical development, but in some cases has the effect of disbursing the work of a single author. An index of persons helps to offset this though. There is also a subject index and an index of the most important geographic names.

171.   Sabourin, Conrad. **Adverbs and Comparatives: An Analytical Bibliography**. Amsterdam: John Benjamins, 1977. 208p. index. (Amsterdam Studies in the Theory and History of Linguistic Science. Series V: Library and Information Sources in Linguistics, Vol.2; ISSN 0165-7267). LC 79-307203. ISBN 90-272-0991-X; 90-272-0993-6.

The two main sections of this bibliography, one on adverbs and adverbials and the other on comparatives and superlatives, are followed by an index of languages and subjects. The entries arranged in each section alphabetically by author are for books, dissertations, and articles, mainly in English and French. There are no annotations other than occasional notes concerning an abstract, review, or discussion appearing in the literature. It covers material appearing in the three decades preceding its publication, selecting titles that deal with not only syntactic, but also semantic, psycholinguistic, stylistic, and logical aspects of adverbs and comparatives.

172.   Salus, Peter H., comp. **Pāṇini to Postal: A Bibliography in the History of Linguistics**. Edmonton, Alberta, Canada: Linguistic Research, 1971. 75p. index. (Linguistic Bibliography Series, No.2). LC 85-116873.

In his bibliography Salus attempts to gather the threads of the history of linguistics running through not only the Western tradition from around 500 B.C. to the present, but also among the Indic, Far Eastern, and Semitic grammarians. Because such a history cannot be confined to a history of those who would have considered themselves linguistics, or even grammarians or rhetoricians, it includes material from the history of lexicography, philosophy of language, and logic.

The organization is both topical and chronological. There are separate sections for the non-Western traditions, each subdivided by country or language. The studies on Western tradition are arranged first by major time periods and then subdivided by topics appropriate to that period. Both monographs and journal articles are included among the nearly 700 entries. There is an index of authors.

As the compiler states in the preface, this bibliography is not complete. Secondary sources in such areas as Chinese, Japanese, and Korean linguistics are far from complete. Moreover, there are imbalances with a lot of material on Sanskrit and Greek grammarians and philosophers, the Modistae, and the nineteenth century, but missing a number of crucial studies of this century such as F. Brunot's *Histoire de la langue française des origines à 1900 à nos jours* (Paris: A. Colin, 1966-1968), an important sourcebook for the history of linguistics in France. Publications of the Prague and Kazan schools as well as the area of Soviet linguistics are inadequately treated, if at all. Coverage of Western studies of the history of linguistics for the 9th and 20th centuries is better covered by E.F.K. Koerner's bibliography (see entry 159).

173.   Schumacher, Helmut. **Valenzbibliographie (Stand: Juni 1988)**. Unter Mitarbeit von Aloys M. Hagspihl. 2. erw. u. verb. Aufl. Mannheim: Institut für Deutsche Sprache, 1988. 265p. index. bibliog. ISBN 3-922641-34-2.

The second edition of this bibliography on valency theory and dependency grammar has 2,377 items published through June of 1988. Schumacher has gathered items written in many languages; many are in German, but works in English are well represented. Entries are annotated with subject terms and name of language(s) under study. An examination of the index of these subject terms and language names reveals an emphasis on the German language, but there are studies of many other languages, from Arabic to Yoruba.

174.   Seifert, Stephan, and Werner Welte. **A Basic Bibliography on Negation in Natural Language**. Tübingen: Gunter Narr, 1987. 327p. (Tübinger Beiträge zur Linguistik, 313). ISBN 3-87808-373-4.

The 3,147 entries in this bibliography are arranged alphabetically by author and provide the usual bibliographic information. Also indicated by means of abbreviations are the languages treated in a work as well as an indication of its contents according to categories such as morphosyntax, sociolinguistics, linguistic theories, and methodological approaches. These categories are subdivided as well. The category of methodological approaches has, for example, the subcategories of descriptive, historical, philological, contrastive, didactical, etc. A register, really a classified index, lists the entries by number under the appropriate categories/subcategories.

The authors did not confine themselves to including purely linguistic research, but took into consideration the related areas of psychology, philosophy, anthropology, and literature. Books, periodical articles, and dissertations in many languages were included regardless of quality with the authors refraining from making any evaluations.

175.   Verschueren, Jef. **Pragmatics: An Annotated Bibliography**. Amsterdam: John Benjamins, 1978. 270p. index. (Amsterdam Studies in the Theory and History of Linguistic Science. Series V: Library and Information Sources in Linguistics, Vol.4; ISSN 0165-7267). LC 78-388097. ISBN 90-272-0991-X; 90-272-0995-2.

The scope of this bibliography is very wide, listing publications on speech act theory, presupposition, implicature, and frame analysis, as well as a variety of other topics not fitting under any of these headings. It includes not only purely theoretical works, but also applications of pragmatic theory. The over 1,500 works listed are mainly from the ten years preceding this work's publication and cover only items in English, French, German, and Dutch. Non-evaluative annotations accompany most items. Arrangement is alphabetical by author with subject and language indexes.

Five annual supplements have been published in the *Journal of Pragmatics* from 1978 to 1982. These supplements not only update this book, but go back and fill in gaps, particularly by including items in a wider variety of languages. *A Comprehensive Bibliography of Pragmatics* by Nuyts and Verschueren (see entry 166) succeeds this work and its supplements.

176.   Weydt, Harald, and Klaas-Hinrich Ehlers. **Partikel-Bibliographie: Internationale Sprachenforschung zu Partikeln und Interjektionen.** Frankfurt am Main: Peter Lang, 1987. 251p. index. ISBN 3-8204-9250-X.

Particles and interjections are the subject of this bibliography that gathers together most types of published works as well as dissertations. Entries are arranged alphabetically and can be annotated with up to nine subject codes. Most entries are in German, with a number in English and French, and a few in other languages. The index has a simple classification scheme which enables a user to look up a particle in a specific language and find which entry(ies) are relevant. In addition there are categories for works dealing with such subjects as contrastive studies and classification of particles which correspond to the subject codes of the annotations. Most works have been published in the 1970s up through 1986 though earlier works are sprinkled throughout and one entry on English is even dated 1655. This bibliography will be of most use to those studying particles in Germanic languages or dialects, less productive for Romance, Slavic, and other languages.

177.   Wiegand, Herbert Ernst, and Werner Wolski. **Gesellschaftsbezogene und sprachgelenkte semasiologie: Marginalien anhand der "Einführung in die Semasiologie" von Thea Schippan; mit einer Arbeitsbibliographie zur Semantik in der Sprachphilosophie, Logik, Linguistik und Psychoinguistik (1963-1973/74), zusammengestellt von Herbert Ernst Wiegand und Werner Wolski**. Hildesheim: Olms, 1976. 938p. index. (Germanistische Linguistik, 1-6/75; 0721-460X). LC 77-481389. ISBN 3-487-06044-2.

An article on semasiology, or semantics, occupies the first 90 pages of this book. The remainder of the book is a bibliography of materials on semantics in the areas of philosophy of language, logic, linguistics, and psycholinguistics. About 8,000 entries are arranged according to an elaborate classification system which takes 16 pages to detail. The compilers provide an extensive list of bibliographies and indexes as well as a 50-page list of serials (with abbreviations) which were used as source material. It is international in scope with a lot of the works written in German as one would expect, but also in a variety of other languages. Cyrillic script has been transliterated. There is an author index plus a topic index which refers readers not to individual entries, but to a section of the bibliography which may have one or more entries listed under it.

178.   Zgusta, Ladislav. **Lexicography Today: An Annotated Bibliography of the Theory of Lexicography**. With the assistance of Donna M.T. Cr. Farina. Tübingen: Max Niemeyer, 1988. 349p. index. (Lexicographica. Series Maior, 18; ISSN 0175-9264). ISBN 3-484-30918-0.

This exceptional work displays the scholarly authority of Zgusta, its author, who also wrote the *Manual of Lexicography* (1971), a book which forms the basis of modern lexicographic theory and practice. The bibliography deals with the theory, methods, and procedures of lexicography, in essence, with what is called in French and German "metalexicography." Zgusta does not repeat references found in his manual, so begins systematic coverage with the late 1960s up to winter 1986/87. Only published works are listed and while the author makes no claim to exhaustive coverage, he does list publications in the major languages of Western and Eastern Europe as well as Chinese. Entries are arranged alphabetically by author and include complete bibliographic information along with annotations that may detail the contents or outstanding features of each item, note the relevance of the work, or place it in a theoretical context. There are four excellent indexes: names of second, third, etc. authors and editors; names of persons occurring in titles and epitomes; languages discussed; and topical. The topical index is exceptional both in providing logical access points, and liberal cross-references. This bibliography has much to recommend it, whether to the student seeking an overview of the field, or to the researcher seeking in-depth materials on a specific aspect of lexicography.

8

Bibliographies of Linguists

179. **Arcadia bibliographica virorum eruditorum**. Fasc. 1- . Bloomington, Ind.: Eurolingua, 1979- . irregular. ISSN 0195-7163.

180. Fasciculus 1: Hegaard, Steven E., comp. **Karl Heinrich Menges Bibliographie**. Wiesbaden: Harrassowitz, 1979. 53p. port. ISBN 3-447-018-35-6.

181. Fasciculus 2: Bayerle, Gustav, comp. **Alo Raun Bibliography**. Köln: E.J. Brill, 1980. 29p. port. ISBN 0-931-922-02-X.

182. Fasciculus 3: Décsy, Gyula, comp. **Erich Kunze Bibliographie**. Köln: E.J. Brill, 1980. 31p. port. ISBN 0-931-922-07-0.

183. Fasciculus 4: Feldstein, Ronald F., comp. **Felix Johannes Oinas Bibliography**. Köln/Bloomington, IN: E.J. Brill/Indiana University, 1981. 51p. port. ISBN 0-931-922-03-8.

184. Fasciculus 5: Walter, Michael, comp. **Helmut Hoffmann Bibliography**. 1982. 28p. port. ISBN 0-931-922-13-5.

185. Fasciculus 6: Al-Ani, Salman H., comp. **Fred W. Householder Bibliography**. 1984. 37p. port. ISBN 0-931-922-16-X.

186. Fasciculus 7: Kontra, Miklós, comp. **Ferenc Fabricius-Kovács Bibliography**. 1984. 40p. port. ISBN 0-931-922-18-6.

187. Fasciculus 8: Vértes, Edith, comp. **György Lakó Bibliographie**. 1985. 42p. port. ISBN 0-931-922-21-6.

188. Fasciculus 9: Meserve, Ruth I., comp. **Denis Sinor Bibliography**. 1986. 63p. port. ISBN 0-931-922-12-7.

189. Fasciculus 10: Brend, Ruth Margaret, comp. **Kenneth Lee Pike Bibliography**. 1987. 56p. port. ISBN 0-931-922-28-3.

190. Fasciculus 11: Cowan, William, and Michael K. Foster, eds. **E.F. Konrad Koerner Bibliography**. 1989. 89p. illus. bibliog. port. ISBN 0-931-922-36-4.

191. Fasciculus 12: Kiss, Antal, comp. **Béla Kálmán Bibliographie 1934-1992**. 1993. 100p. illus. port. ISBN 0-931-922-49-6.

192.   Fasciculus 13: Szabó, Adám T., ed. **Gyula Décsy Bibliography 1947-1995**. 1995. 165p. index. illus. port. ISBN 0-931-922-56-9.

193.   Fasciculus 14: Szöke, István, comp. **Gyula László Bibliography 1928-1994**. 1995. 98p. port. ISBN 0-931-922-55-0.

194.   Fasciculus 15: Deely, John N., ed. **Thomas A. Sebeok Bibliography, 1942-1995**. 1995. 144p. index. port. ISBN 0-931-922-53-4.

This series (with different publishers for fasciculi 1-4) of short bio-bibliographical studies on linguists vary somewhat in format, but all contain bibliographies of the person's publications; they may detail other works such as papers presented, editorial work, translations, reviews, and dissertations for which they have served as adviser. All have a biographical sketch(es) accompanied by a portrait. Fasciculi 15 contains an autobiography. The compilers/editors frequently provide short annotations and/or reviews of the person's published works. With the exception of fasciculi 8 (German, English, Finnish, and Hungarian), 9 (English, French, and German), 11 (English, French, and German), 12 (German), and 14 (English and Hungarian) all are written in English.

195.   Baer, E. Kristina, and Daisy E. Shenholm. **Leo Spitzer on Language and Literature: A Descriptive Bibliography**. New York: Modern Language Association, 1991. 172p. index. LC 91-9845. ISBN 0-87352-195-1.

In their twelve-page introduction Baer and Shenholm chronicle Spitzer's career and ideas. Austrian-born Spitzer was already a well-known scholar and professor of Romance philology at a number of universities in Germany before taking up a position at Johns Hopkins University in 1936. He went on to make further contributions to linguistics in the areas of etymology and lexicology, in grammar, morphology, and syntax, and in semantics. The authors have arranged Spitzer's 1,006 publications in categories for books and monographs, then book reviews. Journal articles are then arranged in categories for the subject areas listed above, further subdivided by language and then chronologically under each language(s) heading. Articles outside of linguistics per se are similarly listed under categories for literary criticism and theory, stylistics, and miscellany. The authors provide detailed tables of contents for books and descriptive, non-evaluative summaries for articles. There are three indexes for persons, titles of works, and words and phrases. The latter index cross-references just the articles, not the books.

196.   Bolinger, Bruce C. **Dwight Bolinger 1907-1992: Writings and Biographical Information**. 1997. port. Available: http://www.lsa.umich.edu/ling/jlawler/bolinger.html#270. (Accessed: September 30, 1997).

Dwight Bolinger, a former professor and president of the Linguistic Society of America in 1972, wrote on intonation; English syntax and semantics; Spanish syntax and semantics; and style, usage, and general linguistics. This Web site devoted to his work and material written about him provides links to two lists: the first is an unannotated bibliography of 339 books and articles written by him, the second list references 20 biographical and autobiographical sources. In addition to the lists, the author of this Web page, Bolinger's son, provides some brief biographical notes, a black and white picture of Bolinger père, and information (with e-mail addresses) about access to his father's papers.

197. Bureau, Conrad. **Bibliographie de Georges Mounin**. Neuville, Québec: Bref, 1994. 147p. illus. (Collection Science, no. 1). ISBN 2-9803997-0-1.

Bureau, a former student of Mounin, compiled this exhaustive bibliography of his works. The 950 entries arranged chronologically from 1935 through 1994 represent some 600 unique titles, the remainder being translations, new editions, and reprints. Mounin, a disciple of André Martinet, the French functionalist, was an Italianist who made numerous and varied contributions in general linguistics, history of linguistics, stylistics, and semiology. In addition he was a translator and did research in the theory of translation. Following his bibliography, Bureau provides a list of publications written in honor of Mounin and another list of recent publications analyzing his work. Entries in all three lists are annotated to indicate type of publication.

198. Buzarov, A. Sh., otv. red. **Professor Zul'karin Uchuzhukovich Blyagoz: Bibliograficheskii ukazatel' po yazykoznaniyu i metodike ego prepodavaniya**. Maikop: Izd vo Adygeiskogo Gosudarstvennogo Universiteta, 1993. 22p. port.

Blyagoz conducted research on both the Russian and Adygei language. This unannotated chronologically arranged bibliography lists 175 of his works published from 1963 to 1993. Introductory and explanatory materials are in Russian.

199. Cannon, Garland Hampton. **Sir William Jones: A Bibliography of Primary and Secondary Sources**. Amsterdam: John Benjamins, 1979. 73p. index. (Amsterdam Studies in the Theory and History of Linguistic Science. Series V: Library and Information Sources in Linguistics, Vol.7; ISSN 0165-7267). LC 80-466598. ISBN 90-272-0998-7.

A total of 497 works by and about Sir William Jones are listed here along with reviews of his works. Some have brief annotations. Jones, a British Orientalist and jurist of the 18th century played a considerable role in the founding of comparative linguistics. Since much of his scholarship was interdisciplinary, the compiler has chosen to include items by him which are outside the bounds of strictly linguistic study. The essays and books about him are arranged in three time periods: up to 1850, 1850 to 1941, and 1942 to 1979. These periods reflect large shifts in Jones' reputation.

There is an index of authors, editors, and translators, but not of subjects. Cannon has omitted the latter because of the wide variety of subjects treated in many of the sources, but this is precisely why an index would have been welcome.

200. Cirtautas, Arista Maria, comp. **Nicholas Poppe: A Bibliography of Publications from 1924-1977**. Seattle: Institute for Comparative and Foreign Area Studies, University of Washington, 1977. 51p. index. (Parerga, 4). LC 78-621146.

Poppe, called by some the dean of Altaic studies, published extensively in the areas of Mongolian, Tungus, Turkic, and comparative Altaic studies. This is the first complete bibliography of his publications for the years 1924-1977, issued in honor of his eightieth birthday. Other works of his have appeared since this cut-off date so it falls short of being a totally complete record of his work. It includes nearly 60 books and several hundred articles, organized by year of publication. A separate section organized again by year of publication lists reviews. There are two indexes. One index is an alphabetical guide (by title) to books and articles. Another indexes names of persons who are either authors of books reviewed, persons mentioned in titles of books and articles, or coauthors with Poppe.

201.   Darnell, Regna. **Edward Sapir: Linguist, Anthropologist, Humanist**. Berkeley: University of California Press, 1990. 480p. index. illus. port. bibliog. ISBN 0-520-06678-2.

Sapir, both an anthropologist and linguist, was an influential figure in American linguistics at the beginning of the 20th century. Several contributions having a wide impact were his book *Language* (1921) and the principles of linguistic determinism and linguistic relativity which came to be called the Sapir-Whorf hypothesis. The main part of this book is Darnell's biography of Sapir accompanied by a list of references cited and a thorough index. Beginning on page 457 there is a complete bibliography of Sapir's work arranged in chronological order beginning in 1906 and ending in 1949. This is followed by a list of coauthored publications and publications based on Sapir's materials dated 1925 through 1964. Though the bibliography is unannotated the index can be used to discover more information about certain publications, such as the nine pages of material concerning his influential book *Language* (New York: Harcourt, Brace, 1921). For another bibliography of Sapir updated through 1984 see Koerner's work (entry 211).

202.   Dutz, Klaus D. **Zeichentheorie und Sprachwissenschaft bei G. W. Leibniz: Eine kritische annotierte Bibliographie der Sekundärliteratur**. Mit einem Anhang: **Sekundärliteratur zur Sprachforschung im 17. Jahrhundert**, von Ulrike Klinkhammer. Münster: Institut für Allgemeine Sprachwissenschaft der Westfälischen Wilhelms-Universität, 1983. 451p. index. (Studium Sprachwissenschaft, Hft.7; ISSN 0727-7129). ISBN 3-89083-007-2.

This is a critical, annotated bibliography of secondary literature on the sign theory and linguistics of Gottfried Wilhelm Leibniz (1646-1716). It is a very detailed, comprehensive work. More than 1,250 entries alphabetized by author make up the main bibliography (and a short addendum). Each entry has up to four parts: the complete bibliographic citation with a minimum of abbreviation, an annotation, a reference number referring to the numbered entries in a subject index of topics and themes, and a reference number referring to the Leibniz titles in an index of his works. Both the subject index and the index of Leibniz's works indicate where they are referenced in the main bibliography.

There is a separate appendix (with 316 entries) by Klinkhammer of secondary literature on linguistics in the 17th century. It has its own subject index which, like the main bibliography, refers the reader from a topic listed there to a bibliographic entry.

203.   Feldstein, Ronald F., comp. **Felix Johannes Oinas, Bibliography**. Köln: E.J. Brill, 1981. 51p. (Arcadia bibliographica virorum eruditorum, Fasc. 4). (Indiana University Folklore Institute Monograph Series, Vol.32). ISBN 0-931922-03-8.

Though Oinas is primarily known as a folklorist, his research until the late 1950s was directed towards the study of Balto-Finnic and Russian linguistics.

This whole range of his own work plus theses written under his direction at Indiana University are covered in this work. Bibliographic information is quite complete with many added explanatory notes. Reviews of works are listed as well. Where titles are not in English, translations are provided. The appendixes consist of six short biographical essays on various aspects of Oinas' life.

204. Gippius, A. A., T. M. Nikolaeva, and V. N. Toporov, red. **Rusistika, slavistika, indoevropeistika: 60-letiyu A. A. Zaliznyaka**. Moskva: Izdatel'stvo "Indrik", 1996. 768p. port. (Institut Slavyanovedeniya i balkanistiki RAN). ISBN 5-85759-034-5.

On pages 749-766 is a 116 item bibliography of Zaliznyaka's publications arranged in chronological order from 1958 through 1995. Essays published on the occasion of the 60th birthday of Zaliznyaka precede it.

205. Gordon, W. Terrence. **C. K. Ogden: A Bio-bibliographic Study**. Metuchen, NJ: Scarecrow Press, 1990. 156p. index. bibliog. LC 90-31264. ISBN 0-8108-2317-9.

Though Ogden did research in various disciplines such as semiotics, philosophy of language, psychology, and anthropology, he is perhaps best known in the field of linguistics for his work in semantics, especially the ideas put forth in a book coauthored with I.A. Richards, *The Meaning of Meaning* (1923) and his development of the system of Basic English which originally elicited some strong support as well as controversy, but is now out of favor. A 55-page biographical essay precedes a nearly 250-item, 42-page classified annotated bibliography of Ogden's publications (books, articles, editorials, notes, reviews, and translations) and a section devoted to secondary sources (commentaries and reviews, plus sequels by other authors). There is a single combined index of topics, names of persons as both subjects and authors, and titles of publications for both the biography and bibliography.

206. Hall, Robert Anderson. **A Life for Language: A Biographical Memoir of Leonard Bloomfield**. Amsterdam: John Benjamins, 1990. 129p. index. illus. bibliog. port. (Amsterdam Studies in the Theory and History of Linguistic Science. Series III: Studies in the History of the Language Sciences, Vol.55; ISSN 0304-0720). ISBN 90-272-4540-1.

Bloomfield's book *Language* (1933) synthesizing the theory and practice of linguistic analysis was a seminal work in the field. His structuralist approach held sway in American linguistics for more than twenty years and engendered many descriptive studies of grammar and phonology. Hall, based on personal knowledge both as a former student then a colleague of Bloomfield, provides insights into his life and works. Following six chapters of a biography centered around various stages of Bloomfield's life, Hall supplies an updated bibliography (pages 105-117) which lists in chronological order Bloomfield's publications from 1909 through 1946 and posthumous publications and reprints published through the end of 1985.

207. Hellmann, Wilhelm. **Charles Bally: Frühwerk, Rezeption, Bibliographie**. Bonn: Romanistischer Verlag, 1988. 266p. illus. port. bibliog. (Abhandlungen zur Sprache und Literatur, 8; ISSN 0178-8515). ISBN 3-924888-28-0.

In Parts I and II Hellmann provides an overview of Bally's scholarly pursuits and a brief biographical sketch and discusses Bally's early works. Bally was both a Romance philologist and one of the earlier linguists to work in the new field of stylistics which emerged between 1910 and 1930. Together with Albert Sechehaye he produced Saussure's *Cours de linguistique générale* (1916) on the basis of lecture notes after Saussure's death. Part III is devoted to some reviews and critical analyses of Bally's major works. There is a classified bibliography on pages 163-250 of Bally's publications together with a variety of materials related to his scholarly endeavors.

208.   Jespersen, Otto. **A Linguist's Life: An English Translation of Otto Jespersen's Autobiography with Notes, Photos and a Bibliography**. Edited by Arne Juul, Hans F. Nielsen, and Jørgen Erik Nielsen. Odense, Denmark: Odense University Press, 1995. 380p. index. illus. port. ISBN 87-7838-132-0.

In the first part of this book Jespersen's autobiography *En Sprogmands Levned* (1938) is translated from the Danish by David Stoner and annotated by Jørgen Erik Nielsen. The second part of the book is a "Bibliography of the Writings of Otto Jespersen during his Lifetime," compiled by Gorm Schou-Rode. The bibliography is a revised and expanded edition of one by C. A. Bodelsen published in 1930 and Niels Haislund's continuation published in 1944; entries are keyed to these earlier bibliographies with an occasional brief note. The chronologically arranged 825 entries published from 1879 through 1943 come close to constituting a comprehensive bibliography of this extraordinarily prolific scholar, only lacking, according to the compiler, articles printed in small Ido periodicals and in the daily newspapers of the time. (See also entry 209 below.)

209.   Juul, Arne, and Hans F. Nielsen, eds. **Otto Jespersen: Facets of His Life and Work**. Amsterdam: John Benjamins, 1989. 154p. bibliog. illus. port. (Amsterdam Studies in the Theory and History of Linguistic Science. Series III: Studies in the History of the Language Sciences, Vol. 52; ISSN 0304-0720). LC 89-17797. ISBN 90-272-4537-1.

Jespersen is perhaps most well known for his 7-volume *A Modern English Grammar on Historical Principles* (1909-1949) and the frequently quoted *Language* (1922), but he also made contributions in such areas as Danish and general phonetics, linguistic theory, language evolution, child language, and even did work on a new international auxiliary language. There are eight chapters in this book, each one devoted to a particular facet of Jespersen's work, with notes and bibliographies. As a complete bibliography already exists in two parts, the editors have not compiled an integrated list of his publications here, though they have counted 487 items all told which cover important facets of his work. For a revised and expanded edition of Jespersen's bibliography see entry 208.

210.   Koerner, E. F. Konrad. **Bibliographia Saussureana 1870-1970: An Annotated, Classified Bibliography on the Background, Development and Actual Relevance of Ferdinand de Saussure's General Theory of Language**. Metuchen, NJ: Scarecrow Press, 1972. 406p. index. LC 76-181700. ISBN 0-8108-0457-3.

This partially annotated and classified bibliography is a useful aid in studying Saussure, a major figure in the development of general, or theoretical linguistics who lived from 1857-1913. It is divided into three parts. Part I contains writings by and about Saussure, such as biographical sources, a list of his writings and their translations, and reviews and general accounts of his work. Part II contains background sources of Saussure's linguistic theory published from 1816-1916. Part III lists writings from 1916-1970 concerning the history of linguistics with particular reference to Saussure and his work. Part I with 1,254 entries attempts to be exhaustive. The latter two parts are not and because of this are less satisfactory in their attempt to set the intellectual scene of the time during which Saussure developed his ideas and to show the importance and relevance of his theory to linguistic study today. There are many annoying errors in spelling and translation, but in general the work is useful.

211. Koerner, E. F. Konrad, ed. **Edward Sapir, Appraisals of His Life and Work**. Amsterdam: John Benjamins, 1984. 224p. index. illus. bibliog. port. (Amsterdam Studies in the Theory and History of Linguistic Science. Series III: Studies in the History of the Language Sciences, Vol. 36; ISSN 0304-0720). ISBN 90-272-4518-5.

Parts I-III of this work provide biographical materials and comments and appraisals of Sapir's life and work. Part IV is a two-part bibliography of his publications in linguistics, anthropology, and other behavioral and social sciences. The first part is a bibliography for 1906-1944 based on *Selected Writings of Edward Sapir in Language, Culture and Personality* (1949), while the second part is an addenda for 1916-1984 that includes all publications in English in linguistics and/or anthropology missed in the first bibliography or republished since then. Much of the material after 1964 is reprints and translations. Koerner makes no attempt to include Sapir's interdisciplinary contributions to scholarship. For another bibliography of Sapir see Darnell's work (entry 201).

212. Koerner, E. F. Konrad, and Matsuji Tajma. **Noam Chomsky: A Personal Bibliography, 1951-1986**. Amsterdam: John Benjamins, 1986. 217p. index. (Amsterdam Studies in the Theory and History of Linguistic Science. Series V: Library & Information Sources in Linguistics, Vol. 11; ISSN 0165-7267). LC 86-26829. ISBN 90-272-1000-4.

Koerner and Matsuji with the collaboration of Carlos P. Otero have compiled a thorough bibliography which can be used as a tool for tracing the development and influence of Chomskian theory, particularly the growth of transformation-generative linguistics from its construction through one major reconstruction in 1965 and another in 1980. It has the widest scope of the numerous bibliographies of Chomsky's work to date. In part it is based on another detailed and comprehensive work which covered publications through 1981 (see entry 222).

Part I of Koerner's book covers Chomsky's writing in linguistics and related fields from 1951 to 1986, while Part II covers his considerable output on political issues and other non-linguistic subjects. While the second part is not comprehensive, it does supply a fairly good picture of this portion of Chomsky's endeavors. Included are translations, reprints, reviews, comments, critiques, excerpts, and even reviews of translations. The notes for many entries provide useful background information, especially as to when something was actually written, as opposed to when it was published. Additionally, there is a third part on interviews and discussions, and finally an appendix detailing the dissertations written under Chomsky's supervision from 1964 to 1986. There is also an index of names.

213. Korhonen, Mikko. **Typological and Historical Studies in Language by Mikko Korhonen: A Memorial Volume Published on the 60th Anniversary of His Birth**. Edited by Tapani Salminen. Helsinki: Suomalais-Ugrilainen Seura, 1996. 255p. illus. bibliog. port. (Suomalais-Ugrilaisen Seuran Toimituksia/Mémoires de la Société Finno-Ougrienne, 223; ISSN 0355-0230). ISBN 951-9403-95-7.

Korhonen was a key figure in Finno-Ugrian linguistics during the second half of this century and published materials dealing with these languages as well as historical linguistics and language typology. The nine articles (in German and English) in this volume typify his work. These are followed by a list of his publications from 1960 through 1994 arranged by date and accompanied by information about reviews.

214. Leopold, Joan. **The Letter Liveth: The Life, Work and Library of August Friedrich Pott (1802-1887)**. Amsterdam: John Benjamins, 1983. 438p. index. illus. port. (Amsterdam Studies in the Theory and History of Linguistic Science. Series V: Library and Information Sources in Linguistics, Vol. 9: ISSN 0165-7267). ISBN 90-272-3733-6.

According to the author's lengthy introduction of 152 pages which highlights Pott's activities, publications, and book collection, there is renewed interest in his contributions to linguistics and increased appreciation of the fact that Pott possessed valuable insights and articulated uncommon positions in Indo-European comparative linguistics, general linguistics, and linguistic ethnology. Though other bibliographies of Pott exist, this is the first claiming to be comprehensive, or nearly so. It lists Pott's works published from 1828 through 1983 though most entries are for publications during his lifetime from the 1830s through the 1880s. The chronologically arranged bibliography on pages 1-60 contain very detailed bibliographic information as well as notes on such things as variant editions, table of contents, and reviews of the item. A major section of the book is devoted to a catalogue of Pott's library collection with its wide range of 18th and 19th century linguistic literature. This is a dense, richly detailed work so the multifarious indices and lists Leopold furnishes are of considerable assistance to the user. They include: periodicals in which Pott published, subjects on which he wrote, and personal names in the titles of his works and in the catalogue of his library.

215. Malkiel, Yakov. **Yakov Malkiel: A Tentative Autobibliography**. With an Introduction by Henry Kahane. Special Editors, Joseph J. Duggan and Charles B. Faulhaber. Berkeley, CA: University of California Press, 1988. 186p. (Romance Philology, Special Issue, 1988-1989). LC 88-27756. ISBN 0-520-06592-1.

Malkiel, a noted linguist and founding editor of *Romance Philology*, has gathered in this autobibliography references to some 800 works which represent 50 years worth of publishing. He arranges entries first by some 21 categories such as books, books edited, notes, journal articles, editorial comments, translations, etc. and then chronologically within each category. Thorough indexes provide good access to topics, languages, lexical terms, authors of books reviewed, and names. While a majority of the studies deal with Romance languages, a significant number of entries concern other languages (English, German, Russian, Polish, Greek, and Hebrew) and linguistics in general.

216. Orlova, V. Ya., and A. M. Gutkina, sost. **Viktoriya Nikolaevna Yartseva**. Avtor vstup. stat'i: V. R. Yastrezhembskii. Moskva: "Nauka," 1993. 71p. index. bibliog. port. (Materialy k biobibliografii uchenykh. Seriya literatury i yazyka, Vyp. 22). ISBN 5-02-011160-0.

Yastrezhembskii is responsible for the chronology of Yartseva's life and the short biographical essay which begin this slim volume. Orlova and Gutkina are the compilers of the chronologically arranged bibliography of works published from 1936 through 1992. There is also a two-part alphabetical list of works by title, the list for works in Russian precedes the list for works written in languages with a Latin script. All biographical material and explanatory features are in Russian.

217. Ramaiah, L. S., and T. V. Prafulla Chandra, comps. **Noam Chomsky: A Bibliography**. Gurgaon, Haryana: Indian Documentation Service, 1984. 92p. (Subject Bibliography Series, 7). LC 84-901135.

Works both by and on Chomsky are gathered here in two sections. The first section of works by him (and with coauthors) lists in chronological order 151 books, articles, mimeographed materials, and some reviews of these works. Only Chomsky's publications concerning linguistics and language are covered here, not any of the work he has done in the realm of politics. The second section lists 502 works on him which are mainly in English, though a few are also in such languages as Russian, Italian, French, German, and Spanish. There are no annotations in either section. Both Koerner and Sgroi's bibliographies (see entries 212 and 222) are more extensive, particularly in listing translations into other languages and pulling together reviews from many publications. This is still useful as a handy compilation of Chomsky's extensive contributions to linguistics from 1951 to 1982.

218. Rudnyckyj, Jaroslav B. **J. B. Rudnyckyj repertorium bibliographicum, 1933-1983**. Ottawa: Ukrainian Language Association, 1984. 296p. index. illus. bibliog. ports.

219. Rudnyckyj, Jaroslav B. **Repertorium bibliographicum addenda, 1984-1994**. Ottawa: Ukrainian Language Association, 1995. p.278-320. illus.

Rudnyckyj is perhaps best known for his development of and contributions to Ukrainian onomastics. The main bibliography of his publications for 1933-1983 (entry 218) was compiled and published by students and friends of this scholar on occasion of the 50th anniversary of his scholarly activities. Preceding this bibliography of 2,102 publications is a chronology of his life accompanied by a list of references for biographical materials. An occasional facsimile title page of one of Rudnyckyj's publications is scattered here and there to liven what is just a simple, chronologically arranged bibliography of books, articles, reviews, notes, and other writings An occasional brief note is sometimes provided for an item and titles not in English are translated for the user.

A subsequent bibliography of his works published from 1984 through 1994 (entry 219) brings the total number of items published by this very productive scholar to 2,967. It, however, lacks translation of titles into English and has no index.

220.   Rudy, Stephen, comp. and ed. **Roman Jakobson 1896-1982: A Complete Bibliography of His Writings**. Berlin: Mouton de Gruyter, 1990. index. LC 90-6607. ISBN 3-11-010650-7.

Jakobson is without doubt one of the great linguists of the twentieth century. Though born in Moscow in 1896, he lived and work in Czechoslovakia for most of the years from 1920 through 1939. During this period of his life, he not only made substantial contributions to Czechoslovak linguistics and poetics and was active in founding the Prague Linguistic Circle, but also laid the foundation for much of his subsequent research in the United States while at Harvard and MIT. He made seminal contributions to general linguistics, the linguistic approach to the study of style, child language and aphasia, semiotics, and Slavonic language studies.

Rudy's comprehensive bibliography of Jakobson has two parts. Part I is a chronologically arranged list of more than 650 original works which span the period from 1915 to 1982, the year of Jakobson's death, and includes posthumous publications to 1988. Rudy lists together with the original under its date of publication the numerous translations (into 15 different languages) and reprints. Part II is an inventory of volumes 1-7 of the thematically arranged, *Selected Writings* (1962-1985) (the complete writings include a volume 8 published in 1988 with 2 more volumes in preparation); these works are cross-referenced under the main entry in Part I. Rudy provides indexes for titles, major collections by language, co-authors, names, and periodicals. This is a very satisfying bibliography in part because the compiler was a close collaborator with Jakobson and has an intimate knowledge of his work.

221.   **Schriftenverzeichnis Leo Weisgerber**. Zusammengestellt von Klaus D. Dutz. Münster: Institut für Allgemeine Sprachwissenschaft der Westfälischen Wilhelms-Universität, 1984. 97p. index. bibliog. port. (Studium Sprachwissenschaft, Hft. 8; 0721-7129). ISBN 3-89083-008-0.

A 20-page biography, *Leo Weisgerber zum 85. Geburtstag*, edited by Helmut Gipper on the occasion of Weisgerber's 85th birthday, precedes a bibliography compiled by Dutz of some 436 publications arranged chronologically from 1925 through 1984. In his very long career Weisgerber, a German scholar born in Metz in Lothringen in 1899, made contributions to theoretical linguistics, historical linguistics, and sematics.

222.   Sgroi, Salvatore Claudio. **Noam Chomsky: Bibliographia, 1949-1981**. Padova: CLESP, 1983. 361p. index.

Chomsky's contributions to linguistic and philosophic as well as to political thought are covered by this bibliography. The first 93 pages of the book are taken up with four introductory essays. The first two, written in Italian and Spanish by G. Cinque and C.P. Otero respectively, are concerned with linguistics while the other two, written in Italian and English by G. Giarrizzo and C.P. Otero respectively, deal with Chomsky's contributions to political and social theory. Each one is footnoted.

The bibliography itself is organized chronologically with the annual list of material from 1966 on also divided into a linguistics and a politics section. For the time period covered this is meant to be comprehensive, listing works whether in microfilm, manuscript, or regular book or periodical format together with all editions, reprints, translations, and reviews. Most items are not annotated. For the few that are, the accompanying notes, often on content of an item, are in Italian.

In an appendix are four tables listing in chronological order works translated into Italian, French, Spanish, and German. There is also a list of Chomsky's work in alphabetical order by title (in original language of publication). Completing the book is an index of names which includes mainly coauthors, translators, interviewers, and reviewers. See also the bibliographies by Koerner and Ramaiah (entries 212 and 217).

223.   Straka, Georges, and Max Pfister, Hrsg. **Die Faszination der Sprachwissenschaft: Ausgewählte Aufsätze zum 70. Geburtstag mit einer Bibliographie.** Tübingen: Max Niemeyer, 1990. 1034p. index. illus. bibliog. maps. ISBN 3-484-52224-0.

Essays written in honor of Baldinger's 70th birthday precede an extensive unannotated bibliography of 2,208 items published from 1950 to 1990 (including works still in press) by or about this scholar who wrote extensively in the area of Romance and French language etymology. The compilers, Karl Brodemann and Nicoline Hörsch, classify the entries by type of publication, then arrange them chronologically. An author and subject index provides thorough access to this voluminous bibliography.

224.   Strohbach, Margrit. **Johann Christoph Adelung: Ein Beitrag zu seinem germanistischen Schaffen mit einer Bibliographie seines Gesamtwerkes.** Berlin: Walter de Gruyter, 1984. index. port. 290p. (Studia linguistica Germanica, 21). ISBN 3-11-009612-9.

Following a short five-page biography of Adelung, Strohbach analyzes the works of this 18th century lexicographer and grammarian of the German language. Among his many contributions is an attempt to create a definitive, comprehensive dictionary of standard (or High) German (1811) and the comparative work on about a thousand New World languages published in the 5-volume *Mithridates* (1806-1817). In a concluding index and bibliography section on pages 269-290 Strohbach provides various lists of his works as well as lists of secondary and biographical works.

225.   Swiggers, Pierre. **Georges Straka: Notice biographique et bibliographique.** Leuven: Centre international de Dialectologie générale, 1993. 60p. illus. (Biobibliographies et Exposés, N.S., 2). ISBN 90-6831-494-7. (This work not viewed by author.)

If this bio-bibliography is similar to other volumes in the series, it characteristically offers a short biography followed by a full, if not comprehensive, bibliography of Straka's publications.

226.   Swiggers, Pierre. **Michel Lejeune: Notice biographique et bibliographique.** Leuven: Centre international de Dialectologie générale, 1993. 86p. index. illus. port. (Biobibliographies et Exposés, N.S., 3). ISBN 90-6831-548-X.

Lejeune is one of the leaders of the French comparativists and displayed a keen interest in ancient Greek, Celtiberian, Etruscan, Phrygian, Italic and ancient Celtic dialects. He is well known for his epigraphical studies, particularly his work with Mycenean. Swiggers supplies a short seven-page biography of Lejeune as an introduction to the 317-item bibliography of Lejeune's published books and articles (excludes proceedings, reports, reviews, and the like) arranged in chronological order from 1929 through 1993 with an appended list of works in press. There are two indexes: one is a type/title of publication index, the other is a subject/language of study index.

227.   Szemerényi, Oswald. **Summing Up a Life: Autobiographie und Schriftenverzeichnis**. Hrsg. von Bela Brogyanyi. Freiburg i. Br.: HochschulVerlag, 1991. 135p. port. ISBN 3-8107-5056-5.

Szemerenyi has been a prominent figure in linguistics research, focusing particularly in the area of Indo-European languages. Here he offers a brief autobiography accompanied by a chronologically arranged bibliography of some 281 works published since 1937. While the preface and autobiography are written in English, the editor's brief introduction and various other materials are in German. Since the bibliography is not annotated or keyed to the autobiographical essay, finding background material in the essay on a particular publication can be tedious.

9

Directories and Lists

The directories of programs, grants, fellowships, memberships, organizations, publishers, and periodicals listed in this chapter generally exclude older directories because the information in such reference works becomes rapidly outdated and is of little use. However, a few older ones still useful for historical or identification purposes are included.

228. Cantrell, Karen, and Denise Wallen, eds. **Funding for Anthropological Research**. Phoenix, AZ: Oryx Press, 1986. 308p. index. LC 85-43472. ISBN 0-89774-154-4.

While focusing on anthropological research, this directory includes many funding sources for linguistic research. Over 700 United States-based program sponsors are listed alphabetically along with their addresses, phone numbers, name of the program, Catalog of Federal Domestic Assistance Program Number for federal programs, eligibility/limitations, fiscal information, application information, deadlines, and subject index terms. Sponsors include corporations, federal agencies, foundations, museums, libraries, nonprofit organizations, associations, professional societies, and universities. A subject index and sponsor type index increase its usefulness. For those wanting to investigate funding sources further there is a bibliography of printed and online materials. Though this is an old directory, it might nevertheless be consulted to identify potential sponsors.

229. **Guide to Grants and Fellowships in Linguistics**. Washington, DC: Linguistic Society of America, 1985- . ISSN 1041-5459.

The former title of this publication was *Guide to Grants & Fellowships in Languages & Linguistics*; the new title ceased with publication of the 1994-96 edition in 1994. This last edition lists grants and fellowships in linguistics sponsored by institutions, associations, and foundations (mainly U.S. and Canadian), as well as U.S. government agencies. Under each entry which lists name, address, and sometimes phone number, programs are described giving such essential information as eligibility, restrictions, duration, amount of stipend/allowances, application procedures, deadline, and selection/evaluation procedures. The *LSA Bulletin* (see entry 234) now provides up-to-date information on grants and fellowships.

230. Harner, James L., ed. **MLA Directory of Scholarly Presses in Language and Literature**. 2nd ed. New York: Modern Language Association of America, 1996. 295p. index. ISBN 87352-680-5.

The second edition of this directory includes information on 315 scholarly publishers from 34 countries who publish works on language or literature. From the more than 1,000 publishers queried via a questionnaire, the editor screened out vanity presses and publishers that issue only a few books in these areas or who publish only textbooks or original poetry, drama, or fiction. Entries are listed alphabetically by publisher except for entries beginning with the word "university," which are alphabetized by the state, city, or other proper name in their titles (except for proper name entries which are listed under the surname (e.g. Walter de Gruyter and Edward Arnold are listed under de Gruyter and Arnold respectively). Though no entry contains information on all details requested, a full entry would consist of 41 items organized into six sections: general information, scope, submission requirements, editorial information, contract provisions, and publication and distribution information. Five indexes of publishing interests, imprints and subsidiary firms, series titles, editorial personnel, and languages of publication other than English complete the directory. By using the index of publishing interests one is able to identify publishers of works for linguistics, specialized areas within linguistics and allied areas, language and languages in general, and specific languages.

231. **Language Organisations and Centres: A User's Guide**. 2nd rev. ed. London: Centre for Information on Language Teaching and Research, 1984. 77p. index. bibliog. (Centre for Information on Language Teaching and Research, Information Guide 10). ISBN 0-903466-95-3.

More than 150 organizations and centers concerned with language, linguistics, language teaching, and research are described in this directory. Those concerned with language teaching are limited to French, German, Italian, Russian, Spanish, and English, the latter mainly as a second or foreign language. The focus is on those associations located within the United Kingdom, but also included are other important European and international associations and centers.

The main part of the directory lists the organizations alphabetically, identifying for each one address and phone number, name of correspondent, aims and scope, activities, and a list of its publications. A bibliography refers the reader to other directories and sources of reference. There are also four indexes: index of names, index of abbreviations and acronyms, index of publications, and a subject index.

232. **Linguistic Programs**. Available: http://www.emich.edu/~linguist/program/. (Accessed: March 8, 1999).

This site, under the aegis of The LINGUIST List (see entry 98), provides a directory of graduate and undergraduate programs in linguistics throughout the world. It not only offers links to home pages of programs organized by geographic location (Africa, Asia, Australia & Oceania, Europe, Middle East, North America, and South America), but is developing a database of linguistics programs which can be searched by word and phrase. Some data is already available, but it is still very much under construction and the visitor to this site is prompted to register as a new user or add/modify linguistics program data already contributed. A program listing will provide such information and data as contact information, degrees offered, number of students, faculty, less commonly taught languages, department strengths, special resources available, department publications, information on financial support, and application procedures and deadlines.

233. **Linguists Directory**. Available: http://www.linguistlist.org/persop. html. (Accessed: March 8, 1999).

A directory of linguists is maintained on this page of The LINGUIST List (see entry 98). It is simply a list in alphabetical order by surname. Linguists themselves submit and update information for a listing by using an online submission form. Information may include: name, affiliation, e-mail, home page, postal address, title, specialty, interests, courses taught, and selected publication titles. With little more than 300 entries, most for linguists in the United States, it does not begin to list all practicing linguists.

234. **LSA Bulletin**. Washington, DC: Linguistic Association of America, 1926- . December issue. ISSN 0023-6365.

A short list of honorary members precedes the main list of active personal members of the Linguistic Society of America now contained in each December issue of the Bulletin. Both these lists are arranged alphabetically by members' names and include mailing addresses and e-mail addresses, if known. A list of active members with just names and e-mail addresses can also be found on LSA's Web site at http://www.lsadc.org/web2/membfr.htm (accessed: March 8, 1999). The Bulletin posts lists of forthcoming conferences and a grants calendar, plus the style sheet for the association's journal *Language*.

235. **1998 LSA Directory of Programs—Foreword**. Available: http: //www.lsadc.org. (Accessed: March 8, 1999).

Formerly published as an issue of the *LSA Bulletin*, then as a separate publication, the directory of programs in the United States and Canada is now maintained by the Society on its Web site. The 10th edition can be found by following the "Ling.Programs" link on the home page (updated October 22, 1998). On the programs page a frame on the right side of the screen is an alphabetical list of institutions for the United States, followed by one for Canada. Those schools providing information to the LSA are hot linked to a page where information is displayed in a set format. At the top following the school name is address, telephone and facsimile numbers, and e-mail address. Listed below is the name of the department with date founded, name of department chair, whether academic year system is semesters or quarters, degrees offered in linguistics, department emphases, special resources and facilities, department's publications, and the URL for the department's home page. Beneath, three year's worth of information is displayed in table format providing numbers of undergraduate and graduate degrees conferred, numbers of students in residence, and numbers of students supported. The frame on the left side of the programs page enables a user to more quickly access the United States and Canadian schools by using A-Z listings. Beneath this is a regional index for the United States which is accessed by clicking on a particular region of a map; this part of the index was not functional when last accessed.

236. Maison des sciences de l'homme, Paris. Service d'échange d'informations scientifiques. **Liste mondiale des périodiques spécialisés: linguistique. World List of Specialized Periodicals: Linguistics**. Paris: Mouton, 1971. 243p. (Maison des sciences de l'homme. Service d'échange d'informations scientifiques. Publications. Série C: Catalogues et inventaires, 4).

The 540 periodicals listed and described here are classified according to their country of origin. Within a given country they are further subdivided into categories. Category A (332 titles) includes those devoted wholly to general linguistics, a special branch of the discipline, or study of a particular language (philology journals being excluded). Category B (152 titles) is composed of periodicals which devote a significant portion of their articles to linguistics, many of which are ethnology journals. Category C (56 titles) lists the periodicals on teaching of languages, or their translation.

For each title in Categories A and B above, the entry provides standard abbreviation, title changes, issuing organization, editor(s), name and address of publisher, frequency of publication, information on tables and indexes, date first published, and a paragraph describing one issue. There are subject, institution and title indexes as well. English text or equivalents are provided throughout the book so one does not need to know French in order to use it. Though dated, it is still useful for identifying foreign publications.

237. **MLA Directory of Periodicals: A Guide to Journals and Series in Languages and Literatures, 1978/79-** . New York: Modern Language Association of America, 1979- . biennial. index. LC 80-640485. ISSN 0197-0380.

The *Directory* is a companion volume to the *MLA International Bibliography* (see entry 88). As such it provides all the information available on the journals and series in the *Bibliography*'s master list. The 1996-98 edition, edited by Andrew F. B. LaCroix, lists 3,402 journals and series. Entries arranged alphabetically by title include such general information as name and address of editor(s), date first published, sponsoring organization, ISSN, and MLA acronym. Additional information under each title is given in separate sections on subscription information, advertising information, editorial description, and submission requirements. Four indexes accompany the directory: subjects, sponsoring organizations, editorial personnel, and languages published. Beginning on page 916 there is a listing of periodicals with author-anonymous submission policies. The directory includes nearly all the major linguistics journals and many of the more specialized ones, particularly those devoted to study of a language or languages. In the subject index under the heading of "Linguistics" more than 250 entries are listed.

238. **NSF: Social, Behavioral and Economic Research**. Available: http://www.nsf.gov/sbe/sber/start.htm. (Accessed: March 8, 1999).

The Division of Social, Behavioral and Economic Research (SBER) within the National Science Foundation supports research in a broad range of disciplines and in interdisciplinary areas; linguistics is included among the 17 fields listed. All programs in SBER consider proposals for research projects, conferences, and workshops. Some programs also consider proposals for doctoral dissertation improvement assistance, the acquisition of specialized research and computing equipment, group international travel, and largescale data collection. A visitor to this division's Web page should follow the "Linguistics" link under Scientific Research Programs for more specific details on the type of research supported and the various grants and other special funding opportunities. The site is a rich source for funding information such as deadline and extension dates, addresses, and online forms, and even includes information on awards from past years.

239.   **PMLA: Publications of the Modern Language Association of America**. New York: Modern Language Association of America, 1884/85- . Issue No.4 (Directory Issue). ISSN 0030-8129.

The Directory issue each year of *PMLA* now includes a list of current members of the Modern Language Association of America. It has addresses and is alphabetically arranged by members' last names. There are separate lists for honorary members and honorary fellows.

240.   Pop, Sever, and Rodica Doina Pop. **Premier répertoire des instituts et des sociétés de linguistique du monde**. Louvain: Commission d'enquête linguistique, 1958. 294p. illus. (Comité international permanent des linguistes. Publications de la Commission d'enquête linguistique, 8). LC 59-7313.

Since this directory is about forty years old, a lot of the information it provides is out-of-date. However, it is still useful as a historical record. About 269 institutes and societies of linguistics in 54 countries are listed alphabetically by their names (in French). Descriptions range from less than half a page to more than several pages long and include the address and name (in original language); circumstances surrounding the founding, such as date, place, and people involved; aims and objectives; and details on some of the organizations' major publications. Institutions no longer in existence (at the time this was published) do not rate an entry. Thus, the Linguistic Circle of Prague is not included since it became part of the Association de Linguistique in 1956.

A unique feature of this directory is a chronological table listing the institutes and societies by date of founding. As a matter of interest, the Séminaires d'Études Linguistiques de l'Université de Munich established in 1472 is ranked the oldest.

241.   Ulving, Tor. **Periodica philologica abbreviata. A List of Initial Abbreviations of Periodicals in Philology and Related Subjects**. Stockholm: Almqvist & Wiksell, 1963. 137p. LC 64-1932.

Essentially this book is just what its subtitle says it is, with "related subjects" taking in linguistics and language study. It lists an abbreviation along with the full name of the corresponding periodical and its place of publication. About 3,250 abbreviations are given, mainly for periodicals, although a certain number are included for institutions, societies, dictionaries, and text editions which are often referred to by abbreviations. It is not a prescriptive list; its sole purpose is to help users identify abbreviations they find reference to in scholarly works. Thus, *Archiv Orientalni* can be found listed under "ArchOr," "ArO," and "AO" because it can be found abbreviated all three ways in the literature.

Though in many cases the place of publication has changed since this list was compiled, it can still serve (usually) as an indication of the country from which it originates. This list is particularly useful for tracing older journals that have ceased publication.

242.   **University Linguistics Departments, Programs and Centers**. Available: http://www.ling.rochester.edu/links/departments.html. (Accessed: March 8, 1999).

The Department of Linguistics, University of Rochester maintains this well-kept Web site (last updated January 14, 1999) which has links to the Web sites of both foreign and American universities where information can be found regarding their departments, programs, and centers. As expected each site is unique and varies from those rich with detail to others which provide a modicum of information. The listings for foreign and American universities are separate with each arranged alphabetically by title, not by geographic or political region. A sorter for entries A-D, E-H, I-L, M-P, Q-T, and U-Z allows a visitor to quickly navigate the two alphabetical lists.

10

Professional Associations and Societies

The emphasis in this chapter is on national and regional associations and societies within the United States whose focus is linguistics and/or the study of modern languages in general. Selected associations in allied areas (particularly applied linguistics), a few Canadian- and British-based societies, as well as some important international societies are also included. Specifically excluded are the many national linguistic societies of other countries, such as the Linguistic Society of India (Ireland, Japan, Brazil, etc); with only a few exceptions, the many national and international associations whose focus is study of a particular language or language family, such as the Society for Caribbean Linguistics; and the many associations for teachers of a language or languages, such as the American Association of Teachers of Arabic.

Used together, the two directories published by Gale, the *Encyclopedia of Associations* and its companion, *International Organizations*, are useful for locating information about major associations and societies worldwide. The ninth edition of the *LSA Directory* (1995), pages 133-47, provides details on a number of societies and associations. Other lists found on the Web include the Summer Institute of Linguistics' list "Associations, Societies, SIGs" available at http://www.sil.org/linguistics/univ.html#assoc (accessed: March 8, 1999) and The LINGUIST List of associations available at http://www.linguistlist.org/associations.html (accessed: March 8, 1999).

243. **American Association for Applied Linguistics (AAAL)**, P.O. Box 21686, Eagan, MN 55121-0686, (612) 953-0805, aaaloffice@aaal.org. Available: http://www.aaal.org/. (Accessed: March 8, 1999).

Founded in 1977 and now 700 members strong, AAAL is a professional association of scholars who are interested in and actively contributing to the multidisciplinary field of applied linguistics. In addition to promoting research and facilitating the distribution and exchange of information it organizes an annual conference in conjunction with the Linguistic Society of America. It is the U.S. affiliate of the International Association of Applied Linguistics/Association Internationale de Linguistique Appliquée. In cooperation with the Center for Applied Linguistics it produces various publications. AAAL jointly sponsors, with the British Association for Applied Linguistics, the journal *Applied Linguistics*. It also publishes a triannual newsletter for its members.

244. **American Association of Phonetic Sciences (AAPS)**, Dr. W. S. Brown, Exec. Sec., P.O. Box 14095, University Station, Gainesville, FL 32604, (904) 392-2046, wsbrown@cpd.ufl.edu.

This association has about 150 members who are students or individuals working in phonetics or related fields. The purpose of AAPS is to encourage research in the phonetic sciences and provide a forum for exchange and development of information about the field. Activities include an annual conference and publication of a semiannual newsletter. It is affiliated with the International Society of Phonetic Sciences (ISPhS).

245.   **American Dialect Society (ADS)**, c/o Allan A. Metcalf, Exec. Sec., English Department, MacMurray College, Jacksonville, IL 62650, (217) 243-3403. Available: http://www.americandialect.org/. (Accessed: March 8, 1999).

Members of this society are interested in furthering the study of the English language in North America and other languages influencing it or influenced by it. It sponsors the *Dictionary of American Regional English* (see entry 714), issues an annual Word of the Year report available on its Web site, and is a constituent society of the American Council of Learned Societies. ADS publishes the quarterly, *American Speech* (see entry 290) and a newsletter 3 times a year which not only reports society news, but contains questions and answers from the public about American English. A monograph series, *Publication of the A.D.S.*, is published irregularly. An annual January meeting is held in conjunction with the Linguistic Society of America and it sponsors sessions at the national conventions of the Modern Language Association of America, the National Council of Teachers of English, the Dictionary Society of North America, the International Linguistic Association, and regional meetings at the regional affiliates of the Modern Language Association.

246.   **Association for Computational Linguistics (ACL)**, c/o Priscilla Rasmussen, P.O. Box 6090, Somerset, NJ 00875, (732) 873-3898, acl@acl-web.org. Available: http://www.aclweb.org/. (Accessed: March 8, 1999).

This association now 2,000 members strong promotes research and activities in the area of natural language and computation. It deals with algorithms, models, and computer systems or components of systems for research on language, applications (translation, documentation, and lexicography), and scholarly investigation (stylistics and content analysis). An annual meeting is held each summer; European Chapter conferences are held in the spring of odd-numbered years. ACL is affiliated with the International Committee on Computational Linguistics, sponsors of COLING conferences and has liaison relations with the Linguistic Society of America, Association for Computers and the Humanities, the Association for Literary and Linguistic Computing, and the Cognitive Science Society. It sponsors the quarterly, *Computational Linguistics*, now published by MIT Press and publishes the annual ACL conference proceedings.

247.   **Association for Computers and the Humanities (ACH)**, c/o Elli Mylonas, Box 1885, Brown University, Providence, RI 02912, (801) 378-3513. Available: http://www.ach.org/. (Accessed: March 8, 1999).

The ACH founded in 1978 and now with 350 members is the major professional society for people working computer applications in the study of language, literature, history, music, archaeology, philosophy, political science, and related social sciences. Acts as a forum for scholars to report on research activities and software and hardware developments in the field. It sponsors the bi-monthly

Computers and the Humanities, published by Kluwer Academic, and the *Humanist* (available at http://www.princeton.edu/~mccarty/humanist/humanist.html), an international electronic seminar on the application of computers to the humanities. Along with the Association for Computational Linguistics (ACL) and the Association for Literary and Linguistic Computing (ALLC), it sponsors *The Text Encoding Initiative (TEI)*, an international project to develop guidelines for the preparation and interchange of electronic texts for scholarly research and for uses by the language industries. It holds an annual meeting in conjunction with ALLC.

248. **Association for Linguistic Typology**, c/o Sec.-Treas. Johan van der Auwera, Linguistiek (GER), Universiteit Antwerpen (UIA), Universiteitsplein 1, B2610 Antwerpen, Belgium, +32-3-8202776, auwera@uia.ua.ac.be. Available: http://148.88.14.7/alt/. (Accessed: March 8, 1999).

Founded in March 1994 and currently with more than 400 members, the purpose of ALT is to advance the scientific study of typology, i.e. of cross-linguistic diversity and the patterns underlying it. In addition to organizing annual or biennial meetings and occasional regional workshops, it regularly awards a prize for outstanding typological research. Under the auspices of ALT, Mouton de Gruyter publishes the journal *Linguistic Typology* three times a year. A newsletter published three times a year is also available on the association's Web site.

249. **Association for Literary & Linguistic Computing (ALLC)**, c/o Dr. David I. Holmes, Faculty of Computer Studies and Mathematics, University of the West of England, Cold Harbour Ln., Bristol, W. Midlands BS16 1QY, England, 44117 9656261, david.holmes@csm.uwe.ack.uk. Available: http://www.kcl.ac.uk/humanities/cch/allc/. (Accessed: March 8, 1999).

ALLC was founded in 1973 with the purpose of supporting the application of computing in the study of language and literature. Since then, its interests have broadened to encompass not only text analysis and language corpora, but also image processing and electronic editions. Its membership of 360 is international and is drawn from across the humanities disciplines. Its quarterly *Literary and Linguistic Computing* is published by Oxford University Press. In collaboration with the Association for Computers and the Humanities (ACH), it sponsors an annual conference. Along with other organizations it is involved with several projects: The Text Encoding Initiative (TEI) and the Advanced Computing in the Humanities (ACO*Hum) Project.

250. **Association Internationale de Linguistique Appliquée (AILA)/International Association of Applied Linguistics**, c/o Andrew D. Cohen, Institute for Linguistics and Asian and Slavic Languages, University of Minnesota, 130 Klaeber Ct., 320 16th St. NW, Minneapolis, MN 55455, (612) 891-3500, pbushee@mr.net.

Founded in 1964 as an international effort to coordinate and encourage research in the field of applied linguistics, AILA now has 38 member national associations of applied linguistics representing 4,500 individuals. It publishes the *AILA Review* annually and *AILA News* 3 times a year.

251.   **Berkeley Linguistics Society (BLS)**, University of California at Berkeley, Department of Linguistics, 2337 Dwinelle Hall, Berkeley, CA 94720, (510) 642-2757/5808, bls@garnet.berkeley.edu. Available: http://www.linguistics. berkeley.edu/lingdept/research/BLS/BLS.html. (Accessed: March 8, 1999).

BLS is organized and operated entirely by student volunteers. They hold an annual meeting in February at the University of California at Berkeley and publish its proceedings (see entry 291).

252.   **Canadian Linguistic Association/Association Canadienne de Linguistique**, c/o Paul Pupier, Département de Linguistique, Université du Québec à Montréal, CP 8888, Succursale A, Montréal, PQ, Canada H3C 3P8. Available: http://www.ucs.mun.ca/~claacl/cla.htm. (Accessed: March 11, 1999).

The primary goal of this association is to advance the scientific study of language and languages in Canada. It has more than 700 individual, institutional, and student members. The Association publishes the quarterly, *Canadian Journal of Linguistics/La revue canadienne de Linguistique* (see entry 294).

253.   **Chicago Linguistic Society (CLS)**, The University of Chicago, 1050 E. 59th St., Chicago, IL 60637, (773) 702-8529, cls@diderot.uchicago.edu. Available: http://humanities.uchicago.edu/humanities/cls/main.html. (Accessed: March 8, 1999).

Established 35 years ago as a part of the Linguistics Department at the University of Chicago and run by its graduate students, CLS is the oldest organization of this kind in the United States. The Society organizes a monthly meeting during the school year featuring invited speakers and an annual spring conference. Papers from the conference are then published (see entry 295).

254.   **Comité International Permanent des Linguistes (CIPL)/Permanent International Committee of Linguists**, c/o Prof. van Sterkenburg, Sec. Gen., Instituut voor Nederlandse Lexicologie, P.O. Box 9515, NL-2300 Leiden, Netherlands, 31 71 5141648, secretariaat@rulxha.leidenuniv.nl.

This prominent international organization was established to assist in the development of linguistic science. It attempts to further linguistic research and to coordinate activities undertaken for the advancement of linguistics. CIPL was founded in April 1928 during the first international congress which took place in The Hague. This congress constitutes an important landmark in the study of linguistics since this was the first time that linguistics had presented itself to the world as an autonomous science. In order to ensure the proper organization of future congresses, CIPL was created. Congresses were then held in 1931, 1933, 1936, 1948, 1952, and every 5 years afterwards; the next is scheduled for 2002. Proceedings of all congresses are published. Its membership now consists of national representatives of organizations in 56 countries along with two international linguistic organizations, Societas Linguistica Europaea and Société internationale de linguistique fonctionnelle. In 1949 it began publication of a major international linguistic bibliography which is still published annually (see entry 78). It coordinates and sponsors various special linguistic projects such as the Endangered Languages Project.

255. **Eastern States Conference on Linguistics (ESCOL)**, Department of Linguistics, 204 Cunz Hall, Ohio State University, 1841 Millikin Road, Columbus, OH 43210-1229, (614) 292-4052, lingadm@julius.ling.ohio-state. edu.

ESCOL sponsors a yearly conference on linguistics for the Eastern United States (roughly bounded by New York to the north, Washington, D.C. to the south, and Ohio to the west). The conference is held each fall at a sponsoring university. The proceedings, available back to 1984, are now published by the Linguistic Department at Cornell University.

256. **Generative Linguists in the Old World (GLOW)**, Tilburg University, GLOW Bureau, Department of Language and Literature, P.O. Box 90153, NL-5000 LE Tilburg, The Netherlands. Available: http://cwis.kub.nl/~fdl/research/gm/glow/index.htm. (Accessed: March 8, 1999).

Founded in 1977 GLOW now has 400 individual and 15 institutional members. In its aim to further the advancement of generative grammar in Europe and beyond it holds a yearly GLOW Colloquium. Among its activities is the sponsorship of an annual meeting held around Easter at a site in Europe and the publication of a twice yearly newsletter.

257. **Indiana University Linguistics Club (IULC)**, Indiana University, 720 E. Atwater Ave., Bloomington, IN 47401-3634, (812) 855-8673, iulc@indiana.edu.

The purpose of this nonprofit organization is to distribute at a reasonable cost new papers in linguistics and related disciplines. Profits from sales are put back into the publication program, used to support outside speaker programs, and to provide financial aid to students. A bibliography lists the papers and dissertations reproduced and distributed by the Club from 1967 through 1991 (see entry 113).

258. **International Cognitive Linguistics Association (ICLA)**, Dr. Marjolijn Verspoor, Sec.-Treas., English Department, University of Groningen, Postbus 716, 9700 AS Groningen, The Netherlands, M.H.Verspoor@let.rug.nl. Available: http://odur.let.rug.nl/orgs/icla/. (Accessed: March 10, 1999).

ICLA offers a forum for research within the perspective of cognitive linguistics. Topics of interest include the structural characteristics of natural language categorization, the functional principles of linguistic organization, the conceptual interface between syntax and semantics, the experiential and pragmatic background of language-in-use, and the relationship between language and thought. It is associated with the *Cognitive Linguistics Journal* published by Mouton de Gruyter (http://www.degruyter.de/journals/cogling/index.html) and sponsors a biannual conference and runs the COGLING listserv. Information about the listserv is available at: http://odur.let.rug.nl/orgs/icla/memoff5.html.

259. **International Linguistic Association**, c/o Hispanic Society of America, 613 West 155th Street, New York, NY 10032. Theodore S. Beardsley, Jr., Treasurer.

Founded in 1943 as the Linguistic Circle of New York, this association, in recognition of its international membership, changed to its present name in 1969. It now has about 1,400 members in every part of the world. Each March or April since 1955 the association has sponsored an annual conference in New York in order to provide a forum for the presentation of research papers and for the informal exchange of ideas among members. During the year, from October through December and February through May (except for the conference month), the group arranges monthly meetings at which guest speakers present papers. Its journal, *Word*, appears 3 times a year.

260.   **International Phonetic Association (IPA)**, J. H. Esling, Sec., CLCS, Arts Building, Dublin, Ireland, 353 1 6081348, esling@uvic.ca. Available: http://www.arts.gla.ac.uk/IPA/ipa.html. (Accessed: March 8, 1999).

The IPA's main purpose is to promote the scientific study of phonetics and its applications. The association has devised a widely used phonetic alphabet which may be used to transcribe any language phonetically. Founded in 1886 it now has 800 members. There is a quadrennial international conference held in conjunction with the Permanent International Committee for Congresses of Phonetic Sciences. Its journal is published twice a year (see entry 312). *The Principles of the International Phonetic Association*, which it first published in 1949, contains a description, with illustrations of its use in 51 languages, of the International Phonetic Alphabet; mid-1999 a Handbook published by Cambridge University Press will replace the 1949 publication (see entry 30). In the meantime, the IPA Web site has the IPA alphabet (also abbreviated as IPA) updated through 1996.

261.   **International Society for Historical Linguistics (ISHL)/Société Internationale de Linguistique Historique**, Dorothy Disterheft, Linguistics Program, University of South Carolina, Columbia, SC 29208, (803) 777-2063, disterh@univscvm.csd.scarolina.edu.

This group organized for scholars in the field of historical linguistics works to advance the study of language change. It holds a biennial conference and publishes its proceedings.

262.   **International Society of Phonetic Sciences (ISPhS)**, Prof. Jens-Peter Koester, Sec. Gen., Universitaet Trier, D-54286 Trier, Germany, 49 651 2012256, koester@uni-trier.de.

The purpose of this society is to provide a forum for individuals interested in phonology, acoustic phonetics, speech perception, language teaching, voice training and use, speech pathology, and related professions. It currently has more than 1,400 members from all over the world. The society operates as a network connecting individuals with similar interests and promotes training and research. Occasionally it sponsors a research conference, usually in connection with some other meeting and publishes a biennial directory and *The Phonetician* three times a year.

263.   **Linguistic Association of Canada and the United States (LA-CUS)/Association de linguistique du Canada et des États Unis**, Sydney Lamb, Chm., English Dept. CB 3520, University of North Carolina, Chapel Hill, NC 27599-3520, (919) 962-0469, cceble@email.unc.edu.

About 300 individuals from 50 countries belong to this association founded in 1974. It supports and promotes both applied and theoretical linguistic studies. One of its activities is an annual August conference, alternating sites between Canada and the United States, the LACUS Forum, at which an award is given to the best paper presented by a nontenured scholar. It publishes the forum proceedings as well as a semiannual newsletter.

264. **Linguistic Association of the Southwest (LASSO)**, Garland Bills, Exec. Dir., Department of Linguistics, University of New Mexico, Albuquerque, NM 87131-1196, (505) 277-6353, gbills@bootes.unm.edu. Available: http://www.unm.edu/~linguist/lasso.html. (Accessed: March 8, 1999).

LASSO now with about 190 individual and 35 institutional members holds its annual meeting in October in a southwest city selected by the membership; southwest in this context takes in the states of Arizona, Arkansas, California, Colorado, Louisiana, New Mexico, Oklahoma, and Texas. Once or twice a year it publishes the *Southwest Journal of Linguistics*. It publishes descriptive and structural studies, as well as some pedagogy and applied linguistics; its specialty is North American Indian languages. LASSO's members also receive a twice yearly newsletter.

265. **Linguistic Society of America (LSA)**, 1325 18th St. NW, Suite 211, Washington, DC 20036-6501, (202) 835-1714, lsa@lsadc.org. Available: http://www.lsadc.org/. (Accessed: March 8, 1999).

Founded in 1924 and now with nearly 7,000 members, LSA is the major scholarly society devoted to the furtherance of scientific research on language in the United States. It is an affiliate of the Permanent International Committee of Linguists, a constituent society of the American Council of Learned Societies, and a member of the Consortium of Social Science Associations, the National Humanities Alliance, and the American Association for the Advancement of Science. Every two years during the summer it sponsors an institute (at a host university) that provides intensive training in applied and theoretical linguistics on both the graduate and undergraduate level. The annual meeting is held each December. It publishes both *Language* (see entry 313), a quarterly journal, and the *LSA Bulletin* four times a year. The latter includes a membership directory, information on grants, and a calendar of events. A directory of programs, formerly a separate publication, can now be found on the Society's Web site.

266. **Linguistics Association of Great Britain (LAGB)**, c/o Dr. Nigel Fabb, Sec., University of Strathclyde, Glasgow G1 1XH, Scotland. Available: http://clwww.essex.ac.uk/LAGB/. (Accessed: March 8, 1999).

LAGB, now with about 600 members, exists to promote the study of linguistics. To this end it holds two conferences per year and publishes the semiannual, *Journal of Linguistics* (see entry 308) and the *British Linguistic Newsletter* which comes out 9 times a year. For its members there is an LAGB mailing list.

267. **Modern Humanities Research Association (MHRA)**, c/o Professor David A. Wells, Hon. Sec., University of London, Birkbeck College, Malet Street, London, WC1E 7HX, England. Available: http://www.mhra.org.uk/. (Accessed: March 8, 1999).

The purpose of this association founded at Cambridge in 1918 is to encourage and promote advanced study and research in the field of the modern humanities, especially modern European languages and literatures (including English). Annual meetings and dinners are held in the United Kingdom and the United States for its 600 members found in all parts of the world. It has an active publication program, publishing various journals, bibliographies, monographs, and other aids to research, among which are the two standard reference works: *Annual Bibliography of English Language and Literature* and *The Year's Work in Modern Language Studies* (see entries 739 and 652). It is affiliated with the International Federation for Modern Languages and Literatures.

268. **Modern Language Association of America (MLA)**, Phyllis Franklin, Exec. Dir., 10 Astor Place, New York, NY 10003, (212) 475-9500, info@mla.org. Available: http://www.mla.org/. (Accessed: March 8, 1999).

MLA was founded in 1883 in order to promote study, criticism and research in modern languages and their literatures, and to further the common interests of teachers of these subjects. It now has more than 30,000 members, most of whom are college and university teachers. Of 81 divisions, those of interest to linguists are Linguistic Approaches to Literature, Applied Linguistics, Language & Society, Language Change, and Language Theory & Teaching Language. There are discussion groups for Comparative Romance Linguistics, General Linguistics, Germanic Philology, Lexicography, Present-Day English language, Slavic Linguistics, and Poetics. It conducts a wide range of programs and activities. A convention is held each year at the end of December. Among its numerous publications are a standard reference work, the multi-volume *MLA International Bibliography* (see entry 88) available in print, online, on tape, and on CD-ROM; a journal, *PMLA*; a newsletter; and various publications of interest to the teaching profession. It is affiliated with the International Federation for Modern Languages and Literatures as well as the International Association of Applied Linguistics.

269. **Northeast Linguistic Society (NELS)**, Graduate Linguistic Student Association, Department of Linguistics, South College, University of Massachusetts, Amherst, MA 01003, (413) 545-6838, glsa@linguist.umass.edu.

NELS is not a membership society as it includes all registered graduate students in the Program in Linguistics at the University of Massachusetts-Amherst. Its purpose is to promote the welfare of the linguistics graduate program and provide a forum for its student. It publishes the proceedings of its annual meeting usually held each November.

270. **Societas Linguistica Europaea (SLE)/Linguistic Society of Europe**, c/o Prof. D. Kastovsky, University of Vienna, Department of English, Universitatsstrasse 7, A-2300 Vienna, Austria, 43 1 401032513, dieter.kastovsky @univie.ac.at.

This European and international society was founded in 1966 with the express purpose of bringing together persons interested in the scientific study of all aspects of language. It presently has about 1,100 individual members from more than 50 countries. Annual meetings have been held since 1967. SLE publishes two semiannuals, *Folia linguistica* and *Folia linguistica historica* (see entry 298) and an annual bulletin. It is affiliated with the Permanent International Committee of Linguists.

271. **Société internationale de linguistique fonctionnelle (SILF)/International Society of Functional Linguistics**, c/o École Pratique des Hautes Études, 4e Section, 45-47 rue des Écoles, F-75005 Paris, France.

Founded in 1976, SILF brings together some 200 linguists and researchers in 15 countries who are interested in the teachings of noted French linguist Andre Martinet. It works to coordinate research and publicize findings, particularly in the study of functional linguistics, publishing the semiannual, *La Linguistique* (see entry XX) and the proceedings of its annual colloquium.

272. **Society for Linguistic Anthropology (SLA)**, c/o American Anthropological Association, 4350 N. Fairfax Dr., Ste. 640, Arlington, VA 22203-1620, (703) 528-1902, (name)@aaa.mhs.compuserve.com.

This association was founded in 1983 as a section of the American Anthropological Association (AAA). Its 512 members, faculty and students, come together to promote the anthropological study of language. The annual meeting is held in conjunction with the AAA and there is also a semiannual meeting and symposium. It publishes the *Journal of Linguistic Anthropology* in June and December.

273. **Society for the Study of Indigenous Languages of the Americas (SSILA)**, c/o Victor Golla, Humboldt State University, Native American Studies, Arcata, CA 95521, (707) 826-4324, gollav@axe.humboldt.edu.

Founded in 1981 and with a membership of about 800, this society's purpose is to further the study of the languages of the Native peoples of North, Central, and South America. Its annual conference is held in alternate years in conjunction with the American Anthropological Association or the Linguistic Society of America. It publishes a quarterly newsletter and an annual membership directory which includes an index of the languages of specialization of members.

274. **Southeastern Conference on Linguistics (SECOL)**, Dr. Marvin K. L. Ching, Co-Exec. Sec., English Department, Patterson Hall, University of Memphis, Memphis, TN 38152, (901) 678-4520, mching@memphis.edu. Available: http://www.people.memphis.edu/~english/secol.htmlx. (Accessed: March 8, 1999).

SECOL, one of the regional linguistic societies in the United States, now has a membership of about 300 individuals. Only linguists of the southeast (Texas, Oklahoma, Arkansas and states west of the Mississippi) may hold office, but anyone may join and deliver papers. It holds 2 meetings each year, usually in March and November and publishes *The SECOL Review* in the fall and spring.

275. **Western Conference on Linguistics (WECOL)**, c/o Grant Goodall, Department of Languages and Linguistics, LART 113, University of Texas at El Paso, El Paso, TX 79968, (915) 747-7023, ggoodall@utep.edu.

WECOL is a regional linguistic society with no membership requirements, but does maintain a mailing list. Its purpose is to sponsor an annual conference open to participation to anyone, from any state or country, and to publish the proceedings (Department of Linguistics, California State University at Fresno).

11

Research Organizations

Because research resources (government, university-based, and corporate) in the United States and abroad are so many and varied, they are difficult to effectively identify and enumerate. Hundreds of units support linguistic research. For some, linguistics and/or languages are their main focus; for others, they are of secondary concern. Many can be found in such standard directories as *The World of Learning* (Europa Publications), and the three Gale publications *Research Centers Directory*, *Encyclopedia of Associations*, and *International Organizations*. The 9th edition of the *LSA Directory* (1995), pages 121-32, also provides details on a number of laboratories, centers, and institutes. Details were taken from these directories as well as any Web sites for these entities.

276. **Alaska Native Language Center**, University of Alaska Fairbanks, Dr. Michael E. Krauss, Dir., P.O. Box 757680, Fairbanks, AK 99775-7680, (907) 474-7874. Available: http:\\www.uaf.edu/anlc/. (Accessed: July 25, 1999).

The center is an integral unit of the College of Liberal Arts at the University. The focus of its research is on the 20 native Indian, Aleut, and Eskimo languages of Alaska, including preparation of comprehensive native language dictionaries which currently cover 12 Alaskan languages. It publishes a variety of materials in journals and in its own research papers, story collections, histories, geographies, dictionaries, and grammars. It sponsors a summer institute for linguists and native language speakers and teachers as well as being extensively involved in providing materials, training, assistance, and consulting services for teachers and workers dealing with native languages.

277. **Center for Applied Linguistics (CAL)**, Donna Christian, Pres., 1118 22nd St. NW, Washington, DC 20037, (202) 429-9292, info@cal.org. Available: http://www.cal.org/. (Accessed: March 8, 1999).

CAL is an independent nonprofit organization which since 1959 has been involved in the study of language and the application of linguistics to educational, cultural, and social concerns. The center sponsors in-depth research, the development of teaching and scholarly materials and technical assistance programs, active participation in language policy formation, publications, and conferences. It acts as a liaison among corporations, government agencies, academic institutions, foundations, and other organizations. CAL carries out a wide range of activities including research, teacher education, analysis and dissemination of information, design and development of instructional materials, technical assistance, conference planning, program evaluation, and policy analysis. In recent years the Center has concentrated its work in six areas: adult language education, cross-cultural communication, language variation, literacy, testing and assessment, and uncommonly taught languages. It operates the ERIC Clearinghouse on

Languages and Linguistics (see entry 283). CAL produces an extensive range of both scholarly and practical publications and audiovisual materials.

278.   **Center for Spoken Language Understanding (CSLU)**, Charlene Edayan, Oregon Graduate Institute of Science and Technology, P.O. Box 91000, Portland, OR 97291-1000, (503) 690-1142, edayan@cse.ogi.edu. Available: http://cslu.cse.ogi.edu/. (Accessed: March 10, 1999).

CSLU is now a distributed center with laboratories at the Oregon Graduate Institute (OGI) and University of Colorado at Boulder. It was established first at OGI in 1990 then at CU Boulder in 1997. Both laboratories will continue to conduct basic research in areas of speech technology, contribute to the development of the CSLU speech toolkit, and continue to develop and distribute language resources.

279.   **Center for the Study of Language and Information (CSLI)**, Prof. John Perry, Dir., Stanford University, Ventura Hall, Stanford CA 94305-4115, (415) 723-1224, mking@csli.stanford.edu. Available: http://wwwcsli.stanford.edu/csli/index.shtml. (Accessed: March 8, 1999).

The center is an interdisciplinary endeavor, bringing together researchers from artificial intelligence, computer science, linguistics, logic, mathematics, philosophy, and psychology. What unites them is their common interest in the nature of information and how it is conveyed, processed, stored, and transformed through the use of language and computation. CSLI was established in 1983 under the impetus of researchers from Stanford University in cooperation with SRI International and Xerox PARC. In order to foster and expand the ties between the university and industry it established an Industrial Affiliates Program. Its basic research is carried out by means of various programs, including the Situated Language Research Program which is by far its largest. CSLI has a report series and a lecture note series, the latter including not only lecture notes, but also monographs and conference proceedings.

280.   **Centre for Information on Language Teaching and Research (CILT)**, Alan Moys, Dir., Regent's College, Inner Circle, Regent's Park, London NW1 4NS, England, 01-486 8221. Available: http:\\www.cilt.org.uk/. (Accessed: July 25, 1999).

CILT is an independent educational charity established in 1966 and maintained principally by central government grants. It collects and coordinates information on all aspects of modern languages and their teaching in the UK, helping individuals and organizations with practical and theoretical concerns including methods and materials, language policy and provision, research, careers, languages, and business. It operates an extensive language teaching library and various in-service training programs and conferences. A catalog, available on request, lists CILT's numerous publications.

281.   **Contrastive Linguistics and Language Typology in Europe (CoLLaTE)**, CONTRAGRAM, c/o Bart Defrancq, Dept. of French Linguistics, University of Gent, Blandijnberg 2, B-9000 Gent, Belgium, +32 9 264 4157, bart.defrancq@rug.ac.be. Available: http://bank.rug.ac.be/contragram/collate.html. (Accessed: March 10, 1999).

CoLLaTE is an international research network set up in 1996 with funds from the Belgian National Science Foundation with the stated purposes of bringing together fragmented research efforts in the field of contrastive linguistics, of bridging the gap between theoretical and applied research, and of archiving bibliographical and other data to make them accessible. The core research group is CONTRAGRAM with Flemish partners, other Belgian partners, and international partners. There are yearly symposia and workshop, an exchange of materials and know-how between the participating research units as well as availability of resources (such as bibliographies, corpora and lexicons in electronic format, and publication of proceedings), and the preparation of joint Flemish and/or European research projects.

282.   **Educational Resources Information Center (ERIC)**, ERIC, Resource Sharing and Cooperation Division, National Library of Education, 400 Maryland Ave. SW, Washington, DC 20202, (202) 205-5015, (800) 4241616, library@inet.ed.gov. Available: http://www.accesseric.org:81/. (Accessed: March 8, 1999).

ERIC is a national information system designed to provide users with ready access to an extensive body of education-related literature. It has been in existence since 1966 and is currently supported by the U.S. Department of Education, Office of Education Research and Improvement, and the National Library of Education. ERIC offers a variety of products and services, such as the ERIC database (see entry 374), and abstract journals, microfiche, computer searches, online access, document reproductions, and digests. There are three components that comprise the ERIC system: 16 subject-specialized clearinghouses (see entry 283), adjunct clearinghouses, and support components which produce, publish, and disseminate system-wide ERIC products and services.

283.   **ERIC Clearinghouse on Languages and Linguistics (ERIC/CLL)**, Dr. Joy Kreeft Peyton, Dir., Center for Applied Linguistics, 1118 22nd Street NW, Washington, DC 20037-1214, (202) 429-9292, (800) 276-9834, eric@cal.org.. Available: http://www.cal.org/ericcll/. (Accessed: March 8, 1999).

The Clearinghouse on Languages and Linguistics, operated by the Center for Applied Linguistics, is one of 16 ERIC Clearinghouses funded by the U.S. Department of Education (see entry 277). ERIC/CLL collects and disseminates information in the following areas: foreign language education (for both commonly and less commonly taught languages); English as a second or foreign language (ESL/EFL); all areas of language and linguistic instruction, pedagogy, and methodology; psycholinguistics and sociolinguistics; theoretical and applied linguistics; bilingualism and bilingual education; intercultural communication and cultural education in the context of language learning; and study abroad and international exchanges. ERIC/CLL provides a wide range of services and materials for language educators, most of them free of charge. These include two-page information digests and short bibliographies, a semiannual newsletter, and a question-answering e-mail service. Ready-made computer searches of the ERIC database are available for a nominal fee. It also publishes a monograph series, Language in Education, which is available for purchase from Delta Systems, Inc.

284.   **Haskins Laboratories, Inc.**, 270 Crown Street, New Haven, CT 06511-6695, (203) 865-6163, haskins@yalevm. Available: http://www.haskins. yale.edu/. (Accessed: March 10, 1999).

Haskins Laboratories is a private, nonprofit research laboratory founded in 1935 and is currently affiliated with CUNY, University of Connecticut, Wesleyan University, and Yale University. Beginning in 1948 it began research on speech communication, studying problems in human communication and related topics, including speech perception, physiology and dynamics of speech production, reading, linguistics, and cognitive science. Speech and reading research is gradually becoming the principal research activity of the institution.

285. **Information Sciences Institute (ISI)**, Edward Hovy or Kevin Knight, University of Southern California, 4676 Admiralty Way, Marina del Rey, CA 90292-6695, (310) 822-1511, hovy@isi.edu or knight@isi.edu. Available: http:\\www.isi.edu/. (Accessed: July 25, 1999).

ISI is a natural language processing research endeavor established in 1980 at USC which consists of various projects mainly of interest to computational linguists. The focus of research is computer-based generation and parsing of natural (i.e. human) language, both as a theoretical study on the nature of language and to develop tools for computational man-machine interfaces.

286. **Linguistics Research Center (LRC)**, Dr. Winfred P. Lehmann, Dir., University of Texas at Austin, P.O. Box 7247, Austin, TX 78713-7247, (512) 471-4566, lrc@utxvms.cc.utexas.edu. Available: http:\\www.dla.utexas. edu/depts/lrc/index.html. (Accessed: July 25, 1999).

Since its founding in 1961 as an integral unit of the University of Texas at Austin, LRC has been primarily involved with the analysis of past and present languages with the aid of computers, including theoretical, descriptive, and historical linguistics, automatic linguistic analysis, lexical semantics, and computational linguistics. Much of its current activity is directed toward the development of the METAL system for machine translation. The center also assists scholars in the humanities and other disciplines with automated text processing and linguistic analysis of language materials. The center has compiled an etymological Gothic dictionary and an analytical dictionary of Nahuatl and produced grammars for Gothic, Old French, and Old Irish.

287. **Summer Institute of Linguistics (SIL)**, Frank E. Robbins, Pres., 7500 W. Camp Wisdom Road, Dallas, Texas 75236, (214) 709-2400, frankrobbins@sil.org. Available: http://www.sil.org/. (Accessed: March 8, 1999).

SIL was founded in 1934 with the objective of studying those languages throughout the world that have never been written, committing those languages to writing, teaching speakers of the language to read and write, and translating into those languages various useful books, including the New Testament. In 1972 the International Linguistics Center was established in Dallas as the international headquarters for this organization and the Wycliffe Bible Translators. The Center now contains the largest linguistics school in the world which operates in conjunction with the University of Texas at Arlington.

Since its founding, SIL has transcribed about 1,200 different languages from nearly 60 countries throughout the world. It currently operates offices and study centers around the world and has a membership of about 5,800 people from 35 countries. SIL publishes many linguistic and ethnographic works written by its members.

12

Core Periodicals

The serials described below are important for study and research in the core areas of general and theoretical linguistics rather than for allied subject areas or for specific languages. However, generally well-known publications with a broad readership and journals of the modern languages are excepted. Seventeen titles have been added to the core periodicals described in the first edition of this book published in 1991; most began publication just prior to or after this date. Some older publications added are the five titles identified in two journal studies. One study on core journals for general linguistics was published in the *Journal of the American Society for Information Science* (1991), volume 42, issue 5, pages 332-340, the other study on core journals for theoretical linguistics published in *Language* (1990), volume 66, number 3, pages 553-557. Only serials currently being published are listed. Citations contain volume numbers and dates for the first issue of a title. The place of publication and the publisher are current as of 1998. The annotations make no attempt to characterize publications over their entire publishing history.

Current issues of each title were consulted to obtain descriptive information. In addition, details were obtained from standard periodical directories; other specialized print directories such as the *MLA Directory of Periodicals* (see entry 237), *Magazines for Libraries*, 9th edition (New York: Bowker, 1997) and *The Fifth Directory of Periodicals Publishing Articles on American and English Language and Literature, Criticism and Theory, Film, American Studies, Poetry and Fiction* (Athens, OH: Swallow Press/Ohio University Press, 1992); and from Web sites such as the Journals page on *The Linguist List* available at http://www.linguistlist.org/journal.html (accessed: February 28, 1999), the Linguistics Journals page (found by following the Publications link) of the Linguistics Society of America's Web site available at http://www.lsadc.org/ (accessed: February 28, 1999), and the Linguistics Resources: Journals and Newsletters page on the Summer Institute of Linguistics' Web site available at http://www.sil.org/linguistics/journals.html (accessed: February 28, 1999).

288. **Acta linguistica hafniensia: International Journal of General Linguistics**. Vol. 9, No. 1- . Copenhagen: Lingvistkredsen, 1965- . irregular. LC 85-641181. ISSN 0374-0463.

The former title of this publication is *Acta linguistica*. It is published irregularly by the Linguistic Circle of Copenhagen, though usually there are two issues per year. It accepts for publication articles in English, French, or German that present original research in all branches of theoretical linguistics. Particular interest is paid to papers dealing with typological aspects of language structure, and those papers presenting documented and critical discussions of the methodology, terminology, and subject matter of linguistics. Most issues publish a few book reviews.

289. **Acta linguistica Hungarica: An International Journal of Linguistics**. Vol. 38- . Dordrecht, Netherlands: Kluwer Academic, published in cooperation with Akadémiai Kiadó, 1988- . quarterly. ISSN 1216-8076.

The former title of this quarterly was *Acta linguistica Academiae Scientiarum Hungaricae* (ISSN 0001-5946). It publishes papers on the subjects of Finno-Ugric, Slavonic, Germanic, Oriental, and Romance linguistics as well as general linguistics. The language of publication is English, French, German, or Russian. A typical issue contains half a dozen articles and about the same number of critical book reviews. On the publisher's Web site recent tables of contents are browsable and searchable at http://www.wkap.nl/journalhome.htm/12168076 (accessed: March 6, 1999).

290. **American Speech: A Quarterly of Linguistic Usage**. Vol. 1- . Tuscaloosa, AL: Published by the University of Alabama Press for the American Dialect Society, 1925- . quarterly. LC 27-21844. ISSN 0003-1283.

While this journal is concerned principally with the English language in the Western hemisphere, there are contributions dealing with English in other parts of the world, with other languages influencing English or influenced by it, and with general linguistic theory. Many articles deal with current usage, others with dialectology, or the history and structure of English. A recurring feature is titled "Among the New Words." Recent issues have dealt with the many new words and meanings spawned by the Internet; the editors note that the Internet has also made their task of looking for citations of new words easier. Issues generally contain a few book reviews, often a miscellany section for short informative articles, and occasionally a response to a previously published article. The American Dialect Society maintains a Web page with a searchable index and tables of contents available at http://www.americandialect.org/amspeech.shtml (accessed: February 28, 1999).

291. **Berkeley Linguistics Society. Proceedings of the Annual Meeting**. 1st- . Berkeley, CA: Berkeley Linguistics Society, 1975- . annual. LC 76-640143. ISSN 0363-2946.

In February each year the Berkeley Linguistics Society, a graduate student organization of the University of California at Berkeley, holds a meeting during which papers are read on topics of general linguistic interest, and, since 1984, also on a particular topic of current interest in a separate parasession. The proceedings are then published in this annual. The parasessions for 1984-1988 were on: subordination; poetics, metrics; semantic typology; grammar and cognition; and grammaticalization, respectively. The general session at the 1994 meeting was dedicated to the contributions of Charles J. Fillmore; the special session was on historical issues in African linguistics.

292. **Bulletin de la Société de linguistique de Paris**. t. 1- . Paris: Librairie C. Klincksieck, 1869- . semiannual. ISSN 0037-9069.

The society now publishes two issues of the bulletin per year. The first issue contains minutes of its meeting for the previous year along with some ten or more research articles on general, descriptive, and historical linguistics, each preceded by an abstract and possibly some short notes and discussion pieces. All are in French.

The second issue consists of lengthy, scholarly reviews of recent publications. Publications are written in English, German, Russian, and other languages.

293. **Cahiers Ferdinand de Saussure/Revue Suisse de Linguistique Générale**. 1- . Genève: Librairie Droz, 1941- . annual. LC 50-57411. ISSN 0068-516X.

The Cercle Ferdinand de Saussure generally publishes each year one issue of this review of general linguistics with regard to Saussurean or Geneva structuralism. The scholarly articles are mainly in French, but others are in English, German, or Italian.

294. **The Canadian Journal of Linguistics/La revue canadienne de linguistique**. Vol. 7, No. 1- . North York, Ontario: University of Toronto Press for the Canadian Linguistic Association/Association canadienne de linguistique, 1961- . quarterly. LC 76-319989. ISSN 0008-4131.

The editors consider for publication manuscripts in either English or French dealing with theoretical linguistics. Explanatory materials are in both languages. Generally, each issue carries two to three lengthy articles and as many as a dozen book reviews along with a list of books received. From 1954 until 1961 it was published under the title *Journal of the Canadian Linguistic Association*. The change in title signaled a broadening in its point of view even though it remains the official association journal.

295. **Chicago Linguistic Society. Papers from the Regional Meeting**. 4th- . Chicago, IL: Chicago Linguistic Society, 1968- . annual. LC 76-27943. ISSN 0577-7240.

Each spring the Chicago Linguistic Society holds its regional meeting. From the 4th meeting in 1968 on, the Society has published its papers in this annual (papers from the 1st-3rd meetings were never published). Beginning with the 20th regional meeting in 1984 it has been published in two parts. Papers from the general session are in part 1; papers from a parasession focusing on one topic are published in part 2.

296. **Cognitive Linguistics: An Interdisciplinary Journal of Cognitive Science**. Vol. 1- . Berlin: Walter de Gruyter, 1990- . quarterly. ISSN 0936-5907.

Cognitive Linguistics provides a forum for linguistic research of all kinds on language from a cognitive perspective. It focuses on language as an instrument for organizing, processing, and conveying information. It publishes mainly research articles. However, there may also be a lengthy review article or a squibs section in some issues. Squibs include short notes on matters of fact and principle, pointing out topics for research, problems, and puzzles as well as remarks and replies with regard to published papers. The international editorial board is composed of prestigious scholars in the field. Tables of contents of recent issues are on the publisher's Web site available at http://www.degruyter.de/journals/journals.html#ling (accessed: February 28, 1999).

297. **Diachronica: International Journal for Historical Linguistics/Revue international pour la linguistique historique/Internationale Zeitschrift für Historische Linguistik.** Vol. 1, No. 1- . Amsterdam: John Benjamins, 1984- . semiannual. LC 86-648462. ISSN 0176-4225.

Diachronica was established as a forum for the exchange and synthesis of information concerning all aspects of historical linguistics and pertaining to all language families. Both theory-oriented and data-oriented research in English, French, or German are included. Each issue contains three to five articles, a review article, and up to ten other reviews. There is also a miscellaneous section with notes, discussions, reports, and a list of publications received.

298. **Folia linguistica: Acta Societatis Linguisticae Europaeae.** T. 1- . Berlin: Walter de Gruyter, 1967- . semiannual. LC 86-11164. ISSN 0165-4004.

This journal publishes articles on phonology, morphology, syntax, semantics, and other topics of general and comparative linguistics in two double issues each year. Both typology and languages in contact have been the subjects of recent special issues devoted to a single topic. Articles are published in English, German, or French. *Folia linguistica historica* is now published once each year as a supplement to this journal. It covers all aspects of historical linguistics in relation to all languages and language families. Tables of contents of some recent issues for both the main journal and its supplement can be found on the publisher's Web site available at http://www.degruyter.de/journals/journals.html#ling (accessed: February 28, 1999).

299. **General Linguistics.** Vol. 1- . Asheville, NC: Pegasus Press, University of North Carolina, 1955- . quarterly. LC 78-5757. ISSN 0016-6553.

Papers in all fields of linguistics—historical, comparative, descriptive—and in such allied fields as psycholinguistics and sociolinguistics are published in this journal. The articles as well as the 20 or so book reviews it publishes each year may be in English, French, German, or Russian. Volume 35, no. 1-4 (1997) was a special volume dedicated to Saul Levin.

300. **Glossa: An International Journal of Linguistics.** Vol. 1- . Burnaby, BC: Glossa Society, Dept. of Modern Languages, Simon Fraser University, 1967- . semiannual. LC 77-318800. ISSN 0017-1271.

Most of the articles, discussions, and notes published here are in English or French though they may be in any language using the Latin or Cyrillic alphabets. The scope of topics covered is quite wide, whereas the focus of the individual articles tends to be narrow and very specific. Tables and charts are frequently used to illustrate the text.

301. **Historiographia linguistica: International Journal for the History of the Language Sciences/Revue internationale pour l'histoire du langage/Internationale Zeitschrift für die Geschichte der Sprachwissenschaften.** Vol. 1- . Amsterdam: John Benjamins, 1974- . triannual. LC 73-88206. ISSN 0302-5160.

As befits an international journal, the editors accept material in a variety of languages: English, French, German, Italian, and Spanish. It is aimed at an audience of scholars interested in the history of the sciences concerned with language, such as linguistics, anthropology, philology, sociology, philosophy, psychology, neurology, and other disciplines. A typical issue may contain six articles, some review articles, a number of lengthy reviews of recent publications, and perhaps some notes, obituaries, and a section on publications received. Occasionally there are issues dealing with special topics. For example, the combined issues of volume 23 (1996) are devoted to the history of Spanish linguistics.

302. **International Congress of Linguists. Proceedings/Congrès international des linguistes. Actes.** 1st- . Leiden: A. W. Sijthoff, 1928- . LC 88-27451. ISSN 0074-3755.

The International Congress of Linguists is organized by the Permanent International Committee of Linguists (see entry 254). The first congress was held in The Hague in 1928, then sporadically until the 7th congress held in London in 1952. Since then, it has convened every five years. This publication prints the papers delivered at each of these congresses. The language of presentation, and thus of the contributions, may be English, French, German, or Italian. The imprint varies with each congress's proceedings depending on where the congress was held. The 16th congress was held in Paris in 1997 (Moskva: INION RAN, 1997).

303. **International Journal of American Linguistics.** Vol. 1, No. 1- . Chicago: University of Chicago Press, 1917- . quarterly. LC 22-9284. ISSN 0020-7071.

The *IJAL* publishes studies on all aspects of the native languages of the Americas: description, history, typology, and linguistic theory. Issues average three to six articles. A reviews section provides signed and footnoted reviews of recent scholarly books. During its long publication history which began with its founding in 1917 by Franz Boas, its sponsorship has changed a number of times. It was published under the auspices of the Linguistic Society of America from 1930 to 1973, in cooperation with the American Anthropological Association from 1944-1973, and by others for various periods. The publisher has also varied during the years, with the University of Chicago Press publishing it since 1974. Tables of contents for some recent issues may be found on the Web at http://www.journals.uchicago.edu/IJAL/ (accessed: February 28, 1999).

304. **International Journal of Corpus Linguistics.** Vol. 1, No. 1- . Amsterdam: John Benjamins, 1996- . semiannual. ISBN 1384-6655.

An editorial in the first issue of this journal explains its raison d'être and provides a review of the field. Corpus linguistics studies text, using explicit algorithms to extract linguistic knowledge from corpora. This journal will publish research based on the analysis of authentic spoken and written texts. As such it will provide a forum where linguists, lexicographers, and language engineers can meet to share their findings. In the emerging global information society, the editors see a growing importance for people to be able to deal with foreign languages. Corpus linguistics has a key role in developing lexicons to be used in natural language processing (NLP) applications and for electronic dictionaries. Besides publishing articles, the journal contains reviews—of both books and corpora—and publishes abstracts of recent articles and books based on studies carried out within the framework of corpus linguistics. The IJCL home page with tables of contents is available at http://solaris3.idsmannheim.de/~ijcl/ (accessed: February 28, 1999).

305. International Journal of Lexicography. Vol. 1, No. 1- . Oxford: Oxford University Press, 1988- . quarterly. ISSN 0950-3846.

First published in 1988, this international and interdisciplinary journal of lexicography is a publication of the European Association for Lexicography (EURALEX). It encompasses all aspects of lexicography—theoretical and practical, diachronic and synchronic, monolingual and bilingual—and deals with the organization of lexicographic projects and of dictionary publishing and the use of dictionaries. Tables of contents are accessible through the journal's online services link on Oxford's Web site: http://www.oup.co.uk/lexico/.

306. International Journal of the Sociology of Language. Vol. 1- . Berlin: Walter de Gruyter, 1974-. bimonthly. ISSN 0165-2516.

Nearly all issues of this international journal are devoted to specific topics pertaining to the study of language use in social behavior using theoretical or empirical approaches. The purpose is to contribute to the growth of language-related knowledge, applications, values, and sensitivities. Six issues are published each year and numbered sequentially from the first. Issue 123, the first number for 1997 is on the topic of Berber sociolinguistics while 128 the last number is on issues in language contact and social power relations. All articles in a subject-issue are commissioned or come as the result of a call for papers on a particular subject. Articles may be in English, French, Spanish, German, or Italian though English predominates. There are book reviews in most issues. Some tables of contents are available on the publisher's Web site available at http://www.degruyter.de/journals/journals. html#ling (accessed: February 28, 1999).

307. Journal of English Linguistics. Vol. 1- . Thousand Oaks, CA: Sage Publications, 1967- . quarterly. ISSN 0075-4242.

Focusing on empirical studies of the English language, the editors consider submissions on both the modern and historical periods of the English language. It publishes synchronic and diachronic studies on subjects from Old and Middle English to modern English grammar, corpus linguistics, and dialectology. Issues may also contain half a dozen or so book reviews. Beginning with volume 24, monographs or topical collections of articles will also be produced as quarterly numbers. The current editor at the University of Georgia maintains a Web page where information and tables of contents can be found: http://hyde.park. uga.edu/jengl/.

308. Journal of Linguistics. Vol. 1- . Cambridge: Published for the Linguistics Association of Great Britain by Cambridge University Press, 1965- . triannual. LC 65-9873. ISSN 0022-2267.

Articles concerned with all branches of linguistics, including phonetics, are published here. The emphasis, however, is on contributions of general theoretical interest. Though this is the official journal of the Linguistics Association of Great Britain, articles are published from nonmembers as well. The usual language of publication is English. In addition to the six or more full-length articles there are as many as 20 review articles and shorter notices in each issue. It has its own annual index.

Beginning in 1999, publication will increase to three issues each year. Cambridge University Press makes the table of contents and other information available on its Web site at http://www.cup.cam.ac.uk/scripts/webjrn1.asp?mnemonic=lin (accessed: February 28, 1999).

309.   **Journal of Logic, Language, and Information**. Vol. 1, No. 1- . Dordrecht: Kluwer Academic, 1992- . quarterly. ISSN 0925-8531.

This relatively new journal—the official organ of the European Association for Logic, Language and Information—concentrates on publishing work situated on the interfaces between the disciplines of logic, linguistics, computer science, and related fields. It provides a forum for researchers interested in the theoretical foundations of these subjects and in particular, their interdisciplinary connections. Book reviews and guest editorials were added in 1997. Tables of contents for recent issues are browsable and searchable on the publisher's Web site at http://www.wkap.nl/journalhome.htm/09258531 (accessed: March 6, 1999).

310.   **Journal of Phonetics**. Vol. 1- . London: Academic Press, 1973- . quarterly. LC 73-644848. ISSN 0095-4470.

The usual type of article published here reports experimental work concerned with problems in phonetics. Theoretical papers are acceptable if they relate to experimental findings; also suitable are papers dealing with technological and/or pathological topics, or papers of an interdisciplinary nature, providing that linguistic-phonetic principles underlie the work. Contributions from other disciplines are published (e.g. linguistics, psychology, speech science, computer science, or even engineering) to the extent they enhance an understanding of phonetics. A theme issue is generally published once a year. Features include letters to the editor, announcements, and book reviews.

311.   **Journal of Semantics: An International Journal for the Interdisciplinary Study of the Semantics of Natural Language**. Vol. 1, No. 1- . Oxford: Oxford University Press, 1982- . quarterly. ISSN 0167-5133.

The subtitle of this quarterly accurately reflects its scope. In the words of its editors, it aims specifically at an integration of philosophical, psychological, and linguistic semantics as well as semantic work done in anthropology and artificial intelligence. Issues generally contain two to three articles with abstracts and possibly a lengthy, evaluative book review. Tables of contents are accessible through the journal's online services link on Oxford's Web site: http://www.oup.co.uk/semant/.

312.   **Journal of the International Phonetic Association**. Vol. 1- . London: The Association, 1971- . semiannual. LC 85-10936. ISSN 0025-1003.

All aspects of the theory, description, and use of phonetics and phonology are reflected in the articles, specimens (annotations of phonetically transcribed samples of languages), correspondence, and reviews published here. Most contributions are in English, the Association's official language. With the first issue of 1987 there was a change in editorship of the journal. The new editors hope to retain the unique qualities of the journal while opening it up to highlight the kinds of research now possible with the new and/or improved tools available, particularly personal computers. Applied phonetics will become a more visible concern of the journal while revision of the International Phonetic Alphabet will remain a recurring theme.

313. **Language**. Vol. 1- . Washington, DC: Linguistic Society of America, 1925- . quarterly. LC 27-11255. ISSN 0097-8507.

Language, the journal of the Linguistic Society of America (LSA), is a major scholarly, general linguistics journal publishing quite technical articles. A typical issue contains from three to seven full-length articles dealing with problems of linguistic science, plus one or two review articles and a number of shorter reviews, all signed. A discussion notes section appears from time to time. Contributors need not be members of the LSA. The *Language* link on the Society's Web site at http://lsadc.org/web2/index.html (accessed: February 28, 1999) provides tables of contents from volume 54 (1978) through volume 74 (1998).

314. **Language in Society**. Vol. 1- . Cambridge: Cambridge University Press, 1972- . quarterly. ISSN 0047-4045.

Language in Society is among the core journals of linguistics and the premier journal of sociolinguistics. Its articles deal with all branches of the study of the theoretical and empirical study of speech and language as aspects of social life and vary from predominantly linguistic to predominately social in context. Each issue carries three or more research articles, preceded by abstracts, and a handful of evaluative book reviews followed by a list of publications received. Cambridge University Press makes the table of contents and other information available on its Web site at http://www.cup.cam.ac.uk/journals/lsy/lsyetoc.htm (accessed: March 1, 1999).

315. **Language Sciences**. New York: Pergamon, 1978- . quarterly. LC 80-646200. ISSN 0388-0001.

Pergamon now publishes this journal. Its purpose is to provide a forum for the free exchange of ideas on theoretical and conceptual issues in all areas of general linguistics, and welcomes contributions from anthropologists, philosophers, psychologists, sociologists and others. Occasionally there are special issues devoted to a single topic; some recent ones were on areal typology, studies in the syntax of universal semantic primitives, and contrastive semantics and pragmatics. On the *Language Sciences* page of the Elsevier Web site available at http://www.elsevier.com/locate/langsci (accessed: March 1, 1999), tables of contents may be found by following the Contents Services link.

316. **Language Variation and Change**. Vol. 1, No. 1- . New York: Cambridge University Press, 1989- . triannual. ISSN 0954-3945.

In the words of its editor this journal is dedicated to publishing original research reports that are based on data of language production, either written or oral, from contemporary or historical sources. It sometimes publishes articles that synthesize or reanalyze research findings; it is expected that all such findings can be replicated from the information provided. Articles have abstracts and many are illustrated with diagrams, maps, tables, and examples. See the Cambridge University Press Web site for tables of contents and other information available at http://www.cup.cam.ac.uk/scripts/webjrn1.asp?mnemonic=lvc (accessed: March 1, 1999).

317. **Languages of the World/Langues du monde/Lenguas del mundo/Sprachen der Welt: An International Journal on Language Typology, Geographical Linguistics and Related Topics**. No. 1- . annual. München: Lincom Europa, 1991- . ISSN 0940-0788.

This journal publishes articles on language typology, comparative linguistics, language policy, and related issues. Issues are numbered sequentially and though it began as a quarterly, in 1994 they began to appear only once a year. A typical number of the journal has 2 or 3 articles on linguistic projects, on new publications, and on new approaches to linguistic theory. "Linguistic News Lines" is a section presenting brief information about past conferences or congresses, plus a handful of evaluative book reviews. Other sections contain information about new and planned publications and announcements of forthcoming books and journals as well as conferences.

318. **Lexicology: An International Journal on the Structure of Vocabulary**. Vol. 1, No. 1- . semiannual. Berlin: Walter de Gruyter, 1995- . ISSN 0946-9400.

The articles and evaluative book reviews in this new semiannual may be written in English, German, or French. Those in English are preceded by an abstract in French or German, while those in German or French are preceded by one in English. It provides a forum for studies on the nature and structure of words and vocabularies. Articles may be concerned with theoretical issues as well as lexical data. Tables of contents may be scanned on the publisher's Web site at http://www.degruyter.de/journals/journals.html#ling (accessed: March 1, 1999).

319. **Lingua**. Vol. 1- . Amsterdam: Elsevier Science, 1947- . monthly. LC 52-36290. ISSN 0024-3841.

This international review of general linguistics, now published by Pergamon, aims to present work of current interest on a variety of subjects. Articles, however, are required to contain general theoretical implications of interest to any linguist, regardless of specialization. The journal also publishes critical book reviews. While most contributions are written in English, there are some in French and German as well. On the *Lingua* page of the Elsevier Web site available at http://www.elsevier.com/locate/lingua (accessed: March 1, 1999), tables of contents may be found by following the Contents Services link.

320. **Linguistic Analysis: A Research Journal Devoted to the Publication of High Quality Articles in Formal Phonology, Morphology, Syntax and Semantics**. Vol. 1- . Vashon, WA: Linguistic Analysis, 1975- . quarterly. LC 75-645644. ISSN 0098-9053.

As its subtitle indicates this research journal publishes articles in the areas of formal phonology, morphology, syntax, and semantics. An issue may have 4 to 5 articles, often illustrated with charts and examples, as well as a review article, a squib or two, and perhaps a "Replies and Rebuttals" section. There is an occasional special issue, for example, volume 27, nos. 3-4, was centered around clause structure.

321. **Linguistic Inquiry**. Vol. 1- . Cambridge, MA: MIT Press, 1970- . quarterly. LC 71-18726. ISSN 0024-3892.

The excellent reputation of this international peer-reviewed journal is well-established. It publishes research on current topics in linguistic theory at the rate of about 4 articles per issue. Among its authors are some of the world's foremost linguists. Less extensive research, not required to propose solutions to linguistic problems, is published in the squibs and discussion section. The publisher generously allows you to browse tables of contents and read article abstracts at http://mitpress.mit.edu/journalhome.tcl?issn=00243892 (accessed: March 1, 1999).

322. **The Linguistic Review**. Vol. 1, No. 1- . Berlin: Walter de Gruyter, 1981- . quarterly. LC 83-4081. ISSN 0167-6318.

This quarterly, the official journal of the Generative Linguists in the Old World, or GLOW (see entry 256), publishes papers in syntax, semantics, phonology, and morphology as well as critical discussions of theoretical linguistics as a branch of cognitive psychology. It also provides lengthy abstracts of doctoral dissertations in these domains. From time to time thematic issues with guest editors are published. The language of publication is English. The publisher allows browsing its tables of contents at http://www.degruyter.de/journals/journals.html#ling (accessed: March 1, 1999).

323. **Linguistic Typology**. Vol. 1- . Berlin: Walter de Gruyter, 1997- . triannual. ISSN 1430-0532.

One volume with three issues will appear each year for this relatively new journal published for the Association for Linguistic Typology. It will attempt to cater to the needs of the typological community which concern, in particular, the empirical dimensions of the typological enterprise and the ensuing demans to coordinate research and keep track of the data and results. Therefore the editors encourage informed dialogue and recording of past and present achievements. An issue may have two to three articles, a review article, and perhaps a few book reviews. Tables of contents can be scanned on the publisher's Web site at http://www.degruyter.de/journals/journals.html#ling (accessed: March 1, 1999).

324. **Linguistics; An Interdisciplinary Journal of the Language Sciences**. No. 1- . Berlin: Walter de Gruyter, 1963- . bimonthly. LC 67-34472. ISSN 0024-3949.

The frequency of publication for this prestigious, international review has varied since it began publication in 1963. It publishes articles in the traditional disciplines of linguistics (semantics, syntax, morphology, pragmatics, and phonology). It also accepts articles from neighboring disciplines engaged in the study of natural language (experimental phonetics, psycholinguistics, neurolinguistics, and first and second language acquisition). Work in logic, artificial intelligence, social interaction, physiology, and neurology is published when of interest to linguists. From time to time an individual issue is devoted to a special topic. It also publishes evaluative book reviews and review articles which may include reviews of more than one book. There are informative notices about conferences and other events for the professional as well as an annual publications received list. The language of publication is usually English with occasional articles in French or German. Tables of contents may be scanned on the publisher's Web site at http://www.degruyter.de/journals/journals.html#ling (accessed: March 1, 1999).

325.   **Linguistics and Philosophy: A Journal of Natural Language Syntax, Semantics, Logic, Pragmatics, and Processing**. Vol. 1- . Dordrecht, Netherlands: Kluwer Academic, 1977- . bimonthly. ISSN 0165-0157.

More than 20 years old now, this journal is for studies focused on natural language that will be of interest to both linguists and philosophers. Contributions are in the form of articles, review articles, remarks and replies, and notes and discussions. The occasional book review is restricted to those publications of the widest possible interest. An issue contains three to seven articles, some with abstracts, or may be a special issue such as volume 20, no. 6 devoted to articles on the mathematics of language. Tables of contents for recent issues are browsable and searchable on the publisher's Web site at http://www.wkap.nl/journal-home.htm/01650157 (accessed: March 6, 1999).

326.   **La Linguistique: Revue de la Société internationale de linguistique fonctionnelle/Journal of the International Society for Functional Linguistics**. Vol. 1- . Paris: Presses universitaires de France, 1965- . biannual. LC 71-415608. ISSN 0024-3957.

While this journal's concern centers on functional theory, its focus is two-fold: one, it publishes articles on functional theory vs. other theories of language, and two, it publishes articles on the application of functional theory to phonology, syntax, morphology, semantics, synchronic linguistics, and diachronic linguistics. Most of the articles and book reviews are written in French with a few in English.

327.   **Linguistische Berichte**. Vol. 1- . Wiesbaden: Westdeutscher Verlag, 1969- . bimonthly. LC 80-963. ISSN 0024-3930.

Most of the articles in this leading German linguistics journal are written in German with a few in English or French. Among the topics covered are syntax, sociolinguistics, phonology, pragmatics, text linguistics, semantics, and morphology. An issue contains an average of 3 articles and provides substantial reviews of several books. A short calendar gives information on upcoming conferences, association meetings, and symposia.

328.   **Lingvisticae investigationes: Revue internationale de linguistique française et de linguistique générale/International Journal of French Linguistics and General Linguistics**. T. 1- . Philadelphia, PA: John Benjamins, 1977- . semiannual. LC 79-642331. ISSN 0378-4169.

The articles, evaluative book reviews, and summaries of theses in this journal of French and general linguistics are usually in French, occasionally in English. Though issued jointly by the Departement de linguistique of the Université de Paris VIII and the Laboratoire d'automatique documentaire et linguistique of the Centre national de la recherche scientifique, the consulting editors are also from institutions in other European countries, Canada, and the United States.

329.   **Natural Language & Linguistic Theory**. Vol. 1, No. 1- . Dordrecht, Netherlands: Kluwer Academic, 1983- . quarterly. LC 83-645682. ISSN 0167-806X.

The aim of this journal is to bridge the gap between descriptive work and work of a highly theoretical, less empirically oriented nature. It provides a forum for discussion of theoretical research based on natural language data in order to facilitate communication between researchers with diverse viewpoints. Illustrations are numerous. Each number publishes four to six articles with substantial abstracts. The last number of each volume has indexes for authors, languages, and subjects as well as contents for each number of that volume. Some issues contain a "Topic . . . Comment" section which is a lively, often witty forum for readers' letters, for example, he letter in volume 15, no. 3 (August 1997) titled "Double Standards" concerns the flap following the Oakland School Board resolution on Ebonics. Tables of contents for recent issues are browsable and searchable on the publisher's Web site at http://www.wkap.nl/journalhome.htm/0167806X (accessed: March 6, 1999).

330. **Natural Language Semantics: An International Journal of Semantics and Its Interfaces in Grammar**. Vol. 1-, No. 1- . Dordrecht, Netherlands: Kluwer Academic, 1992-. triannual. ISSN 0925-854X.

The focus of this journal is on studies of linguistic phenomena as opposed to those dealing primarily with the field's methodological and formal foundations. Example of topics include: quantification, negation, modality, genericity, tense, aspect, anaphora, nominalization, ellipsis, and interrogatives. Articles accompanied by short abstracts and squibs are all written in English. Recent tables of contents are browsable and searchable on the publisher's Web site available at http://www.wkap.nl/journalhome.htm/0925854X (accessed: March 6, 1999).

331. **Papers and Studies in Contrastive Linguistics**. Vol. 1- . Poznań, Poland: Adam Mickiewicz University, 1973- . irregular. LC 80-646643. ISSN 0137-2459.

Published in cooperation with the Center for Applied Linguistics this journal appears irregularly, usually in one or two volumes per year. It aims to be an international review of contrastive studies, publishing contributions in English both from Poland and abroad. A bibliography of English-Polish contrastive studies in Poland appears from time to time.

332. **Phonetica: International Journal of Speech Science**. Vol. 1- . Farmington, CT: S. Karger, 1957- . quarterly. LC 59-31617. ISSN 0031-8388.

The editorial scope of this international journal encompasses papers written in English, French, or German concerned with experimental phonetics, phonology, speech perception and production, acoustic analysis, and speech synthesis. An occasional thematic issue brings together invited papers for a comprehensive discussion of a topic of general interest in basic phonetic research. A few authoritative book reviews are included in most issues.

333. **Phonology**. Vol. 1- . New York: Cambridge University Press, 1984- . semiannual. ISSN 0952-6757.

Beginning in 1988 this journal shortened its title from *Phonology Yearbook* and began publishing two issues per volume. One issue concentrates on one or more themes with the other issue being nonthematic. Themes for future issues are announced inside the back cover. Articles cover all aspects of phonology and related disciplines. Review articles are also included.

334. **Revue québéçoise de linguistique**. Vol. 11, No. 1- . Montréal: Université du Quebéc à Montréal, 1981- . semiannual. LC 84-11721. ISSN 0710-0167.

The former title of this publication is *Cahier de Linguistique* (ISSN 0315-4025). It is addressed to researchers and students of not only linguistics, but also of interdisciplinary fields such as sociolinguistics, psycholinguistics, and those studying the relationship between linguistics and another discipline. Each issue contains articles written around a theme, usually announced a year in advance, plus articles not on the theme, book reviews, notes, remarks, and discussions. Most material is in French, with only an occasional article in English.

335. **Revue roumaine de linguistique**. T.9, No. 1- . Bucarest: Editura Academiei Romāne, 1964- . bimonthly. ISSN 0035-3957.

From 1956 to 1963 this serial was titled *Revue de Linguistique*. It publishes short articles in English, French, German, Italian, Russian, Spanish, and Portuguese in all areas of general linguistics. With tome 20 (1975), 2 additional issues each year appear as fascicles 1 and 2 of *Cahiers de linguistique théorique et appliquée* (ISSN 0007-988X).

336. **Die Sprache: Zeitschrift für Sprachwissenschaft**. Vol. 1- . Wien: Verlag der Wiener Sprachgesellschaft, 1949- . semiannual. LC 51-23293. ISSN 0038-8467.

The focus of this journal is the study of Indo-European languages and linguistics as well as historical linguistics. Articles in German predominate with others in English, French, and Italian.

337. **Sprachtypologie und Universalienforschung (STUF)**. Bd. 46- , Hft. 1- . Berlin: Akademie Verlag, 1993- . quarterly. ISSN 0942-2919.

With the volume year 1993 the former *Zeitschrift für Phonetik, Sprachwissenschaft und Kommunikationsforschung* was replaced by this title with a new focus. It will offer a forum for scholarly debate and information to persons doing research in typologies and language universals, in general and comparative linguistics, and socio-, ethno- and psycholinguistics.

338. **Studia linguistica: A Journal of General Linguistics**. Vol. 1- . Cambridge, MA: Blackwell, 1947- . triannual. LC 50-3420. ISSN 0039-3193.

Formerly serving primarily as a forum for Scandinavian linguists, this journal of general linguistics is now an international forum for the discussion of theoretical linguistic research, primarily within the fields of grammar, cognitive semantics, and language typology. Articles with abstracts are published in English, French, and German. A number of substantive book reviews appear in each issue. Contents of issues may be viewed on the publisher's Web site at http://www.blackwellpublishers.co.uk/asp/journal.asp?ref=00393193 (accessed: March 5, 1999).

339.   **Studies in Language: International Journal Sponsored by the Foundation "Foundations of Language"**. Vol. 1- . Amsterdam: John Benjamins, 1977- . triannual. LC 85-641272. ISSN 0378-4177.

This journal's editorial board formerly issued the title *Foundations of Language* (1965-1976). The fields of research covered by this international publication are: traditional areas of linguistics; linguistic theories derived from various methods of language analysis; contributions to the study of the foundations of language from such allied fields as sociology, psychology, anthropology, and language acquisition; logical systems with strong compatibility with natural languages; methodology of linguistics, etc. In addition to articles, some with abstracts, an issue may contain a "Squibs/Discussions" section, review articles, and other shorter book reviews. The usual language of publication is English.

340.   **Studies in the Linguistic Sciences**. Vol. 1- . Urbana, IL: Dept. of Linguistics, University of Illinois, 1971- . semiannual. LC 79-643436. ISSN 0049-2388.

SLS is intended as a forum for the presentation of the latest original research by the faculty and students of the Department of Linguistics of the University of Illinois at Urbana-Champaign. Invited papers by other scholars are included from time to time. One issue each year is devoted to a specialized topic, for example, East Asian linguistics, historical linguistics, and studies in language variation. Some book reviews are published.

341.   **Syntax and Semantics**. Vol. 1- . San Diego, CA: Academic Press, 1972- . irregular. LC 72-9423. ISSN 0092-4563.

Volume 1 is composed of papers presented at the 1971 Summer Linguistics Conference held at the University of California, Santa Cruz. Volume 2 continued to publish some papers from the summer conference, but also began to broaden by including other papers drawn from national and international sources. Subsequent volumes with individual volume editors are devoted to single topics such as: speech acts, pragmatics, tense and aspect, the grammar of causative constructions, and studies in transitivity. Volume 30 published in 1998 was subtitled *Complex Predicates in Nonderivational Syntax*. Each volume has a subject/language index.

342.   **Theoretical Linguistics**. Vol. 1- . Berlin: Walter de Gruyter, 1974- . triannual. LC 76-645604. ISSN 0301-4428.

Though the language of publication for this journal is English, the contributors as well as consulting editors represent many countries from around the world. Articles on linguistic methodology are included as well as studies on the theory of meaning, syntax, phonology, phonetics and graphics, and pragmatics of language use. Issues (some of which are combined into double issues) sometimes contain a discussion section. Tables of contents can be browsed at the publisher's Web site at http://www.degruyter.de/journals/journals.html#ling (accessed: March 5, 1999).

343.   **Travaux du cercle linguistique de Prague, New Series**. Vol. 1- . Amsterdam: John Benjamins, 1995- . ISSN 1383-7583.

This series is a revival of the *Travaux du cercle linguistique de Prague* which was published in Prague between the two World Wars and continued by

Travaux linguistiques de Prague (ISSN 0564-1578) published between 1964 and 1971. Volumes 1 and 2 together, according to the preface in the second volume, present contributions "witnessing that ideas and results of the classical Prague School of functional and structural linguistics are still alive and serve as starting points for new developments in the context of present day trends in theoretical and empirical linguistics" (p. v). The 36 articles are written mainly in English with a few in French and German. In the next volume the editors plan to publish mainly papers presented at the Prague conference devoted to the 70th anniversary of the Circle and to the 100th anniversary of the birth of Roman Jakobson, one of the Circle's founders.

344. **Voprosy yazykoznaniya**. Moskva: "Nauka," 1952- . bimonthly. LC 54-16157. ISSN 0373-658X.

Articles written in Russian on general linguistics are published in this journal now issued by the Rossiiskaya Akademiya Nauk, Otdelenie Literatury i Yazyka. The table of contents in each issue is translated into English. Reviews of books, primarily works published in Russia, are included in each issue.

345. **Word**. Vol. 1- . New York: International Linguistic Association, 1945- . triannual. LC 55-40019. ISSN 0043-7956.

This journal issued by the International Linguistic Association, formerly known as the Linguistic Circle of New York, publishes research on the structure, function, or historical development of natural languages, or on theoretical questions related to these. No theoretical approach is favored or excluded. Three to 5 articles and a number of reviews appear in most issues. From time to time, two numbers are combined in a double issue containing articles on a specific subject. In the past, double issues have been devoted to such topics as national languages and language planning, text linguistics, and systemic linguistics.

346. **Yearbook of Morphology**. Dordrecht, Netherlands: Kluwer Academic, 1988- . annual. ISSN 0922-3495.

With the renewed interest in morphology due, in part, to its change of position in generative grammar, this yearbook supports research in the area along with its relations to syntax, semantics, phonology, psycholinguistics, and language change. It publishes original research, state-of-the-art papers, and substantial, evaluative book reviews along with book notices. Nearly all contributions are in English. A particular yearbook may be centered around a theme. For example, the 1994 yearbook theme was mechanisms of morphological change. The publisher makes abstracts and tables of contents for each yearbook in the series from 1991 available on its Web site at http://www.wkap.nl/series.htm/YOMO (accessed: March 6, 1999).

347. **ZDL: Zeitschrift für Dialektologie und Linguistik**. Stuttgart: Franz Steiner, 1969- . triannual. ISSN 0044-1449.

This journal publishes articles, notes, reviews, and bibliographies on dialectology and general linguistics. The language of publication is almost exclusively German.

Part 2

ALLIED AREAS

13

Anthropological Linguistics

In brief, anthropological linguistics is the study of language in culture and society using the theories and methods of anthropology. It views language through the prism of culture and seeks to uncover the meaning behind the use of language in its different forms, registers, and styles. Because it emphasizes the study of languages in speech communities that have no writing system or literary tradition, fieldwork is especially important. It overlaps with other allied areas of linguistics study, particularly ethnolinguistics and sociolinguistics. Anthropological linguistics does not have a separately identifiable body of reference literature such as the large number of individual bibliographies that psycholinguistics and sociolinguistics have, or the dictionaries and handbooks of applied linguistics. Many pertinent reference materials for this area of study can be found in other parts of this guide. A selected number of the major reference works within the field of anthropology itself are described in this chapter.

Encyclopedias

348. Levinson, David, and Melvin Ember, eds. **Encyclopedia of Cultural Anthropology**. Sponsored by Human Relations Area Files at Yale University. New York: Henry Holt, 1996. 4v. 1,486p. index. bibliog.

Each of the 340 articles in this four-volume work is written by one of the 310 experts brought together by an editorial advisory board for this first-ever encyclopedia for cultural anthropology. The in-depth essays are signed and have substantial up-to-date bibliographies along with an abundance of cross-references. Many articles are of interest to linguists such as those on linguistic anthropology, historical linguistics, color terminology, four-field approach, sociolinguistics, descriptive (structural) linguistics, writing systems, and dialectology. Volume 4 contains a list of anthropological periodicals and a thorough index of peoples, organizations, concepts, and topics.

349. Levinson, David, ed. in chief. **Encyclopedia of World Cultures**. Boston, MS: G. K. Hall, 1991-1996. 10v. index. bibliog. filmog. maps. ISBN 0-8168-8840-X (set).

Each of the first nine volumes of this set is devoted to a particular geographic region of the world: volume 1, North America; volume 2, Oceania; volume 3, South Asia; volume 4, Europe; volume 5, East and Southeast Asia; volume 6, Russia and Eurasia, China; volume 7, South America; volume 8, Middle America and the Caribbean; volume 9, Africa and the Middle East. The culture summaries, following a standardized outline, are written either by an expert on the culture or by a researcher at the Human Relations Area Files, Inc., working from primary source materials. Specific information for the linguist includes linguistic affiliation (name of language spoken and/or written by the culture, place in the classification system, and internal variation in language use). The regional volumes contain maps, a filmography, glossaries, and indexes of alternate names for the cultural groups. Volume 10 contains the cumulative indexes for the cultures, their alternate names (ethnonym), and a bibliography of selected publications.

Human Relations Area Files

350. **Human Relations Area Files, Incorporated (HRAF)**, 755 Prospect St., New Haven, CT 06511-1225, (203) 764-9401 or (800) 520-4723, hrafmem@hrafmem.mail.yale.edu. Available: http://www.yale.edu/hraf. (Accessed: March 11, 1999).

Since 1949 this nonprofit research and educational organization centered at Yale University has been developing programs and services to encourage and facilitate the worldwide comparative study of culture, society, and human behavior.

The HRAF Archives is a collection of mostly primary descriptive materials (books, articles, manuscripts, some translations, etc.) classified both by the culture or society to which they pertain and the topics discussed in them. Various HRAF publications explain the nature and use of the archives. Among these are George P. Murdock's *Outline of World Cultures* (6th rev. ed., 1983) which provides the key to the now more than 330 historical and contemporary cultures in the full collection, and a companion volume by Murdock and others, *Outline of Cultural Materials* (5th rev. ed., 1982), which details the 700 subject categories by which the collection is organized.

One of the 79 major subject divisions is for language, which in turn is divided into minor subject divisions for speech, vocabulary, grammar, phonology, stylistics, semantics, linguistic identification, and special languages. Most of this language information derives from primarily ethnographic monographs. Very few specialized linguistic studies have been included in the archives except for some sociolinguistic materials.

HRAF currently has two electronic collections. The *HRAF Collection of Ethnography*, available on CD-ROM or via the Web, to members only, and with installment 43 replaces the annual installments of microfiche. Each installment of the *HRAF Collection of Archaeology*, available only via the Web, to members only contains from 12 to 15 randomly selected archaeological traditions, subtraditions, and important sites. In cooperation with SilverPlatter Information, Inc. HRAF also produces the *Bibliography of Native North Americans* (see entry 355).

Indexes, Abstracts, Serial Bibliographies, and Electronic Databases

351. **Abstracts in Anthropology**. Vol. 1- Westport, CT: Greenwood Press, 1970- . quarterly. LC 77-20528. ISSN 001-3455.

More than 100 journals in linguistics and cultural anthropology are now indexed in numbers 1 and 3 of this publication. (Numbers 2 and 4 of each volume are for archaeology and physical anthropology). The entries have a classified arrangement, with those for linguistics arranged under the subheadings of historical, psycholinguistics, sociolinguistics, and theoretical linguistics. The abstracts can be as short as one sentence, but are usually about a paragraph in length. The author and subject indexes are cumulated for the volume year.

352. **Anthropological Index Online (AIO)**. Available:http://lucy.ukc.ac. uk/AIO.html. (Accessed: March 11, 1999).

The title of the print publication preceding this database has varied. For volumes 1-14 (1963-1976) it was known as *Anthropological Index to Current Periodicals in the Library of the Royal Anthropological Institute*, for volumes 15-20 (1977-1982) the title was *Anthropological Index to Current Periodicals in the Museum of Mankind Library*, and for volumes 21-32 (1983-1994), the title became simply *Anthropological Index*. With the October/December issue of volume 32, the print index ceased publication and is only available via the Web.

With the financial support of the William Buller Fagg Charitable Trust, and the practical support of the Centre for Social Anthropology and Computing (CSAC) at the University of Kent at Canterbury (UKC) *AIO* is free of charge for educational non-commercial purposes until the end of 1999. It is a site still under construction with new data being added continuously. It now covers only volumes 22-32 (1984-1994) but will eventually be brought up to date as well as provide retrospective citations to 1963, the beginning date for the print index. It currently indexes the articles in about 750 periodical titles. A user may search the *AIO* using the subject headings (continent, region, subject area); search author, title, or journal fields; or search keywords in any field. Date limiting is also available and the site now supports Boolean searching: "and" is automatic between fields, while "or" can be used within a specific field. Citations from a search can be e-mailed.

353. **Anthropological Literature**. Vol. 1- . Cambridge, MA: Tozzer Library, 1979- . quarterly. ISSN 0190-3373.

Volumes 6 through 10 (1984-1988) of this index were published only in microfiche. It functions as an author and subject index to the serial and edited works received by the Tozzer Library, the anthropology library of Harvard University (formerly the library of the Peabody Museum of Archaeology and Ethnology). It has a section for linguistics in addition to archaeology, biological and physical anthropology, cultural and social anthropology, and research in related fields and topics of general interest. Linguistic coverage, however, is sparse; less than 7 percent of the entries in Volume 11, number 1 were listed in the linguistics section. *AL* is international in scope with emphasis on materials published in European languages. A complete list of the journals and monograph series indexed as of 1998 can be found on Tozzer's Web site at http://wwwhcl.harvard.edu/tozzer/al.html (accessed: March 11, 1999).

As *Anthropological Literature on Disc* it is available on CD-ROM (G. K. Hall) from 1984 on with annual updates. As *Anthropological Literature (ANL)* it can also be accessed online as a CitaDel file (RLG) from 1979 on with quarterly updates. (See introduction to chapter 3 for vendor contact information.)

354. **Bibliographic Guide to Anthropology and Archaeology**. 1987- . New York: G. K. Hall, 1988- . annual. ISSN 0896-8101.

This annual provides an update to the *Author and Subject Catalogues of the Tozzer Library* (see entry 356) for books, serials, microforms, manuscripts, maps and video recordings. The guide for 1988 has more than 2,800 entries for such materials cataloged between June 1987 and August 1988.

355. **Bibliography of Native North Americans (BNNA).** [electronic database]. Norwood, MA: SilverPlatter Information, 1992- . semi-annual. ISSN 1064-5144.

BNNA on CD-ROM and via the Internet can be purchased by any library from SilverPlatter. It encompasses and updates two previous electronic editions as well as the print *Ethnographic Bibliography of North America* published by HRAF until 1990. *BNNA* contains citations to works on the history, life, and culture—and is an excellent source of language and linguistic materials—of native North Americans published from the 16th century to the present (monographs, essays, journal articles, dissertations, U.S. and Canadian government documents, and other publications). SilverPlatter provides semi-annual cumulative updates. (See introduction to chapter 3 for vendor contact information.)

356. Tozzer Library. **Author and Subject Catalogues of the Tozzer Library: Formerly the Library of the Peabody Museum of Archaeology and Ethnology, Harvard University**. 2d enl. ed. Boston, MA: G. K. Hall, 1988. 1122 microfiches. LC 89-955961. ISBN 0-8161-1731-4.

Like the multi-volume catalogs of the first edition, this microfiche set reproduces the library cataloging cards from what is one of the largest anthropology library collections in the world. It is international in scope, with entries for books, serials, maps, pamphlets, microforms, manuscripts, and films. Linguistics coverage is particularly strong for the Western Hemisphere.

It includes materials cataloged through June 1986, with the *Bibliographic Guide to Anthropology and Archaeology* (see entry 354) serving as an updating tool. Since the catalogs have not included periodical literature since 1982, the user should also consult *Anthropological Literature* (see entry 353) for such material after this date.

Internet Sites

357. **American Anthropological Association**. Available: http://www.ameranthassn.org/. (Accessed: March 11, 1999).

The AAA is the primary professional society for anthropologists in the United States. There is a link on their home page to "Anthropology Resources on the Internet" that lists many links to other electronic resources on the Internet of interest to anthropologists; links are listed under headings for general resources, colleges and universities, other AAA sites, and listservs/discussion groups. If a user follows the "Sections/Interest Groups" link on the AAA home page, they will be able to obtain information about the Society for Linguistic Anthropology, a section of the AAA which publishes the *Journal of Linguistic Anthropology*. This recently became a searchable by keyword site.

358. **Anthropology Resources on the Internet**. Available: http://home.worldnet.fr/clist/Anthro/index.html. (Accessed: March 11, 1999).

Bernard-Olivier Clist, a scholar with strong academic credentials, now maintains this comprehensive, award-winning site originally compiled by Allen H. Lutins. His aim is to update it twice a month. A visitor can choose whether to view the site with frames or not. The table of contents provides links to discussion groups, news groups, software and files, Web directories, archaeology, linguistics, cultural anthropology, physical anthropology, museums, academic and other institutions, commercial sites, journals, and other anthropology resources as well as to awards earned by the page. There are occasional short annotations when a site name is not self-explanatory or if it contains unusual types of information.

359. **Linganth Listserv Home Page**. Available: http://www.betatech. com/linganth/. (Accessed March 12, 1999).

The Linganth Listserv contains material related to the Linganth discussion group and its members. Its a modest Web site, but the only one focused solely on linguistic anthropology. The page contains links to course syllabi, biographies of members, shareware, and other information.

360. **ROYAL ANTHROPOLOGICAL INSTITUTE**. Available: http://lucy.ukc.ac.uk/rai/. (Accessed: March 12, 1999).

Founded in 1843 the RAI is the oldest anthropological organization in the world with an international membership. Its core activity is publishing journals: *The Journal of the Royal Anthropological Institute* (incorporating *Man*), a quarterly; and *Anthropology Today*, a bimonthly. Their home page has information on these publications, its history and library as well as the new electronic database *Anthropological Index Online* (see entry 352).

361. **SSLIS Anthropology Guide**. Available: http://www.library. yale.edu/socsci/subjguides/anthropology/. (Accessed: March 11, 1999).

This anthropology subject guide is part of a series issued by the Social Science Libraries & Information Services (SSLIS) at Yale University. Their Web page originally compiled by William J. Wheeler, subject specialist for anthropology, was recently updated and reorganized by Wheeler and Ryan Turner into 11 sections with links to: anthropology departments (worldwide coverage), career opportunities, discussion lists (listservs, discussion groups, and e-mail lists), electronic journals (as well as directories of e-journals), Internet resources, museums, online databases, print resources at Yale Libraries, professional organizations (also associations and societies), teaching resources, and Yale Library collections in anthropology. Brief factual annotations accompany some entries. A search engine with Boolean capabilities is available that can search this site and a number of other Yale Library sites.

362. **Voice of the Shuttle: Anthropology Page**. Available: http://humanitas. ucsb.edu/shuttle/anthro.html. (Accessed: March 11, 1999).

Alan Liu, a professor in the English Department at the University of California at Santa Barbara, is the weaver for the well-maintained *Voice of the Shuttle: Web Page for Humanities Research* (VoS). He has organized information on the Anthropology Page into seven sections: general resources; sites, projects, writings; course syllabi and teaching resources; journals; departments and programs; listservs and newsgroups; and conferences and calls for papers. Rather than trying to be all-inclusive, this site is a selective, eclectic gathering of links, a number of which are not found on other Internet meta-sites. Some links have brief annotations and there is the option of searching this page or any of the other pages of the *VoS*.

14

Applied Linguistics

Since applied linguistics is a general term for the practical applications of linguistic theory or investigation and language theory, it encompasses many topics. In this chapter its scope includes native language teaching and learning; second (or foreign) language teaching and learning along with such closely allied topics as error analysis, transfer and interference, contrastive analysis, and interlanguage studies; bilingualism; language testing; reading; composition; adult language development; translation and translating; and lexicography. Considering the large number of languages in the world, the topic of foreign language teaching (FLT) and learning is immense. Editorial constraints on length make it possible to include only works on teaching the English language though reference works dealing with the general principles of FLT.

The subject of child language is dealt with in the chapter on psycholinguistics. Materials dealing with language contact and language planning are in the chapter on sociolinguistics.

Dictionaries, Encyclopedias, and Handbooks

363. Baker, Colin, and Sylvia Pries Jones. **Encyclopedia of Bilingualism and Bilingual Education**. Clevedon: Multilingual Matters, 1998. 758p. index. illus. bibliog. maps. LC 96-24015. ISBN 1-85359-362-1.

Baker and Jones, together with a team of consulting editors and assistance from various experts, have distilled a lot of information into a very readable, browsable encyclopedia for the nonspecialist. It is a handsome volume with a lot of color and other visual interest such as maps, text boxes, photographs, drawings, and charts. Four sections contain more than 100 one- to five-page articles written in a clear, concise form of English to appeal to an international audience. For those wishing to pursue a topic, short bibliographies at the ends of articles provide direction for further reading. Section 1 deals with individual bilingualism; section 2 takes the broader view of languages in society; section 3 deals with languages in contact in the world from a regional point of view with chapters devoted to a particular area, for example, Africa, Asia, Australia and New Zealand, Caribbean, and the Middle East; while section 4 covers such issues in bilingual education as aims of bilingual education, the bilingual classroom, multiculturalism in education, and bilingualism and second language acquisition. There is a glossary of key terms as well as a bibliography of some 2,000 references.

364.   Baker, Mona, ed. **Routledge Encyclopedia of Translation Studies**.
Assisted by Kirsten Malmkjaer. London and New York: Routledge, 1998. 654p.
index. illus. bibliog. LC 96-44586. ISBN 0-415-09380-5.

The appearance of this first full-length encyclopedia of translation studies
underscores the establishment of this applied field as an important new discipline
for the 1990s. According to its editor in the introduction (p.xiiv), its rise is marked
by an increase in the number of university-level institutions which now offer
degrees in translation and/or interpreting from 49 in 1960 to more than 250 in
1994. Interest in translation ranges broadly across a variety of disciplines, from
linguistics and ethnography to cultural studies and psychology. Baker assembled
a cadre of well-known scholars and experts from around the world to function as
consultant editors and contributors, including Eugene Nida, Umberto Eco, Jean
Delisle, and György Radó (now deceased).

There are two parts to the encyclopedia. In the first part, with more than 80
general articles, Baker has taken a broad view of the discipline to include articles
dealing not only with such traditional approaches as equivalence, shifts of translation, and translatability, but more popular issues such as metaphor of translation
and gender metaphorics in translation, and includes the now burgeoning area of
corpora in translation studies. There are entries for the two most important
associations for practicing interpreters and translators, the "Association internationale des interprètes de conférence (AIIC)" and "Fédération internationale des
traducteurs (FIT)" and an interesting entry for the highly appropriate "Babel,
tower of."

The second part of the encyclopedia contains survey articles covering the
history of translation, both interlingual and intralingual, for some 30 major
linguistic and cultural communities, including African, Arabic, Danish and Norwegian, Indian, Japanese, Romanian, and Russian. Each survey article concludes
with brief biographies summarizing the contributions of prominent translators or
theorists to that particular linguistic tradition.

Articles in both parts are replete with cross-references to other articles of
possible interest and are signed by the authors. Nearly all articles are appended
with suggestions for further reading and "see also" references. This specialized
work will satisfy the needs of scholars and practitioners as well as provide a
fascinating read to both them and the casual reader.

365.   Hartmann, R. R. K., and Gregory James. **Dictionary of Lexicography**. London: Routledge, 1998. 176p. illus. bibliog. LC 97-34079. ISBN 0-415-
14143-5.

In the introduction to this fine dictionary, the authors make a point of saying
that "lexicography, often misconceived as a branch of linguistics, is 'sui generis,'
a field whose endeavours are informed by the theories and practices of information science, literature, publishing, philosophy, and historical, comparative and
applied linguistics." They go on to name a dozen sister disciplines which "provide
the wider setting within which lexicographers have defined and developed their
field." While lexicography can be thought of as dictionary-making in its narrow
sense of the theory and practice of compiling and preparing texts for publication,
the development of electronic media has expanded the need, and at the same time
provided the means, for new types of dictionaries. The authors have culled 2,000
entries from glossaries, textbooks, and specialist works on lexicography which
address the traditions of dictionary-making as well as this changing nature of

dictionary-making. Thus, a user will find definitions for such different types of dictionaries as "calepin" with a reference dated 1502 and "COBUILD" with reference to a Web site. Headwords are confined to nouns and adjectives, and while including names of principal professional bodies, the authors have excluded famous lexicographers, descriptions of well-known dictionaries, and histories and traditions of lexicography in different cultures. An entry displaying all possible features would consist of a headword, definition, elaboration, examples, cross-reference to another headword, further cross-references to related notions, references to English-language publications, sample reference works illustrating the application of the headword concept, and reference to electronic data such as an Internet site. Symbols and different typeface are used to good effect. An up-to-date bibliography of English-language references is appended.

366.   Johnson, Keith, and Helen Johnson. **Encyclopedic Dictionary of Applied Linguistics: A Handbook for Language Teaching**. Oxford: Blackwell, 1998. 389p. index. illus. bibliog. LC 97-24551. ISBN 0-631-18089-3.

A dozen contributors, all scholars from universities within Great Britain, wrote the more than 300 entries for this handbook. Signed entries grouped around the three categories of language, language learning, and language teaching vary in length from six or so pages to just a single sentence, with long entries signaling more important topics, short entries usually less important. Nearly all entries, regardless of length, are accompanied by a bibliography with the most important items marked by an asterisk. Within the text, cross-references are indicated by print in small capital letters. Occasional figures and tables accompany an entry, such as the International Phonetic Alphabet chart, which is used to illustrate the entry for "phonetics" and the diagram illustrating components of writing which accompanies the entry on "teaching writing." There is also a comprehensive index useful for tracking down topics that do not have their own entry.

367.   Jung, Heidrun, and Udo O. H. Jung. **The Dictionary of Acronyms and Abbreviations in Applied Linguistics and Language Learning**. Frankfurt am Main: Peter Lang, 1991. 2v. 802p. (Bayreuth contributions to glottodidactics/Bayreuther Beiträge zur Glottodidaktik, Vol. 1). ISBN 3-631-43867-2.

Though not billed as such, this dictionary is an upgrade and expansion of a 1985 edition with the title *Elsevier's Foreign-Language Teacher's Dictionary of Acronyms and Abbreviations*. To gather the more than 13,000 entries the authors combed the literature of the field in order to find the acronyms and abbreviations in use for the major languages of Europe (English, French, German, Spanish, Dutch, Italian, Russian, Portuguese, Swedish) and a few other European idioms. Volume 1 is much more than a simple alphabetical listing of acronyms and abbreviations with their meanings as entries for organizations, societies, and centers include such information as address, telephone/fax numbers, and periodical publications; some entries may also include bibliographic references for further information, related entries, and new words based on acronyms and abbreviations. Volume 2, an inverted index for the first volume, lists the full forms of the acronyms and abbreviations. The authors concede the difficulty of establishing criteria for inclusion or exclusion for such a broad topic. Despite some uneven coverage this reference work should be of great value to a wide audience of teachers, translators and interpreters, applied linguists, librarians, and administrators.

368. Richards, Jack C., John Platt, and Heidi Platt. **Longman Dictionary of Language Teaching and Applied Linguistics**. Consultant, C. N. Candlin. Harlow, England: Longman, 1992. 423p. illus. bibliog. ISBN 0-582-07244-1.

This dictionary with 2,000 entries is a new edition of the well-received *Longman Dictionary of Applied Linguistics* (*LDAL*) published in 1985. The authors have added more than 500 terms and revised a number of the entries in *LDAL*. In writing the definitions the authors consulted with experts from around the world. The authors have chosen to focus on words which are in common usage in language teaching and applied linguistics with special attention given to English and to examples from English. The authors include terms from introductory linguistics as well as from the field of language teaching—broadly interpreted—and from areas within applied linguistics that include discourse analysis, sociolinguistics, and psycholinguistics. Students and teachers alike will find it useful for specialized terms not found in general dictionaries. The definitions themselves are clear and simple, written in non-technical language with liberal cross-references, examples, and suggestions for further reading where fuller discussion of a term or concept can be found. The authors provide both British and American English pronunciation of headwords.

369. Sofer, Morry. **The Translator's Handbook**. 2nd ed., completely rev. Rockville, MD: Schreiber Publishing, 1998. 400p. index. illus. biblio. LC 97-62510. ISBN 1-887563-42-3.

The beginning sections of this handbook provide valuable, practical information for both the professional translator and translation student, such as requisites for professional translators and a self-evaluation, translation problems for various languages, techniques, equipment, Internet resources, tips on how to be successful as a freelance translator, sources of translation work, and training programs. A series of 8 appendixes, taking up more than half the book, follow. Appendixes 1 and 2 list dictionaries for some 39 languages and where to find them, followed by appendixes on foreign language software sources, sources of translation work, translation courses and programs, translator organizations, translator accreditation, and professional periodicals. A brief bibliography, 9-page glossary with concise definitions, and an index follow.

370. Thorum, Arden R. **Language Assessment Instruments: Infancy Through Adulthood**. With a foreword by Katharine G. Butler. Springfield, IL: Charles C. Thomas, 1981. 288p. index. illus. bibliog. LC 80-17835. ISBN 0-398-04107-5.

Approximately 175 test instruments are described in this book. Of these about one-third were developed between 1960 and 1970. The book begins with a short chapter giving a brief overview of assessment. It is followed by six chapters devoted to assessment instruments for the following categories: developmental and academic; auditory perception; language (infancy through adolescence); language (adults); language (bilingual); and, related areas such as reading skills, cognitive skills, and social adjustment skills. Within each chapter detailed descriptions of the instruments are provided along with basic information such as author, publisher, copyright, age range, normative data, administration time, and cost. A number of appendixes greatly increase its usefulness. For example, one summarizes in a matrix 16 major components of each language assessment instrument. A bibliography and indexes for authors and titles of the assessment instruments complete the book.

Indexes, Abstracts, Serial Bibliographies, and Electronic Databases

371. **CCCC Bibliography of Composition and Rhetoric**. 1987- . Carbondale, IL: Southern Illinois University Press, 1990- . annual. ISSN 1046-0675.

In 1987 on the publication of the first annual covering the years 1984-1985, the title of this bibliography was the *Longman Bibliography of Composition and Rhetoric*. The 1994 edition published in 1996 cites 2,286 works in English gathered by a network of 134 contributing bibliographers. Its coverage has now expanded to cover material from the fields of critical theory, science studies, feminist theory, technology studies, and postmodern theory. It lists with brief descriptive annotations the following types of material: monographs, articles, published collections (of essays, conference presentations, or working papers), dissertations, bibliographies and other reference works, ERIC documents (with ED numbers), various types of audio-visual material, and finally, in a section added with the 1993 edition, lists electronic discussion groups or listservs. Entries are arranged within subdivisions of an outline having six major categories: bibliographies and checklists; theory and research; teacher education, administration, and social roles; curriculum; testing, measurement, and evaluation; and listservs.

372. **Current Index to Journals in Education**. Phoenix, AZ: Oryx Press, 1969- . monthly. ISSN 0011-3565.

More than 775 education and education-related journal titles are indexed in this publication popularly known as CIJE. Together with *Resources in Education* (RIE) it makes up what is known as ERIC (Educational Resources Information Center). Entries, each assigned a unique 6-digit EJ number and accompanied by short abstracts, are arranged according to a classification system. There is a subject index, an author index, and a journal contents index, all of which refer the user to an entry by means of its EJ number. For the years 1969-1984 there is a separately published cumulative author index. For additional information about the ERIC system, the thesaurus, and the *ERIC* electronic database see entry 374.

373. **Education Index**. Vol. 1- . New York: H. W. Wilson, 1929- . monthly. ISSN 0013-1385.

About 325 English-language periodicals in all areas of education, including languages and linguistics, are indexed in this publication. It is useful to search for topics in applied linguistics, sociolinguistics, psycholinguistics, and English as a second or foreign language. Compared to the *Current Index to Journals in Education* it covers fewer journals, does not provide abstracts, and is limited to English-language journals. There is a great deal of overlap between the two indexes. The electronic database is available variously as an index, with abstracts, or full-text on CD-ROM (SilverPlatter, Wilson) and online (OCLC FirstSearch, Ovid, SilverPlatter, Wilson).

374. **ERIC (Educational Resources Information Center)**. [electronic database]. Washington, DC: U.S. Dept. of Education, Office of Educational Research and Improvement, 1966- (for RIE), 1969- (for CIJE).

This immensely popular database corresponds to the two print indexes *Current Index to Journals in Education* (CIJE) which indexes the journal literature and *Resources in Education* (RIE) which covers report literature (see entries 372 and 376). ERIC uses a system of sixteen subject-specialized clearinghouses each of which is responsible for monitoring, acquiring, evaluating, abstracting, and indexing information in its particular fields of education. One of the clearinghouses contributing much material in the area of applied linguistics is the Clearinghouse on Languages and Linguistics, maintained and operated by the Center for Applied Linguistics. Its subject coverage is the general area of research and application in languages, linguistics, and language teaching and learning. Other contributions to ERIC include material on a wide variety of related topics such as: anthropological linguistics, sociolinguistics, psycholinguistics, neurolinguistics, and computational linguistics. The subject indexes of both *CIJE* and *RIE* make use of descriptors listed in the *Thesaurus of ERIC Descriptors* now in its 13th edition (1995). Users should consult this excellent thesaurus before using either the print indexes or the *ERIC* database.

The *ERIC* database is available in its entirety with access to more than 20,000 journal articles and 14,000 documents each year on CD-ROM (Dialog, EBSCO, NISC, SilverPlatter) and online (CSA, Dialog, OCLC FirstSearch, Ovid). (See introduction to chapter 3 for vendor contact information). It can also be searched free from a number of sites through the "ERIC Sites" link on ERIC's home page at http://www.accesseric.org:81/searchdb/searchdb.html (accessed: March 11, 1999).

375. **Language Teaching**. Vol. 15, No. 1- . Cambridge: Cambridge University Press, January 1982- . quarterly. ISSN 0261-4448.

The title of this index has changed a number of times since it was first published as *Language-Teaching Abstracts* (Vol. 1-7, 1968-1974). (This index itself incorporated *English-Teaching Abstracts* published from 1961-1967.) It then became *Language Teaching and Linguistics: Abstracts* (Vol. 8-14, 1975-1981), and finally with volume 15 assumed its present title.

Edited jointly by the British Council and the Centre for Information on Language Teaching and Research, this index focuses on modern language (and especially English language) teaching and learning. Coverage is international with close to 400 journals being regularly scanned. Although there is considerable overlap between this index and *LLBA* (see entry 85), a user would probably want to consult both for comprehensive research.

An English translation of the title is provided when an article is written in a language other than English. All entries have substantial annotations, also in English. Entries are arranged under various subdivisions within four main divisions: 1) language learning and teaching—theory and practice; 2) teaching particular languages (English, French, German, Dutch, Italian, Spanish, Russian, Polish, Chinese, Japanese, Arabic, Hebrew, and other); 3) research in the supporting sciences; and 4) language description and use.

A subject index in each quarterly provides additional subject access. Indexes are cumulated annually. There are a variety of other useful features such as a book review section, a state of the art article, list of bibliographies, and a summary of current research in Europe.

376. **Resources in Education**. Vol. 10- . Washington, DC: U.S. Dept. of Health, Education, and Welfare, National Institute of Education, 1975- . monthly. ISSN 0197-9973.

From 1966-1974 this publication's title was *Research in Education*; both are referred to as *RIE*. *RIE* together with the *Current Index to Journals in Education* (CIJE) make up what is called ERIC (Educational Resources Information Center). *CIJE* covers journal literature while *RIE* covers the ERIC report literature. Lengthy annotations frequently accompany the entries in *RIE*. Each one is assigned a unique ED number. This number is used for reference in the subject, author, and institution indexes. ED numbers are also used to retrieve the reports from the ERIC microfiche collection, available in many libraries. Both *CIJE* and *RIE* are available for searching online and via CD-ROM as part of the *ERIC* database. For additional information about the ERIC system, the thesaurus, and the *ERIC* electronic database see entry 374.

Internet Sites

377. **American Translators Association**. Available: http://www.atanet. org/. (Accessed: March 11, 1999).

The ATA has a well-developed and organized Web site with lots information of interest to those in the profession. The home page has 12 links to the following: membership (includes a directory); a calendar of events; accreditation; ATA Divisions; Chapters, cooperating, and local groups; publications; ATAware; links to areas of interest ; the Chronicle (the ATA's monthly newsletter); conferences; jobs; and a FAQ.

378. **Applied Linguistics Virtual Library**. Available: http://alt.venus. co.uk/VL/AppLingBBK/welcome.html. (Accessed: March 11, 1999).

The home page of this award-winning site maintained under the auspices of the Department of Applied Linguistics, Birkbeck College, University of London has an index to 15 such topics as short courses and workshops, conferences and seminars, electronic journals, publishers, mailing lists, English as a second/foreign language, electronically available papers, jobs, and other resources.

379. **FIT (Fédération Internationale des Traducteurs)**. Available: http://www.fitift.org/. (Accessed: March 11, 1999).

The International Federation of Translators (FIT) maintains this Web site to provide information about its organization, the different committees, members and their activities, and its publications. All information is in French and English. The index is clearly presented in a table with ten boxes, most having to do with the Federation itself, but several provide links to more general information on the profession itself with links to member associations and other links (journals, publishers, international organizations, and shareware.

380. **Internet Resources for Language Teachers and Learners**. Available: http://www.hull.ac.uk/cti/langsite.htm. Accessed: March 11, 1999).

This collection of links to Internet sites for both teachers and learners is part of the comprehensive and up-to-date *CTI Modern Languages* Web site maintained by the CTI Centre for Modern Languages at the University of Hull, UK. Links on the first page are divided into five broad categories with brief descriptions: general, language-specific, multilingual, Internet, search engines, and commercial. From this simple front end, links quickly lead the visitor through several layers to many rich resources.

381. **IoL Home Page**. Available: http://www.iol.org.uk/. (Accessed: March 11, 1999).

The Institute of Linguists (IoL) is the UK's largest membership organization for professional translators, interpreters, language educators, and those using languages in industry and commerce. In addition to providing information for current and potential members, there is a link leading to useful links for linguists, organized into six categories: sites for translators and interpreters; sites for teachers and students of languages (including universities); dictionaries, reference works, glossaries; language bodies; languagespecific sites; and commercial sites.

382. **NCBE Home Page**. Available: http://www.ncbe.gwu.edu/. (Accessed: March 11, 1999).

The National Clearinghouse for Bilingual Education (NCBE) is funded by the U.S. Department of Education's Office of Bilingual Education and Minority Languages Affairs (OBEMLA) to collect, analyze, and disseminate information relating to the effective education of
linguistically and culturally diverse learners in the U.S. NCBE provides such information through its Web site which also includes access to a biweekly news bulletin, *Newsline*, and a topical electronic discussion group. It is an award-winning site, and deservedly so for both its interesting design and rich content. Another plus, is that it can be searched by keyword.

383. **Resources in Applied Linguistics (TESOL)**. Available: http://www.surrey.ac.uk/ELI/external.html. (Accessed: March 11, 1999).

The bright colors and unique presentation of this Web site makes it stand out of the crowd. Ten boxes at the top each with a graphic are simply labeled: archives, virtual libraries, learning English online, ERIC, writing laboratories, language and literature, Email 101-language lists, electronic journals, organizations, and language testing. Beneath, each is again listed along with details of what a visitor will find by following that particular link. This Web page is a link on the English Language Institute affiliated with the University of Surrey, UK home page which indicates it was updated March 1999.

384. **TESOL online!** Available: http://www.tesol.edu/index.html. (Accessed: March 11, 1999).

Teachers of English to Speakers of Other Languages, Inc. is an international professional association of persons and institutions headquartered in Alexandria, VA. A dozen links on their home page are briefly annotated. Some information it provides is of most interest to its members, but much is of value to anyone involved in teaching English to speakers of other languages, such as U.S. advocacy, conventions, education programs and academies, publications (browse through TESOL's extensive catalog publication and materials), and ESL standards for pre-K-12 students. Additional links are listed under "TESOL Services."

385. **Welcome to the Center for Applied Linguistics**. Available: http://www.cal.org/. (Accessed: March 11, 1999).

The Center for Applied Linguistics (CAL) is a private, non-profit group of scholars and educators who use the findings of linguistics and related sciences to identify and address language-related problems. It is a well-organized and maintained site (last updated January 5, 1999) with a lot of substance. In addition to links providing various types of information about CAL, the home page on the left-hand side has links to clearinghouses, centers, products, services, databases/directories, projects, and topics (among the 14 listed are bilingual education, dialects (ebonics), immersion education, language testing, and workplace literacy). The right-hand side of the home page is devoted to current news and reviews of recent publications under the link "Hot off the Press." Features such as book of the month and important news items are in the middle of the home page to catch a visitor's attention, and they do.

Cumulative Bibliographies

386. Afendras, Evangelos A., and Albertina Pianarosa. **Le Bilinguisme chez l'enfant et l'Apprentissage d'une langue seconde: bibliographie analytique/Child Bilingualism and Second Language Learning: A Descriptive Bibliography**. Québec: Presses de l'Université Laval, 1975. 401p. index. (Travaux de Centre international de recherche sur le bilinguisme/Publications of the International Center for Research on Bilinguaism, F-4). ISBN 0-7746-6751-6.

All the prefatory material and the indexes of this 1,661 item bibliography are in both English and French. The authors examined all documents which concerned the child with the problem of bilingualism, whether the documents were written from the sociological, psychological, linguistic, or educational perspective. They did not attempt any quality control over the items chosen to be included, leaving the reader to do the screening. About a fifth of these entries come from the first edition of Mackey's *International Bibliography on Bilingualism* (see entry 417). The authors admit a heavy bias toward research either completed within or concerning the United States where interest in child bilingualism increased explosively in the two decades prior to publication of this work.

The main section lists works alphabetically by author. It also gives the title and bibliographic information followed by a list of terms in English, describing the content. Both the French and English indexes make use of these same descriptors, organizing them into a number of major conceptual fields. The fields are listed just before the main index. Since the index itself is a combination of the descriptors, their occasional synonyms, and a modified thesaurus of the conceptual fields, it lends itself to searching either by a narrow, precise term, or by a broad topic. There is also a very useful index of languages, countries, and peoples. A list of co-authors completes the work.

387. American Council on the Teaching of Foreign Languages. **ACTFL Annual Bibliography of Books and Articles on Pedagogy in Foreign Languages**. New York: American Council on the Teaching of Foreign Languages, 1973-1979. 7v. LC 79-642664. ISSN 0191-3107.

The ACTFL issued this bibliography annually for 11 years. From 1969-1972 it was issued in both the *Foreign Language Annals* (ISSN 0015-718X) and as a fourth volume of the Library Edition of the *MLA International Bibliography* (see entry 88), then from 1973-1979 as a separate publication. It is concerned with pedagogy in modern foreign languages, Latin and Greek, English as a foreign language, and applied linguistics. Entries are for books, articles from a master list of 300 journals (except for the 1979 annual with a reduced list), chapters from collections, including Festschriften, and ERIC documents (for 1969-1973). The arrangement of entries is a classified one which varies somewhat from year to year. It is international in scope. Each year's bibliography has its own author index.

388. Antier, Maurice, et al. **Le Guide des langues: Méthodes et programmes**. BPI, Bibliothèque publique d'information, Centre Georges Pompidou et CIREEL, Centre d'information et de recherche pour l'enseignement et l'emploi des langues. Paris: Groupe Tests, 1983. 568p. index. LC 84-113290. ISBN 2-904479-00-7.

More than a hundred languages are featured in this guide to language learning manuals/materials which more often than not are audio and audio-visual. There is also a selection of reference materials such as grammars and dictionaries and "authentic" sound and visual works (tapes, records, video cassettes, and films). With few exceptions materials are intended for adults, even if a number of them would be suitable for those of school age. The compilers intended for it to be used not only by teachers, librarians, and students, but the general public.

Materials are grouped by language and then subdivided into type of material. Under type of material entries are arranged alphabetically by title. All the information about a title is presented in a unique grid-like format. The titles separated by lines run down the left side of the page; descriptive information also separated by lines runs across the grid. Each grid is helpfully labeled not only at its beginning, but also at the top of each page when a grid runs over from one page to another. The descriptive information includes five types of information: publisher, distributor, editor, and author; description of contents which usually states the language of instruction; medium, indicating such tings as number of books, teachers manual, cassettes, albums, and films; price of material in 1982; and, an evaluative commentary.

At the end of the book is a list of sources for the materials that includes addresses and often phone numbers. Advertisements are scattered throughout the text; there is a separate index to these. An impressive amount of material has been gathered here in a very useable format. A surprising number of the teaching materials are in English.

389. Arjona-Tseng, Etilvia. **A Bibliography of Pedagogy & Research in Interpretation & Translation**. Honolulu: Second Language Teaching & Curriculum Center, University of Hawaii at Manoa, 1993. 115p. (Technical Report, No.4). ISBN 0-8248-1572-6.

The title of this bibliography is descriptive of its subject content. Unannotated entries with the usual bibliographic details are arranged alphabetically by author from Abbe to Zydatiss. Nearly all citations are to materials written in English. A subject index would have made the bibliography more usable, though a determined researcher might be willing to skim the more than 1,200 entries in search of needed material.

390. Baur, Rupprecht Slavko. **Resümierende Auswahlbibliographie zur neueren sowjetischen Sprachlehrforschung (gesteuerter Fremdsprachen-erwerb)**. In Zusammenarbeit mit Lothar Dierkes, et al. Amsterdam: John Benjamins, 1980. 318p. index. bibliog. (Linguistic & Literary Studies in Eastern Europe, Vol.3; ISSN 0165-7712). LC 81-163653. ISBN 90-272-1504-9.

This selective, annotated bibliography of works published in Russian in the Soviet Union concentrates on those works dealing with the teaching of foreign languages in the schools and at institutions of higher learning. Studies on the teaching of foreign languages to preschoolers or on special adult education language programs have been omitted. Because of educational reforms in 1958 and a consequent intensified study of language learning and teaching, this year marked a major turning point in Soviet research on this topic. Only works published from this time on are included here.

One of the motivations for compiling this work is that Soviet studies, and particularly dissertations, have been neglected outside of the Soviet Union with the exception of Eastern Europe. This is partly due to their being published in Russian and partly for lack of a convenient reference tool. The availability of a few translations has done little to alleviate the problem since they fail to reflect the wide range of research being done. This work with its extensive annotations in German and excellent subject indexes provides an excellent overview of the goals, scope, and findings of Soviet research in the sixties and seventies and helps narrow the information gap.

391. Baur, Rupprecht Slavko, and Paul Gerhard Rühl. **Analytische Bibliographie zur sowjetischen Sprachlehrforschung (1970-1981)**. Unter Mitarbeit von Olga Wanzelius. Tübingen: Gunter Narr, 1982. 151p. (Tübinger Beiträge zur Linguistik, 206). LC 82-245549. ISBN 3-87808-589-3.

The time span covered by this analytical bibliography on Soviet research in foreign language teaching and learning is 1970-1981. For books and articles it is selective; for dissertations it strives to be complete.

The 1,143 unannotated entries are arranged alphabetically by author in two sections, one covering 1970-1979, the other to 1981. A section preceding the main bibliography lists and numbers the monographs and journal volumes/issues which are the sources of the entries. Then, for an entry in the main bibliography only a source number, accompanied by page numbers, is used in place of publication information. The entries themselves are numbered as well. Both the source numbers and entry numbers are referenced in the analytical subject index. Annotations for some of the important works listed here can be found in an earlier bibliography by Baur (see entry 390).

392.   Bausch, Karl Richard, Josef Klegraf, and Wolfram Wilss. **The Science of Translation: An Analytical Bibliography**. Tübingen: Tübinger Beiträge zur Linguistik, 1970-72. 2v. index. (Tübinger Beiträge zur Linguistik, 21, 33). LC 73-157371. ISBN 3-87808-033-6(v.2).

Volume I covers materials published from 1962-1969 while volume II covers 1970-1971 with a supplement and corrections for the first volume. Entries total 1,708. Part I of the first volume is a straight alphabetical listing of entries by author. Immediately below each entry is an English translation of the title if published in a language other than English, French, or German. Citations to reviews of a publication appear just below the entry, or title translation if there is one. There are no further annotations. Part II of the first volume contains three registers: list of analytical categories, list of languages discussed, and list of reviewers. The 11 analytical categories cover such topics as theoretical problems, language-pair related problems, comparative descriptive linguistics, and history of translation.

Material selection was determined by a number of considerations, some of which are described below. The authors have not included any works on machine translation or on translation problems connected with terminological and lexicographical questions, nor on foreign-language teaching. With few exceptions, only publications dealing with European languages were listed. Materials in the field of comparative descriptive linguistics was incorporated only if directly relevant to problems of translation of 20th century languages.

Volume II continues the page and entry numbering of the prior volume as well as its two-part arrangement. It is a great convenience to the user that the indexes in this second volume are cumulative for the set. The *Bibliographie du traducteur* published in 1987 (see entry 395) is a more current bibliography, but does not cover material in the variety of languages that this one does.

393.   Center for Applied Linguistics. Library. **Dictionary Catalog of the Library of the Center for Applied Linguistics, Washington, D.C.** Boston: G. K. Hall, 1974. 4v. LC 75-301806. ISBN 0-8161-1114-6.

The Center for Applied Linguistics (CAL) is an independent non-profit organization (for a description see entry 277). The materials listed in this catalog have since been donated to Georgetown University's library and can be found there. CAL's holdings of general works (history, theory, trends, conference proceedings, and publications of a number of linguistic societies) were complemented by various special subject collections. One of these, a unique collection on the teaching of English as a second language consisted of a variety of material, much of it produced by various governments or such organizations as the British Council, Unesco, and the Summer Institute of Linguistics. Other special collections included materials on Arabic language and literature and materials from Russia.

Photocopies of the author, title, subject, and added entry cards from the Library's catalog are arranged here in one alphabetical sequence. Library of Congress subject headings have been used, but are augmented when necessary. In general, the catalog does not provide subject access to periodicals as this is available in other indexes (such as some of those cited earlier in Chapter 3). It does, however, provide access to many manuscripts, working papers, and other unpublished materials difficult to access elsewhere.

394. CoLLaTE (Contrastive Linguistics and Language Typology in Europe). **Contrastive Linguistics: A Selective Bibliography**. Available: http://bank.rug.ac.be/contragram/biblio.html. (Accessed: January 5, 1998).

CoLLaTe is an international research network set up in 1996. One of its objectives is to make available such resources as this bibliography in electronic format. It is based on two earlier independently compiled bibliographies by Bengt Altenberg and Filip Devos. This unannotated bibliography of articles, papers from proceedings, and books prints out to 28 pages, with an estimated 500 citations. Entries are alphabetically arranged within four categories: bibliographies; theoretical studies; descriptive studies; and alignment of bilingual texts, text encoding, tagging, etc. The majority of citations are to works published in English, but with a significant number in German, French, and other European languages such as Danish. They range in date from the 1920s and 1930s to as recent as 1997. While visitors to the site are invited to contribute additions and corrections to the bibliography, they are given no explicit guidelines for what is included.

395. Collectif de l'École de traducteurs et d'interprètes. **Bibliographie du traducteur/Translator's Bibliography**. Ottawa: Presses de l'Université d'Ottawa, 1987. 332p. index. (Cahiers de traductologie, t.6). ISBN 2-7603-0120-6.

Two earlier versions of this bibliography have appeared. One by Lorraine Albert and Jean Delisle was titled *Répertoire bibliographique de la traduction/Bibliographic Guide to Translation* (Ottawa: Morisset Library, University of Ottawa, 1976). A second also by Delisle and Albert was titled *Guide bibliographique du traducteur, rédacteur et terminologue/Bibliographic Guide for Translators, Writers and Terminologists* (Ottawa: University of Ottawa Press, 1979).

The 1987 version is not only an update, but also a substantial revision of the 1979 edition. The major differences are a new section on the Spanish language, a substantial subsection on the specialized area of law, and an increased emphasis on tools that can be used in a large variety of specialized domains. Like its predecessors it should be of interest to professors and students of translation, researchers, professional translators, and writers and terminologists. Though intended primarily for the Canadian translation world and citing mainly French and English language items, there are materials in it that should be of use to translators in every country. It is the most current bibliography in the field.

References are divided into six parts. Part one is a general section dealing with translation, interpretation, and terminology. Parts two through five are devoted to the French language, English language, bilingual dictionaries, and Spanish language and translation, respectively. Part six lists reference works, mainly dictionaries, for specialized domains. An index of authors follows this last part. The foreword as well as the headings are in both French and English.

396. Cooper, Stephen. **Graduate Theses and Dissertations in English as a Second Language, 1975/76-1980/81**. Washington, DC: Center for Applied Linguistics, 1977-81. annual. 6v. ED 175244(1977/78); ED 193973(1978/79); ED 208673(1979/80); ED 210927(1980/81).

The fifth in this series of six annual bibliographies was issued under a variant title, *ESL Theses and Dissertations: 1979-80*. Entries in each annual are for studies completed during the academic year indicated. Cooper provides such information as writer's name, thesis or dissertation title, degree earned, university, year degree was granted, name of thesis adviser, department or program, and writer's address. Most entries also provide a short abstract. They are arranged under such subject headings as bilingualism, phonology, reading and vocabulary, sociolinguistics, and testing. These headings vary somewhat from year to year as does the inclusion of an index for authors and an index for culture and language. Cross-references under each heading are provided at the end of each section.

397.   Dale, Edgar, Taher Razik, and Walter Petty. **Bibliography of Vocabulary Studies**. 3rd rev. ed. Columbus, OH: Ohio State University, 1973. 236p. index. LC 41-52514.

The first edition of this unannotated bibliography on studies of vocabulary development was issued in 1939 then revised and published again in 1949, 1957, and 1963. The present edition includes both published and unpublished works from 1874 through December 1972. Nearly all are in English as well as about the English language. Entries are classified into three broad subject areas: acquisition and development, instructional materials, and research. Each division has a number of subdivisions and they in turn are divided into categories, some 69 in all. For many entries cross-references are provided, not to specific entries, but to related categories. An author index is provided.

398.   Dechert, Hans W., Monika Brüggemeier, and Dietmar Fütterer, comps. **Transfer and Interference in Language: A Selected Bibliography**. Amsterdam/Philadelphia: John Benjamins, 1984. 488p. index. (Amsterdam Studies in the Theory and History of Linguistic Science. Series V: Library and Information Sources in Linguistics, Vol.14; ISSN 0615-7267). LC 84-16830. ISBN 90-272-3735-2.

Transfer and interference is, in a broad sense, the subject of a wide range of disciplines such as cognitive science, psychology, linguistics, applied linguistics, psycholinguistics, sociolinguistics, pragmalinguistics, neurolinguistics, and language planning and policy. In all these disciplines it is the contact and interaction of languages which is basic to the concepts of transfer and interference. While choosing references from all these areas, the compilers have nevertheless been highly selective, directing their main focus towards the psycholinguistics of language contact and interaction.

They drew references for the bibliography from many sources, not only standard reference works, but also more than 50 special bibliographies which are listed in the preface. They gathered books and journal articles, plus ERIC documents, dissertations, and working papers. Most titles are in English, some are in French, German, Spanish, Russian, and other languages. The bulk of the references are dated 1960 through 1983. A list of languages (which are the subject of study) and list of topics provides access by author and date of publication to the unannotated entries in the bibliography.

399.   Devaki, L., K. Ramasamy, and A. K. Srivastava. **An Annotated Bibliography on Bilingualism, Bilingual Education and Medium of Instruction**. Manasagangotri, Mysore: Central Institute of Indian Languages, 1990. 380p. index. (CIIL Documentation Series, No. 10).

While there are a number of other bibliographies on bilingualism and bilingual education (see especially the massive work begun by Mackey and continued by Laforge, entries 417, 413-416), the authors of this work, covering some 855 journal articles, edited books, and monographs, give the reader, for such material published in English from 1950 to 1988, added value with their annotations of each entry stating the purpose of the study, methodology used, and results. They are careful to note foreign language (FL), first language (L1), second language (L2), third language (L3), medium of instruction (MI), and mother tongue (MT). Items are alphabetically arranged by author or main entry; complete bibliographic information is provided with a minimum of abbreviation. There is a thorough subject index based on the descriptors used in the 1987 *Thesaurus of ERIC Descriptors* on the topic of bilingualism.

400. English-Teaching Information Centre. **Theses and Dissertations Related to the Teaching of English to Speakers of Other Languages, Deposited with British Universities, 1961-72**. London: English-Teaching Information Centre, 1973. 90p. index. LC 73-175827. ISBN 0-901618-01-2.

Entries in this bibliography of theses and dissertations completed at British universities are listed under some 14 headings: spoken English, teaching methods, English for special purposes, testing, language learning, and so on. Those works relevant to more than one heading are listed in full under each relevant heading. A full entry consists of author, title, degree, place, institution, and date. An index of authors lists all the sections under which a particular work can be found. It includes almost 800 works for the 12-year period from 1961 through 1972. It will be of limited use to most researchers because of the short time period covered.

401. Goldstein, Wallace L., comp. **Teaching English as a Second Language: An Annotated Bibliography**. New York: Garland, 1975. 218p. index. (Garland Reference Library of the Humanities, No.23). LC 75-17987. ISBN 0-8240-9991-5.

402. Goldstein, Wallace L. **Teaching English as a Second Language 2: An Annotated Bibliography**. New York: Garland, 1984. 323p. index. (Garland Reference Library of Social Science, Vol. 181). LC 83-48197. ISBN 0-8240-9097-7.

Works listed in both the original and updated edition of this bibliography were selected on the basis of their relevancy in helping teachers and administrators to increase their understanding of teaching English as a second language and to improve the programs in which they are involved. The original version contains 852 entries for works, mostly published from 1966 to 1975; the updated version has 935 entries, mostly dating from 1975 to 1982, but picking up a few earlier titles overlooked in the original edition.

The emphasis is on American research with nearly all entries in English. Many different types of material are picked up, including texts and guidebooks; reference materials; articles found in a variety of periodicals and anthologies; speeches and papers presented at conferences; city, state, and federal reports; dissertations; and unpublished writings and speeches. Items entered in the Education Resources Information Center (ERIC) system and available through the ERIC Document Reproduction Service have all been supplied with ED numbers.

In both versions of the bibliography entries, along with their descriptive annotations, are arranged according to some sixteen or seventeen categories such as: audio-visual, curriculum, grammar, language learning, reading, teaching aids, and writing. A new category was added in the updated version to reflect growth in the study of English for special purposes. Cross-references at the end of each category refer the user to entries listed under other categories. Both editions also have a short keyword index and an author index.

403.   Goodman, Kenneth S., and Yetta M. Goodman, comps. **Linguistics, Psycholinguistics, and the Teaching of Reading: An Annotated Bibliography**. 3rd ed. Newark, DE: International Reading Association, 1980. 77p. (IRA Annotated Bibliography Series, No.312). LC 80-16364. ISBN 0-87207-312-2.

The third edition of this annotated bibliography on approaches and contributions to theories of reading and to the teaching of reading reflects the increased application of both linguistics and psycholinguistics to reading. And, the increasing research on discourse analysis in recent years has caused the compilers to add a section for this. The remainder of the 400 books and articles are distributed among 13 other sections such as: general applications of linguistics and psycholinguistics to reading; miscue analysis; the reading teacher and linguistics; syntax, grammar, and intonation; and words. Each section begins with a paragraph explaining its scope. One of the bibliography's shortcomings is the lack of an author, title, or subject index. Another is the lack of cross-references between items relevant to more than one section.

404.   Gunar, Daniel. **Contact des langues et bilinguisme en Europe orientale: Bibliographie analytique/Language Contact and Bilingualism in Eastern Europe: Analytical Bibliography**. Québec: Presses de l'Université Laval, 1979. 391p. index. (Travaux de Centre international de recherche sur le bilinguisme/Publications of the International Center for Research on Bilingualism, F-5). index. LC 80-670029. ISBN 2-7637-6806-7.

Both this specialized bibliography of 1,656 items and one on child bilingualism and second language learning by Afendras and Pianarosa (see entry 386) are follow-ups to a basic 11,000-item international bibliography on bilingualism published in 1972 and expanded ten years later to 19,030 items (see entry 417). The geographic regions surveyed in this work are: Poland, Czechoslovakia, Hungary, Yugoslavia, Rumania, Bulgaria, and the USSR. For the latter, only Slavonic languages have been included, that is, Russian, Ukrainian, and Byelorussian. While items of general interest on bilingualism are listed here, bilingual dictionaries and works concerned with the teaching of foreign languages are excluded. Also gathered here are any works dealing with language contact, not only from a linguistic point of view, but also from a judicial, psychological, or sociological viewpoint. Articles, books, theses, and reports from the countries mentioned above as well as other countries are represented.

The bibliography is organized into three parts: a list of major conceptual fields (descriptors) and subject index in French, a similar list and index in English, and the bibliographic entries themselves. The well designed subject index, in both French and English, usually provides several access points to each entry. Entries are arranged alphabetically by author and provide the usual bibliographic information except that initials are used in place of full given names. Titles for works written in the Cyrillic alphabet are transliterated into the Latin alphabet; titles for works written in a language other than English or French are translated into one of the two. Scholars studying bilingualism or language contact in Central and Eastern Europe would do well to begin their research here.

405. Gutknecht, Christoph. **Kontrastive Linguistik: Zielsprache Englisch**. 1.Aufl. Stuttgart: Kohlhammer, 1978. 109p. illus. bibliog. LC 78-359677. ISBN 3-17-004465-6.

This bibliography deals with contrastive linguistics where English is the target language. It has three sections. The first is an introductory discussion of applied linguistics, contrastive linguistics, and interlanguage. A short bibliography of contrastive-pragmatics items accompanies it.

The second section, the main bibliography, is on contrastive linguistics subdivided by some 18 languages or language families (the native languages of those learning English). The entries for each language subdivision are generally divided into monographs, journal articles, and a separate section on error analysis (both books and articles).

A third section, about half of the book (pages 59-101), is a discussion dealing with problems in the areas of phonetics, syntax, and semantics for English as the target language. There is a short bibliography of 53 items accompanying the text of this third section. Bibliographic entries throughout the book are mainly for works written in English and German, but with a significant number of items in other languages. Most of the research material cited is from the 1960s and 1970s, with occasional references to older material going back to the 19th century.

406. Hammer, John H., and Frank A. Rice, comps. and eds. **A Bibliography of Contrastive Linguistics**. Washington, DC: Center for Applied Linguistics, 1965. 41p. index. ED 130509. LC 65-29014.

A total of 484 items are included in this revised and expanded version of William W. Gage's *Contrastive Studies in Linguistics: A Bibliographical Checklist* (Washington, DC, Center for Applied Linguistics, 1961). A general section is followed by entries arranged alphabetically under some 90 foreign languages. Studies systematically comparing selected linguistic features of two or more languages in order to provide information to teachers and textbook writers are included here; studies which attempt to demonstrate or establish genetic or typological relationships are excluded. Liberal cross-referencing is made to languages other than the first mentioned in the title or text. Most references are to periodical articles, books, and dissertations published in the 1950s and early 1960s. An author index appears at the end.

407. Hoof, Henri van. **Internationale Bibliographie der Ubersetzung/International Bibliography of Translation**. 1. Ausg. Pullach bei Munchen: Verlag Dokumentation, 1973. 591p. index. (Handbuch der internationalen Dokumentation und Information, Bd.11/Handbook of International Documentation and Information, Vol. 11). LC 73-205044. ISBN 3-7940-1011-6.

The introductory material as well as the subject headings in this classified bibliography are written in English, French, and German. It has three main sections: the bibliography, a section on organizations, and a section on publications. The bibliography itself is arranged according to such subject categories as the history and theory of translation, teaching in translation, the translator's profession, typology of translation, and machine translation. Specifically excluded are materials on oral translation. There are some items published in previous centuries, one as early as 1610 A.D., but most entries are for works in the two or three decades prior to the cut-off date of mid-1971. Most of the major languages of Europe are represented here, many being in English, French, or German. The user is advised to watch for minor errors of detail.

408.   Jokovich, Nancy. **A Bibliography of American Doctoral Dissertations in Bilingual Education and English as a Second Language, 1968-1974**. Arlington, VA: ERIC Clearinghouse on Languages and Linguistics/Center for Applied Linguistics, 1977. 24p. (CAL-ERIC/CLL Series on Languages and Linguistics, No.44). ED 136584.

The 225 dissertations listed here are those excluded from another more general bibliography of American doctoral dissertations by the same compiler (see entries 114-115). The subject areas covered here are bilingual language acquisition, psycholinguistics, teaching methods and instructional materials for bilingual education and English as a second language, language competence assessment, the sociolinguistics of bilingualism and bilingual education, and teacher education. The entries alphabetized by author also give title, institution, and date. The lack of annotations or an index limits its usefulness.

409.   Jung, Udo O. H. **An International Bibliography of Computer-Assisted Language Learning With Annotations in German**. Frankfurt am Main: Peter Lang, 1988. 148p. index. LC 88-2686. ISBN 3-8204-1123-2.

Both journal articles and books on computer-assisted language learning (CALL) are included in this international bibliography. Most of the 1,054 entries are for works published after 1980. It complements and continues Stevens bibliography which picks up materials prior to this date (see entry 429). The majority of works are in English, with the rest in French and German plus a variety of other languages from around the world. Annotations in German accompany about 400 of the entries. These entries tend to be the more important works as well as those whose titles are not indicative of their contents. Included is a subject index, with descriptors again in German.

Despite the annotations and descriptors being in German, this bibliography should be useful to a reader of English only since so much of the jargon in this field is quasi-international.

410.   Jung, Udo O. H., and Gothild Lieber. **An International Bibliography of Computer-Assisted Language Learning with Annotations in German. Volume II**. Frankfurt am Main: Peter Lang, 1993. 197p. index. ISBN 3-631-46376-6.

Volume 2 with the addition of nearly 2,000 entries updates Jung's earlier CALL bibliography (see entry 409). Most of the additions cover the time period 1987 through 1991, but there are a fair number of earlier entries for Slavic languages, due to the efforts of Lieber, the co-editor. Approximately 600 entries are annotated in German. In addition to a subject index in German, Jung has added a subject index in English and a proper name index (for example, Athena Project, CompuServ, GPSG, and Zbasic). Together, the 3,051 entries in both volumes of the bibliography constitute "a fairly comprehensive picture of developments in international CALL between 1980 and 1991" (p. v).

411. Jungo, Michael E., comp. **International Bibliography for a Didactics of Early Bilingualism in the Education of Underprivileged Children, Especially Children of Migrant Workers/Bibliographie internationale pour une didactique du bilinguisme précoce dans l'éducation des enfants socialement désavantages, spécialement des enfants de travailleurs migrants/(III.) Bibliographie für eine Didaktik der frühen Zweisprachigkeit zugunsten von Unterschichts-insbesondere Fremdarbeiterkindern.** Einsiedeln: 1982. 140p. 5 microfiches.

The five microfiches in a pocket of this book contain two earlier bibliographies compiled in 1977 and 1978 by Jungo on this same topic. They contain 6,175 entries; the book continues the numbering of these earlier bibliographies. There is a total of 11,614 entries plus an unnumbered section listing American dissertations on bilingual education from 1926 to 1981.

What began as a fairly narrowly focused bibliography has gradually broadened, despite the book's title, to a global view of the problem of early bilingualism. The bibliography is international in scope with all types of materials written in a score or more of languages. Entries are arranged according to a classification system. Some of the main divisions of this system are: socio- psycholinguistics and compensatory education; acquisition of early bilingualism; methods for bilingual, bicultural and binational schools; models of bilingual schools; teaching books for bilingual instruction; and, preparation and training of bilingual teachers.

412. Jungo, Michael E., and Rolf Ehnert. **Frühe Zweisprachigkeit von Kindern fremdsprachiger Minderheiten: Eine kommentierte Auswahlbibliographie.** Frankfurt am Main: Peter Lang, 1985. 253p. index. (Werkstattreihe Deutsch als Fremdsprache, Bd.16; ISSN 0721-4278). ISBN 3-8204-9024-8.

Many of the 297 entries in Part One of this selective bibliography on early bilingualism in the children of foreign-speaking minorities are drawn from a previous bibliography compiled by Jungo (see entry 411). It has substantial annotations and, like the previous bibliography, is international in scope with works in German, English, French, and a variety of other languages. Entries contain complete bibliographic information with a minimum of abbreviation. Where titles are in a language other than German, a German translation is provided. At the bottom of each annotation at least one and as many as six subject terms are noted. An index of these terms can be found at the end of the bibliography.

Part Two of the bibliography with entries numbered 298-348 is a listing of reference sources containing such varied things as abstracts, bibliographies, documents, indexes, journals, organizations, laws, monographic series, and so on.

413. Laforge, Lorne. **Bulletin bibliographique sur la didactique des langues: Banque de données BIBELO.** Québec: Centre international de recherche sur le bilinguisme/International Center for Research on Bilingualism, 1987. 559p. index. (Publication, J-1). ISBN 2-89219-183-1.

414.   Laforge, Lorne. **Bulletin bibliographique sur le bilinguisme et le contact des langues: Banque de données BIBELO**. Québec: Centre international de recherche sur le bilinguisme/International Center for Research on Bilingualism, 1989. 534p. index. (Publication, J-2). ISBN 2-89219-201-3.

415.   Laforge, Lorne. **Bulletin bibliographique sur la linguistique appliquee a l'informatique: Banque de données BIBELO**. Québec: Centre international de recherche sur le bilinguisme/International Center for Research on Bilingualism, 1987. 116p. index. (Publication, K-3 [J-3]). ISBN 2-89219-182-3.

416.   Laforge, Lorne. **Bulletin bibliographique sur la variation linguistique (1960-1986)**. Québec: Centre international de recherche en aménagement linguistique/International Center for Research on Language Planning, 1991. 408p. index. (Publication, J-4). ISBN 2-89219-217-X.

Laforge is the director of the Centre international de recherche sur le bilinguisme and the BIBELO (Bibliographie informatisée sur le bilinguisme et l'enseignement des langues officielles) Project from which this series of four bibliographies emanates. The series covering materials on the topic of language teaching published from 1970 through 1985 continues a massive bibliography of more than 19,000 items compiled by Mackey (see entry 417 for scope and types of materials included). The alphabetically arranged and numbered entries in each of the four bibliographies are accompanied by subject classifications, descriptors, and indication of material type. Laforge improves Mackey's work with the addition of abstracts, variously in French, English, or both languages. He also supplements the subject indexes (in both French and English) with both a classified subject index and a type of material index, for example, proceedings, atlas or dictionary, book, essay, dissertation, article, review.

417.   Mackey, William Francis, ed. **Bibliographie internationale sur le bilinguisme: Avec index analytique sur microfiches/International Bibliography on Bilingualism: With Analytic Index on Microfiche**. 2e éd. revue et mise à jour. Québec: Les Presses de l'Université Laval, 1982. 575p. index(14 microfiche). (Travaux du Centre international de recherche sur le bilinguisme/Publications of the International Center for Research on Bilingualism, F-3). LC 83-133820. ISBN 2-7637-6991-8.

There are two sections to the second edition of this now massive bibliography on bilingualism. The first section, consisting of entries numbered 1 to 11,006, includes all the works from the first edition for the years 1940 to 1970; the second section, going from number 11,007 to 19,030, contains all the titles added for the second edition. While the second edition focuses on materials published from the late sixties through mid-1979 there are some added titles from the earlier period as well. The scope of both editions is essentially the same, encompassing anything having to do with bilingualism, biculturalism, and language contact. It is not exhaustive, however, since it excludes material peculiar to the language professions, that is, translation, interpretation, and language teaching.

The compilers have included articles, books, and book reviews, plus such unpublished materials as manuscripts, theses, dissertations, conference papers, research reports, and briefs presented to official language commissions. The researcher will find works from many different countries gathered here. When titles of works are in a non-Latin script they have been transliterated. Furthermore, when a title is in a language other than English or French, the compilers have usually provided a translation into one or the other. Each of the numbered entries includes the usual bibliographic information with a minimum of abbreviation. One small drawback is the use of initials in place of full given names.

There are no annotations, but there is a well-structured, detailed subject index to the first and second sections/editions, in both French and English, on a set of microfiche that slips into plastic sleeves inside the back cover. Each title has been indexed under a number of keywords, sometimes as many as 14. Under each keyword in the index the number of the relevant item is listed along with all the other keywords under which that item has been indexed. This listing of all keywords makes for a very useful index since at a glance the user can grasp the scope of a particular work. For a related work see entry 416.

418.   Mackey, William Francis. **Le bilinguisme canadien: Bibliographie analytique et guide du chercheur**. Québec: Centre international de recherche sur le bilinguisme/International Center for Research on Bilingualism, 1978. 603p. illus. (Publication, Centre international de recherche sur le bilinguisme, B-75). LC 79-117889.

Works cited in this bibliography on Canadian bilingualism deal directly or indirectly with only the two official languages, English and French. For those researchers interested in languages other than these two, Mackey provides a short list of alternate sources including his own international bibliography on bilingualism (see entry 417). This bibliography has an introduction in French that provides useful background information on bilingualism in general and on the Canadian situation in particular.

There are 14 chapters, each with its own introduction, organized around such areas as: historical studies, political solutions, legal problems, languages and education, the social dimension, the geographic aspect, psychological factors, and so on. The first page of each chapter lists the subject subdivisions under which the unannotated entries for that chapter are organized. Within the subdivisions the entries may be grouped according to type of publication such as books, journal articles, documents, newspaper reports, etc. and then arranged chronologically under this. References are to works in both English and French. Bibliographic information is complete and includes the usual information except for newspaper articles where the absence of page numbers could prove a hindrance to a researcher.

Following the bibliography is a short glossary of 100 or so of the terms of bilingualism. Four appendixes reproduce the text of some documents important to the legal status of languages in Canada: the law concerning the statute of official languages (Canada), the law on the official language (Quebec), the law on official languages (New Brunswick), and the charter of the French language (Quebec).

419.   Markus, Manfred, and Josef Wallmannsberger. **English-German Contrastive Linguistics: A Bibliography**. Frankfurt am Main: Peter Lang, 1987. 108p. index. (European University Studies Series 14: Anglo-Saxon Language and Literature, Vol. 174). ISBN 3-8204-0146-6.

One of the purposes in compiling this bibliography was to enable foreign students and teachers of English and German to bridge the gap between theoretical and applied contrastive linguistics. While the main target group is those who are interested in learning the foreign language on the basis of contrastive rules, the authors expect that this bibliography will also be helpful to theoretical linguists, encouraging them to apply their general insights to English and/or German. Unannotated entries for books, articles, and dissertations are arranged alphabetically by author under eleven headings such as: theoretical aspects, syntax, semantics, pragmatics, translation, and pedagogical applications. Some entries are listed in more than one section. This system works quite well for subject access, since there is no subject index. Nearly all the studies cited are written in German and English. Most are dated in the two decades prior to publication of the bibliography though some earlier important works, even some in the 1800s, are also included.

420.   Meara, Paul M., comp. and ed. **Vocabulary in a Second Language**. 1st ed. London: Centre for Information on Language Teaching and Research, 1983. 90p. index. illus. bibliog. (Specialized Bibliography, 3). LC 85-111213. ISBN 0-903466-554.

421.   Meara, Paul M., comp. and ed. **Vocabulary in a Second Language: Volume 2**. London: Centre for Information on Language Teaching and Research, 1987. 90p. index. (Specialised Bibliography, 4). ISBN 0-948003-86-3.

Meara in the first volume (1983) of his bibliography of research in the fields of vocabulary acquisition and word handling in a second language gathers together citations to books, journal articles, working papers, papers presented at congresses, theses, and dissertations published between 1960 and 1980. Some 280 studies, most with descriptive abstracts, are in the main section. Meara deliberately omits works dealing solely with teaching methods, works dealing with the question of what words should be taught, and works dealing with contrastive semantic analysis, or linguistic studies of the vocabularies of pairs of languages. Entries dealing with these omitted areas, some 103 items, are listed, unannotated, in a supplementary bibliography. Technical terms in abstracts are marked with an asterisk; these terms are defined and discussed in a glossary at the end of the book. Examples of such terms are: Brown-Peterson paradigm, click placement, dichotic listening, paradigmatic responses, semantic differential, and concluding with Zipf's law. There is also a very short subject index and a language index. Volume 2 (1987) with 270 entries and displaying the same format, updates the earlier bibliography with works mainly published between 1980 and 1985.

422.   Palmberg, Rolf. **A Select Bibliography of Error Analysis and Interlanguage Studies**. Åbo: Åbo akademi, 1980. 82p. (Meddelanden från Stiftelsens för Åbo akademi forskningsinstitut, Nr.53). LC 81-464697. ISBN 951-648567-7.

About 800 unannotated items written in English on error analysis and interlanguage studies from 1970 to 1979 (with a few classical works from the late 1960s) are listed in this bibliography. Works dealing with contrastive analysis were included only if they also dealt with either or both of these two fields of linguistics. For more comprehensive coverage of contrastive analysis the author refers the user to a bibliography by Sajavaara and Lehtonen (see entry 426). Palmberg divided this bibliography into four sections: a general introduction to the area of study, list of journals referred to in the bibliography, the bibliography itself, and a list of other bibliographies in the field arranged chronologically. A subject index, and particularly a language index, would have been useful since more than a dozen target languages are represented.

423. Ramaiah, L. S., comp. **Communicative Language Teaching: A Bibliographical Survey of Resources**. With an introductory essay by N. S. Prabhu. Gurgaon, India: Indian Documentation Service, 1985. 130p. (Subject Bibliography Series, 9).

Second-language pedagogy in the last several decades has moved in the direction of communicative language teaching, that is, instruction activities that encourage language output and use of language as a social tool. A short introductory essay by Prabhu discusses both content and methodology of this particular type of language teaching.

The bibliography that follows gathers references gleaned from many of the standard sources. Most entries are dated from the 1970s through 1983 with a few published as early as 1961. The more than 1,000 entries for books, journal articles, chapters in edited collections, theses, and some conference papers are arranged alphabetically by author and provide the usual bibliographic information. The lack of annotations or some sort of subject access limits its usefulness to researchers.

424. **RELC Research in Language Education, 1968-1981**. Singapore: SEAMEO Regional Language Centre, 1982. 217p. index. ISBN 9971-74008-7.

RELC, the Regional Language Centre (formerly the Regional English Language Centre) is an educational project of SEAMEO, the Southeast Asian Ministers of Education Organization. The general object of RELC is to assist SEAMEO member countries in improving the teaching of English and other languages. The Centre located in Singapore conducts a number of courses and training programs. Most RELC courses require each participant to complete a major project. Gathered here are these and other projects and dissertations for the period 1968-1981, 780 in all, covering research on language teaching programmes, problems and practices in Southeast Asia, as well as language teaching materials. An abstract is placed under a country heading according to the country of origin of the author. Most country sections are further subdivided by teaching level and subject headings such as language and language teaching, primary level, secondary level, tertiary level, and special uses of language. The language and language teaching heading includes studies of a linguistic, sociolinguistic, or psycholinguistic nature, plus studies on teaching materials and methods not targeted to a specific educational level. This bibliography should serve as a useful reference work not only to teachers and students, but also to educational planners, administrators, and individuals and organizations involved in language planning and language education.

425. Sabourin, Conrad. **Computer Assisted Language Teaching: Teaching Vocabulary, Grammar, Spelling, Writing, Composition, Listening, Speaking, Translation, Foreign Languages; Text Composition Aids, Error Detection and Correction, Readability Analysis: Bibliography**. With the collaboration of Elca Tarrab. Montréal/Hudson: Infolingua, 1994. 2v. 1067p. index. (Series in linguistics, informatics, communications, 9; ISSN 1198-1083). ISBN 2-921173-13-1 (v.1); ISBN 2-921173-14-X (v.2).

This 2-volume bibliography is part of the Infolingua series published on topics pertaining to any form of computer processing of natural language (see entry 477 for a description of the project and this series). Volume 1 contains the 7,100 entries for this title. Volume 2 is the index.

426.   Sajavaara, Kari, and Jaakko Lehtonen, eds. **A Select Bibliography of Contrastive Analysis**. Jyväskylä: Dept. of English, University of Jyväskylä, 1975. 108p. index. (Jyväskylä Contrastive Studies, 1/Reports from the Dept. of English, University of Jyväskylä, No. 1). LC 77-474088. ISBN 951-677-528-4.

With few exceptions only studies published before 1965 are included here, older material being covered by previous bibliographies on contrastive analysis such as the one by Hammer and Rice (see entry 406). It grew out of research done for the Finnish-English Contrastive Project in the Department of English of the University of Jyväskylä. Compiled with the aim of serving Finnish students and teachers looking for material for contrastive topics, it is not meant to be exhaustive. Materials are classified under three headings: general works; semantics, syntax and morphology; and phonetics and phonology. Within each section entries are arranged in alphabetical order. The majority of studies are in English with the rest in German, French, Finnish, and other languages. Providing subject access to the entries is a topic index containing 56 headings referring to different fields of research or various grammatical categories.

427.   Schecter, Sandra R., and Linda A. Harklau. **Annotated Bibliography of Research on Writing in a Non-Native Language**. Berkeley, CA/Pittsburgh, PA: Center for the Study of Writing, 1991. 66p. index. (Technical Report, No. 51).

This short bibliography of 170 entries, nearly all of which are published in English, is narrowly focused on research on writing in a non-native language, including only data-based publications and excluding studies dealing exclusively with non-standard dialects. Entries accompanied by thorough, descriptive annotations are arranged alphabetically by author within a classified scheme having five main divisions: text features, non-native writing proficiency development, writing process, non-native writing and other language skills, and instructional factors. There is an alphabetical index for first authors of each study.

428.   Spillner, Bernd. **Error Analysis: A Comprehensive Bibliography**. Amsterdam: John Benjamins, 1991. 552p. index. (Amsterdam Studies in the Theory and History of Linguistic Science. Series V: Library and Information Sources in Linguistics, Vol. 12; ISSN 0165-7267). LC 90-22393. ISBN 90-272-3731-X.

Error analysis is an important component of applied linguistics and foreign language teaching and is an aspect of such specialized linguistic domains as psycholinguistics, neurolinguistics, speech pathology and therapy, rhetorical communication, reading research, typography, shorthand research, computation linguistics, and contact linguistics. Given the interdisciplinary nature of research in this area, a bibliography of 5,398 items is not surprising. The author has cast a wide net, covering some 1,350 periodicals, books, doctoral dissertations, and gray literature in more than 30 different languages. The time span ranges from a few entries prior to 1800, from as far back as 1578, through 1990. The peak of interest in this topic appears to be the year 1980 with nearly 400 publications.

There are three indexes which provide access to these unannotated, alphabetically arranged entries: a chronological index, a language index, and a subject and keyword index. Though in some cases an entry is represented by only one keyword where more would be appropriate and terms one would expect to find, such as "error of performance" or "error of competence," are not represented, the index does a preliminary sorting of a great many multidisciplinary titles. Explanatory materials, including the introduction, are in English, German, and French.

429.   Stevens, Vance, Roland Sussex, and Walter Vladmir Tuman. **A Bibliography of Computer-Aided Language Learning**. New York: AMS Press, 1986. 140p. (AMS Studies in Education, No.6; ISSN 0882-438X). LC 86-17450. ISBN 0-404-12666-9.

Language teachers, educators, and computer specialists involved in computer-aided language learning (CALL) are the intended audience for this bibliography. It focuses primarily on information that appeared in the two decades prior to its compilation in books, monographs, research reports, articles, government documents, and reference sources from Australia, Canada, the United States, and Western Europe.

Over 1,700 items are numbered and arranged alphabetically by author, or title if there is no author. Each item is then assigned to a category or categories. Numbers of all related items are listed under each category designation. There are 16 categories for topics (artificial intelligence, computer literacy, computers and English, evaluation, hardware, and the like) and another 19 for specific foreign languages. A special category is for major journals and scholarly and professional associations involved in the area of computers and language education. A related bibliography by Jung complements and updates this one (see entries 409-410).

430.   Tannacito, Dan J. **A Guide to Writing in English as a Second or Foreign Language: An Annotated Bibliography of Research and Pedagogy**. Alexandria, VA: Teachers of English to Speakers of Other Languages, 1995. 533p. index. ISBN 939791-60-9.

Within the study of English as a second or foreign language there is an increasing emphasis on writing. This is partly in response to the large numbers of non-native students studying in English-speaking countries. In his bibliography of 3,461 items arranged alphabetically by author, Tannacito captures citations to relevant bibliographies, monographs, textbooks, periodical articles, dissertations and theses, conference papers, and Resources in Education (ERIC) documents published from 1937 through 1994. The bibliography provides greater depth and breadth of coverage than any other existing bibliography on this topic as it covers all instructional levels from early childhood to adult education. The *CCCC Bibliography of Composition and Rhetoric* (see entry 371) only covers publications on secondary- and post secondary-level ESL writing. Entries are annotated with subject terms that correlate to terms in the subject index and many have an additional, relatively brief, one- to three-sentence descriptive annotation. An index of names lists authors for main entries as well as editors and authors for anthologized essays.

431.   Tjeerdsma, R. S., and M. B. Stuijt, eds. **Bilingualism and Education: A Bibliography on European Regional or Minority Languages**. Ljouwert/Leeuwarden, the Netherlands: Fryske Akademy, Mercator-Education, 1996. 484p. index. (Fryske Akademy, 836) ISBN 90-6171-836-8.

Since the 4,000 entries in this bibliography are not arranged in any particular order, the three indexes of authors and editors (not corporate authors, translators and secondary authors), descriptors, and minority language communities are essential tools for its use. For purposes of this bibliography, the category of European regional or minority languages encompasses languages currently used by groups of speakers in one or more European states and which differ from the language(s) used by the majority, plus those languages which, though official at a state level, are used only in limited social or geographical spheres, such as Luxembourgish in Luxembourg. Though all of Europe, considered to extend from the Atlantic Ocean to the Urals and including the Caucasus and the European part of Turkey, is covered, it is most comprehensive for the European Union. According to the introduction (p. 3), the editors have a broad audience of users in mind from a variety of disciplines such as applied linguistics, didactics, educational studies, sociolinguistics, and language planning so they have included both specialist and more general entries from a diversity of approaches. Most of the cited works (books, articles, reports, and gray literature) are from the 1980s and 1990s and are present in either the Mercator-Education library at the Fryske Akademy or one of the centers participating in the Mercator network. More than half of the publications cited are in English with a significant number in German and French and the remainder in some 40 other languages. Each entry consists of detailed bibliographic information with a minimum of abbreviation along with notes on the languages discussed, geographical areas, and subject descriptors. The editors plan for the entire bibliography to eventually become accessible and kept up-to-date on the Mercator-Education web site (http://www.fa.knaw.nl/mercator).

432.   University College of Wales, Aberystwyth. Faculty of Education. **Bilingualism: A Bibliography of 1000 References with Special Reference to Wales**. Cardiff, University of Wales Press, 1971. 95p. index. (Welsh Studies in Education, Vol.3). LC 73-157257. ISBN 0900768940.

The previous edition of this now revised and extended bibliography was prepared for Welsh-speaking students concerned with the study and promotion of bilingualism in Wales and published as *Bibliography of Bilingualism*. On the occasion of the First International Seminar on Bilingualism in Education held at Aberystwyth in 1960 under the auspices of UNESCO it was distributed to participants in pamphlet format. A growing international interest in the bibliography prompted some changes from the original version and its reissuance.

The introduction, formerly in Welsh, is now written in English. Studies written in the 1960s and up through 1971 have been added, particularly those dealing with sociological aspects of bilingualism and the means of achieving bilingualism with a minimum of effort. The entries from the first edition written in Welsh are retained here for the record even though of little interest to the general researcher. Besides the Welsh entries, most works are in English with a small number in other major languages. A significant amount of the research cited here dates from the 18th and early part of this century. An index classifies the entries according to a few major categories: bilingualism in Wales, bilingualism in universities and colleges, other bibliographies, bilingualism in other countries, and bilingualism in general. These categories are subdivided in some cases, but even these subdivisions sometimes have too many entries listed under them to be of much use to a researcher. For someone interested in early study of bilingualism this book would be a useful supplement to Mackey's international bibliography on bilingualism which begins coverage in 1940 (see entry 417).

433.   Yakut, Atilla. **Cultural Linguistics and Bilingualism: A Bibliography/Kulturlinguistik und Zweisprachigkeit: Eine Bibliographie**. Frankfurt/M.: Verlag Yvonne Landeck, 1994. ISBN 3-89002-016-X.

In the introduction to his work the author explains that cultural linguistics is an interdisciplinary field relating to culture theory, pragmatics, sociolinguistics, ethnolinguistics, semiotics, and many others; here bilingualism and contrastivity are highlighted as two of its central themes (p.5). Most references are to materials published in the 5 to 10 years prior to the bibliography's publication in 1994. Contents are arranged in 5 parts. Part I contains the 2,653 unannotated entries arranged in alphabetical order by author's name. Parts II and III are lists of the titles and authors respectively from the full entries in Part I, but since there is no reference back to these full entries, the lists are virtually useless. Parts IV and V are useful lists of bibliographies and publications the author consulted. Prefatory material is in both English and German. This is a valuable bibliography as few exist specifically on cultural linguistics; but without annotations and with no subject access, it rapidly becomes an exercise in frustration for the user.

Directories of Organizations and Programs

434.   American Translators Association. **ATA Translation Services Directory, 1996-1997**. 11th ed. Alexandria, VA: American Translators Association, 1996. ISBN 0-914175-02-5.

The ATA publishes this directory as a service to its members. Only active and corresponding (or non-U.S.) members meeting certain standards of criteria are eligible for a listing. There are two main sections, each separately paged. The first, a language/subject index, lists language combinations from a foreign language into English, followed by listings from English into a foreign language. Under each language combination translators are listed by subject-area specialties, then grouped by state and country. Thus, one can find a translator for Chinese into English specializing in corporate law located in Florida, or a translator for English into Russian specializing in agriculture living in Iowa. Translator profiles in the next section provide contact information (address, phone, fax, and e-mail), accreditation(s), citizenship, country born in, native language, education, services, equipment, clients, experience, languages, and areas of specialization. A final unpaged advertising section contains display ads from both translation agencies/bureaus, and individuals.

435.   Conru, Paula M., Vickie W. Lewelling, and Whitney Stewart. **Speaking of Language: An International Directory of Language Service Organizations**. Prepared by the ERIC Clearinghouse on Languages and Linguistics. Washington, DC: Center for Applied Linguistics, 1993. 189p. (Language in Education: Theory and Practice, 80). ISBN 0-93-7354-80-5.

The directory, an expanded and updated version of earlier editions by Sophia Behrens, continues to be a valuable aid to teachers, students, and others interested in languages and cultures by providing them with a convenient reference guide to resources and services. The main section alphabetically lists more than 120 organizations along with such information as address, phone, contact person, languages, purpose, subject area, services, and publications. Other sections list addresses and contact persons for International Association of Applied Linguistics (AILA) affiliates; information on where to look for opportunities abroad to teach English as a foreign language; addresses of currently funded Multifunctional Resource Centers involved in bilingual education; contact information and languages taught by currently funded National Resource Centers for foreign language and area studies; and brief descriptions, addresses and phone numbers for some of the providers of resources and the materials they offer.

436. **Directory of Professional Preparation Programs in TESOL in the United States and Canada**. Edited by Ellen Garshick. Arlington, VA: Teachers of English to Speakers of Other Languages, Inc., 1995- . irregular. (This work not viewed by author.)

This title is a continuation of *Directory of Teacher Preparation Programs in TESOL and Bilingual Education* (ISSN 0191-7641) and the *Directory of Professional Preparation Programs in TESOL in the United States*. The 10th edition for 1995-1997 (ISBN 0-939791-61-7), now including Canada, lists 210 institutions that offer over 300 programs in TESOL at the undergraduate, master's, and doctoral levels including programs granting certificates. Each program is described briefly with details of degree offered, program and admission requirements, program length, courses offered, summer sessions, staff, tuition and fees, financial aid, general information, and contact person with address. State and provincial requirements for teaching ESL are included. Geographic and institutional indexes are appended.

437. Edwards, J. A., and A. G. Kingscott, eds. **Language Industries Atlas**. 2nd ed. Amsterdam: IOS Press, 1997. 440p. index. LC 95-81751. ISBN 90-5199-252-1.

Language industries in this work encompass all the commercial, professional, and organizational activities involved with language services, mainly in Europe. It supports communication efforts and work in many of the applied areas of language, such as translation and interpreting, technical writing, computer-assisted language learning, electronic dictionaries, machine translation, natural language processing, computational linguistics, and language for business.

Despite the word "atlas" in the title, it is essentially a cross between a directory and a lexicon, listing in one alphabetic sequence organizations, institutions, and publications (newspapers and journals) as well as subject entries for terms (machine translation, corpus linguistics), names of languages, and abbreviations and acronyms along with their meaning, definition, or a brief description. The index of entries arranged by country, some 38 in all, is useful to quickly zero in on the language industries within a particular country. Also useful is an introductory section on the status of languages in each of the countries of Europe usually listing the official language(s) and sometimes indicating number of speakers and providing information on minority languages also spoken.

438. Harris, Brian, comp. **Translation and Interpreting Schools**. Amsterdam: John Benjamins, 1997. 235p. (Language International World Directory, Vol.2; ISSN 1383-7591). LC 97-38872. ISBN 90-272-1052-4.

In the words of Harris, training of translators and interpeters "has been one of the biggest growth areas in academic circles in the last decade. The reason can be expressed in one word. Globalisation. . . . Translation is no longer something anyone with a smattering of a foreign language and a dictionary can sit down and do. It is a highly sophisticated activity requiring an agile intellect and multi-disciplinary training." (p.vii). Hence the need for and importance of this up-to-date world-wide directory of schools for students, practicing translators, and translation teachers which details translation and interpreting courses and degrees offered.

A page is devoted to each of the 235 schools described in the directory. Its organization is alphabetical, arranged, first by country, then name of school. Information which refers to the academic year 1996/97 includes the following: name, mailing address, telephone, fax, e-mail and/or website, date founded, head/director, tuition fee, full-time/part-time staff, number of undergraduate students, number of graduate students, degrees and diplomas granted, languages/language combinations, specializations, other specialties, and publications. Information was supplied by each school. Appended to the directory is a form which schools can use to become listed or if already listed, to update their information for 1998/99. For a first attempt at a directory of this nature, the compiler has gathered entries from a surprising number of countries, including Algeria, Japan, Latvia, Israel, China, Turkey, and South Africa as well as Australia, the USA, Canada, UK, and many European nations.

439. DeAngelis, Carl, and Sara J. Steen, eds. **English Language and Orientation Programs in the United States: Offered by U.S. Institutions of Higher Education and Private Language Schools**. 11th ed. New York: Institute of International Education, 1997. index. map. 400p. ISBN 0-87206-238-4. (This edition not viewed by author.)

The intent of this now standard directory is to provide a comprehensive listing of programs and courses designed to meet the English language training needs of students preparing to study at U.S. institutions of higher education. Some of the programs listed may be suitable as well for persons preparing for technical training programs or for professionals needing English to practice their profession. For nearly 1,000 programs and courses the directory provides information on proficiency levels taught, dates, costs, instructional facilities and faculty, student services, eligibility and admissions, contact addresses, phone, fax, and e-mail. It should be of use to any organization or agency that sponsors international students in the U.S.

440. Ward, Adrienne Marie, comp. **A Guide to Professional Organizations for Teachers of Language and Literature in the United States and Canada**. 2nd ed. New York: Modern Language Association of America, 1990. 104p. LC 90-31194. ISBN 0-87352-186-X.

Ward is the compiler for this expanded second edition of an earlier guide compiled by Gibaldi and Achtert (1978). In the main body of the guide she provides essential information on 133 professional organizations and societies. In addition to the strictly professional organizations for teachers of language and literature listed in the 1st edition, she covers a wider "variety of membership associations, including those concerned with ethnicity, period studies, political issues, technology, interdisciplinary study, and languages and literatures other than European" (p. v). The entries are arranged alphabetically by the organization's name and list acronym, address, year founded, size, phone number, contact person, and statement of purpose as well as such information as materials published, meetings, and other activities. In a second section of the guide she provides such information as year founded, contact person, address, and size for 81 author societies. An appendix contains a checklist of abbreviations and there is a brief subject index to the main body of the guide.

15

Mathematical and Computational Linguistics

Works on such topics as mathematical, computational, and quantitative linguistics; machine translation; natural language processing (and use of computer corpora or machine-readable corpora); and statistical methods in linguistics are gathered in this chapter.

Dictionaries and Handbooks

441. Gibbon, Dafydd, Roger Moore, and Richard Winski, eds. **Handbook of Standards and Resources for Spoken Language Systems**. Berlin: Mouton de Gruyter, 1997. 886p. index. illus. bibliog. LC 97-22921. ISBN 3-11-015366-1. With CD-ROM. Available: http://www.degruyter.de/EAGLES/degruyt/eagbook.html. (Accessed March 1, 1998).

The handbook is one of the outcomes of the EAGLES, Expert Advisory Groups on Language Engineering Standards initiative to accelerate the provision of standards for developing, exploiting, and evaluating large-scale language resources, both spoken and written, within Europe. EAGLES is a project of the European Commission within Directorate General XIII with five working groups: corpora, machine readable lexicons, grammar formalism, evaluation, and spoken language. The handbook, edited by three distinguished specialists in the areas of speech technology and computational linguistics and with the collaboration of more than two dozen leading scholars in their fields, is the product of the spoken language working group. Intended users include research workers and system developers, corporate end-users, and newcomers to the field, including graduate students; however, the editors caution non-experts that there is a limit to what can be achieved on a do-it-yourself basis.

The handbook covers four main areas: spoken language system and corpus design in Part I, spoken language characterization in Part II, spoken language system assessment in Part III, and spoken language reference materials in Part IV covering specifications of standard formats and practice, from the IPA (International Phonetic Alphabet) and SAMPA (Speech Assessment Methods Phonetic Alphabet) standard transcription and labeling practice to corpus recording and archiving standards. In addition it has a user guide, glossary, list of abbreviations, comprehensive bibliography, a well-designed two-level index, and numerous tables and figures used to good advantage. The hardbound library edition of the handbook is accompanied by a CD-ROM and in a highly unusual move for a publisher, is available without charge on the Web. Each part of the handbook is also available separately in paperback.

442.   Polanski, Kazimierz, ed. **A Terminological Dictionary of Algebraic Linguistics**. Katowice: Uniwersytet Slaski, 1985. 325p. (Prace naukowe Uniwersytetu Slaskiego, Nr.699; ISSN 0208-6336). LC 86-107395. ISBN 82-226-0014-3.

No definitions are given in this dictionary. The main section of the book is a list of English terms with the French, German, Czech, Russian, and Polish equivalents. The other five sections are lists of the equivalents in each of these languages with the corresponding English entry. It contains terms not only from algebraic linguistics and from such related disciplines as logic, statistics, and information theory, but also includes entries dealing with the theory of syntax and semantics which constitutes a major area of investigation in algebraic linguistics. As this is a pioneering dictionary, the editor suggests that in many cases the choice of terms and their equivalents should perhaps be viewed as suggestions rather than a final determination.

443.   Venev, Yvan, comp. **Elsevier's Dictionary of Mathematical and Computational Linguistics in Three Languages: English, French and Russian**. Amsterdam: Elsevier, 1990. 682p. bibliog. LC 89-49200. ISBN 0-444-88063-1.

Prefatory material in this trilingual dictionary is in both English and French. The main section of the dictionary consists of English phrases arranged in alphabetical order followed by their French and Russian equivalents. The terms within a phrase are permuted so that a phrase will appear in the alphabetical listing several times with each occurrence arranged under a different term of the expression. For example, the phrase "algorithm of analysis" is listed under both "algorithm of analysis" and "analysis, algorithm of" and both times it is followed by the French and Russian equivalents. The numbered entries are keyed to the alphabetical lists of the French and Russian phrases found in the second and third sections. Such an arrangement facilitates its use as a tool for translators and interpreters; and, even though it contains no definitions, it should also be of value to students and researchers working in these languages.

Indexes, Abstracts, and Electronic Databases

444.   **ACM Guide to Computing Literature**. New York: Association for Computing Machinery, 1977- . annual. LC 79-643062. ISSN 0149-1199.

All fields of computer science and its applications are covered by this index of books, journal articles, conference proceedings, technical reports, and theses. The entries are indexed by authors, keywords, proper noun subject (such as particular computer languages, hardware models, or persons), categories (a detailed subject classification system), and reviewers for *Computing Reviews* (for which this publication also serves as an index). Sections of the classification scheme of particular interest to linguists are: natural language processing, learning, computer applications, and computers and education.

As *ACM Electronic Guide to Computing Literature* this is available from the publisher on CD-ROM with quarterly updates. The Association also produces the *ACM Digital Library* version, with a full-text option, available via the Web. As *COMPUSCIENCE* online access is available from 1982 to present (STN) with monthly updates. (See introduction to chapter 3 for STN contact information).

445.   **Computer Abstracts**, Vol. 1- . St. Helier, Jersey, British Channel Islands: Technical Information Co., 1957- . monthly. LC 61-2637. ISSN 0010-4469.

Abstracts for current computer literature are provided here for 3 main types of items: 1) articles and papers in periodicals, conference proceedings, etc.; 2) U.S. government reports and patents; and 3) books. Entries for the first two types of items are arranged within some 18 classified sections. Book abstracts appear in a final section. The section on computer applications is subdivided into specific areas of application, one of which is linguistics. An author index and subject index provide additional access points. The publisher also makes available a CD-ROM version with biannual updates.

446.   **Computer and Control Abstracts**. Vol. 1- . London: Institution of Electrical Engineers, 1966- . monthly. LC 76-646598. ISSN 0036-8113.

The aim of this major index is world-wide coverage of journals, books, reports, dissertations, and conference papers in all languages for all aspects of computers and control. Of interest to linguists is its coverage of computational linguistics, language translation, and computer-aided instruction. An entry includes author, author affiliation, title, source (such as journal, report series and number, or conference information), abstract written in English, and number of references. A detailed subject arrangement is used to classify the entries. There are subject and author indexes (cumulated semi-annually) as well as a variety of subsidiary indexes. Its coverage is vast and searching it can be tedious and time-consuming. An alternative is to search it as part of the *INSPEC* database (see entry 448).

447.   **Computer and Information Systems Abstracts**. Bethesda, MD: Engineering Information, Inc./ Cambridge Scientific Abstracts, 1962- . monthly. ISSN 0191-9776.

In the course of its publishing history this title has changed publishers and its title a number of times, variously including the words "Journal" or "Abstracts," both, or neither at the end of the title. Its content provides access to books, journal articles, conference proceedings, and government reports for both theoretical research and many areas of applied computer science which are of interest to linguists. From 1981 on it is available online (CSA, STN) with monthly updates. (See introduction to chapter 3 for vendor contact information.)

448.   **INSPEC**. [electronic database]. Piscataway, NJ: Institute of Electrical and Electronic Engineers.

A number of vendors supply this very large database online (Dialog, OCLC FirstSearch, Ovid, SilverPlatter, STN) with various years of coverage and updates. (See introduction to chapter 3 for vendor contact information). *INSPEC* incorporates citations from *Computer and Control Abstracts*. See entry 446 for coverage. User aids recommended for effective retrieval are a newly updated in 1999 *INSPEC Classification* and *INSPEC Thesaurus*.

449.   **NTIS**. [electronic database]. Springfield, VA: U.S. National Technical Information Service, 1964- .

As this database gives access to unrestricted technical reports from U.S. and non-U.S. government-sponsored research and development, it contains information on almost every conceivable subject. Of primary interest to linguists would be its subject category of computers, control, and information theory covering such topics as natural language processing, computational linguistics, and machine translation. The corresponding print index is *Government Reports Announcements & Index*. It is available online (CSA, Dialog, Ovid, STN) from 1964 to present with monthly or biweekly updates depending on the vendor. (See introduction to chapter 3 for vendor contact information).

Internet Sites

450. **The ACL NLP/CL Universe**. Available: http://www.cs.columbia. edu/~radev/u/db/acl/. (Accessed March 13, 1999).

The Association for Computational Linguistics maintains this well-developed and organized, searchable meta-site with nearly 2,000 links. It can be browsed under 11 categories such as companies and corporate research labs, conferences, professional organizations, subject-specific resources (e.g. phonology, translation), and various resources. Each listing tells a visitor how many links are under that category. The various resources link itself has 476 entries for such items as bibliography (20),corpora (60), dictionaries (26), electronic mailing lists (13), language-specific resources (8), other comprehensive sites (33), and software on the Internet (219). While designed for the members of ACL and those doing work in computational linguistics, it is a site that has much to offer researchers in other areas of linguistics. When last accessed the search engine was not working. Last updated February 16, 1999.

451. **ACM Brings You the World of Computing**. Available: http://info.acm.org/. (Accessed March 13, 1999).

The Association for Computing Machinery founded in 1947 is the world's oldest and largest educational and scientific computing society. It's Web site provides information about its publications—books, journals, and databases (see entry 444), special interest groups, education, awards, and other information for its membership of 80,000 computing professionals in more than 100 countries in all areas of industry, government, and academia.

452. **The Association for Computational Linguistics**. Available: http://www.aclweb.org/. (Accessed: March 13, 1999).

The ACL Web site provides information to its membership and resources such as e-mail updating to the NLP/CL Universe, information about ACL's journal *Computational Linguistics* and online access to the latest issue of their newsletter *The Finite String*, an archive of papers on computational linguistics and related fields, an ACL FTP site, and a survey of the state of the art of human language technology. Last updated November 25, 1998.

453. **CL/MT Research Group Home Page**. Available: http://clwww. essex.ac.uk/. (Accessed: March 13, 1999).

The Computation Linguistics and Machine Translation Group is a research group in the Department of Language and Linguistics at the University of Essex. It has strong links with other such groups in Europe and the United Kingdom. From its home page link to "Linguistic Bibliography Search Facilities" it offers searchable access to a half dozen bibliographic databases and links to sites with quite a number of other relevant bibliographies. In addition it offers links to other online services and other sites. By following the few links on this home page just down a level or so, the visitor will shortly have available a vast array of further links. Last updated December 21, 1998.

454. **The Computation and Language E-Print Archive**. Available: http://xxx.lanl.gov/cmplg/. (Accessed: March 13, 1999).

The archive is a fully automated electronic archive and distribution server for papers on computational linguistics, natural language processing, speech processing, and related fields. Stuart Sheiber, Division of Applied Sciences at Harvard University is project coordinator using the computer facilities of Los Alamos National Laboratory. The site offers preprints of papers as soon as they are submitted and maintains a full-text archive accessible by e-mail, anonymous FTP, gopher, and a Web interface. It also has a selected list of links to Web pages of related interest.

455. **Corpus Linguistics**. Available: http://www.ruf.rice.edu/~barlow/corpus.html. (Accessed March 13, 1999).

Michael Barlow, Department of Linguistics, Stanford University and Associate Director of the Center for the Study of Languages maintains this award-winning website with links to English and non-English corpora organized by language. In addition Barlow also provides links to software, courses in corpus linguistics, a bibliography, and other useful sites and home pages. Some links are annotated.

456. **The ELRA Home Page**. Available: http://www.icp.grenet.fr/ELRA/home.html. (Accessed: March 13, 1999).

ELRA (The European Language Resources Association) is a non-profit organization with the goal of providing a centralized organization for the validation, management, and distribution of speech, text, and terminology resources and tools, and to promote their use within the European R&TD community. It will collect, market, distribute, and license European language resources. ELRA will help users and developers of language resources, government agencies, and other interested parties to exploit language resources for a wide variety of uses. Eventually, ELRA will serve as the European repository for EUfunded language resources and interact with similar bodies in other parts of the world. Language resources include such materials as recorded speech databases, lexicons, grammars, text corpora, and terminological data. They are essential for the development of robust speech and text processing systems with wide coverage. The ELRS Web site caters to the needs of its members, such as listing "Resources Requested" (text, speech, terminology, tools). The "Catalogue" link lists resources available. Has links to many other practical sites. Last updated February 9, 1999.

457. **Statistical NLP / Corpus-based Computational Linguistics Resources**. Available: http://www.sultry.arts.su.edu.au/links/statnlp.html. (Accessed: March 14, 1999).

Last updated March 10, 1999 by its compiler Christopher Manning at the Department of Linguistics, University of Sydney this Web site pulls together and organizes a lot of resources. Major categories are tools; corpora; dictionaries;

lexical/morphological resources/courses; syllabi, and other educational resources; mailing lists; other stuff on the Web. Pithy annotations accompany the seven-pages long home page.

458. **Welcome to ELSNET's Home Page**. Available: http://www. elsnet.org/. (Accessed March 14, 1999).

The goal of the European Network in Language and Speech (ELSNET) is to encourage the development of language technology in Europe by helping to coordinate progress on both the scientific and technological fronts. The long-term technological goal is to build multilingual speech and NL systems with unrestricted coverage of both spoken and written language. The Web page provides information on the network's organization, listserv, publications, services and resources, training opportunities, conferences and events, and projects. The "Related Web Sites" link on the home page provides access to many other projects and associations world-wide as well as to selected language and linguistic metasites. Last updated January 14, 1999.

Cumulative Bibliographies

459. Chizhakovskii, V. A., and K. B. Bektaev. **Statistika rechi, 1957-1985: bibliograficheskii ukazatel'**. Otv. red. P.M. Alekseev. Kishinev: "Shtiintsa," 1986. 109p. index. LC 87-120831.

There are nearly 1,000 entries for monographs, textbooks, manuals, dictionaries, articles, dissertations, and conference papers published from 1957 to 1985 dealing with statistical methods and data processing as related to linguistics. Nearly all of the material cited are written in Russian, not transliterated here. There are two indexes. One index organizes works by author. Under an author's name, entry numbers are cited together with subject classification numbers. A user can take an entry number, look in the bibliography to see what that work is, and then take the subject classification number and look at the classification scheme which precedes the index to find the subject matter of that particular work. This index lends itself to finding out what areas an author publishes in rather than to serving as an efficient subject index. A second index does facilitate access to entries dealing with specific languages.

460. Gazdar, Gerald, et al. **Natural Language Processing in the 1980's: A Bibliography**. Stanford, CA: Center for the Study of Language and Information, 1987. 240p. index. (CSLI Lecture Notes, No. 12). LC 87-27644. ISBN 0-937073-26-1.

References to publications in the field of natural language processing (NLP) and computational linguistics from 1980 through part of 1987 are contained in this bibliography of 1,764 unannotated items. To obtain the references the authors exhaustively covered core sources in the field (listed in the introduction) and supplemented this with papers from numerous other journals, conference and workshop proceedings, edited collections, ad hoc publications, and monographs. In selecting from the non-core literature, publications in languages other than English were excluded. NLP work in the logic programming tradition is well represented while such computational linguistic topics as concordance creation, lexicostatistics, author identification, and the like have not necessarily been included.

The arrangement of entries is alphabetical by author. There is also an index to second and subsequent authors. A keyword-in-context (KWIC) index based on titles provides limited subject access. It is limited, as are all such indexes not enhanced with subject words, since titles are not always indicative of the content of a work; plus, for this book, in order to hold down publishing costs, some frequently occurring words such as "natural" and "language" had to be excluded from the KWIC index.

This bibliography is an ongoing project. An up-to-date online version is kept at Stanford University. The introduction gives instructions for accessing it by computer mail. It also gives information on how to obtain a machine-readable copy of the current main file.

461. House, Arthur S. **The Recognition of Speech by Machine: A Bibliography**. London: Academic Press, 1988. 498p. index. ISBN 0-12-356785-8.

The focus of this unannotated bibliography is research published, mainly in the United States, on automatic speech recognition. The bibliography began as internal reports of the Communications Research Division of the Institute for Defense Analyses in Princeton, New Jersey, and reflects the interests of this unit in the criteria used for identifying pertinent materials, outlined by the author in the foreword. It is idiosyncratic in organization as well. Part 1 is a subject index referring the user to sole or primary authors writing on a particular subject, but not detailed nearly enough to be a satisfactory index for the user, as for example, under the topic "Russian" there are some 28 lines of author names. Part 2 is the bibliography proper with citations arranged alphabetically by author with initials used for given names. Many of the titles in languages other than English, especially those in Russian and Japanese, are translated with original language noted. A few citations are incomplete. Though the dates for inclusion are not stated, most entries are dated in the 1970s and 1980s with a few earlier citations. Part 3 is an index of authors, unduly complicated by a system of italics and indentation to identify sole, primary, and co-authors. Despite its shortcomings, the bibliography gathers together a lot of hard-to-track literature, such as conference proceedings, transactions, institutional and laboratory reports, and theses and dissertations as well as mainstream journal articles and books.

462. Kantrowitz, Mark. **Bibliography of Research in Natural Language Generation**. Pittsburgh, PA: School of Computer Science, Carnegie Mellon University, 1993. 49p.

The 1,224 entries in this bibliography gather together natural language generation (NLG) research found in dissertations and published in conference or workshop proceedings, books, and journals. There are no annotations or indexes, but in the introduction the compiler does point the user to a number of entries as good prior surveys of NLG or some its subfields. Coverage includes a few entries dated prior to 1970, with the majority published in the 1980s and continuing through 1993. The compiler provides instructions to the reader for obtaining the bibliography by anonymous FTP.

463.   Kohler, Reinhard. **Bibliography of Quantitative Linguistics/Bibliographie zur quantitativen Linguistik/Bibliografiya po kvantitativnoi lingvistike**. With the assistance of Christiane Hoffmann. Amsterdam/Philadelphia: John Benjamins, 1995. 780p. index. (Amsterdam Studies in the Theory and History of Linguistic Science. Series V: Library and Information Sources in Linguistics, Vol. 25; ISSN 0165-7267). LC 95-15252. ISBN 90-272-3751-4.

The 6,341 entries in this classified bibliography broadly cover the topic of quantitative linguistics with no restrictions on form, place, language, or date of publication (covering through 1993). The study of quantitative linguistics has been particularly strong in Eastern Europe and Kohler provides substantial coverage of this research. The result is a very comprehensive survey of the field. The compilers have arranged the entries into 28 chapters with subheadings, and then alphabetically by main entry. Each entry is annotated with descriptors and often enriched with additional keywords. Entries in alphabets other than the Roman alphabet are transliterated. There are a number of indexes to assist the user: authors (authors, editors, translators), keywords, subject headings, subheadings, uncontrolled vocabulary, investigated languages (languages, language groups, dialects), and reviewed publications. The entries make extensive use of abbreviations (including journals and languages), but there are lists expanding them.

464.   Mel'chuk, Igor Aleksandrovich, and R. D. Ravich. **Avtomaticheskii perevod, 1949-1963. Kritiko-bibliograficheskii spravochnik**. Moskva, 1967. 517p. index. illus.

465.   Mel'chuk, Igor Aleksandrovich, and R.D. Ravich. **Traduction automatique: 1964-1970/Automatic Translation/Automaticheskii perevod: 1964-1970. Kritiko-bibliograficheskii spravochnik**. Red. A. V. Gladkii. Montreal: Universite de Montreal, 1978. 421p. index. illus. bibliog.

The first edition of this international bibliography on automatic translation and related subject areas covers materials published from 1949 to 1963 in Russian, Polish, Bulgarian, etc., as well as in a number of Western languages. A detailed, descriptive abstract emphasizing above all the linguistic aspects of automatic translation research accompanies each of the 1,430 entries. Diagrams accompany some of the entries which are arranged under about 80 divisions of a classification system. The author index lists an entry number plus the truncated title of that author's particular work; names written in Cyrillic script precede those in Latin script. Following this index are indexes for subjects, languages, journals cited, and organizations, the latter organized by country.

The second edition for 1964-1970 with 1,360 entries is essentially a continuation of the earlier one though it was published in Montreal, not Moscow. The title page, preface and table of contents are in French and English as well as Russian.

466.   The RAND Corporation. **A Bibliography of Selected RAND Publications: Linguistics**. Santa Monica, CA: The RAND Corporation, 1989. 25p. (SB-1035 (1961-1983)).

The RAND publications in this bibliography are on various aspects of computational linguistics, machine translation, and the like. Included among them are 8 bibliographies which themselves have the following RAND Memoranda numbers:

RM-3610-1, RM-3894-3, RM-4479, RM-4523, RM-4986, RM-5345, RM-5733, and RM-6223. Some of these are bibliographies of RAND publications (years covered are 1964-1977) while others are bibliographies with an international scope. Each item has one paragraph describing its contents.

467. Sabourin, Conrad. **Computational Morphology: Morphological Analysis and Generation, Lemmatization: Bibliography**. Montreal/Hudson: Infolingua, 1994. 492p. index. (Series in linguistics, information, communications, 1; ISSN 1198-1083). ISBN 2-921173-01-8.

468. Sabourin, Conrad F. **Computational Parsing: Syntactic Analysis, Semantic Analysis, Semantic Interpretation, Parsing Algorithms, Parsing Strategies: Bibliography**. Montreal/Hudson: Infolingua, 1994. 2v. 1029p. index. (Series in linguistics, informatics, communications, 2; ISSN 1198-1083). ISBN 2-921173-02-6 (v.1); ISBN 2-921173-03-4 (v.2).

469. Sabourin, Conrad F. **Computational Lexicology and Lexicography: Dictionaries, Thesauri, Term Banks; Analysis, Transfer and Generation Dictionaries; Machine Readable Dictionaries; Lexical Semantics; Lexicon Grammars: Bibliography**. Montreal/Hudson: Infolingua, 1994. 2v. 1031p. index. (Series in linguistics, informatics, communications, 3; ISSN 1198-1083). ISBN 2-921173-04-2 (v.1); ISBN 2-921173-05-0 (v.2).

470. Sabourin, Conrad. **Computational Text Understanding: Natural Language Programming, Argument Analysis: Bibliography**. Montreal/Hudson: Infolingua, 1994. 657p. index. (Series in linguistics, informatics, communications, 4; ISSN 1198-1083). ISBN 2-921173-06-9.

471. Sabourin, Conrad. **Computational Text Generation: Generation from Data or Linguistic Structure, Text Planning, Sentence Generation, Explanation Generation: Bibliography**. With a survey article by Mark T. Maybury. Montreal/Hudson: Infolingua, 1994. 649p. index. (Series in linguistics, informatics, communications, 5; ISSN 1198-1083). ISBN 2-921173-07-7.

472. Sabourin, Conrad. **Natural Language Interfaces: Interfaces to Databases, to Expert Systems, to Robots, to Operating Systems, and to Question-Answering Systems: Bibliography**. Montreal/Hudson: Inforlingua, 1994. 2v. 847p. index. (Series in linguistics, informatics, communications, 6; ISSN 1198-1083). ISBN 2-921173-08-5 (v.1); ISBN 2-921173-09-3 (v.2).

473. Sabourin, Conrad. **Machine Translation: Aids to Translation, Speech Translation: Bibliography**. With the collaboration of Laurent R. Bourbeau. Montreal/Hudson: Infolingua, 1994. 2v. 1168p. index. (Series in linguistics, informatics, communications, 7; ISSN 1198-1083). ISBN 2-921173-10-7 (v.1); ISBN 2-921173-11-5.

474. Sabourin, Conrad. **Quantitative and Statistical Linguistics: Frequencies of Characters, Phonemes, Words, Grammatical Categories, Syntactic Structures; Lexical Richness, Word Collocations, Entropy; Word Length,**

Sentence Length: Bibliography. Montreal/Hudson: Infolingua, 1994. 508p. index. (Series in linguistics, informatics, communications, 13; ISSN 1198-1083). ISBN 2-921173-19-0.

475.   Sabourin, Conrad. **Mathematical and Formal Linguistics: Grammar Formalisms, Grammar Testing, Logics, Quantifiers: Bibliography**. Montreal/Hudson: Infolingua, 1994. 612p. index. (Series in linguistics, informatics, communications, 14; ISSN 1198-1083). ISBN 2-921173-20-4.

476.   Sabourin, Conrad. **Computational Speech Processing: Speech Analysis, Recognition, Understanding, Compression, Transmission, Coding, Synthesis; Text to Speech Systems, Speech to Tactile Displays, Speaker Identification, Prosody Processing: Bibliography**. Montreal/Hudson: Infolingua, 1994. 2v. 1187p. index. (Series in linguistics, informatics, communications, 15; ISSN 1198-1083). ISBN 2-921173-21-2 (v.1); ISBN 2-921173-22-0 (v.2).

477.   Sabourin, Conrad. **Computational Linguistics in Information Science: Information Retrieval (Full-Text or Conceptual); Automatic Indexing, Text Abstraction, Content Analysis, Information Extraction, Query Languages: Bibliography**. Montreal/Hudson: Infolingua, 1994. 2v. 1047p. index. (Series in linguistics, informatics, communications, 16; ISSN 1198-1083). ISBN 2-921173-23-9 (v.1); ISBN 2-921173-24-7 (v.2).

The above entries are all part of the Infolingua series in linguistics, informatics, and communications (see also entry 425). The series volumes are printouts of the vast Infolingua bibliographic database incorporating references to publications pertaining to any form of computer processing of natural language. The long titles of each volume describe the subject content for each number in the series. As of January 1994 the Infolingua project totaled some 73,846 entries. Documents of all types are included, regardless of their country of origin or language written in, but coverage is more comprehensive for North America and Western Europe (73% of entries). In the future the publishers aim to include more coverage from outside these areas. Although citations range from 1950 to 1993, about half were published after 1985. To ensure wide coverage the compilers scanned some 400 periodicals and 800 conference proceedings for relevant materials. They also included all references in the bibliographies of selected materials; such inclusion of secondary citations has inevitably introduced some irrelevant citations into the database.

No abstracts or annotations are provided for the alphabetically arranged references. Each reference has an author, title, place and date of publication, and a number for access via the subject index. Each reference is assigned keywords from a thesaurus, designed specifically for this project, of 3,800 terms for both topics and languages. This gold mine of information is best accessed through these indexes of keywords found in each of the series titles. Many keywords have subfields; for example, the keyword "Grammar" is subdivided into more than 360 more specific keywords. While the format of this work is not fancy—it looks simply like what it is, a computer printout—it is readable and includes complete bibliographic information for each entry. Happily for the user, the compilers did not abbreviate names of persons or titles of publications.

478.   Slocum, Jonathan, ed. **Machine Translation Systems**. Cambridge: Cambridge University Press, 1988. 341p. illus. bibliog. LC 87-15111. ISBN 0521351669.

A bibliography by Slocum, "A Machine(-Aided) Translation Bibliography," appears on pages 265-341. It covers materials written in English, French, and German during the years 1973-1986. In addition to covering books and journal articles it does a good job of ferreting out reports and conference proceedings of various associations and institutes. However, entries are not annotated and there is no type of subject access, the entries being listed alphabetically by author.

16

Psycholinguistics

The general topic of psycholinguistics, a term used for psychological studies and experiments attempting to explain language acquisition and competence (including child language), is covered in this chapter. To a much lesser extent it covers neurolinguistics and language and the brain. No attempt has been made to gather research materials specifically on speech disorders and learning disabilities, although such material can be found here in works on the aforementioned topics.

Abstracts and Electronic Databases

479. **Child Development Abstracts and Bibliography**. Vol. 1- . Chicago: Society for Research in Child Development, 1927- . 3 times/yr. LC 46-31872. ISSN 0009-3939.

Both abstracts of articles in professional journals and review of books related to the growth and development of children appear in this publication. Abstracts of articles are classed in six sections. The section of most interest to linguists is on cognition, learning, and perception; it contains research dealing with child language acquisition. Each issue contains an author and subject index, the year-end index cumulating the others.

480. **Psychological Abstracts**. Vol. 1- . Arlington, VA: American Psychological Association, 1927- . monthly. LC 29-23479. ISSN 0033-2887.

References to articles from more than 1,400 journals, monograph series, book chapters, and technical reports can all be found in this important, international index to the literature of psychology and the behavioral sciences. The linguist will find entries dealing with such diverse topics as ethnolinguistics, psycholinguistics, sociolinguistics, semiotics, pragmatics, language development, bilingualism, dialects, and verbal communication. Items are arranged according to a classification system with 16 major sections, some subdivided. An abstract in English is provided regardless of the original language of publication. With each issue there is an author and brief subject index. A variety of cumulated indexes are issued as well. The subject indexes are best approached by using the indexing terms found in the 8th edition of the *Thesaurus of Psychological Index Terms* (1997).

From 1967 to 1979 the electronic database *PsycINFO* corresponds to the printed abstracts, but beginning in 1980 the database contains more citations. There is a historical file of *PsycINFO* covering 1894-1966 and a file covering 1967 to current available online from a variety of vendors (APA, CSA, Dialog, EBSCO, Gale, IAC, OCLC FirstSearch, NISC, Ovid, SilverPlatter, UMI). Another file *PsycFIRST* representing the latest three years of *PsycINFO* is available online also (CSA, EBSCO, NISC, OCLC FirstSearch, Ovid, UMI). The *PsycLIT* database with just articles, books, and book chapters and not technical reports nor dissertations is available from 1887 to present on CD-ROM (EBSCO, NISC, Ovid, SilverPlatter). (See introduction to chapter 3 for vendor contact information.)

Internet Sites

481. **American Psychological Association**. Available: http://www.apa. org/. (Accessed March 14, 1999).

The APA is the largest scientific and professional organization for psychology in the United States with 50 divisions and a membership of more than 159,000 researchers, educators, students, and practitioners. The Web site contains information for potential and current members. In development is a gateway to full-text psychological information on the Web as well as links to the best Internet sites called "PsycPORT."

482. **American Psychological Society (APS)**. Available: http://www. psychologicalscience.org/. (Accessed March 14, 1999).

Founded in 1988 the APS is dedicated to the science of psychology. Its 16,000 member scientists and academics come from the entire spectrum of basic and applied psychological science. Its home page provides a link to selected psychology Web sites (government agencies, psychological societies and associations, and other sites of interest).

483. **Cognitive and Psychological Sciences**. Available: http://www. psych.stanford.edu/cogsci.html. (Accessed March 18, 1999).

The Virtual Library Cognitive Science which formed part of the WWW Virtual Library, supported by Margaret Doll at Brown University, was recently combined with this index edited by Ruediger Oehlmann, a researcher in the Data Archive at the University of Essex, UK. The sites have not yet been integrated; the Brown site now titled *Previous Cognitive Science Links at Brown* is accessible via a link from the Stanford site at http://dawww.essex.ac.uk/~roehl/PsycIndex/cogdir/cognitive.html (accessed: March 18, 1999). The combined sites, maintained in parallel in the Data Archive and in the Stanford Psychology Department, will eventually be an index to Internet resources relevant to research in cognitive science and psychology. Sections include academic programs, organizations and conferences, journals and magazines, Usenet Newsgroups, discussion lists, announcement/distributionists, publishers, software, and miscellany. The latter provides links to various other meta-indexes.

484. **Homepage of the IASCL**. Available:http://www.atila-www. uia.ac.be/IASCL/Inhoud.html. (Accessed: March 14, 1999).

The International Association for the Study of Child Language (IASCL) was founded to promote international and interdisciplinary cooperation in the study of child language. This is accomplished mainly through holding a triennial international congress. Their home page provides just basic information about membership, past and forthcoming congresses, and their publications.

485. **Psychology WWW Virtual Library**. Available: http://www.clas. ufl.edu/users/gthursby/psi/. (Accessed: March 18, 1999).

Sections of this meta-site maintained by Gene Thursby, Associate Professor at the University of Florida, include: e-mail lists and newsgroups, books and publishers, guides to psychology online, online libraries, professional societies, and more. The second level of this Web site is annotated with brief descriptions. Last updated March 3, 1999.

Cumulative Bibliographies

486. Bach, Ulrich, and Dieter Wolff, Hrsg. **Ausgewahlte Bibliographie zur Psycholinguistik und Sprachpsychologie**. Königstein/Ts.: Scriptor, 1980. 434p. index. (Monographien Linguistik und Kommunikationswissenschaft, 47). LC 80-146785. ISBN 3-589-20757-4.

Most of the 6,868 works cited in this selective bibliography on psycholinguistics and the psychology of language are in English. A significant number are in German, with other languages such as French and Italian also represented. A short introductory section of about 400 entries on general works precedes the main bibliography. This introductory section is divided into monographs, collected works, articles, proceedings of congresses, bibliographies, and reviews. All these types of works are also included in the main bibliography which is arranged alphabetically by author within a well-organized, detailed subject classification system. Its four main sections are: ontogenesis of language, psychological research on second language acquisition, linguistic behavior in the adult, and language pathology. Entries are not annotated. An index of authors, co-authors, and editors completes the work.

487. Curat, Hervé, and Lionel Meney. **Gustave Guillaume et la psychosystématique du langage: bibliographie annotée**. Québec: Presses de l'Université Laval, 1983. 235p. index. LC 84-172927. ISBN 2-763777-7029-0.

The books, periodical articles, and reviews by and about Guillaume and his theories in this bibliography cover the time period from 1905 to 1981 and are mostly in French. Many of the 1,534 entries are drawn from the authors' preceding 2-volume work *Bibliographie de la recherche en psycho-systématique du langage* (Québec: Université Laval, 1980-81) and its earlier edition published in 1978. The authors cite 9 other works which they heavily drew on for many of the entries here. In deciding which of the works by Guillaume's followers and critics to include, the authors have chosen to use a broad interpretation. Very brief descriptive annotations accompany perhaps half of the entries. There are indexes for authors, subjects, and reviews (by reviewers).

488. Dimitrijević, Naum, and Radmila Djordjević. **A Bibliography on Neurolinguistics**. Padova: Liviana Editrice, 1980. 131p. index.

To decide what to include in this bibliography the authors relied on a definition of neurolinguistics as that whose subject matter is the relationship that pertains between man's language and his nervous system. Thus, there are entries which are purely neurological, some linguistic, others psychological. Nearly all of the 1,609 entries are in English though the authors acknowledge there is an extensive literature in other languages. They cite several reasons for this language limitation. First, most papers in this field are either written originally in English, or are later translated into English. Second, they reason that most researchers in this area can read English. It updates Peuser's bibliography for English language items by several years as it includes references through 1978 (see entry 499). However, Dingwall's 1981 2-volume bibliography is more complete and up-to-date than either of these (see entry 489).

Unannotated entries are arranged in one alphabetical sequence by first author. An index of coauthors follows. There is also a short subject index of neurological and linguistic topics.

489. Dingwall, William Orr. **Language and the Brain: A Bibliography and Guide**. New York: Garland, 1981. 2v.(1017p.). index. (Garland Reference Library of Social Science, Vol. 73). LC 80-8491. ISBN 0-8240-9495-6.

Dingwall compiled this impressive bibliography and guide for two types of users: beginning students and active researchers. For the student he provides a logical step-by-step introduction to the field with his extensive introductions and recommended readings at the beginning of each of the five main sections. The lists of 30 other bibliographies, 16 societies, and over 100 journals and series provide a guide for keeping abreast of the field and establishing contact with others working in this area. Further, a study of the topic index will enable a student to develop a feel for the kinds of interests and approaches characterizing this discipline. For the active researcher this bibliography should help in obtaining background materials in a variety of languages for the area of interest, plus introduce the scholar to works in unfamiliar areas.

The 5,746 unannotated entries are arranged under the following five headings: background, localization of language and allied functions in the brain, neurological disorders of language and allied capacities, development of language and the brain (ontogenesis), and evolution of the brain and communicative behavior (phylogenesis). In putting together this thorough work Dingwall acknowledges his debt to two previous bibliographies, that of Peuser on language and the brain and that of Hewes on language origins, in so far as the latter relates to the area of evolution of the brain and communicative behavior (see entries 499 and 155). In addition a researcher may also want to consult Dimitrijevic's bibliography for English language items (see entry 488). Dingwall also acknowledges that his own research interests have influenced the emphases in this compilation which are: the historical background of the topic, localization of function, experimental research in neurological disorders, and the evolution of human communication systems. On the other hand, less emphasis has been placed on clinical and applied aspects of research in language and the brain.

490. Dittmann, Jürgen, and Jürgen Tesak. **Neurolinguistik**. Heidelberg: Julius Groos, 1993. 48p. index. (Studenbibliographien Sprachwissenschaft, Bd. 8; ISSN 0938-8648). ISBN 3-87276-696-1.

Dittmann and Tesak have put together a small bibliography of 414 citations of research in German and English on neurolinguistics divided into sections for general works, language and the brain, aphasia, dementia, schizophreOnia, and affective psychoses. Each entry is annotated with abbreviations for subject terms. There is an index of subject terms keyed to the entries as well as an author index.

491.   Higginson, Roy, and Brian MacWhinney. **CHILDES/BIB: An Annotated Bibliography of Child Language and Language Disorders**. Hillsdale, NJ: Lawrence Erlbaum Associates, 1991. 1162p. index. LC 90-48836. ISBN 0-8058-0859-0.

492.   Higginson, Roy, and Brian MacWhinney. **CHILDES/BIB: An Annotated Bibliography of Child Language and Language Disorders**. Hillsdale, NJ: Lawrence Erlbaum Associates, 1994. 693p. index. LC 93-34993. ISBN 0-8058-1478-7.

493.   Higginson, Roy, and Brian MacWhinney. **CHILDES/BIB: An Annotated Bibliography of Child Language and Language Disorders**. Mahwah, NJ: Lawrence Erlbaum Associates, 1997. 669p. index. ISBN 0-8058-2411-1.

The Child Language Data Exchange System (CHILDES) began as a bibliographic database of records for books and articles, the vast majority of which are on normal child language acquisition, not language disorders. Several articles in an issue of the *Journal of Child Language* (Vol. 17, No. 2, 1990) and an article in *American Journal of Speech-Language Pathology* (Vol. 5, 1996) provide additional information on the system. The first printing of CHILDES/BIB in 1991 contains nearly 7,500 records published from a database of records dating back to 1250. Of these some 200 entries date from before 1900 with the majority published from 1970 to 1990. The compilers arranged the entries alphabetically by author, provide the usual bibliographic information, and for many give short descriptive annotations. Studies in languages, or about languages, other than English are identified in the annotation. The contents of a number of earlier cumulative bibliographies have been incorporated, including Adele A. Abrahamsen's *Child Language: An Interdisciplinary Guide to Theory and Research* (Baltimore, MD: University Park Press, 1977) and *Leopold's Bibliography of Child Language*, revised and augmented by Dan Isaac Slobin (Bloomington, IN: Indiana University Press, 1972). In addition it has been updated with relevant items from *Child Development Abstracts*, the journal *Language*, and annual bibliographies published by the Child Research Institute, Department of Scandinavian Languages, Stockholm University. There is both an author (including co-authors) and a subject index based on 1,500 subject keywords in the electronic version. The print version of this otherwise valuable bibliography can be tedious to use as both subject indexes are keyed to page numbers, not entry numbers, and a fair number of the keywords are followed by more than 150 relevant page numbers.

The 1994 supplement adds 3,000 new references covering North American research since 1990 and international research published elsewhere since 1970, as well as a few North American omissions prior to 1990. The 1997 supplement with approximately 2,700 references, most published after 1990, extends the bibliography to more than 13,000 references. The format of the supplements is similar to the first printing except that keywords have been added at the end of each citation, greatly enhancing the bibliography's usability. The 1997 edition also contains a categorical list of the subject keywords arranged into major categories and subcategories.

There is now a well-developed Web site for the CHILDES/BIB database system—readable and searchable—maintained by Brian MacWhinney, a Professor of psychology at Carnegie Mellon University, http://poppy.psy.cmu.edu/childes/index.html (Accessed March 14, 1999).

494.   Kess, Joseph F., and Tadao Miyamoto. **Japanese Psycholinguistics: A Classified and Annotated Research Bibliography**. Amsterdam: John Benjamins, 1994. 357p. index. (Amsterdam Studies in the Theory and History of Linguistic Science. Series V. Library and Information Sources in Linguistics, Vol. 24; ISSN 0165-7267). LC 94-35000. ISBN 90-272-3750-6.

Kess and Miyamoto have compiled a much needed source of information in English about "Japanese psycholinguistics" in both readings of the term—the discipline of psycholinguistics as pursued in Japan itself, and research in psycholinguistics which targets the Japanese language as the focal point of research. This annotated bibliography sheds light on a very substantial body of research carried out in Japan—largely unknown outside its environs—by teams of international and Japanese scholars. The authors have written evaluative, often lengthy annotations summarizing important points or conclusions of research and placing the work in the context of the psycholinguistic research tradition. There are more than 1,000 entries for published materials (dissertations and conference proceedings are omitted). Titles in Japanese are translated into English as well as transliterated by using the Hepburn system. The table of contents serves as the subject index to the entries organized into 17 major sections which (outside of the introduction) represent major interests in psycholinguistic research, such as history of psycholinguistics, syntax and sentence processing, semantics and the organization of meaning, language and thought, lateralization and hemispheric specialization in the brain, first language acquisition, and second language acquisition.

495.   Konopczynski, Gabrielle. **Prosodie du langage enfantin: Une bibliographie thématique/Prosody of Child Language: A Thematic Bibliography/Prosodie der Kindersprache: Eine thematische Bibliographie**. Hamburg: Helmut Buske, 1988. 185p. index. (Beiträge zur Phonetik und Linguistik, Bd. 59; ISSN 0178-1723). ISBN 3-87118-859-X.

While the study of child language dates back to debates in ancient times by philosophers and historians, more recent psycholinguistic and sociolinguistic work dates from the publication in 1941 of *Kindersprache, Aphasie und allgemeine Lautgesetze*, by Roman Jakobson. In this unannotated, classified bibliography the author has taken a broad view of the topic and gathered some 1,800 entries for research written in French, English, and German dating from the late 1800s up through 1985. She includes materials published in books, journals, and conference proceedings as well as dissertations arranged according to a ten-part classification scheme explained in the introduction. This scheme serves as the subject index. There is an index of main authors and co-authors. All referatory material is written in German, English, and Russian.

496.   Lamarche, Rolande M., and Elca Tarrab. **Bibliographie de travaux québécois. Volume I. Psycholinguistique et pédagogie de la langue**. Québec: Office de la langue française, 1988. 176p. index. (Langues et sociétés; ISSN 0821-8099). ISBN 2-550-19244-3.

497.   Lamarche, Rolande M., and Denise Daoust. **Bibliographie de travaux québécois. Volume II. Linguistique générale, linguistique computationnelle, terminologie, traduction**. Québec: Office de la langue française, 1988. 316p. index. (Langues et sociétés; ISSN 0821-8099). ISBN 2-550-19245-1.

The two volumes of this bibliography gather together books, articles, theses, and reports published mainly from 1970 through 1987 by researchers in Quebec. The first volume with 2,040 entries covers psycholinguistics and language teaching; the second with 3,772 entries covers general linguistics, computational linguistics, terminology, and translation. The alphabetically arranged and numbered entries are unannotated, but keyed to an adequate subject index in each volume. (For related works on Canadian French see entries 534 and 535).

498.   Lesser, Ruth, and Peter Trewhitt. **An Annotated Bibliography of Verbal Materials for Use in Psycholinguistic and Neurolinguistic Experimentation**. Newcastle upon Tyne: Grevatt & Grevatt, 1982. 18p. index. LC 82-175541. ISBN 0-9507918-2-2.

Psychologists and neurologists frequently need word and sentence lists for their experiments. In selecting these lists such factors as word frequency, ambiguity, regularity of spelling, and category size need to be considered. They may also need controlled verbal materials with normative data. The references in this short list of 135 items provides the researcher with a selection of the most useful and representative of these studies. The entries are arranged under the following broad categories: catalogues of references, word properties (general), word properties (meaning-dependent), word properties (media-dependent), word properties (grammatical), sentences and sentence structures, texts and discourse, and miscellaneous. Short annotations accompany each entry. The index includes both topics and first authors.

499.   Peuser, Günter. **Sprache und Gehirn: eine Bibliographie zur Neurolinguistik/Language and Brain: A Bibliography on Neurolinguistics**. München: Wilhelm Fink, 1977. 260p. index. (Patholinguistica, Bd. 1). LC 77-481367. ISBN 3-7705-1475-0.

The preface of this work is in both English and German. The studies listed in it are for the most part also in these two languages though there are some in a variety of other languages such as Russian and French. In deciding what to include the author used as a guide the principle of listing "all such works as deal with language disorders due to brain damage or 'consider some aspect of human language or communication in a manner that can be related to the brain or brain function' (Whitaker)" (p.vii). He covers nearly 150 years of study, listing some of the classics though emphasizing research done in the last 15 years.

The 2,762 unannotated entries are arranged alphabetically by author's name. They include monographs, chapters, conference proceedings, and journal articles up through 1976. A very good subject index has keywords in both English and German. For the most part these terms are taken from the indexing system used by the Deutsches Institut für Medizinische Dokumentation und Information. A researcher will probably also want to use a bibliography by Dimitrijević which updates research done in English and the bibliography by Dingwall (see entries 488 and 489 respectively).

500.   Peuser, Günter, and Stefan Winter. **Aphasieforschung: Eine Bibliographie nach Sachgebieten**. München: Wilhelm Fink, 1995. 159p. index. (Patholinguistica, Bd. 17). ISBN 3-7705-3044-6.

Aphasia is impairment or loss of the ability to produce or understand spoken or written language resulting from brain damage. The authors have arranged the entries in this bibliography on aphasia according to a classification scheme detailed in the table of contents. With numerous cross-references it functions as a subject index. The unannotated entries are arranged alphabetically by author within each section. Entries are for research published mainly in German and English, including articles, book chapters, and books dating for the most part from the 1970s forward, but with a considerable number of earlier works, some even dating from the late 1800s. An index of authors and co-authors concludes this well-organized bibliography.

501. Schmidt-Knaebel, Susanne. **Sprache und Schizophrenie: Eine kommentierte Bibliographie zur Schizolinguistik**. Hamburg: Helmut Buske, 1992. 273p. index. ISBN 3-87548-042-2.

The added title to this page is *Language in Schizophrenia: An Annotated Bibliography on Schizolinguistics*. In the introduction, written in both German and English, the author characterizes the relatively new study of schizolinguistics as having three historical phases. The first phase lasting until the end of World War II, the second from 1945 until the end of the 1970s during which major theories on schizophrenic cognition and perception emerged, and the last decade (the 1980s) during which new aspects of schizophrenia research have emerged. The editor aims "to document as thoroughly as possible what amounts to over a hundred years of academic efforts to understand the phenomenon of so-called schizophrenic language" (p. x). In the first section of the book, Schmidt-Knaebel arranges the 4,076 numbered entries of books, chapters, journal articles, and dissertations from A-Z by author and annotates them with keywords. In the second section she supplies an index of these same keywords by which a user can identify pertinent entries.

17

Semiotics

Dictionaries, Encyclopedias, and Handbooks

502. Bellert, Irena, and Peter Ohlin, eds. **Selected Concepts in Semiotics and Aesthetics: Material for a Glossary**. Montreal: Programme in Communications, McGill University, 1978. 206p. index. illus. bibliog. (McGill Studies in Communications). LC 79-311216.

The material gathered here was to be the basis of a future encyclopedic glossary of terms on semiotics and aesthetics. In fact it also includes quite a bit of material on theoretical linguistics and the Prague School of linguistics. It does not contain entries of an explicitly technical nature, the aim being to make concepts clear to the interested non-specialist and scholars doing research outside their own specialty.

Entries are in the form of definitions, essays, or extended classificatory descriptions which are arranged in four sections: symbol, selected concepts in linguistics, selected concepts in logical semiotics, and selected concepts in aesthetics. The section on symbol is a single essay in French with its own short bibliography. The other three sections have entries arranged under subheadings. The second section is written in both French and English while the third and fourth sections are only in English. A bibliography at the end lists the references for these last three sections. A subject index divided into parts corresponding to the sections lists the page numbers where terms are defined, explained, or mentioned. This is done for both French terms and English terms. In spite of the provisional and non-technical nature of this glossary, it might still be of some use to a beginning student or someone seeking a very basic explanation for a term.

503. Bense, Max, and Elisabeth Walther, Hrsg. **Wörterbuch der Semiotik**. Köln: Kiepenheuer & Witsch, 1973. 137p. illus. LC 73-343943. ISBN 3-462-00915-X.

The definitions in this handy little German dictionary of semiotics range from a few lines to a few pages long, some accompanied by illustrations. Liberal use is made of cross-references and there are frequent citations in the definitions to the works of scholars, especially to that of Charles S. Peirce. Many entries have at the end a short bibliography for further reference.

504. Bouissac, Paul, ed. **Encyclopedia of Semiotics**. New York: Oxford University Press, 1998. 702p. index. illus. bibliog. LC 98-23092. ISBN 0-19-512090-6.

Bouissac's 1-volume encyclopedia seeks to complement Sebeok's 3-volume work (see entry 511) "not duplicate, notably with respect to the rich philosophical, psychological, and logical traditions that led to modern semiotics" (p. xi). It covers technical terms, schools of thought, authors and scholars, book titles, and general or specific domains of application. Instead of attempting exhaustive reviews of many topics it picks illustrative examples. The signed articles written by 100 international specialists are free of jargon and written in a style accessible to a wide, educated audience beyond the specialist. All articles conclude with cross-references to other articles as well as a bibliography. Articles range from well-known to lesser-know theorists (Barthes, Eco, Nattiez, Gibson, Riegl) to such subjects as baseball, Buddhism, intentionality, play, and zoosemiotics. A reader will be well-served by its fine subject index.

505. Colapietro, Vincent M. **Glossary of Semiotics**. New York: Paragon House, 1993. 212p. bibliog. (A Paragon House Glossary for Research, Reading, and Writing). LC 92-32621. ISBN 1-55778-502-3.

Colapietro recognizes that semiotics is a field with many newly coined words and idiosyncratic usage of ordinary terms, often frustrating those seeking to have even a basic understanding of its research. In view of this, the author designed this glossary for those relatively new to the field, selecting the terms defined based on their centrality to semiotics and their common occurrence in the indexes to books on semiotics (p. xi). Length of entries ranges from brief definitions to short essays. Though entries are meant to be self-contained, terms in boldface indicate other entries the reader may want to check for a fuller understanding of the term being defined. A selected bibliography of basic readings in the field completes this useful little pocket dictionary.

506. Dutz, Klaus D. **Glossar der semiotischen Terminologie Charles W. Morris'**. Münster: Münsteraner Arbeitskreis für Semiotik, 1979. 169p. index. (Zur Terminologie der Semiotik, II/Papiere des Munsteraner Arbeitskreises für Semiotik e.V., 9). LC 80-472946.

A short biography of Charles William Morris and a bibliography of his works precede the glossary of semiotic terms which are taken from the works listed in the bibliography. The biography and introductory remarks are in German, while the terms and glosses are in English, the language in which Morris wrote. An entry consists of a term, the German equivalent, sometimes a cross-reference or see also reference, and one or more quotations from Morris with a reference to the specific page of the work quoted from. There are two indexes. One is a list of English terms with the German equivalent. The other is a list of German terms with the English equivalent. This work could be used profitably by a reader of either German or English.

507. Greimas, Algirdas Julien, and Joseph Courtés. **Semiotics and Language: An Analytical Dictionary**. Translated by Larry Crist, et al. Bloomington: Indiana University Press, 1982. 409p. index. illus. bibliog. (Advances in Semiotics). LC 81-47828. ISBN 0-253-35169-3.

A team of six translators has produced this English version of the original French dictionary *Sémiotique: Dictionnaire raisonné de la théorie du langue* (Paris: Librairie Hachette, 1979) for which there is now a new edition (see next entry). In the French version English equivalents in italics followed the French headwords. In the course of translation some of these proposed equivalents were changed. A list of the changes appears in the preface of the translation.

This work is an attempt to establish a common ground on which various linguistic and semiotic theories could be brought together, compared, and evaluated. A dictionary form was chosen to do this in spite of the fact that an alphabetic arrangement tends to disperse a body of concepts. This mainly so that they could contribute to the development of a terminology, a conceptual metalanguage, which is a necessary prerequisite in establishing any language theory. A system of cross-references on several levels was developed to compensate for the dispersive effect. To understand this system of cross-referencing and make the best use of the dictionary, a reader should consult the translators' note and the preface where it is explained in detail.

Definitions range from the shortest of one sentence (transphrastic, semanticism) to a paragraph (dysphoria, zoo-semiotics) or a page (linguistics) up to the longest entry (semiotics), 7 pages in length. Following each headword is the French equivalent. An appendix gathers all these French headwords in an alphabetical list and gives the English equivalents. The works of semioticians and linguists, writing in French and English, which were consulted in this dictionary's preparation are collected in a 26-page bibliography.

508.   Greimas, Algirdas Julien, and Joseph Courtés. **Sémiotique: Diction-naire raisonné de la théorie du langage**. nouv. éd. Paris: Hachette, 1993. 454p. index. illus. bibliog. ISBN 2-01-020648-7.

The authors define more than 600 terms in the field of semiotics in this new edition of their dictionary. The French headword is in bold type as well as underlined and is accompanied by the part of speech and the equivalent term in English. Definitions, occasionally illustrated with diagrams, range in length from a sentence to three pages; most conclude with cross-references to other entries in the dictionary. There is a bibliography of works listing mostly French sources, some as recent as 1992.

509.   Nöth, Winfried. **Handbook of Semiotics**. Bloomington, IN: Indiana University Press, 1990. 576p. index. illus. port. bibliog. (Advances in Semiotics). LC 89-45199. ISBN 0-253-34120-5.

In this reworked, updated, and enlarged translation of *Handbuch der Semiotik* (Stuttgart: Metzlersche Verlagsbuchhandlung, 1985) Nöth provides an overview of the field of semiotics, both theoretical and applied. Some 65 essays are arranged in eight sections beginning with the history and classics of modern semiotics and continuing on to include sign and meaning; semiosis, code, and the semiotic field; language and language-based codes; from structuralism to text semiotics: schools and major figures; text semiotics: the field; nonverbal communication; and aesthetics and visual communication. The essays themselves are subdivided with headings that assist the user in zeroing in on a particular facet of a topic. The text is accompanied by interesting illustrations and portraits of major figures in the field. The bibliography of an estimated 3,000 works contains only references referred to in the text of the essays. In addition there is a thorough index of subjects and terms (those in boldface refer to topics which are the subject of whole essays), and an index of names.

510. Posner, Roland, Klaus Robering, and Thomas A. Sebeok, Hrsg. **Semiotik: Ein Handbuch zu den zeichentheoretischen Grundlagen von Natur und Kultur. 1. Teilband/Semiotics: A Handbook on the Sign-Theoretic Foundations of Nature and Culture. Volume 1.** Berlin: Walter de Gruyter, 1997. 1198p. illus. (some col.). (Handbücher zur Sprach- und Kommunikationswissenschaft/Handbooks of Linguistics and Communication Science/Manuels de linguistique et des sciences de communication, Bd. 13.1) LC 96-49024. ISBN 3-11-009584-X. (In progress).

This is the first volume of what is to be a three-volume handbook of more than 3,000 pages with 178 articles written by 175 experts from 25 countries. It offers, in the words of its editors, "a comprehensive survey of contemporary knowledge and methods of research in semiotics" and "documents the current state of research into the sign-theoretic foundations of living nature and culture" (p.1). Volume 1, containing 61 articles, presents a theory-based outline of the field, goes on to deal with the presuppositions and problems of semiotic historiography, and begins the history of Western semiotics from its inception up to the Renaissance. Volume 2 will complete the history of Western semiotics up to the present, treat sign conceptions in non-Western cultures, and cover current trends in the field. Volume 3 will deal with the relationship between semiotics and other interdisciplinary approaches and between semiotics and the individual disciplines, finally focusing on the applied aspects of semiotics, and concluding in an appendix with professional tools (organizations, reference works, and periodicals). The third volume will also contain an index of persons and subjects.

The handbook can be useful to a wide variety of readers, but is especially targeted at specialists in the humanities and social sciences as well as biologists and those studying medicine and the philosophy of science. Every reader should start with the very first chapter in volume 1, written in English by Posner, as it lays the foundation for the structure of the handbook and makes brief comments about each of the articles. Explanatory materials are written in both German and English and the signed articles seem to be about equally divided between being written in German and in English. References are gathered together at the end of each article. Authors are generous in illustrating their writing with a wide variety of black and white drawings and pictures; the volume concludes with 16 color plates.

511. Sebeok, Thomas A., general ed. **Encyclopedic Dictionary of Semiotics.** 2nd ed. rev. and updated. Berlin: Mouton de Gruyter, 1994. 3v. illus. bibliog. (Approaches to Semiotics, 73). LC 93-49813. ISBN 3-11-014229-5.

An international editorial board of prominent scholars compiled this outstanding 3-volume work now revised and updated with a new preface. Revisions made by 45 of the original contributors have not been integrated into the text of this new edition, rather they are appended at the end of each volume which even keep their original pagination (volume 1, A-M, has 25 supplemental pages, volume 2, N-Z, 19 pages, and volume 3, the bibliography, 47 pages). The unchanged text in the first two volumes (1179 pages) contains 426 signed articles arranged in alphabetical order. The articles were written by 236 contributors from all over the world, reflecting the original objective of its general editor not to represent any particular school of semiotic thought. As explained in the preface, some gaps, especially on semiotic theory and practice outside the Western tradition, exist because suitable contributors could not be secured.

The entries comprise three interlaced categories of articles: 1) entries giving the historical background and present usage of terms with recommendations, where appropriate, for standardizing current convention; 2) biographical sketches of those leading figures in semiotic studies who are no longer living, plus assessing works of others outside the field per se who have made pivotal contributions to semiotic studies; and 3) articles explaining the impact of semiotics on, or the penetration of semiotic methods of inquiry into other fields of study. They range in length from over 22 pages each on "Charles Sanders Peirce" and "Semantics" to a single paragraph on "Proposition." Extensive cross-referencing between the articles themselves and between the articles and the bibliography in volume 3 (originally 448 pages in length) facilitates its use as a tool for in-depth study of the discipline and related fields.

While the editors intentionally minimized the entries for linguistics, there are still many articles of interest to linguists, for example, "Aphasia"; "Jakobson, Roman"; "Language, Concept of"; "Language, Origins of"; "Lexicon"; "Meaning"; "Semantics"; "Semiotics and Linguistics"; "Syntax"; "Universals"; and "Whorf, Benjamin Lee." While one applauds the editorial decision not to abbreviate the titles of periodicals in the references, it is regrettable that only the initials and not the full given names of the authors are provided. There are a few errors in dates and spelling of names, but no more than expected for such a voluminous work. These few flaws do not mar an otherwise superb reference work. It represents a significant contribution to the field of semiotics and should be the authoritative source in this field for years to come.

Internet Sites

512. **Semiotics**. Available: http://carbon.cudenver.edu/~mryder/ itc_data/semiotics.html. (Accessed March 18, 1999).

Martin Ryder, Professor in the School of Education at the University of Colorado at Denver, maintains this Web page. The top of the page provides a main menu, or table of contents, for areas on the site followed by a search engine called HIPPIAS. HIPPIAS searches a limited area of philosophy on the Internet. Below the search engine is the annotated version of the main menu. This concise front end leads to a wealth of information on primers (definitions, histories, frameworks), resources (associations, research centers, journals, book reviews, university programs, other Web sites), conferences, people (of the past and present in the field), and readings. Last updated March 7, 1999.

513. **Voice of the Shuttle: Literary Theory Page**. Available: http:// humanitas.ucsb.edu/shuttle/theory.html. (Accessed: March 18, 1999).

This subpage of the Voice of the Shuttle (VoS) Web page, compiled by Alan Liu in the English Department at California State University in Santa Barbara, is devoted to semiotics. It provides the visitor with an eclectic list of briefly annotated links to external resources as well as internal links to other sections of the VoS (media theory and structuralism). There are links to pages for such well-known theorists as Roman Jakobson, Charles S. Peirce, and Ferdinand de Saussure and links to such resources as other people and groups, dictionaries, periodicals, proceedings, research groups, and calls for papers. Finally, there are links to other "Metapages." Last updated March 15, 1999.

Cumulative Bibliographies

514.   Eimermacher, Karl, and Serge Shishkoff. **Subject Bibliography of Soviet Semiotics: The Moscow-Tartu School**. Ann Arbor: Dept. of Slavic Languages and Literatures, University of Michigan, 1977. 153p. index. (Michigan Slavic publications. Bibliographic Series, 3). LC 77-624121.

Eimermacher and Shishkoff have gathered here the widely scattered anthologies, conference proceedings, Festschriften, and periodicals in which the Moscow and Tartu semioticians publish their works. The main scholars of this School include among others V. V. Ivanov, Ju. M. Lotman, V. M. Toporov, and B. A. Uspenskij. The works of these semioticians have been included as comprehensively as possible. For those scholars whose work preceded the emergence of the School, but nevertheless were important in its development, works about, not by them, are listed. The 2,138 unannotated entries are arranged in eight sections covering semiotics, linguistics, text, literature, non-verbal arts, folklore, culture, and writings on Soviet semiotics and structuralism. In addition there is a useful list of major collections of articles published in the West and a listing by entry number of the works translated into English, French, German, Italian, and Polish. An index of authors completes the work.

515.   Eschbach, Achim. **Zeichen, Text, Bedeutung: Bibliographie zu Theorie und Praxis der Semiotik**. München: Wilhelm Fink, 1974. 508p. index. (Kritische Information, 32). LC 75-561235.

This is an impressive international bibliography on the theory and practice of semiotics. It covers over 10,000 studies from the 19th century up to 1974. Entries are arranged according to a classification system explained in the short introduction. This system does not work very well, though, in providing subject access to entries because it is too general. One section is devoted to individual bibliographies of fifteen scholars foremost in the field such as R. Barthes, U. Eco, C. Morris, C. Peirce, and T. Todorov. However, these personal bibliographies are not comprehensive. Books, dissertations, chapters, and articles from nearly 1,000 periodicals are listed. In the unannotated entries the compiler has abbreviated authors' given names and many journal titles. Equivalents for the latter can be found in the introductory pages. There is an index of author names. Another Eschbach bibliography for 1975-1985 partially continues this one (see next entry).

516.   Eschbach, Achim, and Viktória Eschbach-Szabó. **Bibliography of Semiotics, 1975-1985**. With the collaboration of Gabi Willenberg. Amsterdam/Philadelphia: John Benjamins, 1986. 2v.(948p.) index. (Amsterdam Studies in the Theory and History of Linguistic Science. Series V: Library and Information Sources in Linguistics, Vol. 16; ISSN 0165-7267). LC 86-26830. ISBN 90-272-3739-5(set); 90-272-3740-9(v.1); 90-272-3741-7(v.2).

The 10,839 entries listed here for the 10-year period 1975 to 1985 compared to nearly the same number for Eschbach's prior bibliography covering a much greater time span (see previous entry) illustrates the tremendous growth in this field in recent years. Moreover, this bibliography does not cover at all semiotics in the Soviet Union which the prior bibliography did at least to some extent. The first volume contains, in addition to about half the entries, a numbered list of about

700 periodicals. In the entries the number of a periodical is used in place of its title. Volume 2 contains, in addition to the rest of the entries, an index of reviews and a detailed index of subjects and names. This index provides much better access to the entries than the classification system in Eschbach's previous bibliography. Also, this bibliography provides given names of authors, not just initials. Again there are no annotations.

517.   Koerner, E. F. K. **Contribution au débat post-Saussurien sur le signe linguistique**. The Hague: Mouton, 1972. 103p. (Approaches to Semiotics. Paperback Series, 2). LC 72-88221.

This work consists in part of entries extracted from Koerner's *Bibliographia Saussureana 1870-1970* (see entry 210). An extensive twenty-page introduction by the author discusses Saussure's influence on the development of semiotics. It provides the framework for the bibliography following by citing the entries in it. In addition the majority of entries have short descriptive annotations. They range in date from 1916, the year Saussure's *Cours de linguistique générale* was published, up to 1971.

.

18

Sociolinguistics

For purposes of this chapter, sociolinguistics addresses the influences and effects of a society and its language(s) upon one another and provides linguistic analyses of social and cultural patterns. Sociolinguistics views language as a social institution and correlates differences in linguistic behavior with variables defining social groups such as class, sex, age, and race. Language planning, along with political and education policy studies, is included.

Abstracts and Electronic Databases

518. **Sociological Abstracts**. Vol. 1- . San Diego, CA: Sociological Abstracts, 1952/53- . 6 issues/yr. LC 58-46404. ISSN 0038-0202.

The world literature in sociology and material relevant to sociology from related disciplines in the social and behavioral sciences is covered by this major comprehensive scholarly index. *Sociological Abstracts* (*SA*) covers all aspects of sociolinguistics, including material on the influences and effects of a society and its language(s) upon one another, linguistic analyses of social and cultural patterns, and language planning. It contains in-depth, non-evaluative abstracts of articles from over 2,600 journals and other serials, as well as entries for books, book review citations, association papers, conference reports, and dissertations. Its physical make-up as well as frequency has varied over the years. Since 1980, book abstracts and book reviews have been removed from the main section of an issue and put in a section titled *International Review of Publications in Sociology* (IRPS). This section has its own reviews index, source index, and author index.

Until April 1989, the main issues also had one or more supplements containing abstracts of papers presented at various sociological meetings with indexes covering the main section and supplements (cumulated at the end of the volume year). Now the supplements with the meeting abstracts are issued as a separately bound supplement at the completion of the publication year, in December. This change will undoubtedly help the novice users who have found this index difficult to use because of its multi-part organization and system for numbering the abstracts.

In 1986 producers of this abstracting index began to use a thesaurus for subject indexing, the *Thesaurus of Sociological Indexing Terms* (4th edition, 1996). Use of the Thesaurus is highly recommended for current searching and is absolutely essential for effective retrospective searching not only of the print index, but of the online version and CD-ROM. It has in addition to current indexing terms, "history notes" that tell the user what terms were used prior to 1986. A *User's Reference Manual* (5th edition, 1993) describes indexing and editorial practices, classification procedures, retrieval methods, and other information. *Note Us*, a quarterly newsletter, covers current developments.

SA is available as *sociofile* both online from 1963 (CSA, Dialog, Ovid) and as a CD-ROM from 1974 (EBSCO, NISC, Ovid, SilverPlatter). *SocioAbs*, an abridged version covering only the 250 English-languages journals in *SA*, is also available online (OCLC FirstSearch).

Cumulative Bibliographies

519. Brang, Peter, and Monika Züllig. **Kommentierte Bibliographie zur slavischen Soziolinguistik**. Unter Mitwirkung von Karin Brang. Bern: Peter Lang, 1981. 3v.(1639p.). index. LC 86-103403. ISBN 3-261-04958-8(set).

This bibliography of more than 15,000 entries is the first attempt at a comprehensive survey of Slavic and Slavicist publications dealing with sociolinguistics. The concept of sociolinguistics is broadly interpreted here, listing books and articles (and reviews of these books and articles) on wide-ranging aspects of the interdependence between language and society. Titles have been gathered from the earliest times to the present.

Some entries have brief annotations. Those works with titles in the Cyrillic alphabet have been transliterated. Entries are arranged according to an elaborate classification scheme with 158 subject groups. The first 2 volumes comprise the bibliography itself, while the third volume contains lists and indexes. There are 2 abbreviation lists, one for journals and conferences, the other for words and phrases. There are 2 indexes as well, one for authors, the other for subjects. Except for a few headings which are very broad, the subject index works well. For example, the heading for "culture and language" has over 150 entry numbers listed under it and "national language" has more than several hundred under it.

520. Brann, Conrad B. **Language in Education and Society in Nigeria: A Comparative Bibliography and Research Guide**. Québec: Centre international de recherche sur le bilinguisme/International Center for Research on Bilingualism, 1975. 233p. index. illus. (Publication, B-52). LC 76-353934.

What Brann began as a bibliography on language in education he, recognizing the growing interest in the sociology of language in Nigeria, has expanded to include it as well. Because of the wide parameters of this subject he has of necessity been selective in what he includes. Some of the materials specifically excluded are: works on detailed aspects of descriptive linguistics of the many Nigerian languages, all the individual language-teaching tools, and works on education in Nigeria unless they have a direct bearing on the formulation of language teaching policy or method or give historical depth to a view of education in the country.

In the introduction to the bibliography Brann gives the user a good historical background sketch of the complex language situation in Nigeria. Part I of the bibliography is an alphabetical listing of entries. Most are dated in the two decades prior to publication of this work, but a few go back as far as the 1920s. Part II, an analytical index, is not well-constructed. Index terms are often phrases that contain more than one concept, but only the first concept in the phrase is indexed. For example, the index phrase "Arabic as a language of communication" is only under Arabic with no corresponding entries under "language of communication" or "lingua franca." Parts III, IV, and V are a list of journals, list of collections, and list of conferences, respectively. A number of illustrations accompany the text.

521.   Brann, Conrad B. **Language Policy, Planning and Management in Africa: A Select Bibliography**. Québec: Centre international de recherche sur le bilinguisme/International Center for Research on Bilingualism, 1983. 81p. index. bibliog. (Publication, H-2). ISBN 2-89219-136-X.

There are 667 entries in this bibliography dealing with sub-Saharan Africa and to a lesser extent Northern Africa and the adjacent islands. Most works cited date from the 1960s through the 1970s. Introducing the bibliography is a framework for a thesaurus on language policy, planning, and management in Africa which provides the descriptors (geographical location, main languages, practical or theoretical issues dealt with) and type of publication (articles, essays, reports, conference proceedings, theses/dissertations, reviews) with which entries are annotated. Titles of works in languages other than English are translated and put in parentheses following the original title. Completing this slim paperback volume are indexes of languages and countries. For related materials concerned with Nigeria see entry 520.

522.   Braun, Friederike, Armin Kohz, and Klaus Schubert. **Anredeforschung: kommentierte Bibliographie zur Soziolinguistik der Anrede**. Tübingen: Gunter Narr, 1986. 404p. index. (Ars linguistica, 16). ISBN 3-87808-3661.

More than 1,100 entries on the sociolinguistics of forms (terms) of address are gathered here. It is a wide-ranging compilation of material on this subject, covering research on dozens of languages from books, journal articles, conference proceedings, and dissertations dating back to the beginning of the 1800s. A short introduction gives practical hints for using the bibliography. A user would do well to read this introduction in order to make the best use of the indexes.

The entries are arranged in one alphabetical sequence by author. The usual bibliographic information is given with a minimum of abbreviation. Substantial annotations in German, written and signed by one of the three authors, accompany each work. An index for languages and an index for subjects follow. Preceding the classified index for languages is an alphabetical register of languages indicating where in the following index a language or language variant can be found. The language index lists entries under families, branches, groups, and individual languages. In some cases entries for individual languages are further subdivided according to whether they deal with specific time periods or are diachronic studies. Entries under language subdivisions may in turn be arranged under various subjects. These are the same subject headings as those found in the following subject index. Examples of the subject headings are: kinship terms, title, nominative, Mr./Mrs.-words, vocative, indirect address, forms of courtesy, literature, and theory. These indexes provide excellent access to the bibliography.

523.   Canada. Office of the Commissioner of Official Languages. **Annotated Bibliography of the Official Languages of Canada/Bibliographie analytique des langues officielles au Canada**. Ottawa: Office of the Commissioner of Official Languages, 1991. 53p. index.

The 15 themes under which the 88 items in the bibliography are arranged outline the scope of setting up an official bilingualism program in Canada. A brief introduction and the entries themselves are arranged in columns, French on one side, English on the other. Entries, many of which cite Canadian government publications, are dated from 1960-1989 and nearly all have an abstract. There are author and subject indexes, each in French and English.

524. Edwards, John. **The Irish Language: An Annotated Bibliography of Sociolinguistic Publications, 1772-1982**. New York: Garland, 1983. 274p. index. (Garland Reference Library of the Humanities, Vol. 300). LC 81-43335. ISBN 0-8240-9294-5.

The Irish language, once a widespread vernacular, is now a minority language. Irish government efforts to revive it as a national language have been only marginally successful. The references gathered here do not treat the language per se, but deal with its sociolinguistic aspects. Edwards has interpreted sociolinguistics very broadly, gathering works relating to social, historical, psychological, and educational aspects of Irish, including the decline of the language, efforts to restore it, the relationship of language to nationality and religion, and even studies of important figures in the language movement. Because of such a wide scope this bibliography may be of some use to researchers working with other minority languages.

The main entry section contains 810 annotated entries for books, chapters, pamphlets, and articles, nearly all published in English between 1772 and 1982. Reviews are noted for many of the entries. Providing access to the entries is a subject index which covers not only topics and prominent figures in the language movement, but also collects entries which are parts of series. There is a date index showing the breakdown of entries for five-year periods. The time period yielding the most publications is for 1975-1979; it lists 139 publications. Another index shows a breakdown of entries by the 105 journals in which they were published.

525. Fernández, Mauro, comp. **Diglossia: A Comprehensive Bibliography 1960-1990 and Supplements**. Introduction by W. F. Mackey. Amsterdam: John Benjamins, 1993. 471p. index. (Amsterdam Studies in the Theory and History of Linguistic Science. Series V: Library and Information Sources in Linguistics, Vol. 23; ISSN 0165-7267). LC 93-34754. ISBN 90-272-3749-2.

At last, a comprehensive bibliography on diglossia which brings together a wealth of materials published in a variety of languages with no restrictions on language under study. The index of languages cites nearly 200 languages studied. And though Fernández does not agree with all the broader interpretations of the term "diglossia," he nonetheless included any work which uses the word in some form, as for example, "triglossia," "polyglossia," "schizoglossia," or "dysglossia." Most narrowly, diglossia is concerned with the distinction between a high standard form of a language and a low social variant. A six-page introduction by William Francis Mackey provides a brief history of this increasingly prominent field and discusses its social, political, and psychosocial dimensions around which diglossia and its related notions appear to have patterned themselves.

The more than 2,500 entries—37 pre-1959, 156 from the 1960s, 774 from the 1970s and 1,611 from the 1980s—document the rapid development of the field after Charles Ferguson's seminal article in *Word*, Vol. 15, (1959), pages 325-340 coined the term "diglossia." Fernández culled entries from a long list of indexes, electronic databases, and bibliographies, none of which by itself thoroughly covers this topic. Each entry contains complete bibliographic information as well as references to reprints, translations, and reviews. Except for journal titles, some series, and titles of conference proceedings, almost no abbreviations are employed in the text. Brief one- or two-sentence annotations accompany many citations. Six indexes enhance the bibliography's usefulness: index of languages, diglossia in literature, historically oriented works, pedagogically oriented works, theoretical works, and theses and dissertations.

526. Henley, Nancy, and Barrie Thorne, comps. **She Said/He Said: An Annotated Bibliography of Sex Difference in Language, Speech, and Nonverbal Communication**. 1st Know ed. Pittsburgh, PA: Know, Inc., 1975. pp. 205-311. index. ISBN 0-912786-36-1.

This bibliography was first published by Thorne and Henley in *Language and Sex: Difference and Dominance* (Rowley, MA: Newbury House, 1975). The pagination of the bibliography in that book has been kept in this Know edition. The compilers have brought together materials from a wide variety of sources. There are references from popular magazines such as *Ms.* and *Redbook* as well as from the scholarly literature of linguistics, psychology, sociology, anthropology, and English language studies. Books, articles, and papers are all included. Some of the latter are unpublished and probably difficult to obtain now.

Items are annotated, often with cross-references to other items in the bibliography, and arranged by topic. It includes work not only on language about the sexes in a section on sexist bias in the English language, but also on differences in the way men and women use language, such as differences in word choice, phonology, conversational patterns, language acquisition, and verbal ability. The bulk of the references are dated since the late 1960s when the women's liberation movement was in full swing. Completing the book is an author index and a list of the main and most active women's groups in disciplines related to the study of sex differences in language, speech, and nonverbal communication.

527. Key, Mary Ritchie. **Male/Female Language: With a Comprehensive Bibliography**. 2nd ed. 323p. Lanham, MD: Scarecrow Press, 1996. LC 95-36089. ISBN 0-8108-3083-3.

Key's bibliography on male/female language (pp. 181-307) is essentially a selective updating of a comprehensive bibliography published in 1975. She has added numerous items published in popular and news magazines as well as entries treating the problems of legal terminology, an area recently receiving attention in the literature. She centers the bibliography in linguistics, but includes related literature dealing with nonverbal, literary features of language, and sociolinguistics issues as well as more general works showing changing perspectives of males and females. Entries are arranged alphabetically and except for the notation of "review" are unannotated. Most references are to material published in English with a smattering of titles published in Western European languages.

528. Pietrzyk, Alfred, ed. **Selected Titles in Sociolinguistics: An Annotated Preliminary Bibliography of Works on Multilingualism, Language Standardization, and Languages of Wider Communication**. Washington, DC: Center for Applied Linguistics, 1964. 192p. index.

529. Pietrzyk, Alfred, ed. **Selected Titles in Sociolinguistics: An Interim Bibliography of Works on Multilingualism, Language Standardization, and Languages of Wider Communication**. 2nd distribution. Washington, DC: Center for Applied Linguistics, 1967. 226p. index. ED 011120.

Both the preliminary and the following interim versions of this bibliography have a brief introductory section listing bibliographies and reference materials for general aspects of the social sciences and the field of linguistics. They also have a short section on overall aspects of language in society. In both, the main bibliography itself has 700 entries with descriptive annotations. The second distribution provides some minor corrections and also has an addendum of items for 1964-1966. Most studies in both distributions are in English with a few in French, German, and other languages.

530.   Pogarell, Reiner. **Minority Languages in Europe: A Classified Bibliography**. Berlin: Mouton, 1983. 208p. index. LC 83-19421.

Renewed interest in European linguistic minorities which began in the late 1960s resulted in an increase of publications on this subject in the areas of linguistics, sociology, ethnology, politics, law, and education. The author has selected the most important of these works for inclusion. The bulk of the research gathered here is from North America and Western Europe with some representation from Eastern Europe. The title of this book indicates a classified arrangement to the bibliography, whereas, in fact, the 2,400-plus numbered entries are arranged in alphabetical order according to main entry. There is, though, a very useful two-part index of keywords in English (with German and French equivalents in parentheses). In one part keywords of all languages, countries, and regions relevant to the theme are listed with the numbers of the corresponding titles. In the second part there are about 40 keywords representing areas of specific interest to linguistics such as: bilingualism, dialect, interference, language planning, speech islands, trade language, and so on.

531.   Price, Glanville. **The Present Position of Minority Languages in Western Europe: A Selective Bibliography**. Cardiff, Wales: University of Wales Press, 1969. 81p. index. LC 75-471422. ISBN 0900768339.

The minority languages covered here are: Basque, Breton, Catalan, Faroese, Frisian, Irish, Manx, Occitan, Romansh, Sardinian, Scots, Scottish Gaelic, and Welsh. The author has gathered here about 400 entries, some briefly annotated, for works concerned specifically with the present state of the languages in question. They cover such topics as the number of speakers, geographical distribution of the languages, the quantitative and qualitative decline of the languages, their official status, their use, the problem of the creation of standard literary languages, and present standing as literary media. The bulk of the entries, organized by language, are for monographs and journal articles in English, French, German, Italian, and Spanish. There is an index of authors.

532.   Regu, K. **Language Planning: A Select Bibliography**. Kerala, India: Dravidian Linguistics Association, 1988. 64p. (DLA Publication Series, 44).

India with its multiplicity of languages and ethnic groups is a rich source of research on all aspects of sociolinguistics. This particular bibliography with just over 500 entries concentrates on language planning alone and on materials published in English around the world. Entries are arranged alphabetically by author/main entry and have no annotations. Because of its narrow scope and small size, lack of an index is a relatively minor inconvenience to the user.

533. Rubin, Joan, and Bjorn H. Jernudd. **References for Students of Language Planning**. With the assistance of Merle Stetser and Christine Bouamalay. Honolulu, HI: East-West Culture Learning Institute, East-West Center; distr., University Press of Hawaii, 1979. 126p. LC 79-17656. ISBN 0-8248-0686-7.

Over 300 references to studies on language planning are listed here. Good descriptive annotations are provided for all entries except bibliographies and case studies. Included are books, articles, conference proceedings, government studies, reports, dissertations, and even some mimeographed materials. Nearly all are in English, though French, German, Swedish, Czech, and other languages are represented. Some of the references date back to the prior century, but the majority were written in the several decades preceding publication of the bibliography. References are organized under 14 section headings. The headings are grouped around five basic divisions: theory, planning the language corpus, allocating language use, implementation, and examples. Additionally there are sections on language planning bibliographies and planning in general which may be useful to some users. Two fields related to language planning have been deliberately omitted. These are literacy and translation. The authors in all sections along with titles and page numbers are gathered in one alphabetical list. Also provided is a brief list of addresses for government entities and foundations which issued material listed in the bibliography.

534. Sabourin, Conrad F., and Rolande M. Lamarche. **La francité canadienne. Volume 1. Aspects linguistiques: Bibliographie**. Montréal: Université de Montréal, Faculté des sciences de l'éducation, 1985. 395p. index. ISBN 2-920826-00-X.

535. Sabourin, Conrad F., Rolande M. Lamarche, and Elca Tarrab. **La francité canadienne. Volume 2. Sociologie et politicologie de la langue**. Montréal: Université de Montréal, Faculté des sciences de l'éducation, 1987. 460p. index. ISBN 2-920298-51-8.

This 2-volume set on linguistic, social, and political aspects of Canadian French builds on a number of earlier bibliographies including Sabourin and Lamarche's *Le français québécois: bibliographie analytique* (Montréal: Service des publications, Office de la langue française, 1979) and Gaston Dulong's *Bibliographie linguistique de Canada français* (Québec: Presses de l'Université Laval, 1966). Each volume has more than 3,200 entries for books, journal articles, theses, and government reports. Entries are arranged alphabetically by main entry. There are no annotations but each has a serviceable subject index. Unlike many books published in Canada which contain explanatory materials in both French and English, the preface and indexes are in French only.

536. Sabourin, Conrad, and Normand Petit. **Langues et sociétés: bibliographie analytique**. Éd. 1978. Montréal: Service des publications, Office de la langue française, 1979. 583p. index. LC 80-113509. ISBN 2-551-03303-9.

Research from around the world written in a variety of languages is recorded in this bibliography of 5,063 items. It encompasses works on many aspects of language and society such as sociolinguistics, language planning, politics of linguistics, law and jurisprudence in linguistic matters, linguistic demography, ethnolinguistics, and multilingualism.

Books, articles, documents, and dissertations from the mid-1950s through 1978 are arranged alphabetically by author. There are no annotations, but a detailed subject index follows. The descriptors used in the subject index are divided into five categories: areas of research (e.g., anthropology, economics, education, philosophy, psycholinguistics, sociology); different social groups (such as adolescents, children, immigrants, religious groups, and blacks); languages; regions (countries as well as large geographic areas); and nearly 40 other descriptors (such as attitudes, bilingualism, culture, diglossia, interference, national/official language, linguistic legislation, mass media, and social variation). Entries are indexed under a coordination of two descriptors. For example, a researcher investigating aspects of bilingualism in some country would look for the country name under bilingualism, or could begin by going to the country name first and check under that for the term bilingualism. Items are indexed under as many topics as appropriate. This is an excellent bibliography and the index provides good subject access.

537. Silberstein, Sandra. **Bibliography: Women and Language**. Ann Arbor, MI: Women's Studies Program, University of Michigan, 1979. 67p. (Michigan Occasional Paper, No. 12).

Silberstein's bibliography builds on and complements two other bibliographies in particular, one by Henley and Thorne (see entry 526), the other by Mary Ritchie Key in *Male/Female Language* (Metuchen, NJ: Scarecrow Press, 1975); the latter now in a new 1996 edition (see entry 527). It brings together most work written in English on women and language through the summer of 1979. Unannotated entries are arranged under some 20 main topic headings selected as representative current trends in the literature. When relevant, items are listed under more than one topic. References are to published books and articles as well as to unpublished papers, speeches, dissertations, and theses.

538. Simon, Gerd, Hrsg. **Bibliographie zur Soziolinguistik**. Tübingen: Max Niemeyer, 1974. 179p. (Bibliographische Arbeitsmaterialien, 2). LC 74-339113. ISBN 3-484-60038-1.

Almost 3,000 entries gathered by eighteen contributors are listed in this classified bibliography on sociolinguistics. Nearly all references are to works written in German and English. In addition to a general section (bibliographies, abstracts, collections, and introductory and research reports), other sections cover the following topics: political/economic, social/historic, and scientific/theoretical aspects; theoretical and empirical works on analysis and interpretation of class specific language differences; investigations of differences in speech usage of lower class social groups, subcultures and ethnic groups; investigations of age and sex in use of class specific speech variables; sociolinguistic aspects of language changes, language norms, and language planning; and, finally, investigations of effects of prejudice on speech. Although listings in the main bibliography have no annotations themselves, about one-third have references to annotations in other publications such as indexes. An appendix has abstracts for a few references. In addition it contains a short supplement.

There are several drawbacks to this bibliography. First, some citations are incomplete; others are simply inaccurate. Second, it lacks an author and subject index. The latter would be useful despite its classified arrangement.

539. **Studies on Gay & Lesbian Language: A Partial Bibliography**. Available: http://www.ling.nwu.edu/~ward/gaybib.html. (Accessed: March 18, 1999).

Gregory Ward, a Professor in the Department of Linguistics at Northwestern University, maintains this Internet bibliography-in-progress on gay and lesbian language. The 500 or so items include articles, chapters, books, theses, and conference and symposium papers. A few items have brief annotations provided by contributors. Some have links to additional information such as dictionaries, full-text, or reviews; or the e-mail or home page address of the author.

540. Verdoodt, Albert. **Bibliographie sur le problème linguistique belge**. Québec: Centre international de recherche sur le bilinguisme/International Center for Research on Bilingualism in Quebec, 1983. 224p. (Publication, B-121). LC 84-146471. ISBN 2-89219-124-6.

In Belgium the historic division between the Dutch-speaking Flemings of the north and the French-speaking Walloons of the south became a burning issue early in the 1960s. Both groups wanted some form of federal state with autonomous Flemish and Walloon regions. The result was a shift of many thousands of Belgians across a language frontier drawn between the two regions in 1963. This bibliography covers the literature of that time period extensively. Earlier and later materials (up to 1980) are less extensively covered. These are all arranged under one or more of 46 topics. A list of these topics, in both English and French, precedes the 3,331 unannotated entries. Many different aspects of the linguistic problem in Belgium are covered under such topic headings as bilingualism, church, cultural problems, economic problem, Flemish movement, history, pedagogical problems, separation, Walloon movement, and so on. Other topic headings are for cities and provinces. The works cited are mainly in Dutch and French though a few are in English.

Internet Sites

541. **American Sociological Association**. Available: http://www.asanet. org/. (Accessed: March 18, 1999).

The ASA founded in 1905, now with over 13,000 members, maintains this searchable Web site. The Society is dedicated to advancing sociology as a scientific discipline and profession serving the public good. The home page provides links to membership and meeting information, news (last posted March 16, 1999), details about its publications, academic and teaching resources, and opportunity links (grants, research support, data resources, employment).

542. **Sociology Internet Resources**. Available: http://www.wcsu.edu/ socialsci/socres.html. (Accessed: March 18, 1999).

Professor Jerry Bannister in the Social Sciences Department at Western Connecticut State University maintains this award-winning, searchable Web site for sociology. The home page is linked to 14 such topics as culture and society, ethnicity, women, family, general, research, and theory. The "culture & society" link takes a visitor to an eclectic, randomly organized and minimally annotated list of anthropology, communication, cultural, and sociology Internet sites.

543. **SocioSite—Going Dutch Sociology**. Available: http://www.pscw. uva.nl/sociosite/index.html. (Accessed March 18, 1999).

SocioSite is a collaborative project with a network of correspondents and editors, but based in the Department of Sociology at the University of Amsterdam under the direction of Albert Benschop. It is international in scope and aims to become an accurate, comprehensive information system for sociologists around the world covering all areas of sociology. The home page has 24 links to the usual types of information and resources, among which are research centers, associations, newsgroups, mailing lists, and data archives. One link is for "subject areas." If a visitor follows this link, they will find more than 150 links to subject areas within and allied to sociology including culture, communication, language and other areas of interest to sociolinguistics. Last updated March 1, 1999.

544. **WWW Virtual Library: Sociology**. Available: http://www.mcmaster. ca/socscidocs/w3virtsoclib/index.htm. (Accessed: March 18, 1999).

This subpage of the WWW Virtual Library last updated March 11, 1999 is now maintained by Dr. Carl Cuneo, Department of Sociology, McMaster University, Hamilton, Ontario. It has twelve main links on its home page, such as "Discussions: Newsgroups, Listservs, Chats, IRCs," "Research Centres," "Electronic Journals & Newsletters," "Theories," and "Related Fields." The latter link provides access to Web sites in allied areas as well as sub-fields of sociology itself.

Directories and Handbooks

545. Domínguez, Francesc, and Núria López. **Sociolinguistic and Language Planning Organizations**. Amsterdam: John Benjamins, 1995. 530p. index. illus. bibliog. maps. (Language International World Directory, Vol. 1; ISSN 1383-7591). LC 95-23742. ISBN 90-272-1951-6.

In this directory the authors cover organizations dedicated to sociolinguistics, language planning, and language promotion in general. They do not include organizations involved solely with translation, administration, or language teaching. However, they do list institutions conducting research into language teaching and though not listing university departments per se, do include university centers or institutes with research projects. The directory thus updates and expands Joan Rubin's 1979 *Directory of Language Planning Organizations* (Honolulu: East-West Center, 1979).

Section I covers 113 international and multi-country organizations while Section II lists another 509 national organizations (local, provincial, regional and/or state scope) arranged by country, 121 in all, from Afghanistan to Zaire. The authors gathered by means of a questionnaire sent to each organization such information as: official name, address (including telephone, fax, telex, and e-mail), name in English, heads, consulting and opening hours, communications, type of organization, founding date, staff, volunteers, languages planned, geographical coverage, objectives, services provided/activities, publications, works in progress, and future projects. The few organizations not returning their questionnaires are generally listed with just name and address.

Following the two language organizations sections is a "Languages Synopsis" section describing the languages and varieties planned by these institutions and covering such aspects as genetic affiliation, language domain, number of speakers, official status, and a brief sociolinguistic history. Eighteen black and white maps showing language distributions follow. In addition there is a bibliography of sources consulted by the authors and a number of indexes, one of official names and acronyms of organizations, another for languages, and a third for countries. So that they may periodically update the directory, the authors include both a languages synopsis update questionnaire and an organization questionnaire with a request for readers to send them updates of information.

546. Horvath, Barbara M., and Paul Vaughan. **Community Languages: A Handbook**. Clevedon, Avon, England: Multilingual Matters, 1991. 276p. bibliog. (Multilingual Matters, 67). ISBN 1-85359-091-6.

The information on 68 languages in this handbook is meant to assist policymakers and others such as employers, educators, and the media who deal with foreign language communities in English-speaking countries. While not all languages are represented, the authors have attempted to include those that represent the majority of peoples involved in migration movements this century. Chapters are alphabetically arranged by language from Albanian to Yiddish. The information given for each language varies, but profiles usually include basic affiliation and such characteristics as standardization, functional distribution, historical development, the relationship to other languages and variants, and the social evaluation of the language by the speech community and others. A short list of references concludes each language profile.

547. Kloss, Heinz, and Grant D. McConnell, general eds. **The Written Languages of the World: A Survey of the Degree and Modes of Use/Les langues écrites du monde: Relevé du degré et des modes d'utilisation**. International Center for Research on Bilingualism/Centre international de recherche sur le bilinguisme. Québec: Les Presses de l'Université Laval, 1978-98. illus. 5 v. in 8. (Travaux du Centre international de recherche sur le bilinguisme/Publications of the International Center for Research on Bilingualism, E-2). (In progress).

548. **Volume 1. The Americas/Les Amériques**. 1978. 633p. index. ISBN 0-7746-6856-3.

549. **Volume 2. India/Inde. Book/Tome 1: Constitutional Languages/Langues constitutionnelles. Book/Tome 2: Non-constitutional Languages/Langues non constitutionnelles**. Authors/Auteurs: B. P. Mahapatra, P. Padmanabha, G. D. McConnell, and V. S. Verma. 1989. 2v. 1360p. index. ISBN 2-7637-7186-6 (v. 2, bk. 1); 2-7637-7196-3 (v. 2, bk. 2).

550. **Volume 3. Europe Occidentale: Les langues régionales et minoritaires des pays membres du Conseil de l'Europe/Western Europe: Regional and Minority Languages of Member Countries of the Council of Europe**. Directeur du volume/Volume editor: Albert Verdoodt. 1989. 647p. index ISBN 2-7637-7222-6.

551. **Volume 4. China/Chine. Book/Tome 1: Written Languages/Langues écrites. Book/Tome 2: Unwritten Languages/Langues écrites**. Institute of Nationality Studies, Beijing and/et International Center for Research on Language Planning/Centre international de recherche en

aménagement linguistique. Authors/Auteurs: Tan Kergang and Grant D. McConnell. 1995. 2v. 1409p. index. ISBN 2-7637-7433-4 (v. 4, bk. 1); 2-7637-7434-2 (v. 4, bk. 2).

552.   **Volume 5. Afrique Occidentale/West Africa. Tome 1/Book 1 and Tome 2/Book 2**. Centre international de recherche en aménagement linguistique/International Center for Research on Language Planning et/and Conseil international de recherche et d'étude en linguistique fondamentale et appliquée (CIRELFA. Sainte-Foy: Les Presses de l'Université Laval, 1998. 2v. 1099p. index. ISBN 2-7637-7567-5 (v. 5, bk. 1); 2-7637-7568-3 (v.5, bk. 2).

With volume 4, McConnell becomes the sole general editor of this work in progress. Its aim is to present a worldwide sociolinguistic outline of language usage. The editors have tried to include all living languages which are alphabetized; by alphabetized they mean the language has been used in printed writings addressed to the speakers of the languages themselves, thus excluding oral traditions written down by anthropologists and such. All volumes, including prefatory material and indexes, are written in both English and French. The organization and layout of each volume differ somewhat, but all provide a vitality rating for each of the languages investigated. The basis of the vitality calculation is functional use (agents, place, time) in eight domains: schools, religion, mass media, sales and services, justice, administration, manufacturing industries, and socio-political. The more functions used in more domains and on more levels within a domain, the higher the vitality rating of each language. In a nutshell, a language's vitality is its capacity to survive. Information was gathered by means of a questionnaire sent out to various experts and specialists, followed up by letters. The data gathered is presented in tables organized first by country, then by language. Each part of the world surveyed presented its own unique set of problems in gathering the data for the survey which are detailed in the volume introductions.

Part 3
LANGUAGES

19

General and Multi-Language

Manuals, Handbooks, and Encyclopedias

553.   **ALA-LC Romanization Tables: Transliteration Schemes for Non-Roman Scripts**. Approved by the Library of Congress and the American Library Association. Tables compiled and edited by Randall K. Barry. Washington, DC: Cataloging Distribution Service, Library of Congress, 1997. 239p. index. illus. LC 97-012740. ISBN 0-8444-0940-5.

The 1997 edition of this work contains 54 romanization and transliteration tables for more than 150 languages written in various non-Roman scripts. These romanization schemes have been developed over the years by foreign language specialists at the Library of Congress, often in collaboration with other scholars and experts, to support the cataloging of foreign language materials. Development of new romanization schemes for which none exists and revision of existing ones is an ongoing process. Arrangement of the tables is alphabetical by language. Since some tables apply to more than one language, a language index is furnished so the user can locate the pertinent scheme. In addition to the transliteration proper, other relevant information such as characteristics of capitalization and word division may be included as well as a listing of special characters and character modifiers that are used with it. The listings from all the tables are gathered together in one table at the back that shows the graphic, provides the hexadecimal code (used for encoding the characters in USMARC records), and gives the name. Here one can find the name for such special characters as the uppercase Icelandic thorn, lowercase u-hook, and eth; such graphics as the opening curly brace, phono copyright mark, and sharp; and such diacritical marks as the grave, cedilla, breve, and hacek.

554.   Allen, Charles Geoffry. **A Manual of European Languages for Librarians**. 2d impression (with minor corrections). London and New York: Bowker in association with the London School of Economics, 1977. 803p. LC 73-6062. ISBN 0-85935-028-2.

In this manual the author treats 38 languages arranged in 7 language groupings. These are: Germanic; Latin and Romance; Celtic, Greek, and Albanian; Slavonic; Baltic; Finno-Ugrian; and other languages. The examples and data provided are mainly for the aid of librarians who must deal with books in languages they do not know. After providing a specimen of the language and its translation into English, the author generally arranges other information about the language according to an outline that covers general characteristics, bibliolinguistics, alphabet (with transliteration of non-Roman alphabets given), phonetics, spelling, parts of speech, numerals, and word formation. Though the grammatical notes are limited, anyone dealing with, or just curious about, unfamiliar languages would find this a useful, practical aid.

555.   Campbell, George L. **Compendium of the World's Languages**. London: Routledge, 1991. 2v. 1574p. index. illus. bibliog. LC 90-35827. ISBN 0-415-06978-5 (v.1); 0-415-06979-3 (v.2); 0-415-02937-6 (set).

The purpose of Campbell's comparative compendium is to give a brief account in English of how certain languages actually work. A standardized format is used to facilitate easy comparison between languages. In articles for some 300 languages and 40 language families he provides an introduction (background and historical information, affiliation, location and number of speakers, dialects, literature notes), script (if other than Roman, description and display in a chart at the end of volume 2 which contains charts for 48 scripts; see entry 557 for an expansion and revision of these script charts), phonology (inventories given in International Phonetic Alphabet notation wherever possible), morphology and syntax (main sub-headings are article, noun, adjective, pronoun, numerals, verb, pre/postpositions, word order), and illustrative text (when available St. John's Gospel, chapter 1, verses 1 to 8 used). The technique of using a Bible passage or sample text is reminiscent of Nida and Katzner's works (see entries 583 and 576) which are geared more to the student or layperson. A similar scholarly, authoritative work is Comrie's treatment of the world's major languages (see entry 561) which, though covering fewer languages, covers each in greater depth and conveniently provides the reader with references at the end of each article. Campbell on the other hand less conveniently collects sources used in one A-Z bibliography found at the end of volume 2. A user is advised to consult the list of languages at the beginning of volume 1 as it provides many "see" references not found elsewhere and sorts out potentially confusing entries ("Old Irish" is entered under "Irish, Old"; under "Old English" you are directed to see just "English"; and "Old Church Slavonic" is a valid entry); it also sets out the various headings under which a substantial number of individual languages are grouped, for example, "North American Indian Isolates" and "Pidgins and Creoles."

556.   Campbell, George L. **Concise Compendium of the World's Languages**. London: Routledge, 1995. 670p. illus. bibliog. ISBN 0-415-11392-X.

Only about 100 languages are covered in Campbell's concise compendium compared to his original 2-volume compendium containing information on more than 300 languages (see entry 555 above for purpose and type of information provided, both of which remain the same). But, while fewer languages are covered here, many of the articles for languages which are covered are substantially expanded. Entries were largely selected for inclusion based on number of speakers (most spoken by at least 5-10 million people) and socio-political interest and importance (thus some minor languages of political or topical relevance are included). While space limitations precluded having a representative language from each language family, the author found space for 4 minor languages: Navajo, Lappish, Nam, and Nivkh. Dead languages, with the exceptions Classical Chinese and Sanskrit, are excluded. An appendix of scripts, though considerably reduced in size, is retained in the concise compendium, as is a pared down cumulative bibliography now helpfully divided into collective works and individual languages.

557. Campbell, George L. **Handbook of Scripts and Alphabets**. London: Routledge, 1997. 132p. illus. bibliog. LC 96-5765. ISBN 0-415-13715-2.

The 40 script tables in this handbook are, with some revisions and one addition, the same as they originally appeared in the appendix of Campbell's *Compendium of the World's Languages* (see entry 555). The one addition is the script table and commentary for Epigraphic South Arabian. Without the articles in the *Compendium* describing the languages which now use, or once used, these scripts, there is scarcely enough detail in the brief text accompanying the tables to appeal to the beginning student let alone the serious researcher. For transliteration purposes alone, a user would be better served by the *ALA-LC Romanization Tables* (see entry 553).

558. Comrie, Bernard, ed. **The Major Languages of East and South-East Asia**. London: Routledge, 1990. 234p. index. illus. bibliog. maps. ISBN 0-415-04739-0.

The text of this handbook is reprinted from the author's earlier work, *The World's Major Languages* (see entry 561) with the original preface and introduction tailored to the contents of this volume. There are nine chapters on Tai languages, Vietnamese, Sino-Tibetan languages, Japanese, Korean, and Austronesian languages. See entry 561 for a description of chapter contents and index.

559. Comrie, Bernard, ed. **The Major Languages of Eastern Europe**. London: Routledge, 1990. 255p. index. illus. bibliog. maps. ISBN 0-415-0571-X.

The text of this handbook is reprinted from the author's earlier work, *The World's Major Languages* (see entry 561) with the original preface and introduction tailored to the contents of this volume. There are 11 chapters on Indo-European languages (with individual chapters on Slavonic, Russian, Polish, Czech and Slovak, Serbo-Croat, and Greek), Uralic languages (with individual chapters on Hungarian and Finnish), and a single chapter on Turkish and the Turkic languages. See entry 561 for a description of chapter contents and index.

560. Comrie, Bernard, ed. **The Major Languages of South Asia, the Middle East and Africa**. London: Routledge, 1990. 315p. index. illus. bibliog. maps. ISBN 0-415-05772-8.

The text of this handbook is reprinted from the author's earlier work, *The World's Major Languages* (see entry 561) with the original preface and introduction tailored to the contents of this volume. There are 16 chapters on Indo-Aryan languages, Iranian languages, Afroasiatic languages, Tamil and the Dravidian languages, and the Niger-Kordofanian languages. See entry 561 for a description of chapter contents and index.

561. Comrie, Bernard, ed. **The World's Major Languages**. New York: Oxford University Press, 1987. 1025p. index. illus. bibliog. maps. LC 86-12795. ISBN 0-19-520521-9.

Some 44 internationally-renowned experts made contributions to this scholarly, authoritative work. Each of the 50 chapters, devoted to a language family or language, was written by an expert. The emphasis, given the expected readership of this guide, is on Indo-European languages with about half the chapters covering languages of this family. Chapters contain extensive descriptions of the phonological and graphic systems, morphology, word-formation, syntactic patterns, and characteristic features of the lexicon as well as social and historical background. In addition, different and unusual aspects of a language are often highlighted. The result is not only informative, but makes for interesting reading. For example, the chapter on Arabic discusses diglossia, a relatively rare linguistic phenomena; the chapter on Japanese contains a detailed discussion of the grammatical construction involving the particle "wa," an important and unique aspect of its grammar; and the chapter on Danish, Norwegian, and Swedish provides considerable detail on the mutual intelligibility that exists between these mainland Scandinavian languages. Most chapters have references and a bibliography of grammars, surveys, and histories. Figures, maps, tables, and examples are liberally used to illustrate the text. A well-constructed index concludes this handbook.

562. Coulmas, Florian. **The Blackwell Encyclopedia of Writing Systems**. Oxford: Blackwell, 1996. 603p. illus. bibliog. LC 94-47460. ISBN 0-631-19446-0.

Over 400 writing systems, scripts, and orthographies of the world's major languages, both past and present, are concisely described and wonderfully illustrated in this encyclopedia. In addition to the writing systems and their histories, the alphabetically arranged entries deal with technical aspects of writing such as handwriting, printing, and word processing; practical problems of decipherment, alphabet making, and spelling reform; and theoretical issues including distinguishing writing from pre-writing and other notation systems, typology of writing systems, and functions of writing. Length of entries varies from short explanations of terms and concepts to longer, almost essay-length explanations when dealing with theoretical issues or describing individual writing systems. High quality black and white tables and figures dot nearly every page. Keys to the tables and figures enable the user to readily locate the illustration for a particular alphabet or specimen. Coulmas, himself a sociolinguist with an international reputation, acknowledges the assistance of numerous other specialists in putting together this scholarly, authoritative work. Nearly every entry is followed by one or more recommendations for further in-depth research; these references are compiled in a bibliography of some 600 titles at the end of the book.

563. Crothers, John H., James P. Lorentz, Donald A. Sherman, and Marilyn M. Vihman, comps. and eds. **Handbook of Phonological Data from a Sample of the World's Languages: A Report of the Stanford Phonology Archive**. Stanford, CA: Department of Linguistics, Stanford University, 1979. 2v. (Reproduced from typewritten copy).

Volume 1 contains the phonetic inventories, volume 2 the indexes for the Stanford Phonology Archives. See entry 590 for the introductory volume and an explanation of the project.

564. Daniels, Peter T., and William Bright, eds. **The World's Writing Systems**. New York: Oxford University Press, 1996. 920p. index. illus. LC 95-2247. ISBN 0-19-507993-0.

Daniels and Bright, assisted by some 75 other scholars, have compiled a comprehensive work on the world's major scripts, both past and present, that endeavors not only to provide a historical sketch and the table of signforms in their standard order along with their variations, but to describe how the scripts actually work, i.e., how the sounds of the language are represented in writing. Each script is illustrated with a brief text in the language(s) it is used for and provided with the standard transliteration scheme for representing it in a Roman alphabet. Since Roman letters and associated marks can vary in meanings, the transliteration scheme itself is then transcribed using the symbols of the 1989 revision of the International Phonetic Alphabet which can be found in its entirety on the endpapers. In addition the sample text is accompanied by a literal translation as well as a free translation. The 74 articles, each written by one of the contributing experts and arranged in 13 parts, chronicle the history of scripts from their beginning in Mesopotamia and Egypt to modern times. Part 12 is devoted to secondary notation systems such as shorthand, music notation, and movement notation. The final part on imprinting and printing even has a section on analog and digital writing. The liberally illustrated articles are accompanied by bibliographies. The index partially compensates for lack of a key to the many tables and figures.

565.   Décsy, Gyula, comp. **Statistical Report on the Languages of the World as of 1985**. For the Transworld Linguistic Association. Bloomington, IN: Eurolingua, 1986-88. 5v. (Bibliotheca Nostratica, Vol.6/1-6/5; ISSN 0342-4871).

566.   **Part I. List of the Languages of the World in Decreasing Order of the Speaker Numbers with Phyletic and Geographic Identifications**. 1986. 136p. ISBN 0-931922-24-0.

567.   **Part II. List of the Languages of the World Arranged According to Linguistic Phyla with Speaker Number Data**. 1986. 112p. ISBN 0-931922-27-5.

568.   **Part III. List of the Languages of the World Arranged According to Continents and Countries**. 1988. 224p. ISBN 0-931922-31-3.

569.   **Part IV. Alphabetical Index of the Languages of the World Arranged According to Continents**. 1988. 200p. ISBN 0-931922-32-1.

570.   **Part V. Cumulative Alphabetical Index of the Languages of the World**. 1988. 198p. ISBN 0-931922-35-6.

In this statistical report Décsy provides information on number of speakers of languages of the world as of 1985. The subtitles of the parts describe how the data are organized. For most of the more widely spoken languages the compiler took the data (with some reassessment) from official publications of statistical agencies with international scope. Speaker number data for the less widely spoken languages is based, again with some reassessment, on three sources: Voegelin and Voegelin (1977), Ruhlen (1975), and the 8th edition of Grimes (1974) (see entries 591, 587, and 572 for these works or later editions). The author does not intend this statistical report to replace these three sources, but instead to provide a more easily accessible source of data concerning the social status and geographic spread of the languages of the world. According to this report, there are, as of 1985, about 2,800 genuine (unblended) languages in the world spoken by 4,845 million people. The introduction provides a thorough discussion of some of the problems inherent in such a compilation as this and should be read in order to interpret the figures given. In addition to speaker data, Part I contains useful lists of co-languages, blends (pidgins, Creoles, etc.), artificial languages, and extinct languages of the Old and New World.

571.   Gilyarevskii, Rudzhero Sergeevich, and Vladimir Sergeevich Grivnin. **Languages Identification Guide**. Translated from the Russian by Lev Navrozov. Moscow: Nauka, Central Dept. of Oriental Literature, 1970. 343p. index. illus. LC 74-165080.

The Russian title of this work is *Opredelitel' yazykov mira po pis'mennostyam*. For identifying unknown scripts this guide is probably the best source available. More than 200 languages are covered. The languages are grouped in three parts: languages of the nations of the Soviet Union, languages of the nations of other countries, and international artificial languages. The second part, languages of the nations of other countries, is divided into the geographic areas of Asia and Oceania, Africa, and America. Such groupings do not always work well since some languages are widespread. English, for example, is included in the section on Europe although widely used in America and Oceania (Australia). An alphabetical index of languages, however, readily locates any language by name.

For each language a text sample and alphabet are given. If more than one alphabet is widely used, then all of them are shown. Explanatory notes include additional letters and diacritic signs as well as graphic peculiarities and distinctive characteristics. Other information generally includes the region where used, number of people using it, and its place in the genetic classification of languages. The introduction helpfully lists procedures to use in identifying an unknown script. Some of these procedures make use of the numerous tables, indexes, and lists which complete this excellent reference work. Among them are: types of scripts and languages using them, lists of additional letters for Russian and Latin script languages, languages with characteristic letter combinations and auxiliary words, figures of some eastern languages, geographic distribution of languages, and a genealogical classification of languages.

572.   Grimes, Barbara F., ed. **Ethnologue: Languages of the World**. Consulting editors, Richard S. Pittman and Joseph E. Grimes. 13th ed. Dallas, TX: Summer Institute of Linguistics, 1996. 966p. index. illus. bibliog. maps. ISBN 1-55671-026-7. Available: http://www.sil.org/ethnologue/. (Accessed October 11, 1998).

573.   Grimes, Barbara F. **Ethnologue Language Name Index to the Thirteenth Edition of the Ethnologue**. Dallas, TX: Summer Institute of Linguistics, 1996. 288p. 1-55671-027-5. Available: http://www.sil.org/ethnologue/names/. (Accessed October 11, 1998).

574.   Grimes, Joseph E., and Barbara F. Grimes. **Ethnologue Language Family Index to the Thirteenth Edition of the Ethnologue**. Dallas, TX: Summer Institute of Linguistics, 1996. 125p. bibliog. LC 93-86784. ISBN 1-55671-028-3.

Available: http://www.sil.org/ethnologue/families/. (Accessed October 11, 1998).

The 13th edition of this standard reference work "tries to bring together the best information available on the languages of the world" (p.vii) and thus should be useful to linguists, educators, translators, anthropologists, and others. *Ethnologue* is easy to use and read despite the use of abbreviations, or maybe because of them. It also makes good use of different typefaces and bolding. Languages, or probable languages, are listed alphabetically under countries which themselves are organized by five geographical areas—the Americas, Africa, Europe, Asia, and the Pacific. Variants or dialects of a language may be listed under the language and not treated separately. The following information in abbreviated form is provided for each language: its alternate names, number of speakers, location, dialects, linguistic affiliation, availability of word lists, multilingualism of speakers, Bible translation status, and, if known, other demographic and sociolinguistic information. Each language is assigned a unique 3-letter identification code which is the same in all countries in which that language is spoken. This code, in brackets, follows the alternate names in an entry. Other codes indicate the accuracy of data. At the beginning of each country section there is a list of the major sources of information, all of which are consolidated in a bibliography at the end, plus such data as population, literacy rate, number of languages (living, second, extinct), and number of speakers. In the United States alone there are 213 languages, of which 176 are living languages, 2 are second languages without mother tongue speakers, and 35 are extinct. There is an alphabetical index of countries as well as indexes for the more than 100 black and white maps of continents and countries. Continental maps just show where countries are located while the country maps show the areas within a country where a particular language is spoken. Maps are clear and easy to read. A separate table lists languages of special interest and the country under which the user will find more information; these are the gypsy languages, Jewish languages, pidgin and Creole languages, and deaf sign languages. Four questionnaires are appended which readers may use to submit corrections and additions to the editor. The editor plans a new edition approximately every four years.

The main volume is accompanied by two computer-generated indexes. The genetic classification used in the first index to language families is based largely on Bright's *International Encyclopedia of Linguistics* (see entry 13). Language entries give main name, the three-letter language identification code, country with which the language is most identified, and the language family under which it is currently classified. With this information the user can go to the main volume for more information. The second index with 39,304 entries is for the names associated with the 6,703 languages listed in the main volume. It includes all language names and their alternates, and all the dialect names and their alternates. Main names are identified along with the country with which it is mainly identified, plus other countries where spoken.

A searchable version of *Ethnologue* and its two indexes is also available on the Web. The electronic version contains all the material found in the printed volumes with the exception of language maps which will be added later. There is an introduction to the electronic version, plus several pages devoted to searching instructions including Boolean search techniques, and an entirely new section, "Top 100 Languages by Population." This latter section lists languages in rank order with the home country of the language and its population (figures updated from *Ethnologue*, 13th edition).

575. Gunnemark, Erik V. **Countries, People and Their Languages: The Geolinguistic Handbook**. rev. ed. Gothenburg, Sweden: Länstryckeriet, 1992. 291p. index. illus. bibliog. maps. ISBN 91-630-1321-5.

The 1991 and now this revised 1992 edition of *Countries . . .* replace the earlier 1986 *Geolinguistic Handbook* by the same author. Chapter 1 lists more than 210 countries from Afghanistan to Zimbabwe, giving for each: population, official languages, home languages, lingua franca, and languages used for of trade and tourism. A number of illustrations accompany the country entries such as the tables of languages for India; black and white maps show political boundaries. The author estimates the total number of languages in the world to be at least 4,500, perhaps as many as 6,000-6,500. In chapter 2, he lists 300 of these which have large numbers of speakers or which are of special interest, plus 50 of the more than 150 pidgins and Creoles in the world today. For each language he provides such details as total number of speakers, number of speakers by country, script, classification, and varieties. In chapter 3 he provides information about the most important languages numerically, languages with at least one million home speakers, international languages, lingua francas, and planned international auxiliary languages. Chapters 4 and 5 deal respectively with the genetic classification of languages and scripts (with specimens), while chapter 6 contains a glossary of over 70 terms of special interest to geolinguists. A bibliography of some 300 books and journals, plus six appendices chock full of specialized information, and an index of languages complete the handbook. The one irritating feature in the 1992 edition can probably be chalked up to expediency: additions and corrections to the 1991 edition are separated out, not integrated into the text.

576. Katzner, Kenneth. **The Languages of the World**. new ed. London: Routledge, 1995. 378p. index. LC 94-24228. ISBN 0-415-11809-3.

Katzner's handbook first published in 1977 and revised in 1986 is little changed in this new edition except for updates in the number of speakers of each language and revisions necessitated by political changes in the world map. It is primarily useful to the student or layperson in providing an overview of the relationships between languages and in giving some basic facts about individual languages and where they are spoken. Compared with Pei's work (see entry 585) it provides less information about each language, but covers more languages and has more up-to-date figures for estimated number of speakers.

The first of 3 parts is on language families of the world. It begins with a chart of the genetic classification of languages, detailing families, subgroups, and branches, then lists the major and minor languages. Following this are essays ranging in length from seven pages (on Indo-European languages) to just half a page for each of 17 language families, plus sections on American Indian languages, independent languages, artificial languages, and pidgin and Creole languages.

Part II, the heart of the book, provides information on about 200 individual languages. It gives for each one a sample text, written in the appropriate script or characters, along with an English translation. Information on the language itself is brief and varies from language to language, but usually includes the number of speakers and where it is spoken. Other information may include historical notes, official status, relationship to other languages, comments on the script, and distinctive characteristics. Part III is a country-by-country survey of the languages spoken in each country, again giving figures for number of speakers. The author provides both a list of sources for the literary passages and an index of languages and language families.

577. Klose, Albrecht. **Sprachen der Welt: Ein weltweiter Index der Sprachfamilien, Einzelsprachen und Dialekte, mit Angabe der Synonyma und fremdsprachigen Äquivalente/Languages of the World: A Multi-Lingual Concordance of Languages, Dialects and Language-Families**. München: K. G. Saur, 1987. 410p. bibliog. ISBN 3-598-1044-3X.

This index is an attempt to provide a comprehensive checklist of all the known languages and dialects of the world as well as a thesaurus of their foreign language equivalents. German forms of a name are favored with language names translated into English, French, Italian, and Russian (transliterated). The author provides an extensive bibliography of the many sources he consulted. He also includes an outline of the genetic classification of the world's languages. The heading numbers of the source bibliography conveniently correspond to the numbers assigned language families and groups in the classification outline. Before consulting the checklist itself, a user should read the introduction, in both German and English, to determine such things as its limitations, editorial restrictions, conventions for formation of new names, and rules of arrangement of entries.

578. Kloss, Heinz, and Grant D. McConnell, eds. **Linguistic Composition of the Nations of the World/Composition linguistique des nations du monde**. Québec: Presses de l'Université Laval, 1974-1984. 5v. index. bibliog. (Travaux du centre international de recherche sur le bilinguisme/Publications of the International Center for Research on Bilingualism, E-1). LC 76-350521. ISBN 0-7746-6710-9 (v.1); 0-7746-6895-5 (v.2); 0-7746-6881-4 (v.3); 2-7637-6967-5 (v.4); 2-7637-7044-4 (v.5). (In progress).

The first 5 volumes of what is to eventually be a 7-volume set are now published. When finished it will be a complete statistical survey of the demography of the world's languages. In the aim to be comprehensive they have included all types of language figures (first language, second language, bilingualism, ethnic data, etc.) from all available sources (official, secondary, estimates, scientific, etc.). Volumes 1-5 cover Central and Western South Asia, North America, Central and South America, Oceania, and Europe and the USSR, respectively. Volume 6 will cover Eastern and Southeastern Asia, while volume 7 will be devoted to Africa.

Each volume begins with an extensive introduction providing background information on languages of the area. This is followed by a bibliography of sources for the data. The statistical tables listing the data comprise the bulk of each volume. The editors provide an index of statistical offices and a language and country index. Explanatory material and headings throughout the volumes are in both English and French.

579. **Les langues dans le monde ancien et modern**. Ouvrage publié sous la direction de Jean Perrot. Paris: Éditions du Centre national de la recherche scientifique. In 3 pts. pt 1: 1981. 691p. index. illus. bibliog. maps. LC 81-174502.

ISBN 2-222-01720-3; pt. 2: maps (part col.); pt. 3: 1988. 318p. index. illus. bibliog. maps (part col.). ISBN 2-222-04057-4. (In progress).

When completed, this work will replace Antoine Meillet and Marcel Cohen's *Les langues du monde* originally published in 1924 with a new edition issued in 1952 (Paris: Centre national de la recherche scientifique).

Part 1 is the text for *Les langues de l'Afrique subsaharienne. Pidgins et créoles* while part 2 contains its colored maps. The text prepared by some 27 collaborators is also divided into sections and various subparts. The first section of 615 pages, assembled under the direction of Gabriel Manessy, is devoted to the languages of sub-Saharan Africa. The second section, written under the direction of Albert Valdman, is concerned with pidgins and Creoles. The types of information provided for a language group include: classification features, syntax, and dialects. For an individual language there is information on morphology, phonology, and grammar as well as locale, and number of speakers. Some black and white maps as well as various illustrations and sample texts with translation accompany the language articles. There is an index of languages and dialects covering both sections. Part 2 contains a dozen colored maps. Ten are devoted to various language areas or groups in sub-Saharan Africa with another map providing an overview of the whole area. The last map is a planisphere showing world distribution of pidgin and Creole languages. The maps, utilizing a system of color codes and numbers, are well-designed and easy to read. Part 3, *Les langues chamito-sémitiques*, assembled by David Cohen, covers Hamito-Semitic, also known as Afro-Asiatic, languages. It covers these languages similarly to the text and index in part 1. There are several folded maps inside the back cover.

580. Library of Congress. Office for Subject Cataloging Policy. **Index to Languages and Dialects: Classification, Class P, Subclasses P-PM**. 4th ed. Washington, DC: Library of Congress, 1991. LC 90-027240. ISBN 0-8444-0688-0.

The first edition of this was published in 1936, while the second edition originally issued in 1957 was reprinted in 1965 with supplementary pages containing additions and changes. The third edition published in 1983 was simply an integration of the supplementary pages into the second edition. This fourth edition represents a cumulation of the index entries appearing between 1983 and September 1990 and their integration into the third edition. For each language or dialect listed here—which may be qualified by the language group or geographic area to which it belongs—the appropriate Library of Congress subject classification is given. Entries are arranged in alphabetical order with many cross-references provided. While designed for use by cataloging librarians, students doing research on a language or dialect might find this useful to determine the subject classification or subject heading used by the Library, but should not consider the language group or geographic qualifiers as definitive.

581. Malherbe, Michel. **Les langages de l'humanité: une encyclopédie des 3000 langues parlées dans le monde**. Avec la collaboration de Serge Rosenberg. Paris: Robert Laffont, 1995. 1734p. index. illus. bibliog. maps (Bouquins). ISBN 2-221-05947-6.

The original version of this intriguing language encyclopedia for students was published in 1983 (Paris: Seghers). In an attempt to entice the reader to explore new territory, the author has framed the book in terms of taking several trips to explore various aspects of languages. However, the trip metaphor is artificial and does not serve its intended purpose. The first trip, divided into four stages, begins with articles on phonetics, grammar, vocabulary, writing, and examples of a variety of scripts. The second stage of this first trip carries the reader through articles on languages, introduced with overviews of various language groupings—some of which follow genetic classification, others cover geographic areas, while still others are typological (agglutinative, tonal), and finally even articles dealing with sign languages and information languages (binary and computer languages). The reader is then treated to closer examination of individual languages within the groups. The third stage is short with brief articles on etymology, toponymy, Greek words and scientific words, and the origin of Indo-European. The fourth stage dealing with issues of language and society completes the first trip.

The second trip, taking up the major portion of the encyclopedia, describes for 171 individual languages principal characteristics and lists core vocabulary of between 300 and 600 words. The work concludes with five appendices: alphabetical list of countries with information on languages and dialects spoken and numbers of speakers; maps of the second trip showing where each language is spoken; source bibliography; index of languages for the first trip; and an index of maps illustrating the first trip. Black and white illustrations and maps are clear and easy to read.

582. Matthies, Arthur. **Transkriptionen der chinesischen und japanischen Sprache/Transliteration Tables of Chinese and Japanese**. München: K. G. Saur, 1989. 77p. index. bibliog. ISBN 3-598-10789-7.

The foreword and table of contents of this manual are in both English and German. Two transliteration tables make up the bulk of the text. One is for 403 Chinese characters. These are listed with nine romanized transliterations (including Wade/Giles and Pinyin) and in Cyrillic transliteration (Russian based on the palladius system). The other transliteration table for Japanese lists 113 characters (with both Hiragana and Katakana characters) along with 5 transliterations (including the Hepburn system and a Cyrillic transliteration). An index lists in alphabetical order individual syllables found in given forms and refers by item number to the tables.

583. Nida, Eugene Albert, ed. **The Book of a Thousand Tongues**. rev. ed. London: United Bible Societies, 1972. 536p. index. illus. LC 73-160367.

The title of this book is somewhat of a misnomer as it actually covers 1,399 languages. The criteria for inclusion, with few exceptions, is that at least one full book of the Bible has to be published in the language. The organization is alphabetical by language name. Each entry provides a sample of text, usually photographically reproduced, from the Bible. When possible Mark 1:1-4 or Luke 3.1-4 is used. A brief synopsis of the language follows, often giving historical facts and relationship to other languages as well as providing information on where the language is spoken and number of speakers. Beneath this is a chronological list of the major publications of the Bible in that language.

More up-to-date information about translations and numbers of speakers can be obtained from *Ethnologue* (see entry 572). For speaker numbers the user could also consult other more current works (see entries 555, 575, and 576). Nida's book is most valuable now for its excellent text specimens.

584.   Padmanabha, P. **Census of India 1981, Series 1, India, Paper 1 of 1987; Households and Household Population by Language Mainly Spoken in the Household**. Delhi: Controller of Publications, 1987. 903p.

The 1981 census of India asked for the first time the question: "What is the main language spoken in your household?" It was added to the two standard language questions concerning mother tongue and other languages known. Some 96 percent of those questioned speak one of the 15 major languages of India in the home. The remaining 4 percent speak one of a number of other languages, including over 80 other Indian languages, Arabic, and English. Hindi which along with English is one of the official national languages is the majority language with 45 percent of the country speaking Hindi at home. Only a small fraction of 1 percent of the country's population speak mainly English at home, a surprising fact since English plays such a large role as a national and international language. The four tables comprising the volume and presenting a wealth of detail are well-organized and easy to use.

585.   Pei, Mario Andrew. **The World's Chief Languages; Formerly, Languages for War and Peace**. 5th rev. ed. New York: S. F. Vanni, 1960. 663p. index. illus.

This book was designed to present the main facts about the chief languages of the world to students and laypersons interested in acquiring some familiarity with languages they do not know. Besides providing thumbnail sketches of some language groups and widely spoken languages, it has some 16 maps showing language distribution and contains illustrations of various alphabets and scripts.

586.   Price, Glanville, ed. **Encyclopedia of the Languages of Europe**. Oxford: Blackwell, 1998. 499p. illus. bibliog. maps. LC 97-29542. ISBN 0-631-19286-7.

For the purpose of his encyclopedia, Price's definition of Europe includes the islands of Iceland, the Azores, Malta, and Cyprus; in the southeast Europe extends to include Georgia, Armenia, and Azerbaijan; on the east for most of its length the Ural mountains provide a dividing line between Europe and Asia; and then between the southern end of the Urals and the Caspian Sea he considers the border of Kazakhstan Europe's eastern boundary. As for a definition of language, Price includes both living and extinct languages, and in some cases takes a generous view of the distinction between languages and varieties or dialects, including for example Scots and Gascon as separate languages. He further expands the scope of the encyclopedia by including the principal community, or immigrant, languages of Britain, France, and the Netherlands as well as creoles, pidgin languages, artificial languages, and sign languages. Entries in the encyclopedia are alphabetically arranged from Abaza, a Caucasian language, to Zyrian, another name for Komi which is a member of the Permic group of Finno-Ugrian languages. The articles written by Price, a noted scholar of French, or one of some 60 other contributors, range in length from several sentences to a page or two with some of the longer entries being 6 to 10 pages in length. In general, articles cover the external history and sociolinguistic aspects of the language or languages, including such topics as origins and linguistic affiliations, literary use, standardization, scripts and orthography, geographical spread, contacts with other languages, and if applicable, present situation. The encyclopedia is replete with cross-references both within the articles (indicated by bold type and an asterisk) and as "see under" entries. Interspersed throughout the volume are figures illustrating various alphabets and languages (such as Armenian, Hebrew, Linear A, original ogam, runic, and British Sign Language) plus 21 black and white maps showing language distribution. The encyclopedia is written in a lucid style, easily accessible to students while the references listed at the end of most articles provide guidance for further study.

587. Ruhlen, Merritt. **A Guide to the World's Languages. Volume 1: Classification**. With a Postscript on Recent Developments. Stanford, CA: Stanford University Press, 1991. 463p. index. illus. maps. LC 90-21705. ISBN 0-8047-1894-6.

Ruhlen provides a complete linguistic genetic classification of all the world's languages in this revised edition of his now standard 1987 reference work which itself stemmed from the author's earlier, self-published work, *Guide to the Languages of the World* (Stanford: 1975). The genetic classification in this guide is the most comprehensive and up-to-date presently available. Ruhlen intends to publish a second volume on language data and a third on language universals.

Chapter 8 contains the complete classification arranged in terms of 17 independent phyla, plus 4 groupings of languages that cannot be placed in the worldwide classification. These are: language isolates, unclassified, pidgins and Creoles, and invented. Other materials in this chapter include an explanation of the taxonomic principles and geographical distribution of the language families; a table giving an overview of the language phyla showing number of extant languages, number of speakers, location or country, and listing some of the better-known languages; plus an index and outline to the classification.

Chapters 2-6 discuss taxonomic ambiguities, disputes, and uncertainties in the classification from a historical perspective. Language lists, tables, figures, and maps abound throughout the text. Each chapter also has a substantial bibliography. A variety of indexes aid the reader: an index of personal names, a language group index, and a language index. The latter index contains all the approximately 5,000 languages listed in the complete classification section of Chapter 8 and provides cross-references for the most common variants and dialect names. The reader is referred to Voegelin and Voegelin (1977) and Grimes (1984) for indexes to the over 25,000 names associated with the world's languages (see entries 591 and 572, the latter is a later edition of the referenced work).

Leaving the text of the 1987 edition intact, Ruhlen uses a postscript (pp. 379-407) to bring his classification up-to-date. He now breaks up Caucasian into two distinct families, North Caucasian and South Caucasian, using simply the term Caucasian for North Caucasian and the term Kartvelian in place of South Caucasian. He also removes Korean-Japanese-Ainu from Altaic, leaving Altaic with just its traditional constituents: Turkic, Mongolian, and Tungus. In addition he summarizes the work of a growing number of scholars who in the past five years have come to believe "not only that all presently extant languages are related, but that this can be shown by traditional comparative linguistics" (p. 380). In this context he discusses the overlap between the various Nostratic family and Eurasiatic family proposals and goes on to support Greenberg's (1987) revolutionary classification of American Indian languages into just three families. Finally, he touches on the emerging synthesis of historical linguistics, human genetics, and archaeology into a framework for understanding human evolution.

The bibliography of the postscript picks up references left out of the earlier edition and works published during the intervening years.

588.   Sarker, Amal, comp. and ed. **Handbook of Languages and Dialects of India**. With an introd. by Y. M. Mulay. Calcutta: distr., Firma K. L. Mukhopadhyay, 1964. 109p. (Reference and Information Series).

The main part of this handbook is an alphabetical listing of the 782 languages and dialects mentioned in the 1951 Census of India together with brief information on where they are spoken, number of speakers, and in the case of more widely spoken languages an indication of the language group and family. Three appendixes contain various tables and charts. Several alphabet charts provide a key to the transliteration of 13 major Indian languages. An introduction grapples with some of the many problems associated with language classification and enumeration in general and with India in particular.

589.   Summer Institute of Linguistics. **Living Languages of the Americas: Combined Volume**. Dallas, TX: The Summer Institute of Linguistics; distr. International Academic Bookstore, 1995. 1 v. (various paging). ISBN 1-55671-023-2. Available: http://www.sil.org/lla/. (Accessed September 29, 1998).

All the information in this volume was derived from the 12th edition of *Ethnologue: Languages of the World* and the *Bibliography of the Summer Institute of Linguistics* (see entries 572 and 130). It covers languages in North America, Central America, the Caribbean, and South America. Within each of these regions information is arranged in three parts by country (individually paginated with running footers). In the first part, all the languages of a country are listed alphabetically on the left side of each page. Columns moving across the page give language name; language family; population, i.e., number of speakers; and areas spoken in and by whom or whether it is a national language. A second part lists vernacular publications written specifically for mother-tongue speakers while the last part lists technical publications which describe the languages. This is a valuable reference tool which integrates a lot of information from 13 separate volumes into a single easily consulted source. In addition, the Summer Institute of Linguistics has mounted a free searchable, electronic version of this work which supplies the same information as the printed version except that 14 countries have been added. There is a preface to the electronic version which gives instructions for accessing the tables and interpreting the characters representing orthographic transcriptions not supported by the HTML document markup language used on the Web.

590.   Vihman, Marilyn May, ed. **A Reference Manual and User's Guide for the Stanford Phonology Archive**. Stanford, CA: Stanford University, Department of Linguistics, Phonology Archiving Project, 1977. 157p. illus. bibliog.

The *Reference Manual* serves as a general introduction and guide to the Stanford Phonology Archive which is an attempt to create a computerized "storehouse or catalog of information about the phonetics and phonologies of some of the world's languages" (p. 1). The manual explains the archive's coverage, basic philosophy, intent and guiding principles, and describes its approach to standardization and interpretation of grammars. The archive relies on published sources rather than informants and contains copies of all phonologies used as source material. It should prove useful to linguists interested in language universals who might want to consult the data and to analysts and the encoders who create the data stored in the archive. It contains a user's guide, a coding manual, and a technical reference section. An appendix lists the more than 200 languages in the sample. See entry 563 for the 2-volume handbook which contains the phonetic inventories and the indexes.

591.   Voegelin, Charles Frederick, and Florence M. Voegelin. **Classification and Index of the World's Languages**. New York: Elsevier, 1977. 658p. index. bibliog. (Foundations of Linguistics Series). LC 74-19546. ISBN 0-444-00155-7.

This work is based on a survey of the literature, *Languages of the World*, published from 1964 to 1966 in the journal *Anthropological Linguistics* with revisions from a further review of the literature and the incorporation of additional information from readers of the first survey and consultants. Though Ruhlen's classification supersedes this (see entry 587) and various other works contain more up-to-date numbers for speakers of languages, it remains an important reference source, particularly for its index of names.

The main body of the book consists for the most part of alphabetic entries for the names of groups of genetically related languages. After a paragraph or so discussing the internal relationships of the members of the group, the languages belonging to the group are listed. Variant names, alternate spellings as well as names of dialects are given for each language. The dialect names are followed by figures for the number and location of speakers of the language. The authors caution, however, against taking these numbers too literally. If a language or dialect is no longer spoken, an asterisk precedes the name and if inclusion in a language group is doubtful, a question mark follows the name. Finally, the last item for an entry is usually a brief note stating the relationship of the group as a whole to other groups of languages.

An extensive index lists all the names of groups, subgroups, languages, dialects, tribes, and their alternate names which appear in the entry articles and refer the reader to the entry where the language or language group is discussed. A list of references citing works that discuss the classification of groups of languages is included. Though not intended as a full bibliography of the field, the list of references should lead the reader to other research on the classification of languages as well as to descriptive materials of the languages themselves.

592.   Von Ostermann, Georg Frederick. **Manual of Foreign Languages: For the Use of Librarians, Bibliographers, Research Workers, Editors, Translators, and Printers**. 4th ed., rev. and enl. New York: Central Book Co., 1952. (Reprinted 1959). 414p. illus. LC 52-2409.

About 140 languages and dialects are treated in this manual. The main part lists languages in alphabetical order. It is followed by sections for American Indian and African languages. For languages receiving fairly full treatment, for example, German and Hungarian, it covers such points as: alphabet, numbers, capitalization, abbreviations, syllabication, word formation, gender, articles, nouns, verbs, etc. Other languages such as Arabic are sketchily treated. A number of tables useful for quick reference precede the language treatments. The first presents selected library and bibliographical terms (volume, page, edition, part, number/issue, revised, and enlarged) for 36 languages. Another table shows alphabets of Cyrillic origin while two others deal with diacritical marks.

593.   Wemyss, Stanley. **The Languages of the World, Ancient and Modern; the Alphabets, Ideographs, and Other Written Characters of the Languages of the World, in Sound and Symbol**. Philadelphia: Stanley Wemyss, 1950. index. illus. bibliog. LC 50-12123.

The purpose of this work is the same as the guide by Gilyarevskii and Grivnin (see entry 571), that is, to identify unknown languages. The Gilyarevskii work has broader application since it provides more detail on more languages. This book's strength lies, however, in the many excellent drawings and tables illustrating various alphabets, ideographs, and other written characters. There are over 300 in all with references given to the nearly 1,000 languages that make use of them. Other interesting sections deal with the origin and evolution of various alphabets (Roman, early Semitic), types of writing (Egyptian, cuneiform), and Arabic numerals.

Bibliographies and Catalogs

594.   Acharya, K. P., comp. **Classified Bibliography of Articles in "Indian Linguistics"**. Supervisors, D. P. Pattanayak and E. Annamalai. Mysore: Central Institute of Indian Languages, 1978. 106p. index. (CIIL Occasional Monographs Series, 12). LC 79-903006.

This classified bibliography functions as an index to Volumes 1 to 38 of *Indian Linguistics* for the years 1931 to December 1977. It separately indexes the articles, reviews and notices, and miscellany. Author and language indexes are provided for the articles and reviews.

595.   **Bibliographie der Wörterbücher/Bibliography of Dictionaries/Bibliografia słowników/Bibliografiya slovarei**. Vols.1-7 (1945/61-1973/74). Warszawa: Wydawnictwa Naukowo-Techniczne, 1965-76.

The first volume of this set covers 1945/61, the second 1962/64, and then each subsequent volume covers a 2-year period so that volume 7 ends the coverage with 1973/74. Numbering of entries is continuous throughout the volumes. The very long subtitle of this work varies since it indicates country coverage which has changed through the years. Since its beginning, it has included dictionaries published in Bulgaria, Czechoslovakia, the German Democratic Republic, Hungary, Poland, Rumania, and the USSR. It only included Korea in the 1965/66 volume, China from 1945 to 1966, and Yugoslavia from 1962 to 1966. Introductory materials are in Polish, Russian, and German.

The entries are in two sections: one section for single language dictionaries, the other for dictionaries in two or more languages. Each section is arranged according to the universal decimal classification (UDC) with headings in Russian and German. In addition to author, editor, edition, place, publisher, date and size of book, each entry states the number of terms in the dictionary and indicates by means of symbols alphabetic or systematic order, inclusion of definitions, and whether or not there are illustrations. The title of a dictionary is given in the language of publication with both German and Russian titles provided as needed.

There are indexes for languages, authors, titles, and subjects. This work is continued by another title (see next entry).

596. **Bibliografia słowników/Bibliographie der Wörterbucher/Bibliography of Dictionaries/Bibliografiya slovarei**. Vols.8-9 (1975/76-1977/78). Warszawa: Wydawnictwa Naukowo-Techniczne, 1978-81. ISSN 0137-253X.

This title continues the *Bibliographie der Wörterbücher* . . . (see preceding entry) with the same country coverage, format, indexing, and numbering of entries.

597. Brewer, Annie M., ed. **Dictionaries, Encyclopedias, and Other Word-Related Books: A Classed Guide.** . . . 4th ed. Detroit, MI: Gale Research, 1988. 2v. index. LC 87-83314. ISBN 0-8103-0440-6. (This work not viewed by author.)

The new edition of this guide lists about 35,000 works in English and all other languages. They range from general all-purpose works to a number of highly specialized dictionaries and word books including compilations of acronyms, Americanisms, colloquialisms, etymologies, glossaries, idioms and expressions, orthography, provincialisms, slang, terms and phrases, and vocabularies. Entries are arranged according to the Library of Congress classification system. A subject/title index is appended.

598. Collison, Robert Lewis. **Dictionaries of English and Foreign Languages; a Bibliographical Guide to Both General and Technical Dictionaries with Historical and Explanatory Notes and References**. 2d ed. New York: Hafner, 1971. 303p. index. bibliog. LC 78-130513.

This work was first published in 1955 as *Dictionaries of Foreign Languages*. The second edition has been substantially enlarged and now has some 2,000 items. Chapters are devoted to particular languages (English, French, Italian, Russian) or to language families or groups (Celtic languages, languages of Asia, Africa, etc.) when dealing with less commonly known languages. Chief general dictionaries are followed, in order, by these types of dictionaries: etymological, specialist (synonyms, antonyms, etc.), those relating to special periods, slang, dialect, and bilingual. Historical notes, contents, and use are provided along with critical comments. An unannotated list of technical dictionaries and a general bibliography are appended. The index lists in one alphabetical sequence the authors, official bodies, titles, alternative titles and subtitles, languages, dialects, areas and regions, etc.

599. Cop, Margaret. **Babel Unraveled: An Annotated World Bibliography of Dictionary Bibliographies, 1658-1988**. Tübingen: Max Niemeyer, 1990. 195p. index. bibliog. (Lexicographica. Series Maior, 36; ISSN 0175-9264). ISBN 3-484-30936-9.

Coverage of European dictionary bibliographies is especially good in this bibliography of bibliographies. Cop includes both self-contained works as well as bibliographies published as part of other works such as anthologies or periodicals with the caveat that they list at least 50 items (some exceptions were made for lesser-known languages). The 619 annotated entries cover works published over a span of more than 300 years, 1658-1990. Annotated entries arranged alphabetically by main entry contain complete bibliographic information, plus a translation of titles not in English, libraries where the work can be consulted, source for the citation, and a detailed description of the bibliography (languages, content, annotation, arrangement, indexes, time span, number of items, and notes which may include historical or evaluative comments). A system of indexes expands its use: language, chronological, language dictionary types, subject, UDC numbers, dictionary databanks, publishers' and booksellers' catalogs, library catalogs, periodicals regularly announcing/reviewing dictionaries, names. Major sources used in the bibliography's compilation are listed at the end.

600. Geetha, K. R., comp. **Classified State Bibliography of Linguistic Research on Indian Languages**. Mysore: Central Institute of Indian Languages, 1983- . Vol.1- . index. bibliog. (CIIL Occasional Monographs Series, 28). LC 83-904141. (In progress).

This is volume 1 in what the Central Institute of Indian Languages (CIIL) promises will be a 5-volume set of classified bibliographies covering linguistic and language related research on Indian languages for all the States and Union Territories of India.

This first volume covers the Hindi-speaking states of Bihar, Haryana, Himachal Prades, Madhya Pradesh, Rajasthan, Uttar Pradesh, and Delhi. Four main sections deal with: Hindi in general; studies done on Hindi with other languages (includes comparative, contrastive, areal, typological, descriptive, or historical); Hindi and other languages in specific Hindi-speaking States; and, finally, Hindi and other languages of the Hindi-speaking States outside their linguistic territories. The main sections are further subdivided by appropriate languages or geographic areas as well as subject areas. The 4,258 entries for published and unpublished materials range in date from the 1600s to 1981. In the case of non-English titles, the title is followed by a symbol indicating the language and usually an English translation of the title within brackets. All Devanagari script entries are romanized. Bibliographic information is sometimes incomplete and not given in standardized format. This is not surprising considering the difficulties involved in such a massive project and involving so many different languages. To facilitate access to the bibliography the compiler adds indexes for authors, languages, and journals. He also includes a list of languages spoken in Hindi-speaking states and a list of sources.

601. Kabdebo, Thomas, and Neil Armstrong. **Dictionary of Dictionaries and Eminent Encyclopedias Comprising: Dictionaries, Encyclopedias, and Other Selected Wordbooks in English**. 2nd ed. London: Bowker-Saur, 1997. 253p. index. ISBN 1-85739-103-9.

The second edition of this work first published in 1992 now contains about 8,000 titles for dictionaries in a very broad sense of the term. Annotations are mainly descriptive rather than evaluative. It is not meant to be comprehensive and in the words of its compilers "relies on English, both in terms of that being a subject of, or a participant language of, dictionaries" (p. v). It is slanted towards British works to which the American user may not have ready access. Arrangement is alphabetical by some 1,400 headings, or categories, many of which are languages or subjects, but also include a number of explanatory categories for types of dictionaries, their features, and technical or social aspects of the dictionary world. On the one hand, the many idiosyncratic headings makes it an interesting book to browse, but on the other makes the use of its keyword index mandatory for finding a particular topic. There are also author and title indexes.

602. Lengenfelder, Helga, ed. **International Bibliography of Specialized Dictionaries/Fachwörterbücher und Lexika, ein internationales Verzeichnis**. 6th ed. München: K. G. Saur; distr., Detroit, MI: Gale Research, 1979. 470p. index. (Handbook of International Documentation and Information, Vol. 4/Handbuch der internationalen Dokumentation und Information, Bd. 4). LC 82-192823. ISBN 3-598-10501-5(München); 0-89664-061-2(New York).

The 5,719 entries in this international bibliography are for separately published, single- and multi-volume subject-oriented dictionaries as well as general dictionaries in uncommonly known languages which have been published from 1970 to 1979. General dictionaries in common languages, biographical dictionaries, word lists and vocabularies contained in larger works, and many dictionaries of standardized vocabularies are excluded.

The arrangement is alphabetical by main entry according to a 9-part classification system. Section 8.5 for language and linguistics and semiotic dictionaries has 773 entries. Listings include notations on languages and many state the number of terms. Since titles are listed only once, the combined keyword and subject index, in both German and English, is useful for locating titles covering more than one subject. There is also an index of authors, editors, compilers, and translators.

603. Molho, Emanuel. **The Dictionary Catalogue**. 2nd ed. New York: French and European Publications, 1989. 178p. index. LC 89-080287. ISBN 0-8288-0000-6.

Molho lists in his catalog more than 6,000 dictionaries in print at the time of publication. English and French language works predominate, but other widely spoken languages are well-represented as are less widely spoken languages such as Estonian, Greek, Korean, Maori, Persian, and Tulu. Dictionaries are alphabetically arranged under 81 sections consisting of some general categories (bilingual, multilingual, and monolingual), learning professional languages, and technical miscellaneous which are followed by a long list of specialized dictionaries ranging from "abbreviations" to "zoology." A keyword index facilitates access to these specialized, topical dictionaries. Entries are coded for language(s) and include cost and purchasing information, now of course, out-of-date.

604. Navlani, K., and N. N. Gidwani, comps. and eds. **Dictionaries in Indian Languages; a Bibliography**. Jaipur: Saraswati Publications, 1972. 370p. LC 72-908226.

This bibliography of about 3,000 entries aims to be comprehensive for linguistic, scientific, technical, and subject dictionaries in Indian languages. Except for encyclopedias and biographical dictionaries which are specifically excluded, it largely replaces the earlier National Library of Calcutta bibliography. It lists not only monographic works, but items published in periodicals. Lists of bibliographies and surveys of dictionaries are followed by sections for Indo-Aryan, Indian, foreign, and polyglot dictionaries. The Indian and foreign language sections are further divided by language. Bibliographic information for some entries is followed by information about unique characteristics, notes on previous editions, and citations to reviews.

605.   Ramaiah, L. S. **Tribal Linguistics in India: A Bibliographical Survey of International Resources**. Madras: T. R. Publications, 1990. 274p. index. SBN 81-85427-00-3.

In the introduction to this unannotated, classified bibliography Ramaiah explains that according to the 1981 Census of India, there are more than 51,600,000 tribal people who constitute 7.53 percent of the total population in India unevenly distributed throughout the country in 450 tribal communities. The tribal languages are not officially recognized at any level of government even in taluks where their speakers constitute a majority. The 2,812 entries in this bibliography are divided into four main language families: Austroasiatic, 15 languages, 448 entries; Dravidian, 32 languages, 1,012 entries; Indo-Aryan, 14 languages, 121 entries; and Tibeto-Burman, 104 languages, 930 entries. Language families are then broken down into groups and into individual languages. Entries are for books, periodical articles, proceedings, unpublished papers, government reports, book reviews, and dissertations. An index of scholars and a subject index complete the work.

606.   Sakuntala Sharma, J., comp. **Classified Bibliography of Linguistic Dissertations on Indian Languages**. Supervisors, D. P. Pattanayak and E. Annamalai. Mysore: Central Institute of Indian Languages, 1978. 288p. index. illus. (CIIL Occasional Monographs Series, 14). LC 79-901272.

More than 1,200 dissertations and almost 500 master's theses in many areas of linguistic study on Indian languages are gathered here. These areas include: descriptive, historical, sociolinguistics, psycholinguistics, language planning, language teaching, contrastive studies, dialectology, and others. The time span covers from 1921 through 1978. While the bibliography lists theses from other countries (mostly England and the United States) it is particularly useful because of its coverage of the output from Indian universities.

Entries are arranged according to an unusual classification system; a user should read the conspectus (that is, the introduction) before attempting to consult the bibliography. Tables preceding the bibliography itself show the distribution of dissertations in subject areas both by university or institute (Table 1) and by language or dialect (Table 2). The compiler indexes entries by scholar, language (including dialects), author/text (for works linguistically analyzed), and university. A later work by Sharada updates this bibliography (see entry 607).

607.   Sharada, B. A., comp. **Dissertations in Linguistics and on Indian Languages (Available at CIIL)**. Mysore: Central Institute of Indian Languages, Ministry of Education and Culture, Government of India, 1983. 40p. index. LC 84-907034.

This work updates the bibliography compiled by J. Sakuntala Sharma (see entry 606). It lists nearly 400 additional dissertations and theses. A language index is appended.

608.   Sharma, Ran Singh. **Linguistic Studies in Modern India**. 1st ed. New Delhi: Arya Book Depot, 1981. 92p. bibliog. LC 82-900330.

The purpose of the bibliographic essays in this study is to provide the reader with introductory information on linguistic studies in modern India, modern meaning from the time of the noted Indian scholar Dr. Sir Ram Krishna Gopal

Bhandarkar in the 19th century. The text is basically a discussion and evaluation of some of the most important works from this period. There are 7 chapters: Bhandarkar (background and impact), Old Indo-Aryan, Middle Indo-Aryan, modern Indian languages, general linguistics, applied linguistics and miscellaneous studies, and conclusions. The linguistic studies cited in the text (mostly books, but also a few articles and reports) are gathered in a concluding bibliography.

609. Sukhachev, N. L., sost. **Lingvisticheskie atlasy: annotirovannyi bibliograficheskii ukaatel'**. Leningrad: Biblioteka Akademii nauk SSSR, 1984. 158p. index.

More than 200 linguistic atlases are listed in this handy little reference book. The arrangement is by language family, then language, followed by a section with 8 regional atlases. Many are from earlier in this century with even a few published as far back as 1877. Atlases and related publications issuing from the language projects are cited in their original language of publication, but the substantial, descriptive annotations are all in Russian. The editor provides a key to atlas and periodical acronyms as well as indexes of atlas titles; languages, dialects, and geographical names; and authors and editors.

610. Tremblay, Florent A. **Bibliotheca grammaticorum/Bibliography of Grammatical Writings/Bibliographie des écrits grammaticaux**. Lewiston, NY: Edwin Mellen Press, 1996. 7 v. in 15. index. bibliog. ISBN 0-7734-8955-X (set).

Volumes 1 through 6 of this set is a bibliography of grammatical writings from specific time periods: volume 1 (in 2 books) covers antiquity; volume 2 (in 2 books), the classical period; volume 3 (in 2 books), Roman times; volume 4 (in 2 books), the Middle Ages; volume 5 (in 2 books), the Renaissance; and volume 6 (in 3 books), the modern period. Each volume begins with a lengthy introduction giving background material for the time period and sets out its bibliographical, chronological, and geographical boundaries. Entries include complete bibliographic and physical descriptions, plus descriptive and often evaluative summaries in French or German. Volume 7, book 1 is an index of titles, while book 2 is an index of authors.

611. Troike, Rudolph C., comp. **Bibliography of Bibliographies of the Languages of the World. Volume I. General and Indo-European Languages of Europe**. Amsterdam: John Benjamins, 1990. 473p. index. (Amsterdam Studies in the Theory and History of Linguistic Science. Series V: Library and Information Sources in Linguistics, Vol. 19; ISSN 0165-7267). LC 90-426. ISBN 90-272-3743-3. (In progress).

The first volume of this massive bibliography of bibliographies intended to cover all of the languages and language families of the world, covers with just more than 2,500 entries all the Indo-European languages of Europe, plus Etruscan and Basque, as well as general and multi-language references. When published, the second volume will cover all other languages. Troike states that "the primary focus of the bibliography is on 'languages' rather than on linguistics per se, so that purely linguistic bibliographies are generally not included" (p.xvi). Notwithstanding, there is a separate section (under the General heading), selective rather than comprehensive, on special linguistic topics as well as citations to dictionaries, grammars, syntax studies, and many other linguistic works cited under individual languages (e.g. "Catalan, linguistics" and "Slavic, linguistics"). In addition there is some coverage of such allied linguistic topics as anthropological linguistics, applied linguistics, computational linguistics, psycholinguistics, and sociolinguistics. The author intends, within the limitations listed on p.xvi, for the bibliography to be as exhaustive and comprehensive as possible through 1985. Arrangement is alphabetical by main entry under broad categories (General, Indo-European, Celtic, Germanic, Romance, Eastern Europe, Balto-Slavic, Slavic, Albanian, and Greek). Bibliographic data for each entry is full and detailed with annotations usually giving the following information: number of items, arrangement of the items, extent and type of annotation, type of index(es), and relation to other entries (continuing, preceding, superseding, condensing). Titles of works in Slavic and Baltic languages and Albanian are translated and works in non-Roman alphabets are transliterated. An additional aid to the user is the use of one to three asterisks in the name and subject indexes to indicate compilations of 1,000 to 3,000 or more items. This metabibliography should be a useful tool for librarians and students and scholars of the languages it encompasses.

612. Urciuoli, Bonnie, comp. **A Catalog of the C. F. and F. M. Voegelin Archives of the Languages of the World**. Bloomington, IN: Archives of Traditional Music, Indiana University, 1988. 8v. index. bibliog.

This catalog provides access to the collections known as the Archives of the Languages of the World (ALW). The collections contain some 2,300 reels of audiotape and 300 discs representing nearly 300 languages, about one-third of which are native American. The ALW was begun in 1954 by the Voegelins at Indiana University-Bloomington in order to provide primary sources of oral data for linguistic analysis. Though still at the university, the collections have been moved for preservation purposes from the Anthropology Department to the Archives of Traditional Music.

Each of the first 7 volumes is devoted to languages of a particular geographic area: African, Asian and Middle Eastern, Australian, European (including European languages in the Americas), North American Indian, Oceanic, and South American Indian, respectively. In each volume the compiler provides information on where and when a collection was recorded, who the speakers are and where they are from, collection accession number, recording number (tape or disc), duration of each recording, whether or not the material has been transcribed, and provides bibliographic references relating to the collections. Clear instructions for use appear at the beginning of each volume. Unfortunately, use is hampered by lack of page numbers. Volume 8 indexes languages, collectors, and informants for the entire set.

613. Vancil, David E., comp. **Catalog of Dictionaries, Word Books, and Philological Texts, 1440-1900: Inventory of the Cordell Collection, Indiana State University**. Westport, CT: Greenwood Press, 1993. 397p. index. bibliog. (Bibliographies and Indexes in Library and Information Science, No. 7; ISSN 0742-6879). LC 92-30883. ISBN 0-313-28700-7.

Vancil's catalog records both English and other language dictionaries in the Cordell Collection of the Cunningham Memorial Library at Indiana State University. It inventories only the 5,046 pre-1901 titles received by the collection as of December 1991. Arrangement is by main entry with subsequent listings under it arranged by ascending date. Vancil gives information on date, edition, publication statement, physical description, references, and facsimile notation. For English-language entries he also makes reference to O'Neill's catalog number (see entry 707). Following the catalog entries is a subject guide and two indexes, one for date, the other for language.

614. Wellisch, Hans H. **Transcription and Transliteration: An Annotated Bibliography of Conversion of Scripts**. Silver Spring, MD: Institute of Modern Languages, 1975. 133p. index. LC 74-77274. ISBN 0-88499-149-0.

Because this was the first attempt at a bibliography on transcription and transliteration, the author chose to list all the items he found on the subject whether, as he puts it, they were good, bad, indifferent, or outright silly. To be included though, at least one of the languages or scripts dealt with in an item had to be spoken or used today. Each of the more than 750 entries supplies standard bibliographic information. All titles not in English are given an English translation. Wellisch provides annotations for entries of particular importance and for those whose titles are not indicative of subject content. The arrangement is by language. Indexes for author and subject are appended.

615. **World Dictionaries in Print, 1983: A Guide to General and Subject Dictionaries in World Languages**. New York: R. R. Bowker, 1983. 579p. index. ISBN 0-83521-615-2.

The 13,623 titles in this directory can be accessed in four ways: by subject (using Library of Congress subject headings), by title, by author, editor or compiler, and by language. If dictionaries cover two or more languages, then titles are listed under each language. Over 238 languages and nearly 6,000 subjects are covered for dictionaries, wordbooks, glossaries, and thesauri published in about 100 countries. All titles were in print at the time of the directory's publication. The bibliographic information provided for each title is similar in content and format to entries in *Books in Print*. A key to publishers' and distributors' abbreviations contains the complete name, address, and ordering information for the more than 2,500 publishers and distributors. This is an excellent source for identifying foreign language dictionaries on specialized subjects and dictionaries of less commonly studied languages which are often published only in the countries where those languages are spoken.

616. Wortman, William A. **A Guide to Serial Bibliographies for Modern Literatures**. 2nd ed. New York: Modern Language Association of America, 1995. 333p. index. bibliog. LC 95-33134. ISBN 0-87352-965-0.

Serial bibliographies are basic, fundamental tools for linguistic and language research. Wortman has gathered in his expanded second edition some 777 such bibliographies, many of which are of interest to linguists. Another some 100 titles of cumulations and earlier versions can be found in the annotations. Entries are well-organized into 6 chapters and liberally cross-referenced. An appendix provides information on the electronic versions of serial bibliographies described in the chapters. The index of titles, descriptive titles, and names provides thorough access to entries. In the subjects chapter there is a small section on linguistics, language, and language teaching. Other relevant subjects include: comparative literature and translation; composition, rhetoric, and technical writing; computers; education;

folklore; journalism and mass communication; and style. There are other items of interest throughout the chapter on comprehensive bibliographies and general indexes, and the chapters on English and non-English literatures. Though this edition of the guide contains no Internet addresses, Wortman fully expects the next edition to do so. In the meantime he will maintain a Web site for twice-yearly updates and corrections at http://www.lib.muohio.edu/serial-bibliographies. When accessed on December 29, 1998, the site contained a number of corrections and more than 25 new serial bibliographies, some available only on the Internet even though it had last been updated on May 21, 1997.

617.   Zaunmüller, Wolfram. **Bibliographisches Handbuch der Sprach-wörterbücher: ein internationales Verzeichnis von 5600 Wörterbüchern der Jahre 1460-1958 für mehr als 500 Sprachen und Dialekte**. New York/London: Hafner, 1958. 496 columns. index. bibliog.

This bibliography of about 5,600 language dictionaries covers works from 1460-1958 in more than 500 languages and dialects. Entries are arranged by language with long language sections subdivided by dictionary type (such as academy dictionaries; bi- and multilingual; synonym, antonym, and homonym; technical; rhyming; and etymological). Dictionaries for major languages make up about half the entries. Titles are in the original language of publication, transliterated into Latin script when necessary. Some entries have brief annotations. There are author and language indexes, the latter arranged according to continent.

Atlases

618.   **Atlas linguarum Europae (ALE)**. Sous la rédaction de A. Weijnen, et al. Assen, Pays-Bas/The Netherlands: Van Gorcum, 1975-1979. 3v. bibliog. LC 76-458576. ISBN 90-232-1299-1 (v. 1); 90-232-1439-0 (v. 2); 90-232-1697-0 (v. 3).

The purpose of this atlas is to present side by side comparisons of linguistic data taken from the languages on the European continent regardless of whether the languages are related or not. In doing so it hopes to reveal aspects of language contact. The first volume of this set is a polyglot introduction to ALE given in various languages: French, English, Russian, German, and Spanish. It provides background on the origins of the project, the place of the ALE within linguistic research, notes on the organization of the project, contents of the questionnaires, information on the base map and the network of localities, the survey, phonetic transcription, and the mapping of the lexicological data. Volume 2 contains the first questionnaire which is in French; the instructions are also in English and the word lists are in all the languages listed above for the introduction. Volume 3 contains the second questionnaire (only in French).

619.   **Atlas linguarum Europae (ALE). Cartes et Commentaires**. Sous la rédaction de Mario Alinei, et al. Assen, Pays-Bas: Van Gorcum, 1983-1997. 1 v. (in 5 fasc.) bibliog. map. LC 84-166271. ISBN 90-232-2037-4 (set). (In progress).

Each fascicle, or part, of this volume consists of an atlas volume (cartes) and a corresponding volume of text (commentaries). Maps 1-19 plus the base map (in a pocket) are in part 1 of the atlas (1983); maps 20-28 plus 2 other maps (the base map and a map showing the distribution of language families and groups) are in part 2 (1986); maps 29-36 are in part 3 (1988); maps 37-44 are in part 4 (1990); and maps 45-59 are in part 5 (1997). While the introduction in part 1 of the text is in English, notes on maps are all in French.

620.   Comrie, Bernard, Stephen Matthews, and Maria Polinsky, consultant eds. **The Atlas of Languages: The Origin and Development of Languages Throughout the World**. Foreword by Jean Aitchison. New York: Facts on File, 1996. 224p. index. illus. (col.). bibliog. maps (col.). ISBN 0-8160-3388-9.

The audience for this nicely illustrated coffee table book is the general reader wanting an introductory survey of languages with some maps; the text is well-written without jargon or technical language. A number of chapters, including the introduction, are stellar examples of precis writing. However, close examination reveals a too-casual approach, especially with the illustrations, which leads to inaccuracies—for example, a number of maps carelessly drawn and labeled. Inconsistencies in illustrations lead to possibly incorrect interpretation; for example, sometimes language group names are in ovals, ranged horizontally, with lists of the languages below, while other times individual language names are in ovals connected vertically which suggests wrong genetic relationships (p. 62). In addition there are cross-references to wrong pages and dropped lines of text that simple proof-reading would have corrected. A short glossary, bibliography, and index complete the volume.

621.   Grierson, G. A., comp. and ed. **Linguistic Survey of India**. Calcutta, 1903-1928. 11v. in 19. bibliog. maps. (Reprinted Delhi: Motilal Banarsidas, 1967-1968; LC 67-3572).

622.   Volume 1: Introductory; Comparative Vocabulary

623.   Volume 2: Mon Khmer and Siamese-Chinese Families

624.   Volume 3: Tibeto-Burman Family

625.   Volume 4: Munda and Dravidian Languages

626.   Volumes 5-9: Indo-Aryan Family

627.   Volume 10: Specimens of Languages of the Eranian Family

628.   Volume 11: Gypsy Languages

In a language survey that took place mainly between 1897 and 1900 the whole of India was covered with the exception of the Provinces of Madras and Burma and the States of Hyderabad and Mysore. The results were published in this detailed, encyclopedic work which gives estimates of the number of people speaking each language and dialect (based on population figures from the 1891 census). Some 179 languages and 544 additional dialect names are recorded. The volumes contain language specimens and vocabulary lists for many of the languages plus detailed maps. For a summary of the data in this survey see entry 630.

629. Mazel, Christopher, and R. E. Asher, general eds. **Atlas of the World's Languages**. London: Routledge, 1994. 372p. index. illus. bibliog. col. maps. ISBN 0-415-01925-7.

There are eight sections in this atlas, each with its own editor: the Americas, Australasia and the Pacific, East and South East Asia, South Asia, Northern Asia and Eastern Europe, Western Europe, the Middle East and North Africa, and Sub-Saharan Africa. The text beginning each section was written for nonspecialists and covers general linguistic history of the area, genetic relationships and structural features of the languages, statistical and sociolinguistic information, and a selected bibliography which points the reader to more specialized materials. Occasionally sample sentences are given and scripts are mentioned. Format and depth of content varies considerably from section to section. There are 113 maps in which color shows locations of languages and the relationships among them. For Australia and the Americas historical maps represent the languages present at the time of contact—though no dates are given—with European settlers. Complementing the text is an index of languages (in Roman type) and language groups (in italics). The reader should be aware that there are some errors, especially with regard to the maps depicting North American Indian languages and their accompanying text.

630. Varma, Siddheshwar. **G. A. Grierson's Linguistic Survey of India: A Summary**. 1st ed. Hoshiarpur: Vishveshvaranand Institute, Panjab University, 1972-76. 3v. (Vishveshvaranand Institute Publication, 585; Vishveshvaranand Indological Series, 58, 59, 59a). LC 73-900630.

This 3-volume work synthesizes the materials in Grierson's complete survey regarding all the languages and their respective main dialects (see entry 621). For each entry it records name, area, pronunciation, various grammatical categories, and syntax. The summary excludes the maps and details of a non-linguistic nature such as those relating to literature, bibliography, written characters, and folklore specimens.

631. Wurm, Stephen A., Peter Mühlhäusler, Peter, and Darrell T. Tyron, eds. **Atlas of Languages of Intercultural Communication in the Pacific, Asia, and the Americas**. Berlin: Mouton de Gruyter, 1996. 2 v. (in 3 parts). 1622p. (v.2 in 2 parts). index. bibliog. maps (part col.). (Trends in Linguistics. Documentation, 13). LC 96-35866. ISBN 3-11-013417-9.

A note on the title page of this superb, scholarly work states "This atlas was sponsored by the International Council of Philosophy and Humanistic Studies (UNESCO), the Australian Academy of the Humanities, the International Union of Academies, the Research School of Pacific and Asian Studies, and the Australian National University, with financial assistance from UNESCO. Volume 1 contains 151 folded A3 map sheets, each of which contains one large map or two or more smaller maps for a total of 299 maps in all; about one-third are black and white, the remainder in color. For easy reference to the text in volume 2, physically divided into parts 1 and 2, a heading on each map indicates relevant page numbers as well as the map sheet number. At the bottom of each map page is a descriptive title and the map compilers' names. The clear and easy-to-read maps present detailed graphic information on the location and distribution of languages and facilitate understanding of the complex communication patterns in the various areas.

Part 1 of the text volume contains a preface for the general reader; a longer introduction for users with more specialized knowledge follows. In it the editors explain this atlas' relationship to two earlier atlases (see entries 942 and 914) and the rationale for this atlas' coverage of the Pacific hemisphere, the term used by the editors to cover a vast area of the world with the greater Pacific area as its core and including southeast, east and northeast Asia, and the Americas to which they have added the hinterland and far hinterland areas. The editors speculate that a forthcoming atlas might cover the rest of the world, the Atlantic hemisphere, i.e. Europe, Africa, the Middle East including areas as far as the Indian subcontinent, and perhaps parts of the Americas not fully covered by the present atlas. More than 80 experts collaborated with the three editors in writing the 138 chapters of the text which provide explanations and discussions of the information shown on the maps and in some instances describe matters not readily depicted on maps. Topics include native languages, bi- and multilingualism, languages of wider communication (lingua francas, contact languages, mission or church languages, and pidgins and Creoles), metropolitan languages, and languages used by modern media in communication in the Pacific area. The atlas sums up current research and in some cases—such as with pidgins and Creoles and for some of the languages of the Americas—presents new and important facts and theories. Each chapter has bibliographic references and a list of the maps referred to in the text. Part 2 of the text volume concludes with an index the editors label a "subject finder list." Such a list differs from an ordinary index with language names and other one- or two-word items in that it consists largely of phrases and short sentences. For example, the heading "Arctic areas," is divided into "Aleut and the Aleuts in contact with other languages and peoples," "Aleuts, western, semaphoric communication," and "Eskimo interethnic contact, its history and linguistic consequences." Similarly, each of these sub-headings has phrase-listings beneath with page number references. Linguists and geolinguists as well as other specialists such as anthropologists, ethnographers, sociologists, and even political scientists and historians of both culture and economics will find the atlas highly valuable.

Internet Meta-Sites (and More)

632. **Ancient Scripts of the World**. Available: http://alumni.eecs. berkeley.edu/~lorentz/Ancient_Scripts/. (Accessed: March 19, 1999).

Ancient scripts of the world are organized and illustrated at this colorful, interesting site organized in sections by region (Fertile Crescent, Africa, Europe, India, Far East, and the Americas) and by connection (logosyllabic, logographic, syllabic, consonantal alphabetical, and alphabetical). The author is a computer science student with an avocational interest in the field. For a particular language or languages, he summarizes historical background information and displays graphics of the writing system. Other sections of the site are devoted to sounds and phonetics, a bibliography, and a "Resources & Destinations" link which leads the visitor to other Web sites related to writing systems and sources of fonts. A news and updates link last updated December 18, 1998 provides information about recent discoveries and new links. The illustrations and layout of this site make it very appealing to the visitor.

633.   **BUBL Information Service Home Page**.
See entry 94 in chapter 4.

634.   **The Canadian Forces Language School Ottawa—École de langues des Forces canadiennes Ottawa**. Available: http://www.cfls.ndhq.dnd.ca/. (Accessed March 19, 1999).

All information on this site is provided side-by-side in both English and French. Links on the home page include: languages, dictionaries (online multilingual and bilingual), language centers, resources (CALL, education and the Internet, general resources, associations, journals, publishers), and fonts. There are lots of graphics so some pages can be slow in loading. Because of the many levels of links, the visitor needs to be persistent in getting to the many riches of this site. For example, the "Languages/Langues" link leads to a page displaying country flags which if clicked on, leads one to even more links with information about the language(s) and language resources in that country.

635.   **Collection of Web-Dictionaries**. Available: http://dict.leo.org/dict/dictionaries.html. (Accessed: March 19, 1999).

The maintainers of this simple Web site provide an index to bilingual and multi-lingual online dictionaries in many widely and not so widely spoken languages such as Maori, Tongan, Gilbertese, Mingo, and Tibetan. After only a couple of clicks a visitor has access to the desired dictionary.

636.   **CTI Centre for Modern Languages**. Available: http://www.hull. ac.uk/cti/index.htm. (Accessed March 19, 1999).

The Computers in Teaching Initiative (CTI) based in the Language Institutate at the University of Hull, UK maintains this Web site last updated March 17, 1999. The "General" link is subdivided into such sections as fonts, online dictionaries and grammars, software, organizations, and translating and interpreting. There are other language-specific and multilingual links leading to a wealth of language materials useful for language teachers and others. A search engine has recently been added.

637.   **European minority languages**. Available: http://www.smo.uhi. ac.uk/saoghal/mion-chanain/Failte_en.html#directories. (Accessed: March 19, 1999).

The "Other directories worldwide" link on this site's home page provides access to a long list of language meta-sites. In addition it provides two to four comprehensive links for about 78 individual European minority languages. The site available in both Gaelic and English is maintained at Sabhal Mór Ostaig, Scotland's Gaelicmedium Further Education College on the Island of Skye. It was last updated March 8, 1999.

638.   **The Human-Languages Page**. Available: http://www.june29. com/HLP/. (Accessed March 19, 1999).

The Human-Languages Page (H-LP) is one of the top meta-sites for both languages and linguistics. The creator, owner, and maintainer of the English portion of the H-LP is Tyler Chambers, a graduate student at Northeastern University and employee of Harvard Translation; volunteers maintain translated pages. Begun in 1994 with only 30 links available in English, it has continued to grow and mature into an award-winning, complex site with over 1,900 selected links that can be browsed through the AltaVista Translation Services page in German, Spanish, French, Italian, or Portuguese. The WWW Virtual Library Languages page is now contained in the H-LP.

At the top of each page are standard buttons to take a visitor back to the home page or to a form to perform a search of the entire H-LP site (of titles, descriptions or both, using Boolean "and" or "or"). Other buttons allow for such functions as sending e-mail to Tyler, accessing information about H-LP, sampling a random site, submitting a site for addition to H-LP, and browsing book titles for language and linguistics courtesy of amazon.com. Another useful feature is that each resource is preceded by a colored button, purple indicating regular entries, yellow signaling entries added or changed with the last 30 days.

The home page organizes the site into nine categories. A visitor following the link for the "languages and literature" category will find it further organized into an alphabetical list of more than 100 languages. In turn, an individual language page may provide links to a mix of resources such as other meta-sites, software, fonts, associations, language programs, writing scripts, mailing lists, language lessons, and the like, some of which have audio. The category of "schools and institutions" is subdivided into "directories" (language programs, language schools, and universities) and "resources" (alphabetically listed with brief one-sentence or phrase annotations). The category of "products and services" is similarly organized into "directories" (software and translation) and "resources." The categories of "linguistics resources," "organizations," "latest additions," "jobs and internships," "dictionaries" (mono-, bi-, and multilingual), and "language lessons" do not list directories separately, but simply organize resources alphabetically with brief annotations; the search engine only partially compensates for having to scan what are, in some of these categories, long lists of mixed types of sites.

639. **LangLinks**. Available: http://www.ceuc.unican.es/webmaster/langlinks.html. Accessed: March 21, 1999.

Alfredo Reino, himself a student, maintains this well-organized Web site of language resources intended for use of students at the University of Cantabria in Spain. It has not been updated in a while (May 25, 1998), but is nonetheless included here for its valuable content on extinct and constructed languages. Links are listed alphabetically without annotation under headings for languages, extinct languages, courses, dictionaries, conlangs, Esperanto and Ido, newspapers online, and linguistics and guides; the latter are mainly meta-sites. One annoying feature marring an otherwise great site is the use of a black background making the links, especially the purple ones, difficult to read.

640. **The LINGUIST List**.
See entry 98 in chapter 4.

641. **The List of Language Lists**. Available: http://www.indigo.ie/egt/langlist.html. (Accessed: March 21, 1999).

Bernard Comrie and Michael Everson prepared this list of listservs devoted primarily to the linguistic study of individual languages and groups of languages. A few lists for language learners are also included. It is organized by Library of

Congress subject headings and listed in roughly call number order. The authors provide general directions for subscribing and communicating with lists. They last updated the site on September 5, 1998. While making a reference to Diane Kovacs' more general directory of scholarly electronic conferences, the 13th *Directory of Scholarly and Professional E-Conferences*, and giving directions for having it e-mailed, they do not include information about its searchable Web site now available at: http://www.n2h2.com/KOVACS/ (accessed: March 21, 1999).

642. **Other Sites of Interest**. Available: http://www.facstaff.bucknell. edu/rbeard/othrsite.html. (Accessed: March 21, 1999).

There are other more complete meta-sites for languages, but this one compiled by Robert Beard, Professor in the Department of Modern Languages, Literatures, and Linguistics at Bucknell University, is included primarily because of its links to pages (also compiled by Beard) of selected resources on morphology, online dictionaries, and grammars for various languages around the globe. The links on the page for morphology were chosen both for their theoretical significance and content of empirical data. Preceding the alphabetical list of these links is a short list of sites which a visitor can go to for identifying, or making a good guess at, what language a sample is from. The grammar page includes reference, learning, and historical grammars organized alphabetically by language while the dictionaries page indexes online dictionaries, thesauri, and such-like containing words and phrases. For the latter, Beard gives preference to free, high quality dictionary-type resources yet still lists 800 dictionaries in 160 different languages. A grid with language names provides access to mono- and bilingual dictionaries. Other links provide access to multilingual dictionaries, specialized English dictionaries (organized by subject such as business, gastronomy, slang, and philosophy), and various thesauri and other language aids. This excellent site is well-tended and deserving of its awards. It was last updated March 19, 1999.

643. **Reference Shelf**. Available: http://www.library.mcgill. ca/refshelf/swsindex.htm. (Accessed: March 21, 1999).

The "Electronic Reference Shelf" organized by topic and publication type is a link on the McGill University Libraries' home page. It is included here especially for its page of language dictionaries that captures links to many dictionary meta-sites and, in particular, to historical English and other language dictionary projects such as the *Early Modern English Dictionaries Database* and the *ARTFL Project: French-English Dictionary*. Each link is briefly annotated and the few dictionaries only available to McGill University affiliates are clearly marked. The "Language Dictionaries" page was last updated February 16, 1999.

644. **Rivdendel's Links To Useful Resources**. Available: http://rivendel. com/~ric/resources/resources.html. (Accessed: March 21, 1999).

Because of its rich content, excellent organization, continuous addition of good links, and good taste in advertising its services, the Rivendel International Communications Web site is one of the only commercial pages included in this work. While its "Links to Useful Resources" page is organized into some ten categories, the most useful for the visitor needing language information are the links to foreign language dictionaries and translators, free online language instruction, printed language resources (plus software and video), and language chat sites.

645. **SIL Home Page**.
See entry 102 in chapter 4.

646. **Tooyoo Resources and Links**. Available: http://www.tooyoo.L. u-tokyo.ac.jp/deptmnt.html. (Accessed: March 21, 1999).

The Department of Asian and Pacific Linguistics, Institute of Cross-Cultural Studies at the University of Tokyo maintains this Web site rich in content. Its organization can be confusing and is best accessed through the URL cited above rather than through the department home page. This page has just five links and is included here primarily because of two of these.

The first is the "ICHEL Home Page" for the International Clearing House for Endangered Languages" which is itself located at the University of Tokyo. The Web page contains much information specific to the project (such as workshops, a newsletter, grants, progress reports) or of related interest (such as the database on minority languages of Russia joint project) as well as to the Asia and Pacific, Africa, Europe, and Northeast Asia parts of the *UNESCO Red Book of Endangered Languages*; the America section is still in preparation. Each part of the book has a bibliography and various indexes leading to the links for individual languages which, if followed, provide data on the language itself and its endangered state. This page was last modified October 18, 1998.

The second link of special interest is the "Minority/Endangered Languages Links" which points the visitor to an odd mixture of links for language meta-sites, electronic discussion lists, associations and organizations, projects, a site for indigenous peoples of the world, the "Universal Declaration of Linguistic Rights," "The Red Book of the Peoples of the Russian Empire," and the like. This page was last updated February 28, 1999.

647. **Yamada Language Guides**. Available: http://babel.uoregon. edu/yamada/guides.html. (Accessed: March 21, 1999).

The *Yamada Language Guides* site maintained by the Yamada Language Center at the University of Oregon is one of the top resources on the Web for not only finding information on about 115 languages and some 112 fonts for 40 languages, but also technical assistance in using the fonts. The home page provides links to a directory of language-related news groups and a directory of mailing lists. After reaching either directory the visitor has only to click on a language from the list provided to access direct links to relevant news groups or mailing lists. On the home page there is also an alphabetical list of links for individual languages each which may variously provide information on available fonts, news groups, and mailing lists or list other language Web sites. Other links on the home page are for sites for more than one language and a listing of alternate font collections on the Internet.

20

Indo-European

Multi-Indo-European

648. Comrie, Bernard, ed. **The Major Languages of Western Europe**. London: Routledge, 1990. 315p. index. illus. bibliog. maps. ISBN 0-415-04738-2.

The text of this handbook is reprinted from the author's earlier work, *The World's Major Languages* (see entry 561). Aside from a rewritten introduction, it includes no new material. After an initial chapter on Indo-European languages, another 12 chapters are grouped around the Germanic languages, Latin and the Italic languages, and Romance languages. See entry 561 for a description of chapter contents and index.

649. Gamkrelidze, Thomas V., and Vjačeslav V. Ivanov. **Indo-European and the Indo-Europeans: A Reconstruction and Historical Analysis of a Proto-Language and a Proto-Culture. Part II. Bibliography, Indexes**. Compiled by Richard A. Rhodes. Translated by Johanna Nichols. Berlin: Mouton de Gruyter, 1995. 264p. index. (Trends in Linguistics. Studies and Monographs, 80). ISBN 3-11-009646-3.

By providing a translation of a major study on Proto-Indo-European originally published in Russian in 1984, Nichols and Rhodes perform an invaluable service to the English-speaking world. The authors spent some ten years writing the Russian original with another five years in press while the English translation and its typesetting took yet another ten years. The bibliography and indexes in Part II serve as the reference material for the text in Part I and are an indispensable part of the work. Preceding the bibliography are brief synopses of Indo-European languages, followed by even briefer synopses of the non-Indo-European languages in adjacent parts of Eurasia, then notes on transliteration. Abbreviations for languages and dialects, grammatical terms, and sources complete the introductory materials. Unlike the Russian original, the bibliography (pages 1-107) in the translation transliterates the Cyrillic references and merges them with the Latin references. Indexes provide access to the Proto-Indo-European roots, stems, and affixes; semantemes; attested language forms; proper names; and textual citations.

650. **Linguistique balkanique: bibliographie, 1966-1975**. Sous la direction de Petja Assenova [sic]; élaborée par Sima Davidova avec la collaboration du Centre international des recherches scientifiques et de documentation. Sofia: Academie bulgare des sciences, 1983. 265p. index. bibliog.

The Balkans constitute a well-defined linguistic area; the Albanian, Romanian, Bulgarian, and Greek languages form its core. Fundamental work in this area was done earlier in this century by Kristian Sandfeld, N. S. Trubetskoi, and then Roman Jakobson.

In this classified unannotated bibliography of 1,996 items Petia Asenova and others pull together materials on this topic published from 1966 through 1975. Sections of the bibliography are devoted to general and historical works, studies on the theory of Balkan linguistic unity, phonetics and phonology, morphology, onomastics, dialects, etc. In each section entries are arranged in alphabetical order with those in the Latin script preceding entries in Cyrillic, followed by those in Greek. The compilers provide a French translation for titles not in English, French, or German. This is useful since many of the works are in Bulgarian and other lesser known languages. Cross-references are given at the end of sections. There is both a name and geographic index, plus a bibliography of sources consulted. The title page and introductory material are in both French and Bulgarian.

651.   Schaller, Helmut Wilhelm. **Bibliographie zur Balkanphilologie**. Heidelberg: Carl Winter, 1977. 109p. index. LC 77-554071. ISBN 3-533-02552-7.

In his unannotated bibliography of 1,536 items Schaller includes background materials on the Balkans as a linguistic area as well as works dealing with both the Slavonic languages (Bulgarian, Macedonian, Serbo-Croatian) and non-Slavonic languages (Greek, Romanian, Turkish, Albanian) spoken there. Entries for books, chapters of books, articles, and dissertations are arranged alphabetically within a classification scheme. A subject and author index provide additional access. Works cited are in many languages and some date back to the earlier decades of this century.

652.   **Year's Work in Modern Language Studies**. Vol. 1- (1929/30)- . London: Modern Humanities Research Association, 1931- . annual. ISSN 0084-4152.

Both the Oxford University Press and Cambridge University Press have taken turns publishing this critical survey on language and literature since it first appeared in 1931. It has been an annual except for volume 11 which covered the years 1940/49.

Recent research in the form of a running commentary is presented in five main sections: Latin, Romance languages, Celtic languages, Germanic languages, and Slavonic studies—no longer is there a separate section for linguistics (though the first sub-section under Romance languages is for Romance linguistics). Sections are then further subdivided into language and literature sections, often with chronological sub-arrangements. Each subsection is written and signed by a scholar in the particular area of study. Both descriptive and evaluative comments are included. Bibliographic information is complete, but extensively abbreviated. Lists of journal and publisher's abbreviations, revised in volume 59 (1997), appear not only at the end of sections, but also at the end of a volume. There are indexes of subjects and names. Publication lags somewhat, for example, the 1996 annual published in 1997, but not received by libraries until the latter half of 1998, cites material mainly from 1995.

Germanic

Bibliographies of Dictionaries

653. Claes, Frans M., and Peter Bakema. **A Bibliography of Dutch Dictionaries**. Tübingen: Max Niemeyer, 1995. 377p. index. bibliog. (Lexicographica. Series Maior, 67; ISSN 0175-9264). ISBN 3-484-30967-9.

With this bibliography Claes updates and expands his original work, *A Bibliography of Netherlandic Dictionaries* (München: Kraus International, 1980) to include 4,500 items published from 1477 through 1990. Like its predecessor it is a comprehensive listing of monolingual, bilingual, and polyglot dictionaries of all types, but now it also incorporates biographical dictionaries and important encyclopedias. Limitations on size, however, have necessitated the removal of entries for works published as articles or as book chapters. Entries are systematically arranged according to a multi-level thematic classification scheme. Author and language indexes provide additional access points. There is a 2-page bibliography of sources Claes consulted in compiling this work.

654. Claes, Frans M., P. Kramer, and V. van der Veen. **A Bibliography of Frisian Dictionaries**. Grins/Groningen: Frysk Institút RU, 1984. 24p. index. (Us wurk, jiergong 33, jefte 1). LC 84-230518.

All monolingual, bilingual, and polyglot dictionaries or vocabularies of West, East, and North Frisian are included in this classified bibliography. Entries are divided between two main sections, one dealing with Frisian until about 1550, the other continuing from that time until now. Each section is further subdivided by language and dialect. An index of authors follows.

655. Haugen, Eva Lund. **A Bibliography of Scandinavian Dictionaries**. With an Introduction by Einar Haugen. White Plains, NY: Kraus International, 1984. 387p. index. LC 82-48985. ISBN 0-527-38842-4.

More than 2,500 dictionaries published between 1510 and 1980 that are entirely in one of the Scandinavian languages or that translate one of these languages into another language are listed here. All types of dictionaries are covered. Concise notes, including language and direction of translation for bi- and multilingual works, frequently accompany entries. Einar Haugen, a well-known scholar in this area, provides an excellent survey of Scandinavian lexicography in the introduction. Indexes for author, language, and subject further increase the value of this outstanding work.

656. Lemmer, Manfred. **Deutscher Wortschatz. Bibliographie zur deutschen Lexikologie**. Halle/Saale: Max Niemeyer, 1967. 123p. LC 68-76666.

The first half of this work lists over 600 German dictionaries of all kinds, from Gothic and Icelandic to modern technical vocabulary. Most but not all imprints indicate publication in Germany, some going back to the 1700s. The second half of the book is a bibliography of German lexicology. It includes research in both journals and monographs. Only a few entries, in either part of the book, are annotated.

657. Stanze, Britta. **Systematische Bibliographie der deutschen Rechtschreibbücher.** Egelsbach: Hänsel-Hohenhausen, 1994. 220p. index. illus. bibliog. (Deutsche Hochschulschriften, 1045; ISSN 0944-7091). ISBN 3-8267-1045-2.

According to Stanze, this systematic bibliography of orthographic rulebooks for German is the first complete index of German books that contain orthographic rules and/or word lists. The period covered in the bibliography ranges from 1880—the year in which the *Duden* first appeared—to 1993. The first section details the structure of the bibliography and provides a chronological overview plus a source bibliography. The second section contains the classified bibliography itself and an index to the names in the entries.

Atlases

658. Eichhoff, Jürgen. **Wortatlas der deutschen Umgangssprachen.** Bern: Francke, 1977-1978. 2v. index. illus. maps. LC 78-376748. ISBN 3-7720-1337-6(v.1); 3-7720-1339-2(v.2).

The 125 colored maps in these 2 volumes illustrate German colloquial speech. Some text accompanies each. There is an index of place names in each volume and a word index in volume 2.

659. Herzog, Marvin, and others, eds. **The Language and Culture Atlas of Ashkenazic Jewry.** Prepared and published under the aegis of an Editorial Collegium. Tübingen: Max Niemeyer, 1992-4. (In progress).

660. **Volume I. Historical and Theoretical Foundations.** 1992. 136+8p. index. bibliog. maps. ISBN 3-484-73003-X.

661. **Volume II. Research Tools.** 1995. 106+8p. index. bibliog. maps. ISBN 3-484-73004-8.

Volume I provides an introduction to the LCAAJ project which aims to produce a Yiddish dialect atlas of Eastern and Central Europe. Some 500 survivors dispersed throughout the world after the Holocaust were sought out and interviewed using a questionnaire largely crafted by Uriel Weinreich. The 81 three-colored maps illustrate phonological variations. Volume II contains "research tools, particularly those used and developed in the course of collecting, processing, and analyzing the data" (p. 1). Further volumes are expected to emerge from this project.

662. Hotzenköcherle, Rudolf. **Einführung in den Sprachatlas der deutschen Schweiz.** Bern: Francke, 1962. 2v. bibliog.

663. Hotzenköcherle, Rudolf, ed. **Sprachatlas der deutschen Schweiz.** Begründet von Heinrich Baumgartner und Rudolf Hotzenköcherle; in Zusammenarbeit mit Konrad Lobeck, Robert Schläpfer, Rudolf Trüb und unter Mitwirkung von Paul Zinsli. Bern: Francke, 1962-1988. 6v. index. bibliog. map.

This excellent atlas of German spoken in Switzerland (SDS) began publication in 1962. The 6th volume was published in 1988. It consists mainly of colored maps with explanatory notes. An introductory volume published in 2 physical parts (A and B) discusses methodology, transcription used, etc.

664.   König, W. **Dtv-Atlas zur deutschen Sprache: Tafeln und Texte**. Mit 140 farbigen Abbildungsseiten. Graphiker: Hans-Joachim Paul. 9. Aufl. München: Deutscher Taschenbuch Verlag, 1992. 250p. index. illus. bibliog. maps (part col.). ISBN 3-434-03025-9.

Konig's concise account of the history of the German language is now in its ninth edition.

This popular pocket edition is illustrated with numerous maps, charts, and illustrations, many in color, and is complemented by a substantial bibliography of references and source materials as well as an index.

665.   Mitzka, Walther. **Deutscher Wortatlas**. Giessen: Wilhelm Schmitz, 1951-1980. 22v. in 21. maps.

Ludwig Erich Schmitt is a co-author for volumes 5-22 while volumes 11-22 of this set belong to the series Deutscher Sprachatlas, Reihe Wortatlas. The atlas is based on answers to a questionnaire consisting of 200 catchwords relating to concepts, objects, and activities. Regional variants in vocabulary were recorded and superimposed typographically on printed maps of Germany. The maps are very detailed and complex.

666.   Nelde, Peter Hans. **Wortatlas der deutschen Umgangssprachen in Belgien**. Bern: Francke, 1987. bibliog. map. (Wortatlas der deutschen umgangssprachen ergänzungsreihe, Bd. 1). ISBN 3-317-01640-X.

This atlas of German dialects in Belgium contains 60 word maps with keys to each map.

667.   Wenker, Georg, et al. **Deutscher Sprachatlas: auf grund des von Georg Wenker begründeten Sprachatlas des Deutschen Reichs und mit Einschluss von Lexumburg**. In vereinfachter Form bearbeitet bei der Zentralstelle für den Sprachatlas des Deutschen Reichs und deutsche Mundartenforschung unter Leitung von Ferdinand Wrede. Marburg (Lehn): N. G. Elwert, 1926-1956. text (Lieferung 1-21), 344p. illus. maps; atlas, 35p. and 128 maps.

668.   **Deutscher Sprachatlas; regional Sprachatlanten**. Hrsg. vom Forschungsinstitut für deutsche Sprache "Deutscher Sprachatlas." Marburg: N.G. Elwert, 1961- . illus. map. (In progress).

669.   **Kleiner deutscher Sprachatlas**. Dialektologisch bearb. von Werner H. Veith. Computativ bearbeitet von Wolfgang Putschke. Unter Mitarbeit von Lutz Hummel. Tübingen: Max Niemeyer, 1984- . bibliog. maps. ISBN 3-484-24501-8 (Bd. 1, Teil 1); 3-484-24502-6 (Bd. 1, Teil 2); 3-484-24503-4 (Bd. 2, Teil 1).

670.   Mitzka, Walther. **Handbuch zum Deutschen Sprachatlas**. Marburg: Elwertsche Universitätsbuchhandlung, 1952. 180p. LC 52-8839.

Wenker's linguistic atlas of German-speaking countries, the *Deutscher Sprachatlas* (DSA), shows variations in pronunciation throughout Germany, Austria, and Switzerland. A handbook by Mitzka provides an introduction to the history and use of the atlas.

The *Deutscher Sprachatlas; regional Sprachatlanten* provides regional supplements to the DSA. The first of 60 planned volumes was published in 1961. Each volume has an individual title with its own editor(s) and differ somewhat though all have numerous maps and some text. For example, Number 5 in this series, *Linguistic Atlas of Texas German* by G. Gilbert, was published in 1972 by the University of Texas, Austin. Another work in progress supplementing the original DSA is the *Kleiner deutscher Sprachatlas*. Band 1 deals with the pronunciation of consonants, Band 2 with vowels.

Indexes and Serial Bibliographies

671.   **Bibliographie der deutschen Sprach- und Literaturwissenschaft**. Bd. 9- , 1969- . Frankfurt am Main: Vittorio Klostermann, 1970- . annual.

This title is a continuation of *Bibliographie der deutschen Literaturwissenschaft* (1945-1968) which did not include linguistics. It lists primary and secondary material from a wide range of international sources and cites substantial reviews. The arrangement is by topic and/or period. Only a very short section is devoted to German linguistics.

672.   **Germanistik**. 1. Jahrg., Hft. 1- . Tübingen: Max Niemeyer, 1960- . 4 times/year. LC 62-30058. ISSN 0016-8912.

Only a short section of this classified bibliography, like the *Bibliographie der deutschen Sprach- und Literaturwissenschaft* with which it overlaps (see entry above), is devoted to linguistics. Coverage is narrower, however. Its chief value is as a reviewing tool since entries for books often cite reviews or contain signed book reviews by specialists. The fourth issue each year has cumulative name and subject indexes.

673.   **Internationale germanistische Bibliographie: IGB**. 1980-1982. München: K. G. Saur; distr., Detroit, MI: Gale Research, 1981-1984. annual. ISSN 0721-4561.

Only 3 years of this intended annual bibliography of German philology were ever published. It gathers a wide range of materials from many countries and in many languages with the exception of gray literature, microfilm, reviews, theses, audio materials, and research appearing in newspapers. The volume for a particular year includes works from that year and a few years prior. The arrangement is alphabetical by author within a classified scheme. The sections of particular interest to linguists are general linguistics, structural linguistics, onomastics, pragmatics, sociolinguistics, psycholinguistics, area linguistics, historical linguistics, contrastive linguistics, poetics, and applied linguistics. There are name and subject indexes.

674.   **Jahresbericht für deutsche Sprache und Literatur**. Bd. 1-2. Berlin: Akademie-Verlag, 1960-1966. ISSN 0075-2843.

Only 2 volumes of this title were ever published: Band I covers 1940-1945 while Band II covers 1946-1950. This work together with an earlier title, the *Jahresbericht uber die Erscheinungen auf dem Gebiete der germanischen Philologie*, which covered the years 1879-1939 provide an extensive bibliography of the monographic and journal literature for the German language for the period indicated. Each volume has author and name/subject indexes.

Cumulative Bibliographies

675. Augst, Gerhard, ed. **Rechtschreibliteratur: Bibliographie zur wissenschaftlichen Literatur über die Rechtschreibung und Rechtschreibreform der neuhochdeutschen Standardsprache erschienen von 1900 bis 1990.** Unter Mitarbeit von Andrea Höppner. Frankfurt am Main: Peter Lang, 1992. 183p. index. (Theorie und Vermittlung der Sprache, Bd. 15; ISSN 0724-9144). ISBN 3-631-44659-4.

Augst has gathered into this simple, unannotated and alphabetically arranged bibliography works published on German language orthography and spelling from 1900 through 1990. Subject access is provided by a two-tiered index.

676. Bratkowsky, Joan Gloria. **Yiddish Linguistics: A Multilingual Bibliography.** New York: Garland, 1988. 407p. index. bibliog. (Garland Reference Library of the Humanities, Vol. 140). LC 87-34196. ISBN 0-8240-9804-8.

In compiling this work Bratkowsky's goal was to update Uriel and Beatrice Weinreich's *Yiddish Language and Folklore* bibliography (see entry 700) for publications after 1958; though no cut-off date is listed in the introduction, an examination of the more than 7-page long bibliography of works utilized by the compiler shows most coverage is through the 1960s with some coverage of mid- to late 1970s. Nearly 2,200 entries, unannotated except for a few with brief notes, are arranged according to a 12-part classification scheme covering general works, structure and history of Yiddish, dialectology, interaction with other languages, onomastics, stylistics, semiotics, history of linguistics and biographies of linguists, sociolinguistics, psycholinguistics, and applied linguistics. Within subcategories for these 12 parts, entries are further grouped under headings for language of article which, instead of being a convenience to the user, unnecessarily chops up the bibliography and complicates its use. Entries for Hebrew, Yiddish, and Russian works are entirely in the original scripts, though in the index of names, such names are transliterated.

677. Braunmüller, Kurt. **Deutsch-Skandinavisch im Vergleich: eine Bibliographische Übersicht über linguistische und lexikographische Arbeiten (1945-1995).** Revidierte, erw. u. aktualisierte Neuaus. Oslo: Novus Forlag, 1996. 238p. index. (Studia Nordica, 4). ISBN 82-7099-263-1.

The first edition of this bibliography published in 1987 surveying German and Scandinavian comparative linguistics and lexicography covered publications from 1945 through 1985. In this revised and enlarged edition Braunmüller extends coverage through 1995. Two indexes, one for language, the other for subject, provide access to almost 1,400 entries. These entries, some with brief descriptive notes, are arranged in three classified sections: bibliographies of German-Scandinavian comparative linguistics, linguistic works on German-Scandinavian comparative linguistics, and German-Scandinavian dictionaries. Works cited are for books, book chapters, journal articles, and conference papers written mainly in German, Danish, Norwegian, Icelandic, and Swedish; a few other languages such as English and Russian are represented.

678.   Bremmer, Rolf H. **A Bibliographical Guide to Old Frisian Studies**. Odense University Press, 1992. 197p. index. (North-Western European Language Evolution. Supplement, Vol. 6; ISSN 0900-8675). ISBN 87-7492-906-2.

Bremmer's comprehensive bibliography of Old Frisian language and literature is the first such work to be published. The author does not state a beginning coverage date, but at least one citation dates back to 1701; coverage ends in 1992. Part I contains the bibliography itself. It consists of alphabetically arranged citations to books and articles with references to reviews of the cited works. Somewhat curiously, Bremmer has chosen not to include publishers names, especially since he has located many obscure items and this omission may make it difficult for scholars to locate such materials. Part II is an index of the reviewers cited in part I, while part III is a well-executed analytical subject index.

679.   Bunis, David M., and Andrew Sunshine. **Yiddish Linguistics: A Classified Bilingual Index to Yiddish Serials and Collections 1913-1958**. Under the auspices of the Yivo Institute for Jewish Research, New York, NY. New York: Garland, 1994. 194p. index. (Garland Reference Library of the Humanities, Vol. 175). LC 93-34051. ISBN 0-8240-9758-0.

Bunis and Sunshine provide here an exhaustive index of articles on Yiddish linguistics which were published in Yiddish serials and collective volumes between 1913 and 1958; a list of these 24 items preface the bibliography itself. The time period chosen parallels a period of expanded use of Yiddish throughout the world. The work complements Uriel and Beatrice Weinreich's *Yiddish Language and Folklore* (see entry 700). Continued indexing of Yiddish linguistic research articles published in Yiddish and other languages from 1958 on can be found in Bratkowsky's *Yiddish Linguistics: A Multilingual Bibliography* (see entry 676).

Works cited are arranged alphabetically according to an 11-part classification scheme: general, phonology, spelling, grammar, lexicon and lexicography, integration of components (internationalisms, Germanic, Hebrew and Aramaic, and Slavic), sociolinguistics and stylistics, linguistic geography, Yiddish in countries of immigration, influence of Yiddish on other languages, and history. The numbered, unannotated entries are listed both in Yiddish on right-hand pages and again in their transliterated entirety on facing pages, except for article titles which are translated into English. To aid users, the compilers provide indexes of authors, selected subjects (in English only), and lists of words under study.

680.   Eisenberg, Peter, and Alexander Gusovius. **Bibliographie zur deutschen Grammatik, 1965-1986**. 2., überarb. u. erw. Aufl. Tübingen: Gunter Narr Verlag, 1988. 412p. index. (Studien zur deutschen Grammatik, Bd. 26). ISBN 3-87808-367-X.

681.   Eisenberg, Peter, and Bernd Wiese. **Bibliographie zur deutschen Grammatik, 1984-1994**. Unter Mitarbeit von Matthias Butt und Jörg Peters. 3., aktualisierte u. erw. Aufl. Tübingen: Stauffenburg Verlag, 1995. 388p. index. (Studien zur deutschen Grammatik, Bd. 26). ISBN 3-86057-416-7.

The first edition (1985) of this bibliography on grammar of the German language covered works published in the years 1965-1983. The second and third editions together provide coverage from 1965-1994. All follow the same format of unannotated entries arranged alphabetically by author. Most citations are to works in German, with a few in English and other languages. Each edition has a subject index, while the 3rd edition also has an index listing contrastive works by the language with which German is contrasted.

682.   Haeringen, Coenraad Bernardus van. **Netherlandic Language Research: Men and Works in the Study of Dutch**. 2nd ed. Leiden: E. J. Brill, 1960. 120p. index. maps.

The second edition of this work extends the period covered by the survey of Netherlandic language research to material published from 1880 to the first half of 1959. Two black and white line maps show on one the area and main cities of the Netherlands in the 16th century while on the other the area with country and provincial boundaries where Netherlandic is presently spoken as the mother tongue. The survey consists of critical, bibliographic essays on general reference works and periodicals on the language; then a series of 6 essays covers the time periods from Old Netherlandic through to Modern Netherlandic; essays on Netherlandic and foreign languages, dialectology, onomastics, and word studies; and concludes with an essay on special subjects. There are no cumulative bibliographies, whether of the essays or the entire survey, but an index of personal authors, corporate authors, and some main entries and titles, partially compensates for this lack.

683.   Hannich-Bode, Ingrid, comp. **Germanistik in Festschriften von den Anfängen (1877) bis 1973: Verzeichnis germanistischer Festschriften und Bibliographie der darin abgedruckten germanistischen Beiträge**. In Zusammenarbeit mit dem Institute of Germanic Studies (University of London). Stuttgart: Metzler, 1976. 441p. index. (Repertorien zur deutschen Literaturgeschichte, Bd. 7). ISBN 3-476-00329-9.

Some 307 Festschriften dedicated to Germanists are fully analyzed in this index; another 491 are selectively analyzed. It has a classified arrangement with indexes for authors, titles, broad subjects, and personal names as subjects providing additional access.

684.   Hansel, Johannes. **Bücherkunde für Germanisten. Wie sammelt man das Schrifttum nach dem neuesten Forschungsstand**? Berlin: E. Schmidt, 1959. 233p. index. LC 60-1097.

685.   Hansel, Johannes. **Bücherkunde für Germanisten: Studienausgabe**. Bearbeitet von Lydia Tschakert. 8., neubearb. Aufl. Berlin: E. Schmidt, 1983. 209p. index. LC 87-673797. ISBN 3-503-02212-0.

The abridged student's version of this basic guide to research materials for Germanic language and literature is now in its 8th edition. It is of more immediate practical value than the original key work (1959 edition) since only the more important and up-to-date items have been selected for inclusion. All types of reference works including bibliographies, indexes, surveys, dictionaries, guides, histories, and journals are listed along with useful annotations. Charts showing dates of coverage for similar works are particularly helpful. Nearly all the 1,254 entries are for German-language works. The author provides author/title and subject indexes.

686.   Haugen, Einar Ingvald, ed. **A Bibliography of Scandinavian Languages and Linguistics, 1900-1970**. Tove Kangas, David Margolin, and Inger Mette Markey, assistant eds. Oslo: Universitetsforlaget, 1974. 527p. index. LC 74-185312. ISBN 82-00-08997-5.

Haugen emphasizes the linguistic approaches to language in this fairly exhaustive international bibliography. The term Scandinavian here includes all forms of Danish, Faroese, Icelandic, Norwegian, and Swedish as well as all older forms of these back to the time when Scandinavian was still a dialect of Germanic. Descriptor codes indicate the languages and the subject matter of items. There is an index based on these codes. While the codes are cumbersome to work with, they do provide good subject access to the material.

687.   Kelp, Helmut. **Germanistische Linguistik in Rumänien 1945-1985: Bibliographie**. München: Verlag Südostdeutsches Kulturwerk, 1990. 354p. index. (Veröffentlichungen des Südostdeutschen Kulturwerks. Reihe B: Wissenschaftliche Arbeiten, Bd. 49). ISBN 3-88356-060-X.

Articles on Germanic linguistics published over a forty year period from 1945 to 1985 in some 350 journals and collected works as well as theses issued from universities in Rumania for this same time period are cited in this alphabetically arranged bibliography. Nearly all of the more than 5,000 works cited are written in German or Romanian. There are indexes of names (authors, co-authors, editors, subjects), places, and subjects. Though a more detailed subject index would be welcome, Kelp does a service to researchers in bringing together some otherwise not easily identified materials.

688.   McKay, John C. **A Guide to Germanic Reference Grammars: The Modern Standard Languages**. Amsterdam: John Benjamins, 1984. 239p. index. bibliog. (Amsterdam Studies in the Theory and History of Linguistic Science. Series V: Library and Information Sources in Linguistics, Vol. 15; ISSN 0165-7267). LC 84-14597. ISBN 90-272-3736-0.

The author has selected for his guide about 100 of the best and most comprehensive of the reference grammars for contemporary standard Germanic languages, i.e., Afrikaans, Danish, Dutch, English, Faroese, Frisian, German, Icelandic, Norwegian, Swedish, and Yiddish. He specifically excluded grammars organized for learning the language, purely historical grammars, and grammars published before 1900. An extensive introduction, accompanied by a 10-page bibliography, describes the various linguistic theories which have influenced the major Germanic reference grammars of this century. Each chapter deals with one language and begins with a summary introduction to the grammars listed in it. Long, thorough descriptive and evaluative annotations (some with citations to reviews) accompany the entries. A general index of technical terms, linguists, authors, and titles rounds out this excellent reference source.

689.   Markey, Thomas L., R. L. Kyes, and Paul T. Roberge. **Germanic and Its Dialects: A Grammar of Proto-Germanic. III. Bibliography and Indices**. With the assistance of Barbara E. Hagerman. Amsterdam: John Benjamins, 1977. 504p. index. LC 78-351327. ISBN 90-272-0984-7.

Only this third volume of what is to be a 3-volume set has been published. Volumes I and II are to contain the text and maps and commentaries. The 8,298 entries are alphabetically arranged. There are no annotations though variant editions, reprints, and occasionally reviews are noted. Its scope is impressive, covering the whole range of Germanic and its dialects. It includes both published works (books, periodical articles, and Festschriften) and unpublished materials (dissertations, theses, manuscripts, incunabula, and primary textual sources) in a wide variety of languages with a cutoff date of 1976. The compilers have provided excellent, thorough indexes. A word index locates works which deal with specific linguistic forms. It is organized by language/dialect. There are also subject and author indexes.

690.   Moulin-Fankhänel, Claudine. **Bibliographie der deutschen Grammatiken und Orthographielehren**. Heidelberg: Universitätsverlag C. Winter, 1994, 1997. 2v. index. illus. bibliog. (Germanische Bibliothek. Neue Folge, 6. Reihe. Bibliographien und Dokumentationen, Bd. 4, 5). ISBN 3-8253-0225-3(v.1); 3-8253-0226-1(v.2).

Volume 1 of this bibliography of early German grammars and orthography primers details sources from the fifteenth to the end of the sixteenth century, while volume 2 goes on to cover the seventeenth century. Both volumes are alphabetically organized by author, providing biographical information on the author, a bibliography of relevant publications, and references to citations in important linguistic literature which refer to the author's work. No information is given on the content of the works themselves. Occasional illustrations taken from these primary sources illuminate the text. Various indexes, lists of references, and libraries consulted complete each volume.

691.   Munske, H. H., and G. Van der Elst, eds. **Erlanger Bibliographie zur Germanistischen Sprachwissenschaft**. 2., rev. u. erw. Aufl. Erlangen: Palm und Enke, 1993. 94p. index. (Erlanger Studien, Bd. 99; ISSN 0179-1710). ISBN 3-7896-0199-3.

In the second revised and enlarged edition of this short unannotated bibliography the editors cover research on Germanic languages and some general linguistics mainly published in the 1980s. Nearly all works cited are written in German with a few citations to works in English. For subject access a user must rely on the 3-level classified arrangement as there is only a name index.

692.   Newman, L. M. **German Language and Literature: Select Bibliography of Reference Books**. 2nd enl. ed. London: Institute of Germanic Studies, University of London, 1979. 175p. index. (Publications of the Institute of Germanic Studies, 9; ISSN 0076-0611). LC 79-318885. ISBN 0-85457-077-2.

Originally published in 1966 as a teaching aid, this new edition has been updated through the end of 1976. It concentrates on recent publications and those materials from the German Federal Republic since they are more accessible than those from the German Democratic Republic, Austria, or Switzerland. Excluded are bibliographies in monographs, reviews of research, and bibliographies on very specific topics. Its 1,000 entries are arranged in 7 subject sections. The descriptive and frequently evaluative annotations are particularly useful. Name, title, and subject indexes complete this excellent guide.

693.   Ronneberger-Sibold, Elke. **Historische Phonologie und Morphologie des Deutschen: Eine Kommentierte Bibliographie zur strukturellen Forschung**. Tübingen: Max Niemeyer, 1989. 586p. index. (Germanistische Arbeitshefte. Ergänzungsreihe, 3; ISSN 0344-6700). ISBN 3-484-10608-5.

The purpose of this bibliography is to review any book, dissertation, or article which treats any aspect of the history of German phonology or morphology from a structural point of view. The author first organizes the 565 entries for phonology in chronological order for the years 1932 through 1984, then does the same for an additional 201 entries on morphology for the years 1941 through 1984. Works published in German and a variety of other languages such as English, Russian, French, Italian, and Finnish are included. Annotations are substantive beginning with a brief critical summary of contents, followed by pertinent book reviews and review articles, and then a list of subsequent scholarship which takes a position on the work reviewed.

694.   Schindler, Frank, and Eike Thurmann, eds. **Bibliographie zur Phonetik und Phonologie des Deutschen**. Unter Mitwirkung von Christine Riek. Tübingen, Max Niemeyer, 1971. 156p. index. (Bibliographische Arbeitsmaterialien). LC 73-334251. ISBN 3-484-10154-7.

More than 1,700 entries are systematically arranged in this bibliography listing monographs, Festschriften, articles, and theses on the phonetics and phonology of German. The editors include materials dating from 1880 to 1971, mainly written in German, English, and French, on all aspects of the subject. Instead of using cross-references, they list some works under 2 or more subjects. An author index is appended.

695.   Seymour, Richard K. **A Bibliography of Word Formation in the Germanic Languages**. Durham, NC: Duke University Press, 1968. 158p. index. LC 68-18780.

The majority of the approximately 2,000 references to books and articles cited here deal with compounding, derivation by prefixes, suffixes and infixes, gradation, onomatopoeia, root formants, back formations, etc. Entries for dictionaries, glossaries, and word lists have been minimized as have been studies on loan words and borrowings, place names, and personal names. Seymour sometimes provides citations to reviews and short comments (when titles are not indicative of contents). He does not always include the total number of pages nor the full title of some works. The bibliography is meant to be complete through 1964 with some entries for 1965 and 1966, but as this is the first attempt at such a bibliography there are inevitably some omissions. The author provides indexes of the following: dictionaries; words, phrases, and etymologies; grammatical categories; languages; topics; and, specific prefixes, suffixes, etc.

696.   Siegel, Elli. **Deutsche Wortkarte 1890-1962: eine Bibliographie**. Giessen: Wilhelm Schmitz, 1964. 67p. (Beiträge zur deutschen Philologie, Bd. 33).

697.   Siegel, Elli. **Deutsche Wortkarte 1963-1970; eine Bibliographie (Fortsetzung)**. Redaktionelle Betreuung, R. Hildebrandt. Giessen, Wilhelm Schmitz, 1974. 970. (Beiträge zur deutschen Philologie, Bd. 40). LC 74-350232.

698.   Siegel, Elli. **Deutsche Wortkarte, 1971-1978: eine Bibliographie: (Ergänzung)**. Redaktionelle Betreuung, R. Hildebrandt. Giessen: Wilhelm Schmitz, 1981. 38p. index. (Beiträge zur deutschen Philologie, Bd. 40a). LC 82-106522. ISBN 3-87711-041-X.

Each of these 3 successive bibliographies of dialect maps of the German language contain a chronological list of linguistic atlases, together with books, articles, dissertations, and dictionaries which contain word maps. This list is followed by another one, alphabetically arranged, of words treated in the works of the preceding list with references back to the entries. There are name/main entry indexes, with the index in the 1974 edition covering both it and the 1964 edition. Together the 3 editions list 865 works.

699.   Siegrist, Leslie. **Bibliographie zu Studien über das deutsche und englische Adverbial**. Tübingen: TBL-Verlag Narr, 1976. 244p. index. (Forschungsberichte des Institut für Deutsche Sprache, Bd. 33). 244p. index. LC 77-566331. ISBN 3-87808-633-4.

More than 2,000 studies published between 1877 and 1972 are gathered in this classified bibliography on the German and English adverb. Short descriptive notes accompany some of the entries. There is an index of words (adverbs, prepositions, and conjunctions) plus an index of authors.

700.   Weinreich, Uriel, and Beatrice Weinrich. **Yiddish Language and Folklore, a Selective Bibliography for Research**. 's-Gravenhage: Mouton, 1959. 66p. index. (Janua linguarum, Nr. 10). LC 63-1121.

About half of this short unannotated bibliography concerns the Yiddish language. These 253 items are arranged under such topical subdivisions as: the sound system, grammar, important dictionaries, social dialects, and history of the language. Authors are indexed.

701.   Wiesinger, Peter. **Bibliographie zur Grammatik der deutschen Dialekte: Laut-, Formen-, Wortbildungs- und satzlehre, 1981 bis 1985 und Nachträge aus früheren Jahren**. Bern: Peter Lang, 1987. 195p. index. ISBN 3-261-03738-5.

For the years 1981 through 1985 Wiesinger continues coverage of an earlier bibliography (see entry 702) with the same arrangement and indexing.

702.   Wiesinger, Peter, and Elisabeth Raffin. **Bibliographie zur Grammatik der deutschen Dialekte: Laut-, Formen-, Wortbildungs- und satzlehre, 1800 bis 1980**. Bern: Peter Lang, 1982. 515p. index. maps. (Europäische Hochschulschriften. Reihe I. Deutsche Sprache und Literatur, Bd. 509). ISBN 3-261-03201-4.

All types of publications for the time period 1800 to 1980 are included in this closely classified bibliography on the grammar of German dialects (phonology, morphology, word formation, and syntax). With only a few exceptions most of the approximately 5,000 works cited are in German. Other than a section for general works, sections are devoted to particular dialects. There is an index of authors and editors. Five folded maps show areas of various dialect features. See entry 701 for a continuation of this bibliography.

English

Encyclopedias and Handbooks

703.   Crystal, David. **The Cambridge Encyclopedia of the English Language**. Cambridge: Cambridge University Press, 1995. 489p. index. illus. bibliog. LC 94-23918. ISBN 0-521-40179-8.

Colored illustrations—maps, charts, photographs, and reproductions—illustrate nearly every page of this wonderful handbook on the history, structure, and use of the English language. Crystal, a linguistics professor and author of other outstanding reference works (see entries 18, 19, and 20), provides much to delight the casual reader or the scholar. The work is divided into six parts: history (origins, Old English, Middle English, Early Modern English, Modern English, and English varieties and dialects around the world); vocabulary (nature, sources, etymology, structure of the lexicon, and lexical dimensions); grammar (grammatical mythology, structure of words, word classes, and the structure of sentences); spoken and written English (the sound and writing systems); using English (varieties of discourse, and regional, social and personal variations); and learning about English (as a mother tongue and new ways of studying it). The parts, chapters, or segments can be read sequentially or separately. Appendixes include a glossary, special symbols and abbreviations, references for the text, ideas for further reading, and three indexes of linguistic items, authors and personalities, and topics.

This work complements another fine reference work, *The Oxford Companion to the English Language* (see entry 704). The emphasis in both is on British English, not American English and they each provide a thorough discussion of variations between the two. The different organization of these works can be illustrated by examining how each treats the history of the English language. Part I with six chapters—consisting of some 100 pages—of the Cambridge work is devoted to this topic, while the Oxford volume treats history as a theme with several hundred entries (listed together on page 475) scattered throughout the alphabetical sequence. The latter does provide, however, under the heading "history of English," a more than five-page chronology dating from 55 B.C., the Roman military expedition to Britain by Julius Caesar, to 1989, the publication of the second edition of *The Oxford English Dictionary*.

704.   McArthur, Tom, ed. **The Oxford Companion to the English Language**. Feri McArthur, managing ed. Oxford: Oxford University Press, 1992. 1184p. index. illus. map. ISBN 0-19-214183-X.

705.   McArthur, Tom, ed. **The Concise Oxford Companion to the English Language**. Roshan McArthur, editorial assistant. Oxford: Oxford University Press, 1996. 1053p. illus. ISBN 0-19-860052-6 (pap.).

When published in 1992 this encyclopedic dictionary was the first major 1-volume reference work on the English language. It was followed in 1995 by a Cambridge publication (see entry 703). The editor's aim was to provide an accessible work, neither overly popular nor too academic and technical. In this they have succeeded. Each entry is signed by one of more than 90 contributors and some of the longer entries may include a short bibliography. Three types of entries are arranged alphabetically: essays, either concise or extensive with subsections; brief dictionary entries for definitions or other explanations; and biographical entries of varying lengths. Quite often hybrid entries combining characteristics of two types can be found. There are occasional black and white illustrations and one map showing the distribution of English throughout the world. The work is peppered with cross-references, partially the result of its organization around 22 themes or topic areas which often overlap; plus many entries may belong to more than one theme. Among the themes are: geography, history, name, style, grammar, writing, language, usage, and variety. All the entries for a particular theme are listed together under that heading in the dictionary. For example, the hundreds of individual entries under the "language and languages" heading take up three columns of text and are subdivided into two listings, one for language and linguistics, the other for languages. This latter listing is then divided into language groups and individual languages. An index of persons (either mentioned in the entries or appearing in the bibliographies of entries) concludes this substantial, scholarly work.

The concise edition of the Oxford companion has—according to McArthur in its introduction—been shortened for the most part by keeping only the core entries and reducing the entries on the many varieties of world English. Little has been added except for some minor textual adjustments and updates to reflect the changing political world. In addition, nearly all of the illustrations and the map have been deleted, entries are not signed, and bibliographies have been deleted as well as the index of persons.

Bibliographies and Catalogs of Dictionaries

706.   Kister, Kenneth F. **Kister's Best Dictionaries for Adults & Young People: A Comparative Guide**. Phoenix, AZ: Oryx Press, 1992. index. bibliog. LC 91-40679. ISBN 0-89774-191-9.

In his guide Kister provides evaluations of 300 English-language dictionaries for adults and young people and brief descriptions or mentions of approximately 200 other titles. It supersedes his 1977 *Dictionary Buying Guide*. Information provided is current as of August 1991 and with the exception of some substantial or well-known dictionaries, titles reviewed are in print. Electronic and CD-ROM versions are also reviewed. An introductory section provides useful background information on dictionaries, covering such topics as what a dictionary is, some historical facts about English-language dictionaries, the difference between a descriptive and prescriptive dictionary, developments regarding electronic dictionaries, and what points to consider when choosing a dictionary.

The dictionary reviews are divided into two sections. The largest section is devoted to general English-language dictionaries for adults subdivided into unabridged dictionaries, college desk dictionaries, family and office desk dictionaries, pocket and paperback dictionaries, and a comparison chart. The shorter section of reviews is for general English-language dictionaries for children and young students. Reviews are evaluative and comparative. Evaluations for unabridged works are substantive and lengthy (e.g., the entry for *Webster's Third New International Dictionary* is about nine pages long), providing comments on purpose and scope, authority, vocabulary treatment, encyclopedic features, graphics, physical format, a summary, and references to other critical opinions. Simpler dictionaries, e.g. the *Chambers Concise Dictionary* with a review only three sentences in length, have appropriately shorter evaluations. A comparative chart at the end of each of the two sections provides in convenient tabular format: title, edition, date published, and number of volumes; publisher or distributor, number of entries, price, and a grade of A through F. Five appendixes provide information on dictionary and language associations; additional sources for evaluating dictionaries; informative publications and nonprint materials about dictionaries; selected publications on language; and a directory of dictionary publishers and distributors. This reliable work concludes with an author-title-subject index.

707. O'Neill, Robert Keating. **English-language Dictionaries 1604-1900: The Catalog of the Warren N. and Suzanne B. Cordell Collection**. New York: Greenwood Press, 1988. 480p. index. (Bibliographies and Indexes in Library and Information Science, No. 1; ISSN 0742-6879). ISBN 0-313-25522-9.

O'Neill's catalog of the 2,300 pre-1901 English-language materials in the Cordell Collection complements Vancil's catalog of both English- and foreign-language titles in this collection (see entry 613). The very detailed entries consist of seven basic parts: main entry, title, publication statement, collation, notes, provenance, and references. A subject index concludes the work.

708. Pierson, Robert M. **Desk Dictionaries: A Consumer's Guide**. Chicago, IL: American Library Association, 1986. 32p. LC 86-3384. ISBN 0-8389-3316-5 (paper).

Long descriptive and critical annotations accompany entries for seven college-level dictionaries. Nine other desk dictionaries are compared. There is a brief discussion of four related works that serve as supplements to any or all of the dictionaries previously discussed. This pamphlet could be considered an update of the abridged and pocket dictionaries section of Kister's guide (see entry 706).

709. Robertson, H. Rocke, and J. Wesley Robertson. **Collection of Dictionaries and Related Works Illustrating the Development of the English Dictionary**. Vancouver, BC: University of British Columbia Press, 1989. 74p. illus. ISBN 0-7748-0344-4.

Basically, this is a catalog of the Robertsons' collection of 352 dictionaries and related works which were gathered to "illuminate the main steps in the development of the English dictionary from its precursors, through the primitive stages, to the various types of modern dictionary." Works are fully and meticulously described and most have annotations. The foreword contains five tables which provide chronologies. Some 27 illustrations, facsimile reproductions from the dictionaries, enliven the text. See entry 710 for a related work.

710. Starnes, DeWitt T., and Gertrude E. Noyes. **The English Dictionary from Cawdrey to Johnson 1604-1755**. New edition with an introduction and a select bibliography by Gabriele Stein. Amsterdam: John Benjamins, 1991. 299p. index. illus. bibliog. (Amsterdam Studies in the Theory and History of Linguistic Science. Series III: Studies in the History of the Language Sciences, Vol. 57; ISSN 0304-0720). LC 91-13445. ISBN 90-272-4544-4.

Stein has augmented the already invaluable work of Starnes and Noyes (Chapel Hill, NC: The University of North Carolina Press, 1946) in this new edition—with the same title—by providing in part I an introduction; in part II a new up-to-date dictionary census; and in part III a select bibliography that includes the most significant publications complementing the original bibliography by Starnes and Noyes. A facsimile reproduction of the original work follows this new material. As Stein states in her introduction, their work has "provided us with a full-scale account of the major monolingual English dictionaries for that time" (p. vii-viii) from Cawdrey's "Table Alphabetical" in 1604 to Samuel Johnson's dictionary in 1755. For a related work see entry 709.

711.   Wynar, Bohdan S., ed. **ARBA Guide to Subject Encyclopedias and Dictionaries**. Heather Cameron and G. Kim Dority, assistant eds. Littleton, CO: Libraries Unlimited, 1986. 570p. index. LC 86-10264. ISBN 0-87287-493-1.

This book is a guide to selected subject encyclopedias and dictionaries in English which, for the most part, were still in print at the time of its compilation. Some 43 broad subject areas are covered in separate chapters. A chapter usually begins with a section for general works and then is followed by subdivisions appropriate to that subject. It excludes general encyclopedias and dictionaries, works on individuals, and polyglot dictionaries, plus place-name dictionaries, genealogical works, travel guides, and field guides. The annotations accompanying the 1,354 works provide critical evaluations and often comparisons to similar works and/or previous editions. Most annotations were taken from *American Reference Books Annual* (ARBA), though thoroughly revised and brought up-to-date. Citations to reviews are also given. Author/title and subject indexes complete the guide.

Atlases and Related Materials—
The United States and Canada

The Linguistic Atlas of the United States and Canada (LAUSC) was a project initiated in 1931 under the direction of Hans Kurath. It was originally sponsored by the American Council of Learned Societies and later assisted by the Rockefeller Foundation, the American Philosophical Society, various universities and colleges, and others. The idea of a single atlas has since evolved into autonomous regional projects and dialect surveys. Of these, probably only the *Linguistic Atlas of New England* (LANE) and the *Linguistic Atlas of the Middle and South Atlantic States* (LAMSAS) can properly be designated as components of the initial project. Other projects follow the general principles and procedures of LAUSC, but because they each reflect the state of the art at their time of inception, the atlases differ in particular aims and methodology.

The major regional atlases published and designated as *Linguistic Atlas of . . .* are listed below with associated handbooks and interpretative materials. The numerous spin-off publications (including preliminary and follow-up studies) from these atlases and other associated dialect surveys—some of which has not yet been published—are not listed, for example, the Linguistic Atlas of the Pacific Coast (LAPC), the Linguistic Atlas of the Pacific Northwest (LAPN), the Linguistic Atlas of Oklahoma (LAO), and the Linguistic Atlas of the Rocky Mountain Region (LARMR). A Web site maintained at the University of Georgia at http://hyde.park.uga.edu/matlas/main_atlas.html (accessed January 16, 1999) will eventually allow one to browse or search the collection of dialect data from LAUSC; currently only the LAMSAS region is fully functional.

Another major national effort, sponsored by the American Dialect Society, the *Dictionary of American Regional English* (see entry 714) is listed. For an overview of regional dialect studies in the United States see Harold B. Allen's article "Regional Dialects, 1945-1974" in *American Speech*, Vol. 52, Nos. 3-4 (1977), pages 163-261. More recent information can be found in the preface to the 1994 handbook of LAMSAS (see entry 718).

A more recent effort is the Telsur Project at the Linguistics Laboratory at the University of Pennsylvania resulting in the *Phonological Atlas of North America* (see entry 724).

712.   Allen, Harold B. **The Linguistic Atlas of the Upper Midwest**. University of Minnesota Press, 1973-1976. 3v. index. illus. bibliog. maps. LC 72-96716. ISBN 0-8166-0686-2(v.1); 0-8166-0756-7(v.2); 0-8166-0789-3(v.3).

The Linguistic Atlas of the Upper Midwest (LAUM) presents the social and regional distribution of various features of pronunciation of the native English of representative lifelong residents of the states of Minnesota, Iowa, North and South Dakota, and Nebraska. It also includes the Canadian border districts in Ontario, Manitoba, and Saskatchewan. Most of the fieldwork for this project was done between 1947 and 1954. Though continuing in the tradition of the LANE, the LAUM project differed in that it supplemented the usual field interviews (responses by 208 informants to more than 800 questions) by data from mailed checklists (replies of 1,064 respondents to 136 lexical items).

Volume 1, Part A contains background information including the methodology, the worksheets and checklists used, etc.; Part B contains the lexicon followed by a full word index. Volume 2 is concerned with grammatical features. Volume 3 devoted to phonology offers an analysis of those features of pronunciation that are, or show promise of being, socially or regionally distinctive.

713.   Davis, Alva Leroy, Raven I. McDavid, and Virginia G. McDavid, eds. **A Compilation of the Work Sheets of the Linguistic Atlas of the United States and Canada and Associated Projects**. 2d ed. Chicago, IL: University of Chicago Press, 1969. LC 78-100481. ISBN 0-226-13806-2.

The first version of this compilation of the worksheets used in the questionnaires of the LAUSC and other projects was issued in a small mimeographed edition in 1951. It was intended as a convenience to other dialectologists planning surveys of dialects of English. It would show them the kinds of questions that had proved useful in eliciting data on pronunciation, grammar, vocabulary, and meanings. This second edition incorporates not only the material of the regional questionnaires of the first edition, but also the contents of all subsequent ones (up to time of publication) based on LAUSC techniques that have been used to survey English dialects in the New World. The sole exception to this is the one used by David DeCamp for the Linguistic Atlas of Jamaica. Thus, it serves as a useful summary, up to 1969, of Atlas and associated projects.

Individual items (words, phrases) listed are accompanied by codes for the surveys in which they were used. Various other mechanisms are used to indicate such things as the context in which an item should normally be obtained, directions for field workers, and words or phrases known to be regional or social variants.

714. **Dictionary of American Regional English**. Frederic G. Cassidy, chief ed. Cambridge, MS: The Belknap Press of Harvard University Press, 1985- . 903p. (v. 1); 1175p. (v. 2); 927p. (v. 3). illus. maps. LC 84-29025. ISBN 0-674-20511-1 (v.1); 0-674- 20512-X (v. 2); 0-674-20519-7 (v. 3) . (In progress).

Thinking and planning for this work began with members of the American Dialect Society long before the official project start date in 1965. The dictionary, or DARE, as it has become known, is the rich reward for a massive effort by hundreds of contributors aided by funding from government and nongovernment sources, and the generous support of various institutions. Volume 1 (extensive introduction and letters A-C) was published in 1985, volume 2 (D-H) in 1991, and volume 3 (I-O) in 1997. The editors expect volumes 4 and 5 to appear in six- to seven-year intervals.

The purpose of DARE is to describe regional and folk language of the entire United States (words, expressions, metaphors, and similes); it does not cover standard language. The introduction defines the term "regional" and describes in detail the scope of the work. The data were collected by fieldworkers in interviews with some 2,777 informants in 1,002 communities throughout the country using a questionnaire with a total of 1,847 questions. The text of the questionnaire and a list of the informants are part of the first volume. In addition to the interviews, written materials (diaries, letters, novels, histories, biographies, newspapers, and government documents) covering history from the colonial period to the present were reviewed and cited in individual entries to illustrate how words have been used from the seventeenth century to the end of the twentieth. Other prefatory material includes an explanation of the DARE maps which accompany some of the strikingly regional word and phrase entries and show their geographical distribution.

An entry begins with the basic information: headword or words, part of speech, pronunciation using the International Phonetic Alphabet (only when DARE has supporting oral data), variant spellings, etymology, geographical labels, usage labels, cross-references, and editorial notes. This information is followed by the meanings, numbered and with alphabetic subdivisions if neces- sary. Last come dated quotations supporting the meanings. Additional informa- tion about DARE is available on the Web at http://polyglot.lss. wisc.edu/dare/dare.html (accessed December 27, 1998).

There are already many interpretative publications associated with the DARE project. One is Craig M. Carver's *American Regional Dialects: A Word Geography* (Ann Arbor: University of Michigan Press, 1987) which analyzes data from the project and provides 92 maps and information on about 1,500 lexical items. Publication number 77 of the American Dialect Society, *An Index by Region, Usage, and Etymology to the "Dictionary of American Regional English," Volumes I and II* (Tuscaloosa: Published for the Society by the University of Alabama Press, 1993) provides indexing for DARE as indicated by the title.

715. Kurath, Hans, et al. **Linguistic Atlas of New England**. Miles L. Hanley, associate director, Bernard Bloch, assistant editor, Guy S. Lowman, Jr., principal field investigator, and Marcus L. Hansen, historian. Providence, RI: Brown University, 1939-43. (Reprinted New York: AMS Press, 1970). 3 v. in 6. maps. (Linguistic Atlas of the United States and Canada). LC 77-037507. ISBN 0-404-10040-6.

716.   Kurath, Hans. **Handbook of the Linguistic Geography of New England**. With the collaboration of Marcus L. Hansen, Bernard Bloch, and Julia Bloch. 2d ed., with a new introduction, word-index, and inventory of LANE maps and commentary by Audrey R. Duckert, and a reverse index of LANE maps to worksheets by Raven I. McDavid, Jr.. New York: Published by arrangement with the American Council of Learned Societies by AMS Press, 1973. 527p. illus. bibliog. 70-37508. ISBN 0-404-10047-3.

Supervised by Hans Kurath, fieldwork for this seminal American survey took place between 1931 and 1933. It was finally published in 3 volumes with an accompanying handbook just before the end of World War II. Both the atlas and handbook have since been reprinted. Each volume of the atlas, also known as LANE, is in 2 parts. They contain double maps showing how residents pronounce certain words. The words are divided into topical areas such as time, family, farm, weather, and social relations. The handbook outlines the regional and social dialects of New England and provides a background for the critical evaluation and historical interpretation of the materials in LANE.

717.   McDavid, Raven I., Jr., ed. in chief. **Linguistic Atlas of the Middle and South Atlantic States**. Raymond K. O'Cain, associate editor; George T. Dorrill, assistant editor; Guy E. Loman, Jr., principal field investigator. Chicago: University of Chicago Press, 1980. 2 fascicles. maps. ISBN 0-226-55742-1 (Fasc. 1); 0-226-55744-8 (Fasc. 2).

718.   Kretzschmar, William A. Jr., Virginia G. McDavid, Theodore K. Lerud, and Ellen Johnson, eds. **Handbook of the Linguistic Atlas of the Middle and South Atlantic States**. Chicago: University of Chicago Press, 1994. 454p. illus. bibliog. maps. LC 93-15245. ISBN 0-226-45282-4.

Together with the Linguistic Atlas of New England (LANE) this Linguistic Atlas of the Middle and South Atlantic States (LAMSAS) provides a full phonetic record of the primary dialect survey of the area of American colonial settlement. The Middle and South Atlantic States take in the area to the west of New England from Ontario in the north to Florida in the south. Major fieldwork on LAMSAS began in 1933 and continued for 7 years; it was finally completed in 1949. Responses from 1,216 informants in 518 communities make up the field records. Modified short worksheets of LANE were used for the questionnaires. The data in the 2 fascicles now published deal with geographical names. For reasons of economy, the data are, regrettably, presented in lists rather than on maps. A base map is included which researchers can copy and use to do their own charting. After publication of the first two fascicles in 1980, work on two more fascicles was completed by 1982 and microfilmed from 1982-1986. Additional details are given on this microfilming as well as computerization of the project and future plans for LAMSAS in the preface to the handbook edited by Kretzschmar and others. The handbook, similar to Kurath's handbook of LANE, is an essential guide to LAMSAS.

719.   McDavid, Raven I., Jr., and Richard C. Payne, eds. **The Linguistic Atlas of the North-Central States: Basic Materials**. With the assistance of Duane Taylor. [microform]. Chicago, IL: University of Chicago Library, 1976-1979. 9 pts. maps. (Microfilm Collection of Manuscripts on Cultural Anthropology, Series 38, No. 200-208).

The Joseph Regenstein Library, University of Chicago, filmed this atlas after Albert H. Marckwardt, the director of the project died in 1975. Exploratory survey work on the project, also known as LANCS, began in 1938. Some 15 fieldworkers conducted 350 interviews; with later work to fill gaps and to support doctoral dissertations the eventual number of interviews rose to 500. The various parts of the atlas are: 1) Wisconsin (No. 200); 2) Michigan (No. 201); 3) Ontario (No. 202); 4) Illinois (No. 203); 5) Indiana (No. 204); 6) Ohio (No. 205); 7) Kentucky (No. 206); 8) long work-sheet interviews (Ohio, Wisconsin, Ontario, Kentucky) (No. 207); and 9) appendix containing all the LANCS interviews for which tape recording survive, in the original fieldworkers' transcriptions, together with new transcriptions by Raven I. McDavid Jr. and Lee Pederson.

720.   Pederson, Lee, et al., eds. **Linguistic Atlas of the Gulf States**. Athens, GA: University of Georgia Press, 1986-1992. 7v. index. illus. bibliog. map. ISBN 0-8203-0715-7(v.1); 0-8203-0972-9(v.2); 0-8203-1182-0(v.3); 0-8203-1231-2(v.4); 0-8203-1276-2(v.5); 0-8203-1345-9(v.6); 0-8203-1447-1(v.7).

721.   Pederson, Lee, et al., eds. **The Linguistic Atlas of the Gulf States: The Basic Materials**. [microform]. Ann Arbor, MI: University Microfilms International, 1981. 1199 microfiches. maps.

722.   Pederson, Lee, Susan Leas McDaniel, and Marvin Bassett, eds. **The Linguistic Atlas of the Gulf States: A Concordance of Basic Materials**. Editorial and research assistants, Waqas Ahmed, et al. Ann Arbor, MI: UMI, 1986. 157 microfiches.

723.   Smith, Vicki L., and Jean Hoornstra, comps. **Linguistic Atlas of the Gulf States: The Basic Materials: An Introduction and Guide to the Microfiche Collection**. Ann Arbor, MI: University Microfilms International, 1981. 11p. LC 82-103430. ISBN 0-8357-0239-1(paper).

The Linguistic Atlas of the Gulf States (LAGS) reports findings of a general dialect survey over a 10-year period in the 8 southern states of Tennessee, Georgia, Florida, Alabama, Mississippi, Louisiana, Arkansas, and East Texas. The basic materials include a handbook, the survey data gathered in the field on magnetic tape and recorded in phonetic notation by 8 scribes, and other materials (see entry 721 above). University Microfilms International published a short guide to this collection (see entry 723 above). A concordance (see entry 722 above) functions as an alphabetical finding list of every word and phrase of the phonetic texts in the basic materials transliterated into conventional spelling. The seven volumes of LAGS (see entry 720) are comprised of a handbook (1986), a general index (1988), technical index (1989), regional matrix (1990), regional pattern (1991), social matrix (1991), and social pattern (1992) respectively. More descriptive materials may be forthcoming.

724.   **Phonological Atlas of North America**. Available: http://www. ling.upenn.edu/phono_atlas/home.html. (Accessed: March 19, 1999).

The Telsur Project at the Linguistics Laboratory at the University of Pennsylvania is responsible for creation of this atlas. Telsur is a telephone survey of the major urbanized areas of the U.S. and Canada supported by the National Science Foundation and the National Endowment for the Humanities. William Labov, a professor in the Department of Linguistics at the University of Pennsylvania, is director of the Linguistics Laboratory and principal investigator. Sampling is now complete and the phonemic categories of 640 subjects have been analyzed on the basis of minimal pairs and other elicited forms. Maps have begun appearing on these atlas pages together with discussion of geographic and linguistic patterns. Acoustic analyses of the vowel systems of 300 subjects will follow. There are links on this Web page to regional and phonological maps, a list of staff, information on sampling methods, and other related materials including the full-text of several papers given by Labov and others about the atlas project. The maps and analyses on these Web pages are works in progress.

Atlases and Related Materials—Great Britain

725. Fischer, Andreas, and Daniel Ammann. **An Index to Dialect Maps of Great Britain**. Amsterdam: John Benjamins, 1991. 150p. bibliog. (Varieties of English around the World. General Series, Vol. 10; ISSN 0172-7362). LC 91-7244. ISBN 90-272-4868-0.

A lengthy introduction to the index describes the different surveys that form the basis of the index and is a succinct description of the Lowman Survey of central and southern England (LS), the Survey of English Dialects (SED), the Survey of Anglo-Welsh Dialects (SAWD), the Linguistic Survey of Scotland (LSS), and the three surveys of English dialects in Ireland (the latter not indexed in this work). The main part of the book is the index itself arranged in three columns: word, question, and source. The word column is alphabetical with the word being the answer elicited by the question. For example, the question "What does a bird peck its food up with?" might elicit the word "beak." The question column details the respective questionnaire number of a survey while the source column then lists the map(s) in which it can be found whether in an atlas or another type of publication. A bibliography includes publications containing dialect maps (whether indexed or not) plus works mentioned in the index's introduction.

726. Laing, Margaret. **Catalogue of Sources for a Linguistic Atlas of Early Medieval English**. Cambridge: D. S. Brewer, 1993. 186p. index. bibliog. ISBN 0-85991-384-8.

The compilation of this catalog is seen as the first step towards producing a linguistic atlas for the Early Middle English period, complementary to *A Linguistic Atlas of Late Mediaeval English* (LALME). It is an inventory of English texts from about 1150 to 1300. Manuscripts are listed by repository alphabetically from Aberystwyth, National Library of Wales to Zwettle (Lower Austria). Indexes by author/title and incipit follow.

727. McIntosh, Angus, M. L. Samuels, and Michael Benskin. **A Linguistic Atlas of Late Mediaeval English**. Aberdeen: Aberdeen University Press, 1986. 4v. index. maps. ISBN 0-08-032437-1 (set).

728.   McIntosh, Angus, M. L. Samuels, Michael Benskin, Margaret Laing, and Keith Williamson. **Guide to a Linguistic Atlas of Late Mediaeval English**. Aberdeen: Aberdeen University Press, 1987. 23p. bibliog. maps. ISBN 0-08-035076-3.

This atlas represents the results of research, within the framework of the Edinburgh Middle English Dialect Project, initiated by McIntosh, later joined by Samuels, in the early 1950s. In the course of their research they examined several thousand manuscripts written in Middle English—from England and parts of Wales and Southern Scotland—for the late mediaeval period of about a century from 1350 to 1450.

Volume 1 contains a general introduction, index of sources, and dot maps; volume 2, item maps; volume 3, the linguistic profiles; and volume 4, the county dictionary. The questionnaire reproduced in the separately published guide lists the items and sub-items for which the forms in the linguistic profile (LP) were collected. The county dictionary presents the contents of the LPs arranged by item with all variant forms. The item maps display, at the assigned LP locations, all of the various regional forms corresponding to a specific item. The 1,200 dot maps give a simple graphic representation of the geographical distribution of a form or set of forms collected in the LPs. The index of sources details the sources for the linguistic materials presented as LPs in volume 3. The atlas is a gold mine of information for scholars of Middle English and of the cultural history of mediaeval England but only if they are willing to spend the necessary time and do some hard digging.

729.   Orton, Harold, and Eugen Dieth. **Survey of English Dialects**. Leeds: Published for the University of Leeds by E. J. Arnold, 1962-1971. 4v. and introd. in 13. illus. maps. LC 67-6774.

730.   Orton, Harold, Stewart Sanderson, and John Widdowson, eds. **The Linguistic Atlas of England**. London: Croom Helm, 1978. ca. 450p. index. maps. LC 79-304375. ISBN 0-85664-294-0.

731.   Kolb, Eduard. **Phonological Atlas of the Northern Region: the Six Northern Counties, North Lincolnshire and the Isle of Man**. Bern: Francke, 1966. 390p. index. maps.

732.   Kolb, Eduard, Beat Glauser, Willy Elmer, and Renate Stamm. **Atlas of English Sounds**. Bern: Francke, 1979. index. maps. ISBN 3-7720-1423-2.

733.   Orton, Harold, and Nathalia Wright. **A Word Geography of England**. London: Seminar Press, 1974. 302p. index. illus. maps. LC 74-10331. ISBN 0-12-785608-0.

734.   Upton, Clive, David Parry, and J. D. A. Widdowson. **Survey of English Dialects: The Dictionary and Grammar**. London: Routledge, 1994. 506p. index. LC 93-020391. ISBN 0-415-02029-8.

735.   Upton, Clive, Stewart Sanderson, and John Widdowson. **Word Maps: A Dialect Atlas of England**. Cartography by David Brophy. London: Croom Helm, 1987. 228p. index. bibliog. maps. LC 87-675293. ISBN 0-7099-4410-1.

736.   Upton, Clive, and J. D. A. Widdowson. **An Atlas of English Dialects**. New York: Oxford University Press, 1996. 193p. index. bibliog. maps. LC 95-33736. ISBN 0-19-869274-9.

737.   Viereck, Wolfgang, ed. **The Computer Developed Linguistic Atlas of England**. Dialectical editor: Wolfgang Viereck in collaboration with Heinrich Ramisch. Computational production: Harald Händler, Petra Hoffmann, and Wolfgang Putschke. Tübingen: Max Niemeyer, 1991- . 21p. index. bibliog. maps. ISBN 3-484-40122-2 (v. 1). (In progress).

Orton and Dieth together designed a questionnaire to elicit information about current dialectal usages of older members of the farming communities throughout rural England. The results of the fieldwork carried out in 313 localities between 1948 and 1961 are published in the *Survey of English Dialects* (SED). Part (A), an introductory volume, provides background material and reprints the Dieth-Orton questionnaire. The basic materials are published in part (B) which is made up of four volumes. Volume I contains material for the six northern counties and the Isle of Man, volume II the west midland counties, volume II the east midland counties and East Anglia, and volume IV the southern counties.

Another purpose of the questionnaire was that the information, when mapped, would illustrate the nature of the regional distributions of those features of speech which had persisted from early times. These results are interpreted and published in *The Linguistic Atlas of England* (LAE). The atlas has 4 types of maps: phonological, lexical, morphological, and syntactical. The 3 appendixes provide an index to questions, notes on the mapped lexical responses, and unmapped lexical responses. An index lists, for each mapped questionnaire notion, a reference to the correct map.

A number of other publications are based on the SED. Two atlases which are confined to the phonological part of the basic materials are Kolb's *Phonological Atlas of the Northern Region* (PA) and the *Atlas of English Sounds* (AES). In each atlas symbol maps represent individual items, the AES covers only stressed vowel sounds, while the PA maps short vowels, long vowels and diphthongs, unstressed vowels, and the consonants. The outline maps are in green with black and red symbols. Orton and Wright's *A Word Geography of England* (WGE) presents a series of lexical items from the basic material. The word maps are simple black on white with symbols denoting a particular word or words. The base map is an outline of England with county boundaries and the Isle of Man. Dots represent each of the 313 places investigated; areas of lexical distribution are indicated by means of isoglosses.

Upton's *Word Maps* (WM) is yet another atlas based on the SED. Though also using isoglosses to present information, WM differs from the LAE and WGE in that it was produced with less complicated maps so as to be readily understood by a wider audience. There are some 200 of these maps, some showing vocabulary, others pronunciation. The vocabulary maps show different words used for the same thing, for example, "brow," "forehead," "forred" while pronunciation maps show variation in pronouncing a specific word, for example, there are three ways to pronounce the "th" in "thumb." The 1996 *Atlas of English Dialects* is a popular version of the *Word Maps*. It has just 90 maps with accompanying commentaries divided into three groups: pronunciation (maps 1 to 25), grammar (maps 26 to 35), and vocabulary (maps 36 to 90). Map 44 shows the relatively small area where the Standard English word "molars" is used and the pockets of the country where the more descriptive words "grinders," "jackteeth," "jawteeth," "eyeteeth," "doubleteeth," "axleteeth," "backteeth," and even "chockteeth" predominate.

In *A Structural Atlas of the English Dialects* (SAED), also based on material in the SED, Anderson attempts to identify the structural patterns which exist in the sound systems of the dialects of England. The SAED consists of text and 114 black on white maps grouped into categories for Middle English short vowels, long vowels, diphthongs, and consonants. There is an index of words used arranged by Middle English phoneme along with SED references as well as an index of words used.

The 169 maps in this first volume of *The Computer Developed Linguistic Atlas of England* (CLAE) is yet another work based on data collected for the SED. It is the first of a projected 12-volume set. In the introductory pages the editor describes the project, including problems encountered in computerizing the data. Symbol maps show the geographical distribution of dialect forms. A transparent plastic overlay (found in the back pocket of the atlas) with locality codes can be placed over each of the maps. The maps and symbols are well-designed and legible despite the presentation of a lot of complex data. The legend appears on the page facing the symbol maps; this legend offers complete documentation of the dialect forms together with all status information. In the indexes are lists of the localities where data were recorded, the map titles, and the response types included in the maps. The bibliography is a listing of most of the publications that deal with the discussion, presentation, and interpretation of the data of the England-wide SED, the earlier Lowman Survey covering central and southern England, and the more recent *Atlas Linguarum Europae* (see entries 618 and 619) for which new data were collected in England.

Upton, Parry, and Widdowson's *Survey of English Dialects: the Dictionary and Grammar* with more than 18,000 entries weighs in as the latest publication dealing with materials from the SED. The authors present here lexical, phonological, morphological, and syntactical data based on computer analysis of some 404,000 items of information collected in that survey. It can best be used with the SED in hand.

738.   Penhallurick, Robert J. **The Anglo-Welsh Dialects of North Wales: A Survey of Conservative Rural Spoken English in the Counties of Gwynedd and Clwyd**. Frankfurt am Main: Peter Lang, 1991. 413p. bibliog. maps. (Bamberger Beiträge zur Englischen Sprachwissenschaft/University of Bamberg Studies in English Linguistics, Bd./Vol. 27; ISSN 0721-281X). ISBN 3-631-43759-5.

According to Penhalurick, "The presentational design of this study is intended to be entirely compatible with that of the *Survey of Anglo-Welsh Dialects* (SAWD) volumes 1 and 2, so as to facilitate comparison of the data" (p. i). As the SAWD is not yet published, this analysis of the material—based on interviews between 1980 and 1981 of 75 informants, elderly natives in 17 localities in rural North Wales—is the first publication from that project. Investigators used, with some modifications, Orton and Dieth's questionnaire from the *Survey of English Dialects*.

Serial Bibliography and Database

739.   **Annual Bibliography of English Language and Literature**. 1920- . Cambridge: Bowes & Bowes, 1921- . annual. LC 22-11861. ISSN 0066-3786.

ABELL, the common abbreviation for this important annual, is published under the auspices of the Modern Humanities Research Association. It is a classified bibliography with unannotated entries arranged alphabetically within sections or subsections. The English Language section is subdivided into general studies (including history of linguistics), phonetics and phonology, grammar, vocabulary, lexicography, names, meaning, medium and register, dialects, and translation and comparative linguistics. *ABELL* is available on a CD-ROM published by Chadwyck-Healey Ltd. as well as through that publisher's *Literature Online*, or *LION*, service available over the Web and will be updated regularly throughout the year. This is a major advantage since publication of the print version had a considerable time lag.

Cumulative Bibliographies

740.   Aggarwal, Narindar K., comp. **English in South Asia: A Bibliographical Survey of Resources**. With an introductory essay by Braj B. Kachru. Gurgaon: Indian Documentation Service, 1982. 188p. index. LC 82-154162.

An extensive 70-page essay summarizing the history and situation of En-glish in South Asia precedes the main annotated bibliography with 1,181 entries. Divided into 19 sections it covers such topics as the structure of South Asian English, writing, reading, language planning, teaching of English, contrastive studies, and code-switching. There is good coverage of material, most in English, from India, including that of its Central Institute of English and Foreign Languages.

741.   Alston, Robin Carfrae, comp. **A Bibliography of the English Language from the Invention of Printing to the Year 1800: A Systematic Record of Writings on English, and on Other Languages in English, Based on the Collections of the Principal Libraries of the World**. Leeds, England: Printed for the author by E. J. Arnold, 1965- . index. bibliog. LC 66-38399. (In progress).

742.   Alston, Robin Carfrae, comp. **A Bibliography of the English Language from the Invention of Printing to the Year 1800: A Corrected Reprint of Volumes I-X**. Ilkley, England: Janus Press, 1974. 10 v. in 1. (This work not viewed by author.)

When completed, this multi-volume work is intended to supersede Kennedy's bibliography (see entry 750). It will cover all aspects of the English language, including language teaching. So far, 12 volumes of the projected 20 volumes are completed (1965-1987). The publisher varies. Also published is a supplement (The University of Leeds, 1973) containing additions and corrections to the first 10 volumes. Entries provide detailed bibliographic information, notes on copies located in libraries in Europe and North America, references to secondary material and reviews, and brief notes on the contents of books. Most volumes include indexes of anonymous titles, authors, subjects, editors, revisers, and translators. The 1-volume corrected reprint (see entry 742 above) of the first 10 volumes contains not only corrections and additions, but also cumulative indexes.

743. Avis, Walter Spencer, and A. M. Kinloch. **Writings on Canadian English, 1792-1975: An Annotated Bibliography**. Toronto: Fitzhenry & Whiteside, 1978. 153p. index. LC 79-309078. ISBN 0-88902-121-X.

Short descriptive annotations accompany the 723 entries in this work. Since the arrangement is alphabetical by author, lack of a subject index limits its usefulness. The bibliography by W. C. Lougheed updates this work (see entry 751).

744. Brasch, Ila Wales, and Walter Milton Brasch. **A Comprehensive Annotated Bibliography of American Black English**. Baton Rouge, LA: Louisiana State University Press, 1974. 289p. LC 78-83908. ISBN 0-8071-0069-2.

Most entries in this bibliography are annotated. The compilers include not only studies on American Black English, but also primary research materials for folklore, slave narratives, and literature. Unfortunately, it is arranged alphabetically by author with no subject index.

745. Brenni, Vito Joseph, comp. **American English, a Bibliography**. Philadelphia: University of Pennsylvania Press, 1964. (Reprinted Westport, CT: Greenwood Press, 1981). 221p. index. LC 63-15008.

Brenni lists here nearly 1,500 works published through 1961 on American English, that is, the English language as spoken in the United States. He devotes chapters to: general and historical; spelling; pronunciation; grammar, syntax and usage; dialects; slang; loan words; dictionaries; and, miscellaneous. Dictionaries represent a selection of the more important works in regard to authority, thoroughness, and usefulness. Descriptive annotations accompany major studies in book form. Entries are listed only once, but those covering more than one subject may be located through the excellent author/subject index.

746. Cameron, Angus, Allison Kingsmill, and Ashley Crandell Amos. **Old English Word Studies: A Preliminary Author and Word Index**. Toronto: Published in association with The Centre for Medieval Studies, University of Toronto by University of Toronto Press, 1983. 192p. 5 microfiches in pocket. (Toronto Old English Series, 8). ISBN 0-8020-5526-5.

The indexes published here are an offshoot of the Toronto *Dictionary of Old English* (DOE) project. The author index is in book form, divided into three parts: first, a list of 16th and 17th century manuscripts; second, a list of Old English dictionaries, concordances, and glossaries to specific texts; and third, and by far the largest part of the index, is a list of vocabulary studies arranged alphabetically by author and date of publication. The third part of the author index is itself indexed according to the words discussed. This word index is on the 5 microfiches. After the publication of the DOE, the authors expect to publish a revised edition of the indexes with entries keyed to the headwords used in the Dictionary.

747. Fisiak, Jacek, comp. and ed. **A Bibliography of Writings for the History of the English Language**. 2nd ed. Berlin: Mouton de Gruyter, 1987. 216p. index. LC 87-24015. ISBN 0-89925-057-2.

In compiling this unannotated classified bibliography for use by students, Fisiak concentrates on material published in the 20th century, covering only the most important works from the 19th century. While most studies are in English, representative material in a wide variety of other languages is included. There are 15 chapters dealing with such topics as lexicography, phonology, grammar, word-formation, vocabulary and semantics, varieties and dialects of English, and sociolinguistics. Where appropriate, chapters have subdivisions for Old English, Middle English, and Modern English. Though there are 3,641 numbered entries, the actual number of citations is less since many entries are double-listed when they deal with more than a single topic. Authors and editors are indexed. A subject index would have been useful.

748.   Glauser, Beat, Edgar W. Schneider, and Manfred Görlach. **A New Bibliography of Writings on Varieties of English 1984-1992/93**. Amsterdam: John Benjamins, 1993. 208p. index. (Varieties of English Around the World. General Series, Vol. 12; ISSN 0172-7362). LC 93-41367. ISBN 90-272-4870-2.

For the 10-year period of 1984-1993 this bibliography on varieties of English continues and augments (with a few earlier publications incompletely listed or not included) an earlier one for the period 1965-1983 (see entry 762). There are 2,715 unannotated entries arranged in four sections: general entries; England, Wales, Scotland, Ireland; the USA and Canada; and the rest of the world. The index listing topics, languages, and geographic names in one alphabetic sequence is serviceable, but could have been improved if the authors had subdivided some of the index terms having dozens of entries such as "American Black English," "pronunciation/phonology," and "dictionaries/lexicography."

749.   Gneuss, Helmut. **English Language Scholarship: A Survey and Bibliography from the Beginnings to the End of the Nineteenth Century**. Binghamton, NY: Medieval and Renaissance Texts and Studies, 1996. 152p. index. (Medieval and Renaissance Tests and Studies, Vol. 125). LC 94-45610. ISBN 0-86698-130-6.

The subject of this survey and bibliography is "the history of the science of the English language" (p. 7). In part I Gneuss devotes more than 60 pages to an overview of this history. This survey is an expanded, revised version of a paper published in German, *Die Wissenschaften von der englischen Sprache: ihre Entwicklung bis zum Ausgang des 19. Jahrhunderts: vorgetragen am 3. February 1989* (München: Verlag der Bayerischen Akademie der Wissenschaften, In Kommission bei C. H. Beck, 1990). Part II is a select bibliography of books and articles about the study of English published up to the end of 1993 with a few publications from 1994 and 1995 which is intended as a bibliographical guide to the fields covered by the survey in part I. There are separate author/editor indexes for each part.

750.   Kennedy, Arthur Garfield. **A Bibliography of Writings on the English Language from the Beginning of Printing to the End of 1922**. New York: Hafner, 1961. (Reprint of 1927 edition). 517p. LC 61-08940.

This comprehensive classified bibliography is an important source for the history of English. Some 13,402 books, pamphlets, and articles are arranged in 10 chapters: general collections, general and historical writings, English paleography, English and other languages, Middle English, Modern English, recent tendencies in English, history of its study, and theory and method of the study and teaching of English. Entries within the topical subdivisions of the chapters are generally listed chronologically. Though there are no annotations, the author does provide numerous references to critical reviews. Authors, reviewers, and subjects are all indexed. The bibliographies of Fisiak and Tajima update this work (see entries 747 and 760). See also entry 104.

751. Lougheed, William Clinton. **Writings on Canadian English, 1976-1987: A Selective, Annotated Bibliography**. Kingston, Ontario: Strathy Language Unit, Queen's University, 1988. 66p. index. (Occasional Papers, No. 2; ISSN 0834-5341). ISBN 0-88911-510-9.

This reference work listing about 300 items is an update of an earlier bibliography by Avis (see entry 743). Its scope and arrangement are the same except for the inclusion of an index here that provides some subject access.

752. McMillan, James B., and Michael B. Montgomery. **Annotated Bibliography of Southern American English**. Tuscaloosa, AL: University of Alabama Press, 1989. 444p. index. LC 88-36856. ISBN 0-8173-0448-7.

This work is an updated, greatly expanded version of McMillan's earlier bibliography with the same title (University of Miami Press, 1971). Southern English as defined here encompasses 14 states south and west of the Mason-Dixon Line from the Delaware Bay to Texas and also includes the District of Columbia. The authors list books, articles, dissertations, master's theses, and ERIC documents. They drew from research in many fields: linguistics, speech, rhetoric, sociology, folklore, anthropology, language teaching, reading, and others. The 3,833 entries are divided among 12 chapters. Chapter 1, the longest, covers general studies. Chapters 2-12 cover such topics as historical and creole studies, phonetics and phonology, morphology and syntax, place name studies, literary dialect, and speech act and style. "See also" listings at the ends of chapters 2-12 refer the reader to related items in other chapters, particularly chapter 1. Entries have short, descriptive annotations plus citations to reviews. An index of authors is included.

753. Mitchell, Bruce. **A Critical Bibliography of Old English Syntax to the End of 1984 Including Addenda and Corrigenda to "Old English Syntax"**. Oxford: Basil Blackwell, 1990. 269p. index. illus. LC 90-36594. ISBN 0-631-13275-9.

Mitchell's bibliography of Old English syntax is intended to be complete through 1984 and as such supplements the selective bibliography found in his 2-volume *Old English Syntax* (Oxford: Clarendon Press, 1985). The 1,084 references to books, dissertations, articles, notes, and reviews are arranged in 10 chapters, most accompanied by critical annotations. There is a subject index and an index for authors and reviewers.

754. Pulsiano, Phillip. **An Annotated Bibliography of North American Doctoral Dissertations on Old English Language and Literature**. East Lansing, MI: Colleagues Press, 1988. 317p. index. (Medieval Texts and Studies, No. 3). ISBN 0-937191-06-X.

Although Pulsiano limited the scope of his bibliography to doctoral dissertations written in the United States and Canada through 1986, he did include foreign dissertations listed in *Dissertation Abstracts International* (DAI). The main focus of the bibliography is on the language and literature of Old English, but the author also cites dissertations on Old Saxon, Old Frisian, Primitive and Proto-Germanic, and runes and runic inscriptions. The annotated entries are arranged in three parts: general works, poetry, and prose. Items of interest to linguists can be found scattered throughout the bibliography and especially in the section on studies in style and language found in part 1 on general works. There are many cross-references, including citations to DAI, as well as author and subject indexes.

755. Ramaiah, L. S. **Indian English: A Bibliographical Guide to Resources.** Delhi: Gian Publishing House, 1988. 137p. index. LC 88-904298. ISBN 81-212-0236-1.

English was introduced in India with the English trading in the 17th century and gradually became the language of communication between the British and the Indians. The subsequent Indianization of English led to the development of a variety of English called Indian English. This bibliography encompasses a wide variety of material, nearly all in English, on all aspects of the topic through the end of 1987. It is particularly useful for identifying conference papers and material published in India. Unannotated entries are organized into 10 chapters. Author and subject indexes provide additional access.

756. Reichl, Karl. **Englische Sprachwissenschaft: Eine Bibliographie.** Mit einem Anhang von Helmut Gneuss. Berlin: Erich Schmidt, 1993. 251p. index. (Grundlagen der Anglistik und Amerikanistik, 17). ISBN 3-503-03068-9.

There are nearly 2,000 books, articles, and dissertations listed in this classified bibliography on English linguistics. Some items have brief descriptive annotations. While the introduction, annotations, headings, and introductions to sections are in German, many, if not most, citations are to works written in English. There is an index of authors/main entries.

757. Schäfer, Jürgen. **Early Modern English Lexicography. Volume I: A Survey of Monolingual Printed Glossaries and Dictionaries 1475-1640.** Oxford: Clarendon, 1989. 488p. index. bibliog. ISBN 0-19-812847-9.

In volume 1 on pages 18-68 Schäfer lists 134 dictionaries and glossaries of early modern English produced between the years 1475 and 1640. (Volume 2 lists additions to the *Oxford English Dictionary*). He provides detailed descriptions including glossary title, STC number, the number of lemmas, the range of lemmas, the system of arrangement, a sample entry, the role the work played in *Oxford English Dictionary* documentation, edition notes, and references to scholarly treatment of the work. An index of titles, translators, compilers, and editors follows as well as a source bibliography. The remaining nearly 400 pages of the volume are given over to a comprehensive alphabetical list of some 20,000 lemmas from the works described earlier. (See also entries 613 and 707.)

758. Scheurweghs, Gustave. **Analytical Bibliography of Writings on Modern English Morphology and Syntax, 1877-1960.** Louvain, Belgium: Nauwelaerts, 1963-1979. 5v. index. LC 72-14127.

The scope of this whole 5-volume set is limited to studies dealing with the morphology and syntax of the standard English of adult native speakers from the

16th century to the present time. It excludes works dealing mainly with language teaching.

The first two volumes record publications of the United States and Western and Northern Europe from 1877 to 1960. Volume 1 is limited to periodical articles (with an appendix for Japanese publications) while volume 2 (published in 1965) lists monographs, dissertations, theses, and conference papers (with appendixes for Japanese and Czech publications). Volume 3 (published in 1968) covers works published in the Soviet Union for the period 1917 to 1960 and studies published in Bulgaria, Poland, Rumania, and Yugoslavia. Personal names in Cyrillic script are transliterated; the remainder of each entry is translated into English. All three of these volumes provide brief annotations for entries as well as indexes for authors and subjects. Volume 4 (published in 1968) contains an addenda and general indexes for all four volumes.

The fifth volume, edited by Emma Vorlat and not published until 1979, covers articles in periodicals for the period 1961-1970. The arrangement of entries in this volume is an unusual one: periodicals titles, from which articles are cited, are arranged alphabetically with articles then listed below in a chronological fashion. Fortunately, indexes provide author and subject access.

759.   Stein, Gabriele. **English Word-Formation over Two Centuries; in Honour of Hans Marchand on the Occasion of His Sixty-Fifth Birthday, 1 October 1972**. Tubingen: Tubinger Beitrage zur Linguistik, 1973. 356p. index. (Tubinger Beitrage zur Linguistik, Bd. 34). LC 73-175834. ISBN 3-87808-034-4.

Just under 2 centuries worth of publications on English word formation are covered by Stein's bibliography listing material from 1803 to 1972. Specifically excluded are studies on place names and personal names. In a carefully classified arrangement entries are arranged in 2 parts. Sections in Part I are for general studies, and for types of word formation such as compounding, derivation (affixation, prefixation, and suffixation), back-formation, and reduplication. Part II lists the material of Part I again, along with additional studies, according to the aspects studied within English word formation. It has sections dealing with graphemics, phonemics, and contrastive studies. Another section is for studies on word formation in specific authors or in specific works. Most studies are in German, English, or Russian with the titles of the latter being translated into English. Annotations are limited to short notes often pointing the reader to especially pertinent pages in a work or to reviews.

760.   Tajima, Hatsuji, comp. **Old and Middle English Language Studies: A Classified Bibliography, 1923-1985**. Amsterdam/Philadelphia: John Benjamins, 1988. 391p. index. (Amsterdam Studies in the Theory and History of Linguistic Science. Series V: Library and Information Sources in Linguistics, Vol. 13; ISSN 0165-7267).

With a beginning coverage date of 1923 this important bibliography is designed to update for Old and Middle English Kennedy's comprehensive and detailed bibliography which was for all English studies through 1922 (see entry 750). Coverage is thorough up through 1985. Tajima excludes all publications in Slavic languages and most in Japanese. The 3,913 entries are arranged into 14 broad categories, including histories of the English language, grammars, phonology and phonetics, morphology, syntax, onomastics, dialectology, and linguistic stylistics. Within each category, works covering both Old and Middle English and general/historical are listed first followed by those for Old English (to about 1100 A.D.) and finally those for Middle English (about 1100-1500 A.D.). Scope and/or content notes are added to some entries where titles are unclear. Additional notes include cross-references to related items, information on reprints, and references to reviews. An index of names lists all authors, editors, translators, reviewers, etc.

761.   Tsuzaki, Stanley M., and John E. Reinecke. **English in Hawaii; an Annotated Bibliography**. Honolulu, HI: Pacific and Asian Linguistics Institute, University of Hawaii, 1966. 61p. index. (Oceanic Linguistics, Special Publication, No. 1). LC 68-4603.

The majority of entries in this bibliography deal with the variety of English in Hawaii often called pidgin English. It covers the most significant works in this field from 1818 to 1965. Short evaluative annotations accompany the alphabetically arranged entries. It concludes with a chronological index.

762.   Viereck, Wolfgang, Edgar W. Schneider, and Manfred Gorlach, comps. **A Bibliography of Writings on Varieties of English, 1965-1983**. Amsterdam/Philadelphia: John Benjamins, 1984. 319p. index. (Varieties of English Around the World. General Series, Vol. 3). LC 84-218560. ISBN 90-272-4861-3 (paper).

Each of the three compilers is responsible for a section in this unannotated bibliography covering books, chapters, theses, and periodical articles published from 1965 to 1983. Viereck covers varieties of English spoken in England, Wales, Scotland, and Ireland and attitudes towards them; Schneider covers American and Canadian English; Gorlach covers English as a world language. Each section has its own index of topics, ethnic groups, and specific areas. Nearly all works cited are in English. For a continuation of this bibliography see entry 748.

Classical

763.   **Deltion Bibliographias tes Hellenikes Glosses/Bibliographical Bulletin of the Greek Language**. Vol. 1-3, 1973-1975/76. Athens: University of Athens, 1974-1978. annual. LC 86-16417.

Unfortunately, only 3 years of this bibliographic index were ever published. It was issued by the Department of Linguistics of the University of Athens at the end of each year and included the previous year's international work on the entire Greek language (Ancient, Byzantine, and Modern) for every kind of research (synchronic, diachronic, and historical-comparative). Entries are arranged in 20 subject categories with brief annotations in English, notes concerning reviews, and a code indicating the period of the history of the Greek language. For entries in the Greek language authors' names are transliterated and English titles are provided.

764.   Steitz, Lothar. **Bibliographie zur Aussprache des Latein**. Saarbrücken: Institut für Phonetik, Universität des Saarlandes, 1987. 148p. index. (Phonetica Saraviensia, Nr. 9; ISSN 0721-6440).

Steitz has gathered 1,404 references to books, articles, and dissertations in this unannotated bibliography on the pronunciation of Latin. Works cited are in a variety of languages. Arrangement is alphabetical by author within 6 chapters, plus there is an author index.

765. Swanson, Donald Carl Eugene. **Modern Greek Studies in the West; a Critical Bibliography of Studies on Modern Greek Linguistics, Philology, and Folklore, in Languages Other Than Greek**. New York: New York Public Library, 1960. 93p. index. LC 59-14103.

Most of the 980 citations in this bibliography are to works published since 1860 and written in German, French, English, and Italian with a few others in East European languages; works in Greek are excluded. More than half of the books and articles cited are for linguistic studies (phonology, morphology, syntax, word-formation, etc.). Some entries have brief annotations and references to reviews. It has the following indexes: authors and editors, words and names discussed, Greek regions and localities, and miscellaneous (subjects).

766. Tremblay, Florent A. **Bibliotheca Lexicologiae Medii Aevi**. Lewiston, NY: Edwin Mellen Press, 1988-1989. 10v. index. LC 87-26515. ISBN 0-88946-208-9.

Tremblay's 10-volume computer-generated bibliography encompasses all publications and manuscripts that have to do with Latin lexicology in the Middle Ages which the author states as extending more or less from the 5th to the 16th century. It is intended to be comprehensive except for eastern Europe. While this work is complete in itself, it is a companion to Rodrigue LaRue's thesaurus of Greek and Latin bibliography, the *Clavis scriptorum Graecorum et Latinorum* (Trois-Rivières: Université de Québec à Trois-Rivières, Service de la Bibliothèque, 1985. 4v.).

The first eight volumes are topical with volume 1 covering classics and education; volumes 2 and 3 lexicons; volume 4 grammars; volume 5 the rise of vernacular languages; volume 6 influence of vulgar Latin; and volumes 7 and 8 lexicographical manuscripts, and journals and periodicals. Entries in each volume are arranged by author, or for anonymous works by title, and may include detailed bibliographical information, an abstract of the work, incipit of a mediaeval manuscript and place where it can now be consulted, comments, evaluation and book reviews, bibliographical sources and recensions, century during which the mediaeval document was produced, reference to *Clavis*, and descriptors (keywords). There are 12 such descriptors each associated with a main idea, a genre, or a category. Most entries are coded with one to four descriptors. Volume 9 contains author and title indexes. Volume 10 has four more indexes: geographical, abbreviation, chronological, and incipits. There is no comprehensive subject index.

Romance

Encyclopedia

767. **Lexikon der Romanistischen Linguistik (LRL)**. Hrsg. Günter Holtus, Michael Metzeltin, and Christian Schmitt. Tübingen: Max Niemeyer, 1988-1998. v.2-7. ISBN 3-484-50250-9(set). (In progress).

Only volumes 2-7 have been published of what is to be an 8-volume encyclopedia of Romance languages and linguistics. Volume 2, part 1 (1996) covers Latin and Romance, an historical-comparative grammar of Romance languages; volume 2, part 2 (1995), the individual Romance languages and their regions of implantation from the Middle Ages to the Renaissance; volume 3 (1989), the individual Romance languages and language areas from the Renaissance to the present—Romanian, Dalmatian/Istro-Romanian, Friulian, Ladin, Rhaeto-Romanic; volume 4 (1988), Italian, Corsian, Sardinian; volume 5, part 1 (1990), French; volume 5, part 2 (1991), Occitan, Catalan; volume 6, part 1 (1992), Aragonese/Navarrese, Spanish, Asturian/Leonese; volume 6, part 2 (1994), Galician, Portuguese; and volume 7 (1998), language contact, language migration and artificial languages, contrastive analysis—classification and typology of Romance languages. The LRL provides essays written and signed by numerous specialists with extensive bibliographies. There are illustrations, maps, charts, and tables throughout. Not yet published are volumes 1 and 8 which will deal with the history of Romance philology and its methodology, and provide bibliographies and indexes respectively.

Bibliographies of Dictionaries

768.   Alvar Ezquerra, Manuel. **Lexicología y lexicografía: guía bibliográfica**. Salamanca: Almar, 1983. 283p. index. (Colección Guías bibliográficas, 1). LC 84-152555. ISBN 84-74550-42-4.

In the first part of this bibliographic guide the author annotates a number of studies on lexicology and lexicography. The second part contains long critical evaluations for selected, available general language dictionaries. He includes both mono- and bilingual dictionaries.

769.   Dworkin, Steven N., and David J. Billick. **Lexical Studies of Medieval Spanish Tests: A Bibliography of Concordances, Glossaries, Vocabularies and Selected Word Studies**. 2nd ed., rev. and expanded. Madison, WI: Hispanic Seminary of Medieval Studies, 1993. illus. 207p. (Bibliographic Series. Hispanic Seminary of Medieval Studies, No. 11).

In this second edition the authors have revised and expanded their 1987 bibliography of the same title and with the same publisher from 513 entries to 802. They intend for their work to aid the compilation of a comprehensive medieval Spanish lexicon. Citations to all the types of works described in the bibliography's title which were published as journal articles, books, appendixes, and theses are arranged chronologically from the 11th and 12th centuries through the 15th century with separate sections for general works, Judeo-Spanish texts, and Aljamiado texts. The authors attempted to list citations to all reviews of separately published glossaries, vocabularies, and concordances. Within each section the order is alphabetical by editor or compiler. There are indexes for authors and editors, reviewers and titles.

770.   Fabbri, Maurizio. **A Bibliography of Hispanic Dictionaries: Catalan, Galician, Spanish, Spanish in Latin America and the Philippines; Appendix: A Bibliography of Basque Dictionaries**. Imola: Galeati, 1979. 381p. index. (Biblioteca di Spicilegio moderno. Collana bibliografica, 1). LC 80-495551.

This bibliography is a compilation of over 3,500 dictionaries, vocabularies, glossaries, and word-lists of the Spanish language and its dialects. The book is divided into 5 sections: Catalan, Galician, Spanish, Spanish in Latin America, and Spanish in the Philippines and surrounding areas. There is an appendix for Basque dictionaries. The chapters and appendix are further divided into monolingual, bilingual, and polyglot. These parts are further subdivided into appropriate categories. A table of contents precedes each chapter and the appendix. Likewise, each has its individual indexes of authors, languages, and subjects. For each work listed, the author provides full bibliographic information and details on reprints, new editions, revisions, and updates. For multilingual dictionaries a system of arrows, symbols, and language names indicate the direction of translation, base languages, and associated languages.

771. Instituto Nacional del Libro Español. **Diccionarios españoles**. Madrid: INLE, 1980? 207p. index. LC 80-126780. ISBN 84-85635-07-8.

Some 975 dictionaries in Spanish are listed in this classified bibliography. It covers general monolingual and bilingual dictionaries as well as specialized dictionaries in all subject areas that were in print (for the most part) at the time of compilation. A description of contents accompanies long encyclopedic works. Authors and subjects are indexed.

772. Klaar, R. M., comp. **French Dictionaries**. London: Centre for Information on Language Teaching and Research, 1976. 71p. index. (Specialised bibliography). LC 77-377405. ISBN 0-903466-11-2.

Some 60 monolingual dictionaries and 37 bilingual dictionaries in print as of December 1975 are listed here. With one exception the bilingual dictionaries are all French-English and English-French. Various criteria were used to determine which dictionaries to include, but in general, specialized dictionaries and encyclopedias proper were excluded, while general, etymology, phonetics, place name, proper name, and slang dictionaries were included. Full bibliographic details and analytical notes are provided. Both a title index and an index of authors, compilers, and editors are appended.

773. Mormile, Mario. **Storia dei dizionari bilingui italo-francesi: la lessicografia italo-francese dalle origini al 1900; con un repertorio bibliografico cronologico di tutte le opere lessicografiche italiano-francese e francese-italiano pubblicate**. Fasno, Br., Italia: Schena, 1993. 174p. index. illus. bibliog. (Biblioteca della ricerca. Traduttologia, 4). ISBN 88-7514-645-4.

The first part of this work is taken up with a history of the bilingual Italo-French dictionary and Italo-French lexicography from its origins in the 15th century to 1900 and a list of references. The second part (on pages 103-58) offers a chronological listing from 1578 to 1900 of Italian-French and French-Italian lexicographic works. There are no annotations per se since the history section deals with each of the works; accordingly, the index of names refers the reader only to the history, not the chronological list.

774. Wartburg, Walther von, Hans-Erich Keller, and Robert Geuljans. **Bibliographie des dictionnaires patois galloromans (1550-1967)**. Nouv. éd.

entièrement revue et mise à jour. Genève: Droz, 1969. 376p. index. (Publications romanes et françaises, 103). LC 77-471077.

More than 1,100 published and unpublished dictionaries, textual glossaries, etc. of the Gallo-Romance dialects compiled between 1550 and 1967 are listed in this impressive bibliography. The arrangement is by dialect and region. Brief descriptive or, for the more important works, longer critical annotations accompany the entries. Indexes of authors and localities complete this comprehensive survey.

Atlases

775.   Araya, Guillermo, et al. **Atlas lingüístico-etnográfico del sur de Chile: (ALESUCH)**. Valdivia: Instituto de Filología de la Universidad Austral de Chile, 1973. 1v. maps. LC 75-527730.

This dialect atlas of Chile consists mainly of maps, three-quarters of them in red and black. A few introductory pages contain word lists and explanatory details.

776.   **Atlas linguistiques de la France par régions**. Paris: Éditions du Centre national de la recherche scientifique, 1939- . (In progress).

These separately published and edited works on the regions of France form a series of regional volumes, all having a title that begins *Atlas linguistique et ethnographique...* except for the *Atlas linguistique des Pyrénées orientales*.

777.   **Atlas Lingüístico de la Península Ibérica**. Madrid: Consejo superior de investigaciones científicas, 1962. 1v. maps. LC 63-80032.

Only volume 1, *Fonética*, of this linguistic atlas of the Iberian Peninsula (ALPI) has been published. Its 75 colored maps cover the Spanish, Portuguese, and Catalan languages.

778.   Gilliéron, Jules, and Edmond Edmont. **Atlas linguistique de la France.** Paris: Honoré Champion, 1902-10. 7v.

779.   **Notice servant à l'intelligence des cartes**. 1902. 55p.

780.   **Table de l'Atlas linguistique de la France**. 1912. 519p. (Vol. 8).

781.   **Atlas linguistique de la France. Suppléments**. 1920.

782.   **Atlas linguistique de la France. Corse**. 1914-15. 4 fasc. of 800 maps.

This linguistic atlas of France (ALF) was originally published in seven volumes containing 1,920 maps. Additional parts of the atlas (listed above) were subsequently issued by the same publisher. It was reprinted in 10 volumes (Bologna: Forni Editore, 1968-69).

783.   Instituto Caro y Cuervo. Departamento de Dialectología. **Atlas lingüístico-etnográfico de Colombia**. Director, Luis Florez. Bogotá: Instituto Caro y Cuervo, 1981-1983. 6 v.; suppl. to v.3 with text, 92p. and 2 records. illus. maps.

This linguistic-ethnographic atlas for Colombia (ALEC), contains colored illustrations and maps. A manual for it was issued by the director of the institute in 1983; a glossary compiled by Jose Joaquin Montes Giraldo and others was published in 1986.

784. Jaberg, Karl, and J. Jud. **Sprach- und sachatlas Italiens und der Südschweiz**. Die mundartaufnahmen wurden durchgefürht von P. Scheuermeier, G. Rohlfs, und M. L. Wagner. Zofingen, Schweiz: Ringier, 1928-40. 8v. in 16. maps. LC 30-2108.

The authors separately published an introduction to this language atlas of Italian in southern Switzerland (Halle: Max Niemeyer, 1928); still later they published an index to it (Bern: Stampfli, 1960).

785. Lope Blanch, Juan M., director. **Atlas lingüístico de México**. México, D.F.: El Colegio México: Fondo de Cultura Económica, 1990. 4v. (Serie Estudios de dialectología mexicana dedicada a Pedro Henríquez Ureña, 4). ISBN 968-12-0450-6 (obra completa); 968-12-0461-1 (Tomo I); ISBN 968-12-0650-9 (Tomo II).

786. Tomo I. Fonética. Volumen I. 1990. maps 1-119. **Lista de informantes**. 30p. in pocket.

787. Tomo I. Fonética. Volumen II. 1992. maps 120-276.

788. Tomo I. Fonética. Volumen III. 1994. maps 277-441.

789. Tomo II. Morfosintaxis. Volumen IV. 1996. maps 442-613.

Introductory material in the first volume gives a history of the project from its inception in 1965 to the completion of the phonetic maps in 1985, describes the methodology and questionnaire used which addressed morphosyntactic problems as well as lexical isoglosses, and lists publications related to the project. The fold-out red and black line maps are clear and easy to read.

Serial Bibliographies

790. **Bulletin analytique de linguistique française**. Centre national de la recherche scientifique, Institut national de la langue française. No. 1- , 1969- . Nancy, France: Klincksieck, 1969- . quarterly. ISSN 0007-408X.

Books, Festschriften, articles, and theses are all included in this international classified bibliography on French linguistics. It employs an elaborate but clear classification system. In addition to works in all areas of general and theoretical linguistics, it includes the allied areas of sociolinguistics, psycholinguistics, applied linguistics, and studies with interdisciplinary approaches. Brief annotations in French accompany entries. The author index for each quarterly is cumulated annually.

791. **Romanische Bibliographie**. Vol. 77/78- . 1961/62- . Tübingen: Max Niemeyer, 1965 - . annual. ISSN 0080-388X.

This important classified bibliography on Romance linguistics, language, and literature is a supplement to the *Zeitschrift für romanische Philologie*. With the volumes for 1961/62 it began to be issued, though still a supplement to the

Zeitschrift, with its own title. It is presently an annual, but frequency of publication has varied.

The bibliography is made up of three volumes. The first volume contains author, reviewer, name, and subject indexes in addition to listing journals and complete bibliographic information for analyzed monographic works (congresses, collected works, Festschriften, etc.). The second and third volumes contain the bibliography itself. The closely classified arrangement scheme is reproduced in the front of each volume. The second volume on linguistics and language is of most interest here. It has sections for: general linguistic studies, Latin, general Romance, and a section for each language (Rumanian, Italian, French, Occitan, Catalan, Spanish, and Portuguese). Entries are unannotated, but in some instances provide references to reviews.

Cumulative Bibliographies and Guides

792. Alvar López, Manuel. **Dialectología española**. Madrid: C.S.I.C., 1962. 93p. index. LC 67-125012.

This bibliography on Spanish dialects packs a lot of information within its few pages. More than 1,000 works are classified by dialect. It covers not only the dialects of Spain, but also American Spanish, Papiamento, Filippino Spanish, and Judeo-Spanish. Information on the historical situation, morphology, syntax, and phonetics usually precedes the entries in each dialect section. No notes accompany items other than references to reviews. It concludes with an author index.

793. Bach, Kathryn F., and Glanville Price. **Romance Linguistics and the Romance Languages: A Bibliography of Bibliographies**. London: Grant & Cutler, 1977. 194p. index. (Research Bibliographies and Checklists, 22). LC 78-319221. ISBN 0-7293-0055-2.

This exceptionally fine bibliography of bibliographies begins with a chapter on general Romance, proceeds to cover individual Romance languages and dialects (including Vulgar Latin), then concludes with a chapter on creoles and pidgins. Chapters are divided into sections and subsections; within each subsection the arrangement is chronological. The authors list some 650 items with concise descriptive or critical annotations. Cross-references are provided at the beginning of each chapter, section, or subsection. Besides including formal bibliographies published as books, serial publications, or articles in journals, the authors list dissertations and other works such as surveys which are not bibliographies per se, but are useful sources of bibliographical references. The cut-off date is roughly 1975.

794. Bahner, Werner. **Kurze Bibliographie für das Studium der romanischen Sprachwissenschaft; mit besonderer Berücksichtigung des Französischen**. Halle, Saale: Max Niemeyer, 1962. 106p. LC 74-25668.

The most important books, articles, and periodicals in the field of Romance linguistics have been selected for this international bibliography with some 1,400 entries. A section on general Romance linguistics (which includes Latin) is followed by sections for each of the Romance languages. Each section is subdivided into the various areas of linguistic study. The Portuguese section includes Brazilian while Spanish American and Judeo-Spanish are discussed in the Spanish section. Canadian French is not included.

795. Bal, Willy, Jean Germain, Jean Klein, and Pierre Swiggers. **Bibliographie sélective de linguistique française et romane**. 2nd ed. Louvain-la-Neuve, Belgium: Duculot, 1997. 324p. col. maps. index. (Champs linguistiques). ISBN 2-8011-1160-0.

The second edition of this work has a slightly modified title—"française" now precedes "romane"—from the first edition (Paris: Duculot, 1991) which itself was based on an earlier work by Bal and Germain, *Guide bibliographique de linguistique romane* (Louvain-la-Neuve, Belgium: Cabay, 1982). As the switch in the title words indicates, the authors explain in the introduction that the French section of this edition constitutes the most important part of this classified bibliography of monographs. Chapter 1, dealing with languages of the world, Indo-European languages, and Latin is quite short. The main part of the book is chapter 2, itself subdivided into Romance languages in general and then into the individual languages (Romanian, Dalmatian, Italian, Sardinian, Rhaetian, French, Francoprovençal, Occitan, L'ibéro-roman, Catalan, Spanish, and Portuguese). Most sections begin with a brief introduction to the particular language(s) with a short list of distinguishing features and go on to list standard reference works (bibliographies, journals, manuals, handbooks), then works dealing with synchronic and historical studies, onomastics, versification, and anthologies of literary texts. Outside of references to journals or serial bibliographies, most citations are to monographs, or chapters in monographs, written in one of the Romance languages. Following an index of authors some 11 full-page colored maps show distribution of the Romance languages and other features.

796. Berthaud, Pierre Louis, and Jean Lesaffre. **Bibliographie occitane, 1943-1956**. Paris: Les Belles Lettres, 1958. 69p.

This work and an earlier one by Berthaud covering publications for 1919-1942 (Paris: Les Belles Lettres, 1946) are the first and second in a series of Occitan bibliographies continued by Lesaffre and others (see entries 819, 820, and 821).

797. Bialik Huberman, Gisela. **Mil obras de lingüística española e hispanoamericana; un ensayo de síntesis crítica**. Madrid: Playor, 1973. 812p. index. (Coleccion Plaza Mayor Scholar). LC 74-356705. ISBN 84-359-0092-4.

Slightly more than 1,000 works are critically annotated in this bibliography on the linguistics of the Spanish language. The arrangement is a classified one with most of the parts and subsections beginning with a valuable introduction. All areas of general linguistics are covered including syntax, morphology, semantics, grammar, phonology, and phonetics, plus historical considerations and outside influences on the language. One part is devoted to American Spanish. The annotations range in length from a sentence to more than a page, depending on the importance of a work. A word index and a combined name/subject index contribute to the usefulness of this important work.

798. **Bibliografia de linguística portuguesa**. Núcleo de Estudos da Linguística Contrastiva da Faculdade de Ciências Sociais e Humanas da Universidade Nova de Lisboa. Lisboa: Litoral Edições; distr. Sodilivros, 1987. 147p.

More than 200 periodicals and serials were analyzed to find the over 1,900 entries for this classified bibliography of studies in Portuguese linguistics which is arranged by author in 21 sections. Citations are to works in English, German, and various Romance languages published mainly in the 1950s through the early 1980s with a few earlier references such as a dictionary published in 1887-1889.

799. Bleznick, Donald William. **A Sourcebook for Hispanic Literature and Language: A Selected, Annotated Guide to Spanish, Spanish-American, and United States Hispanic Bibliography, Literature, Linguistics, Journals, and Other Source Materials**. 3rd ed. Lanham, MD: Scarecrow Press, 1995. 310p. index. LC 94-47011. ISBN 0-8108-2981-9.

The third edition of this work has a slight change in the wording of its subtitle— "Chicano" becomes "United States Hispanic." Section 10 on Hispanic linguistics has subsections for: bibliographies (with cross-references to entries in other sections); general works; development of the Spanish language; dialectology; phonology and phonetics; grammars, morphology, and syntax; and dictionaries. Materials in some other sections are also relevant. Many entries have evaluative annotations. This work overlaps somewhat with Woodbridge's guide (see entry 839).

800. Carlier, An. **Guide de la documentation bibliographique en linguistique générale et française**. Namur: Bibliothèque universitaire Moretus Plantin, distr. Presses universitaires de Namur, 1987. 99p. index. bibliog. (Bibliothèque universitaire Moretus Plantin. Publication, No. 4).

Carlier has put together a bibliography of 305 annotated entries for linguistic materials classed in sections: general linguistics, Romance language, French, Spanish, Italian, the history of linguistics, historical and synchronic linguistics, theses, and linguistic terminology (dictionaries and encyclopedias). Materials cited are mainly in French, but also in other Romance languages, German, and English. There is an index of authors and periodical titles.

801. Davis, Jack Emory. **The Spanish of Argentina and Uruguay: An Annotated Bibliography for 1940-1978**. Berlin/New York: Mouton, 1982. 360p. index. bibliog. (Janua linguarum. Series maior, 105). LC 82-2345492. ISBN 90-279-3339-1.

This bibliography with descriptive, frequently critical, annotations is comprehensive for books, journals, newspapers, book reviews, Festschriften, dissertations, and conference reports dealing with the Spanish language of Argentina and Uruguay for the years 1940 through 1978. The first section covering lexicography, semantics, and etymology is the most extensive with 941 entries out of a total of 1,227. Other sections cover inter-language influence, phonology and phonetics, grammar, and miscellaneous studies. An author index is appended.

802. Dietrich, Wolf. **Bibliografia da Língua Portuguesa do Brasil**. Tübingen: Gunter Narr Verlag, 1980. 292p. index. (Tübinger Beiträge zur Linguistik, 120). ISBN 3-878-8-120-0.

Nearly 1,500 works are cited in this comprehensive bibliography on the Portuguese language in Brazil. Except for the section on the history of vocabulary up to 1930 which is in chronological order, the remaining 31 sections are alphabetical. The author included articles, books, chapters, conference proceedings, and theses, mostly written in Portuguese, but other Romance languages and

English are represented as well. Some items have short descriptive notes and references to reviews of the cited work.

803.   Ferreira, José de Azevedo. **Bibliografia selectiva da língua portuguesa**. Lisboa: Instituto de Cultura e Língua Portuguesa, Ministério da Educação, 1989. index. bibliog. (Identidade: Língua portuguesa).

The 2,217 entries in this classified bibliography on the Portuguese language are unannotated except for references to reviews. Entries for monographs, articles, and dissertations are arranged in 41 sections. A broad range of topics is covered including structural and historical linguistics, language tools such as dictionaries and grammars, applied studies on the teaching of Portuguese both as a native and foreign language, dialectology (Galego and Brazilian Portuguese), and Portuguese Creoles. An appended bibliography details the 240 periodicals analyzed. There is a name index which lists persons—authors as well as persons who are the subject of study—and a subject index.

804.   Flasche, Hans. **Romance Languages and Literatures as Presented in German Doctoral Dissertations, 1885-1950: A Bibliography/Die Sprachen und Literaturen der Romanen im Spiegel der deutschen Universitätsschriften, 1885-1950: Eine Bibliographie/Langues et littératures romanes dans les publications universitaires allemandes, 1885-1950: Une bibliographie**. Charlottesville, VA: Bibliographical Society of the University of Virginia, 1958. 299p. index.

The table of contents for this bibliography of 4,688 unannotated entries is in German, Grench and English. Entries are classed first under two main parts, linguistics and literary science, then by language and subject. There are name and subject indexes.

805.   García Gondar, Francisco. **Repertorio bibliográfico da lingüística galega: desde os seus inicios ata 1994 inclusive**. Equipo de investigacíon: María Teresa Araújo García, Inés Diz Gamallo, María Teresa Monteagudo Cabaleiro, Pilar Vázquez Grandas. Publicacións do Centro de Investigacións Lingüísticas e Literarias Ramón Piñeiro, 1995. 609p. index.

Published works of all types are included in this comprehensive bibliography of Galician linguistics with 5,109 entries arranged in a very finely classified listing. Extensive cross-referencing is accomplished by listing the entry numbers of other items of interest at the ends of subsections. In addition to general works, it covers such topics as: phonetics, phonology, and orthography; morphology and syntax; lexicology and lexicography; dialectology; historical aspects; sociolinguistics, and applied linguistics. There is a somewhat unusual index for works dealing with the various dialects of Galician, plus an index of authors.

806.   Golden, Herbert Hershel, and Seymour O. Simches. **Modern Iberian Language and Literature; a Bibliography of Homage Studies**. Cambridge, MA: Harvard University Press, 1958. 184p. index. LC 58-12978.

A total of 424 Festschriften are analyzed in this volume which is similar in scope and format to the authors' work on Italian (see entry below). Part II which deals with language has 796 entries subdivided into sections on: Romance linguistics, the Iberian Peninsula, Catalan and Valencian, Galician and Portuguese (including Brazilian), Basque, and Spanish (including Spanish-American).

807.   Golden, Herbert Hershel, and Seymour O. Simches. **Modern Italian Language and Literature; a Bibliography of Homage Studies**. Cambridge, MA: Harvard University Press, 1959. 207p. index. LC 59-14742.

Some 474 Festschriften spanning a time period from the Renaissance through 1957 are analyzed in this bibliography. Citations for all the analyzed homage volumes are listed, arranged alphabetically by name of person or institution honored. Section II is of most interest to linguistics; it covers language in 2 parts: Romance linguistics (84 entries) and Italian language (another 265 entries). An index keyed to the numbered entries references authors as well as persons, works, and subjects treated in the articles.

808.   González Pérez, Rosario, and Ana María Rodríguez Fernández. **Bibliografia de sintaxis española (1960-1984)**. Con la colaboración de F. Javier Herrero Ruiz de Loizaga. Santiago de Compostela: Universidade de Santiago de Compostela, 1989. 245p. index (Verba. Anuario Galego de Filoloxía. Anexo, 31). ISBN 84-7191-5715.

The introduction to this bibliography on Spanish language syntax details the 5-level classification scheme. The largely unannotated 3,271 entries for monographs, articles, and theses are about evenly divided between materials written in English and Spanish with a few materials in other languages such as Japanese and Russian; for these other languages the authors transliterate titles into the Roman script and provide translations in Spanish. Short annotations generally consist of references to reviews of the cited materials or abstracts in *Dissertations Abstracts International*. There is an index of authors.

809.   Griffin, Lloyd W., Jack A. Clarke, and Alexander Y. Kroff, comps. **Modern French Literature and Language: A Bibliography of Homage Studies**. Madison, WI: University of Wisconsin Press; Ann Arbor, MI: Produced and distributed on demand by Xerox University Microfilms, 1976. 175p. index. (Monograph publishing on demand, imprint series). LC 75-26480. ISBN 0-299-06990-7.

This work is a revision and extension through 1974 of the Golden and Simches bibliography with the same title published in 1953. It provides access to the articles in 588 Festschriften, 834 of which are listed in its French language section. A name index includes both authors of articles and personal names appearing as subjects.

810.   Grossmann, Maria, and Bruno Mazzoni. **Bibliographie de phonologie romane**. The Hague: Mouton, 1974. 115p. index. (Janua linguarum. Series practica, 232). LC 74-186968.

In their bibliography the authors list about 1,200 works published through the end of 1970 on the phonology of the Romance languages. Besides chapters for each of the Romance languages there is one for Romance languages in general. Entries are listed chronologically within chapters. Works are generally not annotated except for citations to reviews. The good use of cross-references partially compensates for lack of a subject index; authors are indexed.

811. Hall, Pauline Cook. **A Bibliography of Spanish Linguistics**. Baltimore, MD: Linguistic Society of America, 1957. 162p. index. (Language Dissertation, No. 54; Supplement, **Language**, Vol. 32, No. 4, Pt. 2, October-December, 1956). LC 57-1838.

Articles published between 1887 and 1953 in over 300 periodicals on peninsular Spanish linguistics (not American Spanish) are covered in this classified, separately published, bibliography. Some 1,930 entries are listed in 10 sections: general, Old Spanish, phonology, morphology, word formation, syntax, vocabulary, personal and place names, foreign influences, and dialects. Each section has numerous subdivisions. Unfortunately the classification system is complex and there is no general table of contents listing the headings. Some entries are enhanced with content notes. There are, however, author, word, and subject indexes.

812. Hall, Robert Anderson. **Bibliografia della linguistica italiana**. 2. ed. riv. e aggiornata. Firenze: Sansoni Antiquariato, 1958. 3v. index. (Biblioteca bibliografica italica, 13-15). LC 58-42410.

813. **Primo supplemento decennale (1956-1966)**. Firenze: Sansoni Antiquariato, 1969. 524p. index. (Biblioteca bibliografica italica, 35).

814. **Secondo supplemento decennale (1966-1976)**. Pisa: Giardini, 1980. 388p. index. (Orientamenti linguistici, 13).

815. **Terzo supplemento decennale (1976-1986)**. Pisa: Giardini, 1988. 620p. index. (Orientamenti linguistici, 23).

In the second edition of this outstanding, scholarly work Hall has revised and enlarged the 1941 edition from some 4,000 to nearly 6,900 items. The three volumes (divided into 4 parts) now include material published since about 1860 to 1956. Volume 1 contains Parts 1 and 2, on the history and description of the Italian language. These 2 parts are subdivided by linguistic categories. Volume 2, containing Part 3, is devoted to Italian dialectology, subdivided by dialect. Volume 3, containing Part 4, concentrates on the history of Italian linguistics and is arranged chronologically. The third volume also contains five indexes which cover the whole set: authors and titles (for anonymous works), localities and dialects, words, etyma, and subjects. Each of the supplements contains corrections to the second edition and earlier supplements and has the same format and indexing as the main 3-volume set. The third supplement brings the total number of entries to 19,242.

816. Hall, Robert Anderson. **Bibliografia essenziale della linguistica italiana e romanza**. Firenze: Sansoni, 1973. 230p. (Orientamenti). LC 74-309083.

This unannotated bibliography contains 1,875 entries in 4 main sections, each extensively subdivided: history of Italian and Romance languages in general, description of Italian, dialectology, and the history of Italian and Romance linguistics. Hall provides both an author/title index and a subject index. In comparison to his 3-volume 1958 bibliography and supplements (see entries 812 and 815), the coverage of Italian here is much more selective, including only basic works.

817.   Heydenreich, Titus. **Bibliographie der Hispanistik in der Bundes-republik Deutschland, Österreich und der deutschsprachigen Schweiz**. Frankfurt am Main: Vervuert, 1988-1994. 4v. index. (Vols. 1-3: Editionen der Iberoamericana. Reihe II, Bibliographische Reihe, 4-6) (Vol. 4: Editionen der Iberoamericanana. Serie D, Bibliografien, 1). ISBN 3-89354-704-5(v.1); 3-89354-705-3(v.2); 3-89354-706-1(v.3); 3-89354-707-X(v.4).

Volume 1 (1981) covers material published in 1978-81, volume 2 (1988), 1982-86, volume 3 (1990), 1987-89, and volume 4 (1994), 1990-1992. Unannotated entries on Spanish, Portuguese, Catalan, Basque, and Galician linguistics, philology, and literature are listed in a classed arrangement. It includes a name index.

818.   Klingebiel, Kathryn. **Bibliographie linguistique de l'ancien occitan (1960-1982)**. Hamburg: Helmut Buske, 1986. 185p. index. (Romanistik in Geschichte und Gegenwart, Bd. 19; ISSN 0341-3209). LC 86-209382. ISBN 3-87118-767-4.

With only a few exceptions this bibliography does not include references on modern Occitan, only Old Occitan (from its origins up to the 16th century). Its 804 unannotated entries are arranged in some 14 sections with indexes for subjects and authors. Many items are cross-referenced under more than one section.

819.   Lesaffre, Jean. **Bibliographie occitane, 1957-1966**. En collaboration avec Irénée-Marcel Cluzel. Paris: Les Belles Lettres, 1969. 69p. index. LC 77-484704.

820.   Lesaffre, Jean, and Jean-Marie Petit. **Bibliographie occitane: 1967-1971**. Montpellier: Université Paul Valéry, Centre d'études occitanes, 1973. 110p. index. LC 75-506054.

821.   Lesaffre, Jean, and Jean-Marie Petit. **Bibliographie occitane, 1972-1973**. Montpellier: Université Paul Valéry, Centre d'études occitanes, 1974. 86p. index.

These three unannotated bibliographies of Occitan continue a series begun by Berthaud (see entry 796) that cover publications from 1919 through 1973. All are similar in arrangment and presentation. The sections of linguistic interest are: general works, bibliographies, linguistic studies, and grammars and dictionaries. Lesaffre provides author indexes.

822.   McKay, John C. **A Guide to Romance Reference Grammars: The Modern Standard Languages**. Amsterdam: John Benjamins, 1979. 126p. index. bibliog. (Amsterdam Studies in the Theory and History of Linguistic Science. Series V: Library and Information Sources in Linguistics, Vol. 6; ISSN 0165-7267). LC 80-503772. ISBN 90-272-0997-9.

In this guide McKay briefly describes and evaluates what he considers to be the best reference grammars and comprehensive works on syntax of contemporary Catalan, French, Italian, Portuguese, Spanish, and Rumanian. He excludes grammars organized for learning the language, purely historical grammars, and most grammars published before 1900.

In an introductory survey (with its own bibliography) McKay discusses various aspects of linguistic theories which have influenced the grammars discussed in the following chapters. Each chapter deals with one language and begins with a summary introduction. Except for Catalan each chapter has a section on grammars and another section on syntactic works. Thorough evaluative annotations accompany each work. There are also descriptive notes and often citations to reviews. An index of technical terms and of linguists cited covers both the introductory survey and chapters. The author/title index covers just the chapters.

823. Martin, Robert, and Éveline Martin. **Guide bibliographique de linguistique française**. Paris: Klincksieck, 1973. 186p. index. (Bibliothèque française et romane. Série D: Initiation, textes et documents, 6). LC 74-177951. ISBN 2-252-01534-9.

Short evaluative annotations accompany most of the approximately 1,000 books and periodical articles in this bibliography of French linguistics. A system of symbols indicates type of work, degree of difficulty, and importance. The arrangement is in 5 main sections, each with numerous subsections. In its attempt to include not only all aspects of French linguistics from historical to modern, but also general linguistics, coverage of some topics is rather thin; however, it is adequate as an introduction for students. Author and subject indexes are appended.

824. Mourin, Louis, and Jacques Pohl. **Bibliographie de linguistique romane**. 4. éd., remaniée et mise à jour. Bruxelles: Presses Universitaires de Bruxelles, 1971. 178p. index. illus. maps.

This bibliography of Romance linguistics originated as a guide to students at the universities of Brussels and Ghent. Entries are arranged in 4 parts: general linguistics, Latin, other Romance languages (with a chapter for general Romance and individual chapters for each Romance language), and stylistics. Contrastive linguistics is covered in an addendum. Each part or chapter is then subdivided into appropriate topics. A detailed table of contents and an author index aid retrieval of information. A set of 11 maps roughly outline various language and dialect areas. The practice of underlining not only titles, but all headings and subheadings, plus underscoring authors' and co-authors' names with double-dashed lines is rather disconcerting to the user.

825. Muljačic, Žarko. **Scaffale italiano: Avviamento bibliografico allo studio della lingua italiana**. Scandicci, Firenze: La Luova Italia, 1991. 374p. index. illus. (Biblioteca di Italiano e oltre, 7). ISBN 88-221-0974-0.

With entries published between 1970 and 1991 Muljačic's work provides an important supplement to Hall's bibliography on Italian linguistics that was discontinued after 1986 (see entries 812 and 815). The bibliography itself with 1,300 numbered entries begins on page 265 following a critical bibliographic essay that offers an overview of and a guide to Italian linguistics. The author provides only an index of authors.

826. Niederehe, Hans-Josef. **Bibliografía cronólogica de la lingüística, la gramática y la lexicografía del español (BICRES): desde los comienzos hasta el año 1600)**. Amsterdam: John Benjamins, 1994. index. bibliog. (Amsterdam Studies in the Theory and History of Linguistic Science. Series III: Studies

in the History of the Language Sciences, Vol. 76; ISSN 0304-0720). ISBN 90-272-4563-0.

With this bibliography Niederehe has produced a fundamental contribution for scholars of the history of linguistics in Spain. It provides an enormous amount of useful and fascinating information dealing with printed books and manuscripts prior to 1600 including studies of languages the Spanish encountered in the New World and studies of 16th century Spanish in Europe. Criteria for inclusion is that works much deal with Spanish linguistics, interpreted in its broadest sense, and the presence of Spanish, either as the object of study or the language of description. Meticulous care has gone into the physical descriptions of works. In addition there are fields for compilers' comments, location in libraries, and bibliographical sources. The bibliographical sources are gathered in a comprehensive source bibliography (pages 291-337). There are 985 entries arranged in chronological order beginning with 920? up to 1993, the latter being a republication of a 1599 dictionary. The author provides four helpful indexes for titles, places of publication or production, publishers and printers, and authors.

827.   Nuessel, Frank. **Theoretical Studies in Hispanic Linguistics (1960-): A Selected, Annotated Research Bibliography**. Bloomington, IN: Indiana University Linguistics Club, 1988. 355p. index.

Preceding the alphabetical listing of published works and theses for the years 1960 through 1986, Nuessel provides a useful overview of Spanish linguistic research and issues. The overview is followed by its own list of references and a source list for the bibliography itself. His is a selective bibliography of only the most significant theoretical works during the stated time period with useful, descriptive and often critical, annotations. Subject and author indexes follow.

828.   Palfrey, Thomas Rossman, Joseph G. Fucilla, and William C. Holbrook, comps. **A Bibliographical Guide to the Romance Languages and Literatures**. 8th ed. Evanston, IL: Chandler, 1971. 122p.

The eighth edition of this long-standing guide for students and researchers first published in 1939 now contains 1,824 entries in a detailed classified arrangement. A general Romance section contains a lot of general reference tools in addition to more specialized Romance materials. It is followed by language and literature sections for French (including Provençal, Belgian, and French-Swiss); Italian; Portuguese and Brazilian; and Spanish, Catalan, and Spanish-American. These language and literature sections are further subdivided by language and historical periods, if appropriate. All types of material are cited: general bibliographies, serial bibliographies, periodicals, dictionaries, encyclopedias, histories, grammars, and general treatises. Some entries have brief annotations. It lacks an index, but has a detailed table of contents and a thorough system of cross-references.

829.   Perl, Matthias, Hrsg. **Bibliographie zur romanischen Sprachwissenschaft in der DDR (1949-1990)**. Wilhelmsfeld: Gottfried Egert, 1995. 79p. index. ISBN 3-926972-45-9.

More than 650 entries in this bibliography on works dealing with Romance linguistic studies in the German Democratic Republic are arranged alphabetically in nine sections. One section is on general Romance linguistics followed by sections devoted to individual Romance languages. It is an expansion of Perl and

Barbel Plotner's earlier bibliography covering the years 1949-1986 (Leipzig: Karl-Marx-Universität Leipzig, Sektion Theoretische und angewandte Sprachwissenschaft, 1987). Included are monographs, chapters, journal articles, conference proceedings, and theses. There is an index of authors.

830.   Quilis, Antonio. **Fonética y fonología del español**. Madrid: C.S.I.C., 1963. 101p. index. (Cuadernos bibliográficos, 10). LC 65-76864.

The table of contents sets out the headings of this classified bibliography on Spanish phonetics and phonology. It lists 1,414 works published through 1962. Studies dealing with the phonetics of the various Spanish dialects in Spain and around the world are covered, including American Spanish. Except for occasional brief scope notes and citations to reviews, entries are not annotated. An author index is appended.

831.   Regueira Fernández, Xosé L., et al. **Guía bibliográfica de lingüística galega**. Vigo, [Spain]: Xerais de Galicia, 1996. 249p. index. (Universitaria. Manuais). ISBN 84-8301-032-7.

Some 2,400 entries are listed in this classified bibliography on Galician, a dialect found in the north-west corner of Spain and closely related to Portuguese. Nearly all of the unannotated entries are to works in Spanish. In addition to linguistic and lexical studies on the dialect itself, historical and sociolinguistic aspects are treated.

832.   Rohlfs, Gerhard. **Manual de filología hispanica; guía bibliográfica, crítica y metódica**. Traducción castellana del manuscrito aleman por Carlos Patiño Rosselli. Bogotá, 1957. 37p. (Publicaciones del Instituto Caro y Cuervo, 12). LC 58-47099.

Rohlfs includes studies dealing with the languages of the Iberian Peninsula from prehistoric times to the present. There are sections for general Ibero-Romance, Spanish, Catalan, and Portuguese. He includes research on all aspects of the languages plus works on their history, folklore, and dialect studies. The section on Spanish has a chapter on Spanish in America; the Portuguese section has a chapter on Brazilian Portuguese. Though varying somewhat in format, chapters often begin with text accompanied by footnotes and cross-references to works in other chapters. This text is sometimes followed by lists of supplementary materials; these materials often have brief annotations. The splitting of references among footnotes, text, and lists makes it somewhat difficult to use. Good indexes (for authors, subjects, words, and proper names) somewhat compensate for this.

833.   Sala, Marius. **Le judéo-espagnol**. The Hague/Paris: Mouton, 1976. 117p. bibliog. (Trends in Linguistics, State-of-the-Art Reports, 7). LC 77-460744. ISBN 90-279-3445-2.

This work, important for the study of Judeo-Spanish, a dialect of Spanish, consists of bibliographic essays in a classified arrangement. The 4 main parts are: background, structure of the language, history of the language, and texts (including Ladino). Sala discusses research, ranging in date from 1857 to 1972, from all over the world in numerous languages (though specifically omitting material written or published in Hebrew). References from the essays are gathered in an author-arranged bibliography at the end of the text. Wexler's bibliography updates this (see entry 838).

834.   Serís, Homero. **Bibliografía de la lingüística española**. Bogotá, 1964. 981p. index. (Publicaciones del Instituto Caro y Cuervo, 19). LC 65-80395.

This extensive bibliography is an indispensable tool for students of any aspect of Spanish linguistics. Its nearly 8,000 items continue the numbering sequence of the author's *Manual de bibliografía de la literatura española*. It has a very detailed classified arrangement with some 800 subsections contained in 7 main sections: general linguistics, Romance linguistics, Spanish linguistics, peninsular languages, Spanish dialects, Spanish in America, and the teaching of Spanish. Some entries are accompanied by critical annotations and there are often citations to reviews. Cross-referencing is extensive. Few of the items are for works published after 1958. A detailed table of contents and lengthy index are particularly valuable.

835.   Solé, Carlos A. **Bibliografía sobre el español de América (1920-1986)**. Bogotá: Instituto Caro y Cuervo, 1990. 348p. (Publicaciones del Instituto Caro y Cuervo, 88).

Some 3,558 monographs, articles, and theses published from 1920 through 1986 are listed in Sole's 1990 bibliography on Spanish of the Americas (North, Central, and South). It updates two earlier bibliographies covering 1920-1967 and 1967-1971 (Washington, DC: Georgetown University Press, 1970; Austin: University of Texas, 1972). It has a detailed classified arrangement which is laid out in a table of contents; there are no indexes. General and multiple-country sections are followed by sections for individual countries, each with appropriate subsections. Many entries, particularly the most important works, are descriptively and critically annotated with quotes from important reviews and references to others. The preponderance of entries are to materials in Spanish and English.

836.   Stevenson, John. **Catalán, gallego, vascuence: Ensayo bibliográfico de estudios lingüísticos, publicados o realizados en España (1970-1986)**. Sydney, Australia: School of Spanish and Latin American Studies, The University of New South Wales/Universidad de Nueva Gales del Sur, Sydney, 1989. 235p. index. ISBN 0-85823-786-5.

Some 5,228 unannotated entries are listed in 21 sections in this bibliography concerned with the Spanish, Catalan, and Basque languages and the Gallegan dialect. Coverage of books, journal articles, conference papers, and theses begins in 1970 and goes through 1985 though a few entries are dated later than this.

837.   Teschner, Richard V., general ed. **Spanish and English of United States Hispanos: A Critical, Annotated, Linguistic Bibliography**. Garland D. Bills and Jerry R. Craddock, associate editors. Arlington, VA: Center for Applied Linguistics, 1975. 352p. index. LC 75-21564. ISBN 0-87281-042-9.

This bibliography is a continuation of Hensley C. Woodbridge's 1954 article "Spanish in the American South and Southwest," published in volume 3 of *Orbis* which itself is a continuation of Madaline W. Nichols' *A Bibliographical Guide to Materials on American Spanish* (Cambridge, MA: Harvard University Press,

1941). The latter was for years the standard reference guide to all aspects of Western Hemisphere Spanish.

The major categories of persons of Hispanic background that Teschner's bibliography deals with are: Chicanos, Puerto Ricans, Cubans, Louisiana Canary Islanders, Spaniards, and Sephardic Jews. The scope is not confined to the field of linguistics, but includes language-related items from anthropology, sociology, education, folklore, psychology, and other areas. Many items that deal with the English spoken by Hispanos and the code-switching behavior of bilinguals are also included. The 675 entries are for books, chapters, dissertations, theses, articles, and parts of Festschriften. Long, frequently critical annotations often contain citations to previously published annotations and reviews. Each of the various subsections of this classified bibliography are prefaced by a very useful "reader's guide" that points out the most important items and lists cross-references to items elsewhere in the bibliography. An author index completes this excellent work.

838.   Wexler, Paul. **Judeo-Romance Linguistics: A Bibliography (Latin, Italo-, Gallo, Ibero-, and Rhaeto-Romance Except Castilian)**. New York: Garland, 1989. 174p. index. (Garland Reference Library of the Humanities, Vol. 890). LC 88-24276. ISBN 0-8240-4531-9.

In the introduction to his book Wexler provides a rationale for a bibliography of Judeo-Romance separate from a general bibliography of Romance linguistics. He argues that even if one does not subscribe to the existence of a Judeo-Romance family of languages, a separate bibliography is justified in that both the potential audience and range of topics in Judeo-Romance are much broader than in Romance linguistics. The more than 1,600 entries in this bibliography are listed in a classified arrangement divided first into chapters covering each of the Judeo-Romance languages. Citations to reviews are noted directly below each entry. Cross-references appear at the end of sections. A number of entries are for works in Hebrew.

839.   Woodbridge, Hensley Charles. **Guide to Reference Works for the Study of the Spanish Language and Literature and Spanish American Literature**. With three indexes by Elline Long. 2nd ed. New York: Modern Language Association of America, 1997. 236p. index. (Selected Bibliographies in Language and Literature, 5). LC 96-35093. ISBN 0-87352-967-7.

The 2nd edition of this guide to reference works updates the earlier 1987 edition which covered materials published between 1950 and 1985. It is a selective work intended for graduate students and librarians. Of chief interest to the linguist are the chapters dealing with language and linguistics of the Spanish of Spain and American Spanish. The latter chapter, subdivided by country, mainly lists dictionaries and lexicons. A few entries outside these chapters cover general bibliographies of both literature and language. Most entries are accompanied by descriptive, and sometimes evaluative, annotations. There are three indexes: authors, editors, compilers, and translators; author bibliographies, glossaries, concordances, and anonymous works; and, titles.

Celtic

840.   Baumgarten, Rolf. **Bibliography of Irish Linguistics and Literature, 1941-1971**. Dublin: Dublin Institute for Advanced Studies, 1986. 776p. index. ISBN 0-901282-81-2.

Baumgarten's work continues Best's two bibliographies (see entries 841 and 842). It contains 9,312 entries for books, articles, theses, and conference proceedings arranged according to a 3-level classification scheme. There is some duplication of entries under more than one heading. Many entries have short descriptive annotations. Indexes of words and proper names, first lines of verse, sources, and authors facilitate use.

841.   Best, Richard Irvine. **Bibliography of Irish Philology and of Printed Irish Literature**. Dublin: Published for the National Library of Ireland by H.M.S.O., 1913. 307p. index. (Reprinted New York: Johnson, 1970; LC 70-18829).

842.   Best, Richard Irvine. **Bibliography of Irish Philology and Manuscript Literature: Publications 1913-1941**. Dublin: The Dublin Institute for Advanced Studies, 1942. 253p. index. LC 45-882. (Reprinted Oxford at the University Press, 1969).

Best's 1913 bibliography covers works published through 1912, the 1942 volume those from 1913 to the end of 1941. Of most interest to the linguist is the Irish philology section in each which covers lexicography, grammar (Old Irish, Middle Irish, phonology, Modern Irish, and dialects), metrics, inscriptions, Old Irish glosses, and manuscripts. Both have detailed indexes. For a continuation of works published from 1941 through 1971 see Baumgarten's work (entry 840).

843.   Broudic, F. **Langue et littérature bretonnes: dix ans de bibliographie, 1973-1982**. Brest: Brud Nevez, 1984. 288p. index. LC 85-197384. ISBN 2-86775-025-3.

The material in this bibliography on Breton language and literature represents material from 7 articles previously published in the *Bulletin de la Société Archéologique du Finistère* from 1974 to 1982. The articles are reprinted here with only one change; the index of authors at the end of each article has been replaced with a cumulated author index. Within each article the entries are classified into some 20 to 36 sections. Many of the earlier entries are provided with long descriptive annotations which, particularly after 1976, dwindle to short notes. In all just over 2,500 books, dissertations, and articles are cited. It includes material on phonetics, phonology, etymology, semantics, morphology, grammar, syntax, stylistics, as well as on teaching and items concerned with the social situation.

844.   Mather, J. Y., and H. H. Speitel, eds. **The Linguistic Atlas of Scotland. Scots Section**. Cartography by C. N. Leslie. Hamden, CT: Archon Books, 1975 (v.1); London: Croom Helm, 1977 (v.2), 1986 (v.3). index. maps. LC 74-22345. ISBN 0-208-01475-6(v.1); 0-85664-111-1(v.2); 0-85664-716-0(v.3)

The material published here is based on work carried out for the Linguistic Survey of Scotland (Scots section) in the Faculty of Arts at the University of

Edinburgh. Data were collected by means of questionnaires from Scotland, the 2 northern counties of England bordering on Scotland (Cumberland and Northumberland), the six counties of Northern Ireland, and some neighboring parts of Eire. Material consists of word (and phrase) lists and the word-location maps. Volume 2 contains indexes to both volumes with Index A for the lexical maps and Index B the listed words. The third volume covers phonological findings from field research with 175 maps for words and 120 maps for phonemes.

845. Wagner, Heinrich. **Linguistic Atlas and Survey of Irish Dialects**. Dublin: Dublin Institute for Advanced Studies, 1958-1969. 4v. maps.

Volume 1 contains an introduction and 300 maps showing distribution of dialect forms of given words and expressions based on a survey using a 2,000 item questionnaire at 88 locations done between 1949 and 1956. Volumes 2-4 contain material on the dialects of Munster, Connaught, and Ulster and the Isle of Man, respectively. The latter volume also has specimens of Scottish Gaelic dialects and phonetic texts of East Ulster Irish.

Slavonic

Manuals

846. De Bray, Reginald George Arthur. **Guide to the Slavonic Languages**. 3rd ed., rev. and expanded. Columbus, OH: Slavica Publishers, 1980. 3v. bibliog. LC 80-154015. ISBN 0-89357-060-5(v.1); 0-89357-061-3(v.2); 0-89357-062-1(v.3).

The third edition of this standard work, originally published in 1951, has been substantially revised and expanded. It is intended not as an indepth treatment of each language for the specialist, but as an overall guide and synthesis of the individual languages to aid the learner already familiar with one of the Slavonic languages. Hence, specialized terminology has been minimized.

It is organized into 3 parts, or volumes: Part 1 covers the South Slavonic languages, Part 2 the West Slavonic languages, and Part 3 the East Slavonic languages. A short bibliography at the beginning of each part provides a selective list of grammars, dictionaries, and other study aids for the languages examined in that part. A detailed table of contents serves as an index for each part. A language section (within one of the parts) begins with a brief summary of the history of the development of the language together with references to its main writers. This history is followed by subsections dealing with the alphabet, pronunciation, a summary of its characteristic features presented in historical perspective, main dialects, morphology, word order with enclitics, vowel gradation and vowel lengthening, and a few pages of selected texts.

847. International Organization for Standardization. **International System for the Transliteration of Cyrillic Characters**. Prepared by the Technical Committee ISO/TC46. 1st ed. Geneva: 1955. 7p. (ISO Recommendation, R9).

The table in this recommendation provides for the transliteration into Latin characters from Bulgarian, Russian, Ukrainian, White Russian, and Serbian. This system, closer to European practice than American, is only one of a number of transliteration systems in use.

848.   Shaw, Joseph Thomas. **The Transliteration of Modern Russian for English-Language Publications**. Madison, WI: University of Wisconsin Press, 1967. 15p. illus. LC 66-22858.

The 4 systems of transliteration presented in this manual range from one suitable for general, popular works to those suitable for works in various specialized fields. A short description of each system with recommendations for its use is followed by a transliteration chart. The author also discusses special problems and offers some suggested solutions.

Bibliographies of Dictionaries

849.   Aav, Yrjö. **Russian Dictionaries: Dictionaries and Glossaries Printed in Russia, 1627-1917**. Zug, Switzerland: Inter Documentation Co., 1977. 196p. index. bibliog. (Bibliotheca Slavica, 10). LC 83-159082. ISBN 3-85750-019-0.

The collections of the Helsinki University Library, rich in Russian material published from 1830 to 1917, supplemented by bibliographies and booksellers' catalogs, form the base of this bibliography. It lists 1,537 general dictionaries and vocabularies published in Russia from 1627 to 1917 as books or in Russian newspapers, periodicals, or series. The main arrangement is by monolingual (subdivided by general, general dialect, regional dialect, and such special dictio-naries as etymological, Old Russian, and slang), bilingual (subdivided by language), and polyglot. Titles of all works are transliterated from Cyrillic script. Content notes accompany many entries. Name and language indexes are appended.

850.   Franolić, Branko. **A Bibliography of Croatian Dictionaries**. Paris: Nouvelles editions latines, 1985. 139p. index. illus. ISBN 2-7233-0302-0.

The author introduces this comprehensive bibliography of Croatian dictionaries with an historical outline of Croatian lexicography ranging from the earliest recorded forms of Croatian found in the glosses that go back to the 11th-12th centuries up to the many general-purpose and specialized bilingual dictionaries of the 20th century. Entries are sorted into monolingual (type/field), bilingual (by language), and polyglot (general and special) lists then arranged alphabetically by author. Brief descriptive annotations accompany some titles. Adding interest to the work are facsimiles of title page from some older works. Author, language, and subject indexes are appended.

851.   Lewanski, Richard Casimir, comp. **A Bibliography of Slavic Dictionaries**. 2d rev. & enl. ed. Bologna: Editrice Compositori, 1972-73. 4v. index. illus. (Johns Hopkins University, Bologna Center Library, Publications, 7). (World Bibliography of Dictionaries). LC 7-189489.

The second edition of this selective bibliography now contains entries for more than 11,200 monolingual, bilingual, and polyglot dictionaries. Volume 1 deals with Polish dictionaries. Volume 2 covers other Slavic dictionaries except for Russian which is in volume 3. Volume 4 supplements all of them. Each volume contains its own author, language, and subject indexes. The compiler notes various editions and reprints, adds the number of entries for many titles, and indicates the language from which and into which all bi- and multilingual dictionaries proceed. He gives the contents and paging of multi-volume sets as well.

852. Stankiewicz, Edward. **Grammars and Dictionaries of the Slavic Languages from the Middle Ages up to 1850: An Annotated Bibliography**. Berlin: Mouton, 1984. 190p. index. illus. bibliog. LC 84-985. ISBN 3-11009778-8.

The author intends his bibliography to be a guide to the history of Slavic grammatical thought as reflected in the grammars and dictionaries of both Slavic and non-Slavic scholars from about 1400 to about 1850. The cut-off date of 1850 was chosen as most Slavic literary languages, except for Byelorussian and Macedonian, were formed by then. For works from the second half of the 19th century the reader can consult Stankiewicz and Worth's *Selected Bibliography of Slavic Linguistics* (see entry 878). Works on Church Slavonic and works that deal with artificial all-Slavic languages are excluded except where they bear on the development of the Slavic national languages. Also omitted are works of secondary importance (such as "azbukovniki," primers, and school grammars) as well as dictionaries of exotic languages.

Grammars and dictionaries are grouped separately from each other under a language and then listed chronologically. The annotations are descriptive with frequent cross-references to works in an appended secondary bibliography. This is an authoritative work by one of the preeminent scholars in the field.

853. Zalewski, Wojciech. **Russian-English Dictionaries with Aids for Translators: A Selected Bibliography**. New York: Russica Publishers, 1981. 101p. index. ("Russica" Bibliography Series, No. 1). LC 81-50870. ISBN 0-89830-041-X.

This bibliography includes most of the significant Russian-English dictionaries published after World War II up through 1979. Since the principal audience of this book is intended to be the translator of Russian into English, only a few English-Russian dictionaries are listed. The main emphasis is on subject dictionaries though a selected number of general dictionaries are also included. A section on translators' aids lists bibliographies of dictionaries, monolingual dictionaries, personal name dictionaries, and other reference tools.

Slavic Linguistic Atlas

854. Mezhdunarodnyi komitet slavistov. Komissiya obshcheslavyanskogo lingvisticheskogo atlasa. Rossiiskaya akademiya nauk. Institut russkogo yazyka. **Obshcheslavyanskii lingvisticheskii atlas. Vstupitel'nyi vypusk: Obshchie printsipy. Spravochnye materialy/Atlas linguistique slave. Introduction: Principes de Base. Materiel d'information/The Slavic Linguistic Atlas. Introductory Issue: General Principles. Reference Materials**. 2nd ed. rev. and supplemented. Initiators of the OLA project: R. I. Avanesov, et al. Moskva: "Nauka," 1994. 181p. index. bibliog. ISBN 5-02-011544-4.

855. Institut russkogo yazyka. Akademiya nauk SSSR. **Obshcheslavyanskii lingvisticheskii atlas; materialy i issledovaniya, 1965-1984**. Moskva: Nauka, ?-1988. annual. illus. maps. LC 79-532260.

856. **Obshcheslavyanskii lingvisticheskii Atlas. Seriya fonetiko-grammaticheskaya**. Vypusk 1- . Belgrad: Serbskaya Akad. Nauk i Iskusstv, 1988- .

857. **Obshcheslavyanskii lingvisticheskii Atlas. Seriya leksiko-slovoobrazovatelnaya.** Vypusk 1- . Belgrad: Serbskaya Akad. Nauk i Iskusstv, 1988- . (This work not viewed by author).

Work on the Slavic linguistic atlas (OLA) is an ongoing international effort. It began with the decision of the Fourth International Congress of Slavists in Moscow in 1958 when the OLA commission, which included prominent slavists from different countries, was organized. Initially, commissions in Bulgaria, the GDR, Poland, Czechoslovakia, the USSR, and Yugoslavia were organized to carry out the field work in the territory of their language or state. Other countries subsequently joined the effort. The OLA has been actively supported by a great number of scientific organizations, institutes, colleges, and universities. Material was collected mainly from 1965 to 1975; reports were published annually from 1965 to 1984 (see second entry above). These annuals reported progress of the work, research in dialectology and linguistic geography, and discussed theoretical and practical problems of OLA cartography.

An introductory issue to the atlas, finally published in 1978 and now in a second revised edition, provides a history of the project, discusses its theoretical base, and details major problems (see first entry above). There is also information on the localities where data were collected, the persons from whom the material was obtained, information on the field workers, and other reference data. The introduction and table of contents are in English and French as well as Russian.

Beginning in 1988 atlas materials are issued in numbered series (see last two entries above). One series includes the lexicon, word derivation, and semantics, the other series concerns grammar, phonetics, and phonology. Each issue of the latter series deals with a particular sound or sounds. Volume 1 (1988) is concerned with the reflexes of *e and has 70 colored maps.

Serial Bibliographies

858. **Bibliografie české lingvistiky**. 1945/50- . Praha: Československe akademie ved, 1950- . quinquennial. ISSN 0862-1462.

Publication of this ongoing classified bibliography of general linguistics, Indo-European, Slavonic, and Czech linguistics has changed from a five-year cumulation to an annual. The title has also varied. It is now an annual with a table of contents in both Czech and English and includes citations to monographs, chapters in books, and articles with only occasional brief descriptive annotations of contents. Most citations are to materials written in Czech, German, and English. The bibliography for 1991 published in 1994 had 1,640 entries. There are indexes of authors and words.

859. **Slavyanskoe yazykoznanie; bibliograficheskii ukazatel' literatury, izdannoi v SSSR s 1918 po 1960 gg**. Moskva: Izd. Akad. Nauk SSSR, 1963. 2v. index. LC 64-41581.

The above is an ongoing classified bibliography with supplements covering 1961-1965 (1969), 1966-1970 (1973), 1971-1975 (1981), 1976-1978 (1985), and 1979-1981 (1988) issued by the Akademiya Nauk SSSR (with varying editors and compilers for each cumulation). It is the best available source for books, articles, surveys, and reviews published in the Soviet Union on Slavic linguistics. It contains materials written in Russian, Ukrainian, or Belorussian, covering all areas of the field. Its publication lag, however, limits its usefulness for current research. Author indexes accompany the sets.

860.   Terry, Garth M. **East European Languages and Literatures: A Subject and Name Index to Articles in English-Language Journals, 1900-1977**. Oxford: Clio Press, 1978. 275p. LC 79-315595. ISBN 0-903450-21-6.

861.   Terry, Garth M. **East European Languages and Literatures II: A Subject and Name Index to Articles in Festschriften, Conference Proceedings, and Collected Papers in the English Language, 1900-1981, and Including Articles in Journals, 1978-1981**. Nottingham, England: Astra Press, 1982. 214p. (Astra Soviet and East European Bibliographies, No. 1). ISBN 0-946134-00-6.

Subsequent supplements/volumes of this ongoing bibliography (with some minor variations in title) in the Astra series continue to be published every three years as follows: III covering materials for 1982-1984 (1985), IV for 1985-1987 (1988), V for 1988-1990 (1991), VI for 1991-1993 (1994), and VII for 1994-1996 (1997). Terry's purpose is to facilitate research by gathering in one place references to works on Slavonic and East European languages and literatures published in English, mainly in Great Britain and North America. Even if published in English, East European studies are omitted since the focus here is on Western scholarship and thought in the Slavonic field.

Main subject sections are subdivided. For example, a language section may have subsections for: general and miscellaneous, bibliographies, history, languages in contact, lexicography, morphology, onomastics, phonology, semantics, semiotics, study and teaching, syntax, and translation. Entries in each subsection are arranged chronologically with the most recent materials listed last. A name index includes authors, compilers, editors, translators, and any person mentioned in the entries.

Cumulative Bibliographies

862.   Avilova, N.S., et al. **Bibliograficheskii ukazatel' literatury po russkomu yazykoznaniyu s 1925 po 1880 god**. Glav. red., V. V. Vinogradov. Moskva: Izd. Akad. Nauk SSSR, 1954-1959. 8v. index. LC 55-22007.

This set contains annotated listings for works on linguistics published in Russia between 1825 and 1880. Though it mainly covers the Russian language it also has some material on other Slavonic languages and general linguistics. Each of the first seven volumes is devoted to one or more subjects. Volume 8 is a main entry index.

863.   Andreesen, Walter, and Frank Heidtmann. **Wie finde ich slawistische Literatur**. Berlin: Berlin Verlag Arne Spitz, 1986. 316p. index. illus. (Orientierungshilfen, Bd. 29). ISBN 3-87061-213-4.

Although this book is organized as a guide to doing research for the Slavonic languages and literatures, it is also an excellent up-to-date source for key reference materials in this subject area. Part 2 of the classified arrangement contains sections for general Slavonic and the individual Slavonic languages. Sections are further subdivided and contain listings for such reference tools as: national bibliographies, cumulative bibliographies, subject bibliographies, serial bibliographies, handbooks, dictionaries, encyclopedias, descriptive grammars, historical grammars, and so on. Many entries have descriptive and/or evaluative comments. An index of main entries (plus co-authors and editors) increases its usefulness as a research tool.

864. Bamborschke, Ulrich. **Bibliographie slavistischer Arbeiten aus deutschsprachigen Fachzeitschriften 1964-1973: einschliesslich slavistischer Arbeiten aus deutschsprachigen nichtslavistischen Zeitschriften sowie slavistischen Fest- und Sammelschriften 1945-1973**. Unter Mitarbeit von W. Werner und E. A. Hilf. Berlin: Osteuropa-Institut; Wiesbaden: In Kommission bei Otto Harrassowitz, 1976. 2v. index. (Bibliographische Mitteilungen des Osteuropa-Instituts an der Freien Universität Berlin, Hft. 13). ISBN 3-447-01832-1(v.1); 3-447-01833-X(v.2).

This work continues an earlier bibliography by Seemann and Siegmann (see entry 877); it has the same arrangement and indexing. In addition to Slavonic studies from German-language periodicals it includes for the years 1945 to 1973 both studies from non-Slavic journals and from Slavic Festschriften and collected works. (See entry 865 for a supplement.)

865. Bamborschke, Ulrich, and Waltraud Werner. **Bibliographie slavistischer Arbeiten aus den wichtigsten englischsprachigen Fachzeitschriften, sowie Fest- und Sammelschriften 1922-1976**. Berlin: Osteuropa-Institut an der Freien Universität Berlin; Wiesbaden: In Kommission bei Otto Harrassowitz, 1981. 189p. index. (Bibliographische Mitteilungen des Osteuropa-Instituts an der Freien Universität Berlin, Bd. 19). LC 83-116844.

The title on an added title page reads *Bibliography of Slavonic Studies Selected from the Most Important Periodicals and Miscellanies Published in the English-Speaking World 1922-1976*. It supplements two earlier bibliographies (see entries 864 and 877), continuing their arrangement and indexing. There is considerable overlap in coverage between this work and Terry's bibliographies on East European languages and literatures (see entries 860 and 861).

866. Collins, Daniel E., comp. **Slavic Linguistics; a Bibliographic Guide to Materials in the University of Virginia Library, Charlottesville, Virginia**. Edited by Angelika S. Powell. Charlottesville, VA: University of Virginia Library, 1986.

Though compiled as a guide to acquaint researchers in Slavic linguistics with the major holdings of the Library of the University of Virginia, it should be of value to others since it pulls together so much material in a classified arrangment. Entries cover materials through early 1986. The main divisions are: general and comparative Slavic linguistics, common Slavic (including the question of a Balto-Slavic linguistic unity), South Slavic and Balkan linguistics, West Slavic linguistics, and East Slavic linguistics. There are further subdivisions within the individual language categories.

867. Grubišić, Vinko. **Bibliography on the Croatian Language**. Norval, Ont.: HIŠAK-CSAC, Croatian Schools of America-Australia-Canada-Europe, 1987. 183p. index. (Priručnici za učenje hrvatskog jezika i kulture izvan Hrvatske/Manuals of the Study of the Croatian Language and Culture outside Croatia, Bk. 12). ISBN 0-919817-14-9.

The preface to this unannotated bibliography with 2,300 entries is in English, French, German, and Croatian; a table of contents is in English only. After sections listing bibliographic sources and general studies, other works cited are organized in sections dealing with such topics as the name of the Croatian language, diachronic and synchronic studies, dialects and dialectology, Croatian outside Croatia, orthographic studies, teaching Croatian, and onomastics. Cross-references can be found at the end of each section. Grubišić supplies an author index.

868. Kaiser, Eleonore, and Alfons Höcherl. **Materialien zu einer slavistischen Bibliographie; Arbeiten der in Österreich, der Schweiz und der Bundesrepublik Deutschland tätigen Slavisten (1963-1973)**. München: Otto Sagner, 1973. 243p. index. LC 74-327202. ISBN 3-87690-078-6.

Kaiser and Höcherl's bibliography with 2,756 entries is a continuation of an earlier one by Mahnken and Pollok (see entry 873). Both cover materials published in Austria, Switzerland, and the Federal Republic of Germany, the former for 1945 to 1963, this one for 1963 to 1973. The arrangement and indexing are the same.

869. Kaiser, Eleonore, and Ernst Hansack. **Materialien zu einer slavistischen Bibliographie: Arbeiten der in der Bundesrepublik Deutschland, Österreich und der deutschsprachigen Schweiz tätigen Slavisten (1973-1983)**. Unter Mitarbeit von Sabine Mahr und Raphael Sterl; hrsg. von Erwin Wedel. München: Otto Sagner, 1983. 424p. index. ISBN 3-87690-268-1.

This bibliography listing 4,813 works published from 1973 to 1983 continues, with the same arrangment and subject coverage, Kaiser and Hocherl's previous bibliography and a still earlier one by Mahnken and Pollok (see entries 868 and 873).

870. Koschmieder, Erwin, and Helmut Schaller. **Bibliographie zur slavischen Sprachwissenschaft: eine Einführung**. Frankfurt am Main: Peter Lang, 1977. 89p. index. (Symbolae Slavicae, Bd. 1; ISSN 0170-852X). LC 79-388836. ISBN 3-261-02347-3.

The authors designed this short selective bibliography for the student. It covers the Slavonic languages plus related Balkan and Baltic studies. Among its entries are studies on historical grammar, phonetics and phonology, morphology, syntax, dialectology, and orthography. Some dictionaries and textbooks are also listed. A simple classified arrangement is used for the 1,251 unannotated entries. The journal articles and books listed are in a wide variety of languages; Cyrillic titles are transliterated. The authors provide an author index.

871. Lencek, Rado L., and Miloš Okuka. **A Bibliography of Recent Literature on Macedonian, Serbo-Croatian, and Slovene Languages**. München: Slavica Verlag Dr. Anton Kovač, 1990. 95p. index. (Geschichte, Kultur und Geisteswelt der Südslaven, n.s., Bd. 1). ISBN 3-927077-00-3.

The organization of this unannotated bibliography is rather strange. It seems to be two separate works, each having its own title page, and one having an appendix. On pages 19-54 is Lencek's "Bibliography of the Publications of American Slavists in Macedonian, Serbocroatian, and Slovene Language, 1940-1985" followed by an appendix on pages 55-58, "A Survey of Doctoral Dissertations Accepted by American Universities through January 1985." Entries in the bibliography are listed alphabetically by author while the dissertations in the survey are listed chronologically. This is then followed by Okuka's work on pages 59-90, "A Contribution to the Bibliography of Works on Serbocroatian Language Published Outside Yugoslavia, 1976-1985," which has yet another type of organization, entries arranged alphabetically under six section headings. All rather confusing for the user. A name index thankfully serves for all three parts.

872. Magner, Thomas F., comp. **Soviet Dissertations for Advanced Degrees in Russian Literature and Slavic Linguistics, 1934-1962**. University Park, PA: Dept. of Slavic Languages, Pennsylvania State University, 1966. 100p. LC 68-66174.

In his bibliography of Soviet dissertations Magner first lists those submitted for the "Doktor nauk" degree and then those for the lower degree of "Kandidat nauk." (These are not equivalent to, but are probably somewhat higher than the American doctorate and master's degrees). The linguistics section under each degree contains 26 and 419 entries, respectively. The majority are concerned with the Russian language, the remainder with general linguistics and other Slavonic languages.

873. Mahnken, Irmgard, and Karl-Heinz Pollok. **Materialien zu einer slawistischen Bibliographie; Arbeiten der in Österreich, der Schweiz und der Bundesrepublik Deutschland tätigen Slawisten (1945-1963)**. München: Otto Sagner, 1963. 257p. index. LC 64-36447.

T'his bibliography covers works in Slavic studies published from 1945 to 1963 in Austria, Switzerland and the Federal Republic of Germany. Materials are arranged in sections for general works, various area studies (such as east Slavic), and the individual Slavic languages. Linguistic materials can be found in language subsections as well as through use of the subject index. It also has an author index. Two bibliographies by Kaiser and others continue this compilation (see entries 868 and 869).

874. Milivojević, Dragan, and Vasa D. Mihailovich, eds. **Yugoslav Linguistics in English 1900-1980: A Bibliography**. Columbus, OH: Slavica Publishers, 1990. 122p. index. ISBN 0-89357-213-6.

The authors have gathered in their bibliography 80 years of linguistic research written in English on the three official languages—Serbo-Croatian, Slovene, and Macedonian—of the former country of Yugoslavia. Linguistics is interpreted very broadly to include stylistics, poetics, and literary translation as well as sociolinguistics and pedagogical materials. The nearly 1,200 references for books and articles, along with reviews of such works, are organized first into general categories, then subdivided by language. Some entries have short annotations explaining their content. Some cross-referencing is done for works belonging under more than one heading.

875. Schaller, Helmut Wilhelm. **Bibliographie der Bibliographien zur slavischen Sprachwissenschaft**. Frankfurt am Main: Lang, 1982. 115p. index. (Symbolae Slavicae, Bd. 15; ISSN 0170-852X). LC 82-190341. ISBN 3-8204-5781-X.

Schaller's bibliography of bibliographies is the first of its kind for Slavic linguistics. It is a handy guide to the field covering works from the first decade of this century up through 1978. He includes bibliographies published as books, parts of books, single articles in periodicals, as regularly occurring features of yearbooks and other periodicals, and as sections of serial bibliographies. The 1,333 unannotated entries are arranged according to a classification scheme, then alphabetically by author. Works in many languages are cited, all in the original language of publication. Those in the Cyrillic alphabet are transliterated. First names of authors are not given, only initials. There is a short subject index, name index for biobibliographies, author index, and a title index for cumulative serial bibliographies. Though a quick check revealed a few works in English that are missing, it comes close to being comprehensive.

876. Schaller, Helmut Wilhelm. **Bibliographie zur russischen Sprache**. Frankfurt a.M.: Peter Lang, 1980. 204p. index. (Symbolae Slavicae, Bd. 8; ISSN 0170-852X). LC 80-504640. ISBN 3-8204-6400-X.

Most of the 2,719 entries in this bibliography on the Russian language are for books, periodical articles, and dissertations written in Russian, though some material in other languages is also included. The two main divisions of its classified arrangement are: 1) theoretical (phonetics, phonology, morphology, syntax, sociolinguistics, contrastive linguistics, etc.), and 2) practical (studies in teaching, teaching materials, grammars, textbooks, dictionaries, stylistics, transliteration, and the like). A short concluding section lists bibliographies on Russian linguistics. Entries are indexed by subject and author. This work will be of particular interest to teachers of Russian.

877. Seemann, Klaus-Dieter, and Frank Siegmann. **Bibliographie der slavistischen Arbeiten aus den deutschsprachigen Fachzeitschriften, 1876-1963**. Berlin: Osteuropa-Institut; Wiesbaden: in Kommission bei Otto Harrassowitz, 1965. 422p. index. (Bibliographische Mitteilungen des Osteuropa-Instituts an der Freien Universität Berlin, Hft. 8). LC 66-54761.

In this unannotated classified bibliography Seemann covers Slavonic studies published in German-language periodicals from 1876 to 1963. A general section precedes individual sections for the various Slavonic languages. An author index is appended. (See entry 864 for a continuation and entry 865 for a supplement).

878. Stankiewicz, Edward, and Dean S. Worth. **A Selected Bibliography of Slavic Linguistics**. The Hague: Mouton, 1966-70. 2v. (Slavistic Printings and Reprintings, 49). LC 65-26005.

While this selective bibliography of the most important contributions to Slavic linguistics emphasizes contemporary research with a structuralist approach, major works with other approaches are included as well.

Volume 1 covers origins and migrations of the Slavs, Balto-Slavic, common and comparative Slavic, Old Church Slavonic, South Slavic (general studies, Bulgarian, Macedonian, Serbo-Croatian, and Slovenian). Volume 2 deals with West Slavic (general studies, Polish, Pomeranian, Polabian, Lusatian, Czech, and Slovak), East Slavic (Belorussian, Russian, and Ukrainian), and includes a section on bibliographies of bibliographies and history of research.

The language sections in each volume are further divided by form and subject, such as synchronic studies, diachronic studies, texts, dictionaries, onomastics, and syntax. The general cut-off date is 1962, although a few later works of special importance are included. The authors double-list works instead of giving cross-references and provide a number of entries with reviews to compensate for the lack of annotations. For each Slavic entry the title, author's name, and place of publication are given in modernized spelling; Cyrillic titles are transliterated.

879. Unbegaun, Boris Ottokar. **A Bibliographical Guide to the Russian Language**. With the collaboration of J. S. G. Simmons. Oxford: Clarendon Press, 1953. 174p. index. LC 53-2211.

In this selective, classified bibliography Unbegaun provides descriptive and often evaluative annotations for general, historical, and descriptive works on the Russian language published in all major languages. It is particularly useful for the information it provides on Russian dictionaries, especially those issued up to 1953 by the USSR Academy of Sciences. Bibliographic information is given in the original language and script. There are frequent cross-references. An author index is appended.

880. Worth, Dean S. **A Bibliography of Russian Word-Formation**. Columbus, OH: Slavica Publishers, 1977. 317p. index. ISBN 0-89357-041-9.

A detailed classified arrangement is used for the more than 3,000 numbered entries in this unannotated bibliography. The actual number of studies cited is quite a bit less than this since the numerous cross-references are also given entry numbers. Those sections with the most entries are: morphology, derivational types and models (accounting for more than half of the studies), semantics of derivation, and derivation of and from parts of speech. Books and articles in many languages are cited, though Russian-language works predominate. Section 8 is an author index.

Baltic

881. Kubicka, Weronika. **Języki bałtyckie; bibliografia/Baltic Languages; Bibliography**. Łódz, Poland: Biblioteka, Universytet Łódzki, 1967-1977. 4v. in 5. index. (Wydawnictwa bibliograficzne Biblioteki Uniwersyteckiej w Łódzi, 10, 11, 12, 16a, 16b). LC 75-216670.

The preface and table of contents as well as the headings of the classified arrangment in each of these volumes are in English as well as Polish. Together the volumes constitute an exhaustive bibliography of Baltic languages. Volume 1 (1,065 entries, some annotated) is an introduction to Baltic linguistics. Volume 2 (1,097 unannotated entries) covers Baltic onomastics from its beginnings to 1966. Volume 3 (3,108 entries, some with content notes) deals with both the history and structure of the Lettish language up to 1967. Volume 4 (3,849 entries) covers in Parts A and B the Lithuanian language. Part A is on the history of the language; Part B contains material on the literary language. All volumes have name and subject indexes. Volumes 2-4 also have word indexes.

Indo-Iranian

A number of works containing material on Indo-Iranian languages can also be found among the general and multi-language entries in chapter 19.

Cumulative Bibliographies

882. Aggarwal, Narindar K., comp. **A Bibliography of Studies on Hindi Language and Linguistics**. Rev. and enl. ed. Gurgaon, Haryana: Indian Documentation Service, 1985. 321p. index. LC 85-904349.

In 1978 this bibliography appeared with about 1,700 entries. It has been enlarged to 2,926 entries in this new edition. Coverage is for books, theses, dissertations, articles, and published and unpublished papers on Hindi language and linguistics from the early 1950s to about 1982. The classified arrangement has been expanded in a number of places and now includes a new area of research, that of Hindi in the international context. Other revisions include the addition of a list of major sources and cross-references at the end of some sections. A few entries include content notes and citations to reviews. The compiler supplies an author index.

883. Aggarwal, Narindar K., comp. **Studies on Nepali Language and Linguistics: A Bibliography**. Gurgaon, Haryana: Indian Documentation Service, 1991. 93p. index. bibliog. (Subject Bibliography Series, 15).

Though a number of general bibliographies on Nepal exist, until 1991 there were none on just Nepali language and linguistics. Now there are two, this one and another issued by the Linguistic Society of Nepal (see entry 888) with which there is considerable overlap. Here Aggarwal has gathered articles, books, papers (some unpublished), and theses on such topics as theoretical linguistics, sociolinguistics, historical linguistics, lexicography and lexicology, pedagogy, and language planning written in Nepali, Newari, and English. Newari and Maithili are also spoken in Nepal, thus the author decided to include research on these languages also, but only found material on Newari. A quick check of dates reveal some works cited from the late 1800s and up to 1989. Only a few of the 726 entries are annotated. There is a source bibliography and an index of authors.

884. Koul, Omkar N., and Madhu Bala. **Punjabi Language and Linguistics: An Annotated Bibliography**. Patiala: Indian Institute of Language Studies, 1992. 107p. index. bibliog. ISBN 81-85231-16-8.

Koul has brought together in this unassuming, little bibliography a wealth of research from the 19th century to the present time on Punjabi language and linguistics. The reviews at the beginning of the ten sections plus substantive annotations add to its value for students, researchers, teachers, and librarians. Articles written in Punjabi, English, and Hindi come from journals and edited books. Some dissertations are cited as well. Topics covered include: genealogical classification, phonetics and phonology, morphology and syntax, semantics, pedagogical materials, sociolinguistics, stylistics, semiotics, lexicography, and script. A source bibliography and author index are additional features.

885. Laddu, Sureshachandra Dnyaneshwar, and Kamal Lochan Kar, comps. **A Select Bibliography on the Development of Sanskrit Language.** Edited by S. P. Sharma. 1st ed. Badaun, Uttar Pradesh?: S. P. Sharma, 1983. 49p. LC 85-903233.

This limited bibliography of monographs, dissertations, and journal articles is an attempt to provide a chronology of the different trends and stages in the development of the Sanskrit language. Some 512 unannotated entries are classed by 15 topics such as: surveys of Sanskrit grammar, pre-Paninian, Panini, Vyakarana and other Darsanas, non-Paninian Schools, ancient Indian phonetics, and the philosophy of language. Two addenda list 117 more entries on Sanskrit grammar and linguistic studies. Unfortunately, place of publication and frequently also the publisher are omitted for references to books.

886. Mahmud, Shabana. **Urdu Language and Literature: A Bibliography of Sources in European Languages.** London: Mansell, 1992. 331p. index. ISBN 0-7201-2143-4.

A linguist will find the nearly 950 entries in the chapter on Urdu language most useful in this bibliography. The chapter is subdivided into sections on dictionaries, grammar, history, and study and teaching. The largely unannotated entries, except for a few content notes, cite monographs, journal articles, Festschriften, symposiums, and conference proceedings. An index of authors also lists editors and translators.

887. Satyaprakash, ed. **A Bibliography of Sanskrit Language and Literature.** Gurgaon, Haryana: Indian Documentation Service, 1984. 296p. (Subject Bibliography Series, 5). LC 84-900581.

This unannotated bibliography gathers together more than 3,500 research and general interest articles (including book reviews) from 137 journals and 2 newspapers (*The Times of India* and *The Economic Times*) published from 1962 to 1983. Articles are cited in full twice, first in a classified subject arrangement, then in an alphabetical listing by author. Lack of a list of the headings used in the classified arrangement hinders subject access.

888. Toba, Sueyoshi, ed. **A Bibliography of Nepalese Languages and Linguistics.** Kirtipur, Kathmandu: Linguistic Society of Nepal, Tribhuvan University, 1991. 120p. index. bibliog.

Entries in this largely unannotated bibliography are arranged alphabetically by author, then chronologically. Instead of each entry being numbered, Toba numbers only the 448 authors. To facilitate subject access to the entries, there is a language index (families and specific languages) and a subject index. Types of material and dates covered are similar to another bibliography on Nepali language and linguistics (see entry 883) with this work having a few items also written in French, German, Hindi, Hungarian, Japanese, Maithili, Russian, and Sanskrit in addition to English, Nepali, and Newari.

21

Uralo-Altaic

889. Allworth, Edward. **Nationalities of the Soviet East: Publications and Writing Systems. A Bibliographical Directory and Transliteration Tables for Iranian- and Turkic-Language Publications, 1818-1914, Located in U.S. Libraries**. New York: Columbia University Press, 1971. 440p. index. (The Modern Middle East Series, No.3). LC 73-110143. ISBN 0-231-03274-9.

The bibliographical directory, the first part of this book, contains citations to publications in all areas of scholarship that are written in Iranian and Turkic languages of the Soviet East. Only a few are concerned with the languages themselves. The reason this work is included here is that the second part contains transliteration tables for each of the 26 languages covered in the first part from Altay to Yakut. Cyrillic, Latin, Arabic, and Hebrew writing systems are all represented. Since many of the alphabets vary depending on the time period, there are for some languages as many as five tables (representing up to 3 different writing systems).

890. Grant, Bruce K. **A Guide to Korean Characters: Reading and Writing Hangŭl and Hanja**. Elizabeth, NJ: Hollym International Corp., 1982. 367p. index. bibliog. ISBN 0-930878-13-2.

Though this book was designed as a guide for those wanting to learn how to read and write hangŭl, the Korean alphabet, and the 1,800 Chinese characters taught in Korean schools, it can also function as a character dictionary since its entries are arranged in stroke-count order and has both a radical and a phonetic index. The introduction functions as the tutorial. It is followed by the 1,800 basic characters and appendixes containing a number of useful lists: Korean surnames, easily confused characters, commonly abbreviated characters, characters with multiple readings, and the 900 Middle School characters in textbook order. The end-papers just inside the front and back covers display hangŭl-in-a-hurry charts for consonants and vowels, hangul writing models, and syllable writing models.

891. Halasz de Beky, I. L., comp. **Bibliography of Hungarian Dictionaries, 1410-1963**. Toronto: University of Toronto Press, 1966. 148p. index. bibliog. LC 66-3059.

The compiler includes here both language dictionaries (505 titles) and subject dictionaries (520 titles). The language dictionary section is divided into 2 parts. Part 1, listing mono- and bilingual dictionaries, is further classified by language. Part 2 contains polyglot dictionaries arranged alphabetically by author. The subject dictionaries section lists titles under more than 100 subject headings. The compiler appends both a language and a subject index.

892.   Hazai, György, ed. **Handbuch der türkischen Sprachwissenschaft. Teil I**. Wiesbaden: Otto Harrassowitz, 1990. 493p. bibliog. (Bibliotheca orientalis Hungarica, 31). ISBN 3-447-02921-8. (In progress?).

The 13 chapters in this handbook on Turkish linguistics are variously written in German or English and cover such topics as structure, history, phonetics and phonology, lexicography, and grammar. Each is authored by an expert and concludes with a substantial bibliography.

893.   Hazai, György, ed. **Sovietico-Turcica; Beiträge zur Bibliographie der türkischen Sprachwissenschaft in russischer Sprache in der Sowjetunion, 1917-1957**. Übers. von A. T. Varga. Budapest: Akadémiai Kiadó, 1960. 319p. (Bibliotheca orientalis Hungarica, 9). LC 63-39493.

This bibliography lists by main entry 2,749 works on the Turkish language written in Russian and published in the Soviet Union from 1917 through 1957. Following each Cyrillic script entry is the transliteration of all information except for the title which is translated into German. An index in German provides subject access to the entries.

894.   Kerek, Andrew, comp. **Bibliography of Hungarian Linguistic Research in the United States and Canada**. New Brunswick, NJ: American Hungarian Foundation, 1979. 28p. (Hungarian Reference Shelf, 5). LC 79-102217.

This short unannotated bibliography with 249 items gathers together the work of North American linguists on the Hungarian language, particularly for the decade preceding its publication. Textbooks and teaching materials are included when they supply information on grammar and other aspects of language structure. Readers, word list, and dictionaries are not included.

895.   Loewenthal, Rudolf, comp. **The Turkic Languages and Literatures of Central Asia; a Bibliography**. 's-Gravenhage: Mouton, 1957. 212p. index. (Central Asiatic Studies, 1). LC 58-18354.

The purpose of this preliminary bibliography is to gather materials in, and relating to, Turkic languages and literatures of the region extending from Sinkiang in the east to Russian or Western Turkestan and the Caucasus in the west. Osmanli Turkish spoken in the Balkans is specifically excluded. Most of the 2,093 unannotated entries are for books and articles published in Russian and pertaining to the Russian geographic area. These titles are transliterated. In addition, the compiler supplies English titles for all works in non-European languages. The main sections of the classified arrangement are: bibliographies and biographies (general); Old Turkic (Old and Middle Uigur, Orkhon, and Yenisei); Middle Turkic; and, Modern Turkic. Author, person, and subject indexes provide additional access points.

896.   Lucas, Alain. **Linguistique coréenne: bibliographie 1960-1985**. Avec las collaboration de Yim Seong-sook et le concours de L. R. Kontsevich pour les publications d'URSS. Paris: Collège de France, Centre d'études coréennes, 1989. 234p. index. bibliog. (Mémoires du Centre d'études coréennes, Vol. 8; ISSN 0298-0436). ISBN 2-905358-13-0.

Monographs, journal articles, and dissertations in a wide variety of languages from English and French, to Czech, Russian, Japanese and more' have been gathered together in this unannotated bibliography on Korean linguistics. The 1,781 entries arranged in 20 sections span a wide variety of topics covering not only historical and theoretical linguistics, but pragmatics, sociolinguistics, writing of Korean, transliteration, psycholinguistics, pedagogy, rhetoric, stylistics, poetics, and translation. Names of authors are romanized while titles remain in the script in which they were written. Arrangement with each section is simply chronological by date of publication. Since there is a dearth of reference works on this subject, a user will probably not begrudge the time it takes to scan the all the entries—sometimes in the hundreds—under the desired section heading. There is an index of authors.

897.   Ojama, Airi, comp. **Fennistics and Uralistics: Linguistic Bibliography 1975-1981/Fennistiikan ja uralistiikan bibliografia 1975-1981**. Helsinki: Kotimaisten kielten tutkimuskeskus, Valtion painatuskeskus, 1985. 209p. index. (Kotimaisten kielten tutkimuskeskuksen julkaisuja, 35; ISSN 0355-5437). ISBN 951-859-828-2.

The foreword and contents of this classified, unannotated bibliography of 2,662 entries are written in both Finnish and English. It includes all types of published materials dealing with research on the Finno-Ugric and Samoyedic languages which appeared during the years 1975-1981 in Finland and elsewhere, except for the Soviet Union and Hungary. Titles not in English are provided with an English translation except for works in German. The classification scheme begins with bibliographies, personalia, congresses, institutes, and general linguistics. The remaining sections are organized by languages. There is an author index.

898.   Schlachter, Wolfgang, and Gerhard Ganschow, eds. **Bibliographie der uralischen Sprachwissenschaft, 1930-1970**. Munchen: Wilhelm Fink, 1974-1986. 3v. index.

This finely classified bibliography of Uralic linguistics is the first of its type. It incorporates nearly 50,000 works from Europe, the Soviet Union, and North America published from 1830-1970. Volume 1, issued in 5 parts, is devoted to Hungarian, while volume 2, also issued in 5 parts, covers other Finno-Ugric languages (Lapp, Finnish, and Estonian) as well as Volga-Finnish, Permian, and Samoyed. The editors provide many cross-references and citations to numerous reviews. Volume 3 is an author index.

899.   Yakupova, G. K. **Bibliografiya po tatarskomu yazykoznaniyu (1778-1980)**. Kazan': Tatarskoe knizhnoe izdatel'stvo, 1988. 134p. index. bibliog.

The 2,086 entries in this classified, unannotated bibliography on linguistics, Turkic languages, and the Tatar language are arranged in 21 broad categories such as lexicology, syntax, onomastics, phonetics and phonology, and grammar. All entries are in Cyrillic script. A source bibliography and author index are provided.

900.   Yoshizaki, Yasuhiro, comp. **Studies in Japanese Literature and Language: A Bibliography of English Materials**. Tokyo: Nichigai Associates; distr., Kinokuniya Book Store, 1979. 451p. index. (Nijisseiki bunken yōran taikei, 8). LC 80-463960.

Part II of this unannotated bibliography contains materials on the Japanese language arranged according to author in the following sections: dictionaries; lexical studies and dialects; phonological studies; grammatical studies; pedagogic studies and language texts; and comparative, sociolinguistic, regional, and historical studies. It is particularly valuable to the user who reads only English, since it just lists books, articles, and dissertations written in English. Part III contains reference material: bibliographies, journals, a directory of institutions, and a directory of scholars. The index is for authors and titles (and authors of literary works in Part I). A subject index is needed.

22

Dravidian

901. Agesthialingom, S., and S. Sakthivel. **A Bibliography of Dravidian Linguistics**. 1st ed. Annamalainagar: Annamalai University, 1973. 362p. (Annamalai University, Dept. of Linguistics, Publication, No. 30). LC 75-901318.

Section 1 of this unannotated bibliography lists some 3,706 books, articles, theses, conference papers, and unpublished materials. Another section lists more than 200 dictionaries, while a third section contains book reviews. Material dates from the mid-19th century and is in a wide variety of languages. Since the arrangement of entries is alphabetical by author, lack of a subject index limits its usefulness.

902. Andronov, Mikhail Sergeevich. **Materials for a Bibliography of Dravidian Linguistics**. Kuala Lumpur: Dept. of Indian Studies, University of Malaya, 1966. 52p. LC 74-151765.

First published as a journal article, this is a modest first attempt at a bibliography of Dravidian linguistics. In the main part the author provides a list, alphabetically arranged by author, of 729 books and journal articles. Most of the studies are in English, French, German, and Russian. Entries are not annotated, but Appendix 1 lists reviews for books. Appendix 2 contains a short bibliography of 81 Dravidian language dictionaries.

903. Dhamotharan, Ayyadurai. **Tamil Dictionaries: A Bibliography**. Wiesbaden: Franz Steiner, 1978. 185p. index. (Beiträge zur Südasienforschung, Südasien-Institut, Universität Heidelberg, Bd. 50). ISBN 3-515-03005-0.

In his bibliography Dhamotharan provides a comprehensive listing for both language and technical dictionaries in, and related to, Tamil from the earliest published up to 1975. He compiled it largely on the basis of secondary sources, some 60 of which are listed in an introductory section. This is followed by a section with 432 entries for language dictionaries, vocabularies, polyglots, etc. A final section lists 238 technical dictionaries. In addition to printed works, information on about 60 manuscripts available in European libraries is provided. An occasional entry has a brief annotation. Four name and title indexes provide unusually good access to the entries.

904. Rajannan, Busnagi, comp. **Dravidian Languages and Literatures: A Contribution Toward a Bibliography of Books in English and in a Few Other European Languages, on, About, and Translated from the Dravidian Languages**. 1st ed. Madurai, India: Madurai University, 1973. 279p. illus. LC 75-902240.

The long title and subtitle of this work provides an accurate description of its scope and contents except for not indicating that it covers material dating as far back as 1554. Many of the entries have descriptive annotation and notes concerning various editions and reprints. Bibliographic information is incomplete for some entries.

The classification scheme has 18 parts. One part is for studies on the language family as a whole (and studies dealing with more than one language), while the remaining 17 parts are for each of the Dravidian languages. The parts for Kannada, Malayalam, Tamil, and Telugu are subdivided. Most of the works cited are for books and include: bibliographies, journals, dictionaries, vocabularies, histories, surveys, manuals, grammars, and materials for teaching. Indian as well as British and American sources were consulted in the compilation. Regrettably, there are no indexes.

905. Ramaiah, L. S., general ed. **An International Bibliography of Dravidian Languages and Linguistics**. Madras: T. R. Publications. (In progress).

906. **Volume 1. General and Comparative Dravidian Languages and Linguistics**. 1994. 173p. map. index. ISBN 81-85427-25-9.

907. **Volume 2. Tamil Language and Linguistics**. 1995. 403p. index. map. ISBN 81-85427-26-7.

908. **Volume 3. Telugu Language and Linguistics**. 1998. index. 359p. (This work not viewed by author).

Three additional titles in this series not yet published will address Kannada, Malayalam, and non-literary Dravidian languages and linguistics. Together they will contain more than 15,000 entries. At the beginning of the first volume the compiler lists the more than 200 bibliographical tools used for researching the series. Unannotated entries in each volume are arranged according to a classification system tailored to fit the volume's subject. In addition each has an individual introduction and indexes for scholars and subjects.

909. Thasarathan, A. **An Annotated Bibliography on Modern Tamil Grammars and Tamil Handbooks**. 1st ed. Trivandrum, India: International Printers & Publishers; Madurai: Marketed by Estee Books International, 1983. 48p. index. bibliog. LC 83-907295.

This short bibliography lists 142 Tamil grammars, handbooks, readers, and textbooks from the last 200 years. Though entries are arranged alphabetically by title, an author index is provided. Many entries have descriptive annotations.

910. Thomas, Annie Mrithulakumari. **Dissertations on Tamilology**. Madras: International Institute of Tamil Studies, 1977. 289p. index. (International Institute of Tamil Studies, Publication, No. 10). LC 77-905517.

Thomas lists here only those dissertations and theses submitted to Indian universities. The work is divided into 3 sections: grammar and linguistics, literature, and other studies. Abstracts or content notes are provided for most entries. She appends author and title indexes.

23

Sino-Tibetan

Manuals

911. Dougherty, Ching-yi, Sydney M. Lamb, and Samuel E. Martin. **Chinese Character Indexes**. Berkeley, CA: University of California Press, 1963. 5v. bibliog. LC 63-12210.

The impetus for compiling these indexes was the need for a tool that would convert Chinese characters into code symbols for use in machine translation and machine-aided linguistic analysis. Each volume in the 5-volume set has characters arranged in a particular way: 1) in sequence by the Telegraphic Code number, 2) in alphabetical order by romanization of the pronunciation(s), 3) in traditional order by radical number and residual-stroke count, 4) in sequence according to the total number of strokes, and 5) in sequence by the Four Corner System. An attempt was made to include all categories of characters, that is, those from the classics, the modern standard vernacular, technical and scientific, and simplified forms adopted by the Communist Chinese government. The authors use the National Romanization (GR) system of alphabetization for the indexes.

912. **A Romanization Guide to Standard Chinese in Wade-Giles Romanization**. Project staff, Henry H. C. Lin, director, et al. New Haven, CT: Yale University Library, East Asian Collections; distr., Far Eastern Publications, Yale University, 1975. 115p. bibliog. (Yale University Library East Asia Series, 1). LC 75-315621. (This work not viewed by author.)

The text of this guide is in Chinese. An introduction is in English.

913. Seymour, Nancy N. **How to Identify Chinese Characters**. Metuchen, NJ: Scarecrow Press, 1989. 427p. bibliog. LC 89-24343. ISBN 0-8108-2278-4.

The purpose of this guide is to enable the user, by means of the modified stroke count method, to identify characters and thus the Pinyin word. With this knowledge non-Chinese readers will have access to Chinese dictionaries. Chapter 1 introduces the reader to the structure of Chinese characters while the second chapter teaches the stroke count method. Chapter 3 lists the 4,000 most frequently used characters, plus the 1,600 variants listed according to the method described in the previous chapter. Chapter 4 is a Pinyin character index. Appendixes contain information on simplified Chinese characters, comparative Romanization tables (Pinyin, Wade, and Yale), and a selected bibliography.

Atlas

914.   Wurm, S. A., et al., general eds. **Language Atlas of China. Part 1.** Hong Kong: Longman Group, 1988. 1 atlas case. ISBN 0-581-04986-5.

The overall language situation in China is very complex, especially in the details of the distribution and classification of languages and dialects. The Han nationality use the Chinese language which is commonly spoken in all parts of the country as well as in communities outside China. Of the 55 minority nationalities the Hui and Manchu use the same Chinese language while each of the other 53 has its own spoken language. These languages represent many of the major language families, including Sino-Tibetan, Altaic, Indo-European, Austroasiatic, as well as Austronesian languages spoken in Taiwan. The dialects of Chinese are equally complex.

There is a Chinese version and an English version of the atlas; this annotation is based on this author having seen only part 1 of the English version. It is contained, unbound, in an atlas case with 30 unbound color map plates on glossy, heavy white paper and with accompanying texts and front matter on non-glossy blue paper with generally one blue sheet of text corresponding to one map plate. In the whole of the atlas, maps A1-5 are general maps of China showing the total language situation, all of the Chinese dialects, all of the minority peoples, and all of the minority languages as well as a map of just Guangxi Zhuang Autonomous Region; maps B1-16a and b are dialect maps, while maps C1-14 show other languages and related dialects of the national minorities. Part 1 includes only a selection of the A, B and C maps.

Cumulative Bibliographies

915.   Chien, David. **Lexicography in China: Bibliography of Dictionaries and Related Literature**. Exeter, England: University of Exeter, 1986. 237p. (Exeter Linguistic Studies, Vol. 12). ISBN 0-85989-263-8.

This book contains 2 separate bibliographies. The first is on lexicography in China. It lists over 1,000 monographs and papers written by lexicographers and linguists from, or published in, the People's Republic of China (PRC) from 1949 to 1986. Titles of papers or monographs, names of periodicals, and places of publication for monographs are in Pinyin transcription. An English translation is provided for titles. Subject and language codes accompany the entries. Indexes of cited dictionaries and subject fields are contained in 2 appendixes. To help the user become familiar with the official Chinese romanization system a third appendix lists conventions of Chinese Pinyin in comparison with the Wade-Giles system.

The second bibliography is a classified one, covering both ancient and modern Chinese language dictionaries published in the PRC during the three and a half decades prior to the bibliography's publication. Among the 630 entries are monolingual, bilingual, and multilingual works. When relevant, the author provides dictionary titles in Chinese characters, in Pinyin transcription, and in English translation.

916.   Chinese-English Translation Assistance Group. **Chinese Dictionaries: An Extensive Bibliography of Dictionaries in Chinese and Other Languages**. James Mathias, managing ed.; Thomas Creamer and Sandra Hixson,

comps. Westport, CT: Greenwood Press, 1982. 446p. index. ISBN 0-313-23505-8. LC 82-923.

This work is based on two prior compilations: "List of Chinese Dictionaries in All Languages," issued in 1967 by the U.S. Department of State, Office of External Research and *A Compilation of Chinese Dictionaries* by J. Mathias and S. Hixson (Yale University Press, 1975). To these are added materials from surveys of 12 university libraries, recent acquisitions of the Library of Congress, and new publications gleaned from publishers' catalogs. As such it updates but does not completely replace a bibliography of Chinese-English and English-Chinese dictionaries published by the Library of Congress in 1977 (see entry 917); that work still lists a few dictionaries not included here, plus provides useful annotations.

This work is meant to be a comprehensive listing of Chinese monolingual, bilingual, and polyglot dictionaries. One section contains 727 general dictionary titles. Another section lists 1,750 specialized dictionaries, subdivided into subject areas; some may be listed more than once if they deal with more than one subject category. An appendix with the same arrangement as the two main sections provides an additional 251 unique titles.

Each entry includes title (in both Chinese characters and romanized), English translation of title, full bibliographic information, plus location codes for libraries holding a copy (the 12 libraries surveyed, plus the Library of Congress). The main part of the bibliography is indexed by title and language while the appendix is indexed just by title.

917.   Dunn, Robert, comp. **Chinese-English and English-Chinese Dictionaries in the Library of Congress: An Annotated Bibliography**. Washington, DC: Library of Congress, 1977. 140p. index. LC 76-608329. ISBN 0-8444-0220-6.

The scope of this bibliography is limited to the holdings of the Orientalia Division and the general collections of the Library of Congress. Chinese-English and English-Chinese dictionaries and glossaries as well as some polyglot and multilingual dictionaries with English and Chinese entries are included. Excluded are dictionaries limited to the Chinese language and Chinese dictionaries with equivalents in other languages, but not in English. It lists almost 400 special subject dictionaries, arranged by subject. These are followed by 172 general language dictionaries. Descriptive annotations ranging from a sentence to several paragraphs or more accompany the entries. Author and title indexes include both English and Romanized Chinese entries intermixed. There is a separate Chinese character index. A bibliography by the CETA Group updates this work (see entry 916).

918.   Kim, T. W., and A. Wawrzyszko. **A Bibliographical Guide to the Study of Chinese Language and Linguistics**. Carbondale, IL: Linguistic Research, Inc., 1980. 89p. index. (Current Inquiry into Language and Linguistics, 39). ISBN 0-88783-040-4.

The authors prepared this bibliography of textbooks, dictionaries, works on study and teaching, linguistic research (especially phonetics, phonology, and grammar), material on the writing system, and bibliographies so as to be of particular interest to those involved in learning Mandarin Chinese. Thus it concentrates on recent and easily accessible publications. Informative and sometimes critical annotations accompany entries.

919. LaPolla, Randy J., and John B. Lowe. **Bibliography of the International Conferences on Sino-Tibetan Languages and Linguistics I-XXV**. 2nd ed. Berkeley, CA: Sino-Tibetan Etymological Dictionary and Thesaurus Project, Center for Southeast Asia Studies, University of California, 1994. 308p. index. (STEDT Monograph Series, No. 1A). LC 94-072182. ISBN 0-944613-22-5.

Since complete proceedings of the International Conferences on Sino-Tibetan languages and Linguistics have never been produced, this bibliography provides a valuable service in documenting many of the developments achieved over the years from 1968 to 1992 in Sino-Tibetan linguistics. A prior bibliography published in 1989 covered the conferences through XXI. This edition not only extends coverage through XXV, but includes additional information when available on any of the papers which were published subsequent to the conferences. In the bibliography proper, citations are in order first by author's name, by conference, and by title. For Chinese titles the paper is cited by English title, with the Chinese titles in parentheses using Pinyin Romanization. In addition, the compilers provide a list of papers by conference, an index by author, list of subject headings, index by subject, index by title-subject keyword, and an index to Chinese characters used in titles.

920. Lucas, Alain. **Linguistique chinoise, bibliographie, 1975-1982/ Chinese Linguistics: A Bibliography, 1975-1982/Han, yū yū yen hsūeh lun chu mu lu, 1975-1982**. Paris: Editions Langages croisés, CRLAO, 1985. 315p. index. (This work not viewed by author.)

921. Shafer, Robert, ed. **Bibliography of Sino-Tibetan Languages**. Associate editors: Pentti Aalto, et al. Wiesbaden: Otto Harrassowitz, 1957-1963. 2v. LC 58-17521.

The arrangement of entries in both volumes of this set is the same: alphabetical by author under some 400 language/dialect names, themselves arranged alphabetically. In amongst the language names the editor inserts the following additional categories: Daic, Karenic, maps, Sino-Tibetan, unclassified, wide field (a number of languages), and wider relationships (than Sino-Tibetan). The section on the Chinese language as well as some of the other major language sections are subdivided: grammars (includes phonology), dictionaries, dialects, etc. The first volume (1957) is more selective than the second (1963) in that it was intended to be primarily a scholar's bibliography. The second volume picks up material published since the first volume and adds some 200 specialized dictionaries and vocabularies as well as grammars of Chinese in English.

922. Wang, William S-Y., and Anatole Lyovin, comps. **CLIBOC: Chinese Linguistics Bibliography on Computer**. Cambridge, England: University Press, 1970. 513p. maps (Princeton-Cambridge Studies in Chinese Linguistics, 1). LC 74-85740. ISBN 0-521-07455-X.

The focus of this bibliography is primarily on linguistic aspects of the Chinese language and, secondarily, on closely related linguistic matters. The main section has 3,000 entries arranged alphabetically by author. It is followed by a topical index. There are pocket maps showing the distribution of Sino-Tibetan languages and Chinese dialects. A logograph section lists those entries involving

Chinese logographs or Japanese kana. In still another section abstracts are provided for some entries.

923.   Yang, Paul Fu-mien. **Chinese Dialectology: A Selected and Classified Bibliography**. Hong Kong: Chinese University Press, 1981. 189p. index. LC 84-102927. ISBN 962-201-211-6.

This bibliography with 2,275 entries is a companion volume to the author's earlier bibliography on Chinese linguistics (see entry immediately below). It has the same scope and format though the appended material here is limited to a list of Chinese and Japanese publishers and a romanized index for authors.

924.   Yang, Paul Fu-mien. **Chinese Lexicology and Lexicography: A Selected and Classified Bibliography**. Hong Kong: Chinese University Press, 1985. 361p. index. ISBN 962-201-312-0.

Some of the 4,165 entries in this classified bibliography have a descriptive annotation. Romanized transcriptions and English translations are given for Chinese, Japanese, and Korean titles. Entries are arranged in two parts, Chinese lexicology and Chinese lexicography, then each is further subdivided. Various aspects of traditional, pre-modern, and modern standard Chinese are represented. Concluding the work is a Romanized index of authors.

925.   Yang, Paul Fu-mien. **Chinese Linguistics: A Selected and Classified Bibliography**. Hong Kong: Chinese University of Hong Kong, 1974. 292p. index. LC 73-92411.

Yang includes among the 3,257 entries in his well-classified bibliography all important studies in the principal languages of the world on the Chinese language in general, its history, present status, writing system, and its genetic relationship with other Sino-Tibetan languages. Dialectology is omitted since the author has written a separate bibliography devoted to that field (see entry immediately above).

This bibliography mainly covers books, articles, and dissertations published from 1900 to the time of compilation. Titles in Chinese, Japanese, and Korean characters are given along with romanization and an English translation. Russian titles are transliterated and translated as well. While entries are not annotated, there are sometimes references to reviews along with additional remarks about contents (including illustrations and maps), series, and collections titles. Various materials are appended: a list of Chinese, Japanese, and Korean publishers; a romanized index of authors; a character index of Oriental authors and Chinese names for Western authors; and, a paper on Chinese linguistics in the 20th century by Chou Fa-Kao.

926.   Yang, Winston L. Y., and Teresa S. Yang, comps. **A Bibliography of the Chinese Language**. New York: American Association of Teachers of Chinese Language and Culture; distr., New York: Paragon Book Gallery, 1966. 171p. index. LC 66-27975.

The authors include more than 2,000 works on the Chinese language published in western languages, primarily English, French, or German. They also list a few studies written in Japanese or Chinese that have summaries in a western language. Entries for books, articles, and theses are arranged under 18 broad form and subject headings (such as, bibliographies, language dictionaries and vocabularies, phonology, grammar, dialects, and study and teaching). While the emphasis is on recently published material up to the beginning of 1966, there are a number of works from the 1800s as well. The authors provide a main entry index.

24

Austroasiatic

927. Ghosh, Arun. **Bibliotheca Austroasiatica: A Classified and Anno-tated Bibliography of the Austroasiatic People and Languages**. Calcutta: Firma KLM, 1988. 130p. index. (Netaji Institute for Asian Studies. Monograph Series I).

Works on all Austroasiatic languages spoken in South and Southeast Asia published up to 1987 are included in this bibliography, thus it has a broader geographic scope than the work of Nagaraja (see entry 929) and includes more languages. About half of the approximately 600 entries are annotated. The references are arranged in a ten-part classification covering such topics as descriptive and historical linguistics, applied linguistics, lexical and etymological studies, and sociolinguistics. It is supplemented by language and scholar indexes.

928. Indigenous Languages of Thailand Research Project, Central Institute of English Language, Office of State Universities. **Bibliography of Tai Language Studies**. Bangkok: The Project, 1977. 78p. LC 87-125889.

The purpose of this bibliography is to update through 1976 the Tai language section of Shorto's bibliography (see entry 931). It contains books, articles, and theses on Tai phonetics and linguistics as well as dictionaries and treatises on grammar. The entries are divided into 2 sections: 1) works in a variety of non-Tai languages, and 2) works written in Thai. In each section the arrangement is alphabetical by author.

929. Nagaraja, K. S. **Austroasiatic Languages: A Linguistic Bibliog-raphy**. Pune, India: Deccan College, Post-Graduate & Research Institute, 1989. 147p. index. illus. bibliog.

Nagaraja restricted his bibliography to the Austroasiatic languages spoken only in India. That means it covers the Munda languages spoken in central and northeastern parts of India and then south to the Godavari River, the Khasi language of the Mon-Khmer branch spoken in Khasi and the Jaintia Hill Districts of Meghalaya State and Nicobarese spoken in the Nicobar Islands. Part A lists descriptive studies of individual languages/groups, part B contains general studies, while part C lists comparative studies. This work builds on a number of earlier bibliographies which the compiler carefully acknowledges and lists in the introduction. About 200 of the 547 entries have annotations, some lengthy and evaluative. There are also language and author indexes.

930. Nguyễn, Nhủ Ý. **Thủ mục ngôn ngữ học Việt Nam: tiếng Việt, tiếng Ánh, tiếng Pháp, tiếng Nga/Bibliography of Vietnamese Linguistics: Viet-namese, English, French, Russian**. [Ha Noi?]: Văn Hóa, 1994.716p.

More than 6,200 books, articles, and dissertations written on the Vietnamese language and the languages of Vietnam's ethnic minority groups from the early part of the 20th century up to 1993 in Vietnamese, English, French, and Russian are compiled in this bibliography. Monolingual and bilingual Vietnamese dictionaries as well as language teaching materials are included. Works are simply alphabetized by main entry within three sections for materials written in Vietnamese, English and French, and Russian. An English translation is provided for both Vietnamese and Russian titles.

931.   Shorto, H. L., Judith M. Jacob, and E. H. S. Simmonds, comps. **Bibliographies of Mon-Khmer and Tai Linguistics.** London: Oxford University Press, 1963. 870. index. (London Oriental Bibliographies, Vol. 2). LC 63-25033.

This compilation contains two bibliographies. The first on Mon-Khmer linguistics, compiled by Shorto and Jacob, is organized by language/dialect with entries arranged chronologically under each language. An index of these languages precedes the bibliography itself. The compilers list nearly 450 works (books, articles, and chapters in collected works and Festschriften) published up to 1961. The second bibliography on Tai linguistics, compiled by Simmonds, cites almost 500 studies published through 1959. Its arrangement is geographical. Descriptive notes accompany many entries in both bibliographies. A consolidated author index completes the volume.

932.   Thongkum, Theraphan L., comp. **Bibliography of Minority Languages of Thailand**. Report submitted to the Research Division of the Faculty of Arts, Chulalongkorn University. Bangkok: 1984. 145p.

Though some of the books, articles, chapters, conference papers, and dissertations cited in this unannotated bibliography are in Thai, the majority are in English or other widely known languages. Materials date from the last century through the early 1980s. The classified arrangement has 6 main divisions further subdivided by language: SEA (Southeast Asian) linguistics, Sino-Tibetan, Tai, Mon-Khmer, Malayo-Polynesian (Austronesian), and Meo-Yao. The arrangement is then alphabetical by author. Though the headings in the classification system are in both Thai and English, prefatory material is in Thai only.

25

Austronesian and
Indo-Pacific (Oceanic)

Manuals, Guides, and Handbooks

933.   Dixon, Robert M. W., and Barry J. Blake, eds. **Handbook of Australian Languages**. Canberra: Australian National University Press, 1979. 390p. (v. 1); Amsterdam: John Benjamins, 1981, 1983. 427p. (v. 2), 531p. (v. 3); South Melbourne, Australia: Oxford, 1991. 410p. (v. 4). illus. bibliog. maps. ISBN 0-7081-1201-3; 90-272-2004-2; 90-272-2002-6; 019-553097-7. (In progress).

In the introduction of volume 1 Blake and Dixon provide an overview of the nature of Australian languages. In volume 4 there is a slightly revised, updated introduction covering phonology, grammar, and some notes on historical reconstruction. The remainder of the handbook presents short grammatical sketches of individual languages written by various contributors in a standard format, including a sample text, if available, and a vocabulary list. Maps showing language distribution accompany the text while references for each volume are cumulated at the back. Volume 1 covers Guugu Yimidhirr, Pitta-Pitta, Gumbaynggir, and Yaygir; volume 2 covers Wargamay, the Mpakwithi dialect of Anguthimri, Watjarri, Margany and Gunya, and Tasmanian; volume 3 covers Djapu (a Yolngu dialect), Yukulta, Uradhi, and Nyawaygi; while volume 4 covers Woiwurrung (the Melbourne language), Panyjima, Djabugay, and Mbabaram. Volumes 5 and 6 are not yet published.

934.   Hollyman, K. J., comp. **A Checklist of Oceanic Languages (Melanesia, Micronesia, New Guinea, Polynesia)**. Auckland: Linguistic Society of New Zealand, 1960. 32p. bibliog. (Te Teo Monographs). LC 61-36093.

This book is an alphabetical checklist of about 1,500 languages and dialects spoken in Oceania. Each entry notes the linguistic family, where it is spoken, and frequently provides a reference to a published work about it. Among the entries in the checklist are geographic terms. Each term is followed by names of all relevant languages and dialects.

935.   McGregor, William. **Handbook of Kimberley Languages**. A project of the Kimberley Language Resource Centre. Canberra, Australia: The Australian National University, Department of Linguistics, Research School of Pacific Studies, 1988. 2v. index. illus. bibliog. maps. (Pacific Linguistics. Series C, No. 105; ISSN 0078-7558). ISBN 0-85883-374-3.

Aboriginal languages, including those dying or dead, traditionally spoken within the Kimberley region of northwest Western Australia are covered in this 2-volume handbook. The introduction of volume 1 contains a guide for the reader which explains the standardized format used to provide information about the languages. Each of its seven sections is devoted to a particular language family and illustrated with a black and white map; sections are then subdivided into individual languages. Details for each language are arranged under 12 headings among which are names of the language, classification, number and distribution of speakers, orthography, word lists, grammar, and language learning and literacy materials. Another section covers the post-contact languages of Aboriginal English, Kriol, Pidgin English, and Broome Pearling Lugger Pidgin. A bibliography cumulates works referred to throughout the sections and subsections. Indexes of language names and linguists who have done substantial work on languages spoken in the Kimberley complete volume 1. Volume 2 contains the word lists (this volume not viewed by author).

936.   Menning, Kathy, comp. **Sourcebook for Central Australian Languages**. Edited by David Nash. Pilot ed. Alice Springs, Australia: Institute for Aboriginal Development, 1981. 125 columns (Pt. I); 181 columns (Pt. II). index. map. ISBN 0-94965-901-0.

Menning's sourcebook gathers together basic information on Australian Aboriginal languages within about 500 miles of Alice Springs. A single page black-and-white line map shows present-day locations of the languages. The text is divided into 2 parts. In Part I Menning gives for each language brief general information (language name variants, location and number of speakers, current research) and a listing of written material about and in the language. In Part II Menning provides a list of about 168 basic words in each language and an annotated phoneme chart. The introduction to this part describes the derivation of the word list. An index at the end of Part II facilitates access to both parts of the sourcebook.

937.   Reid, Lawrence Andrew, ed. **Philippine Minor Languages; Word Lists and Phonologies**. Honolulu, HI: University of Hawaii Press, 1971. 239p. (Oceanic Linguistics Special Publication, No. 8). LC 70-150659. ISBN 0-87022-691-6.

In this work the editor treats some 43 of the minor languages of the Philippines. He provides an introductory section containing summary information on each language represented in the word lists. The information includes: language name abbreviation, data source, geographical location, bibliographical reference to source of phonological information, a phonemic chart, 2 sets of pronouns, and 2 sets of demonstratives.

The basis for the word list of 372 items is a list developed by members of the Summer Institute of Linguistics for use in dialect survey work (which itself contains 170 items from the Swadesh basic vocabulary list). The word lists are arranged so that the English glosses, numbered and in alphabetical order, run across the tops of pages, 3 to a page. Abbreviations for the 43 languages run down the left side of each page; equivalents then run across the page being placed under the appropriate English glosses. An asterisk before a form in one of these lists indicates that additional information relating to that entry can be found in the footnotes which are gathered together at the end of the book.

938. Thieberger, Nicholas. **Handbook of Western Australian Aboriginal Languages South of the Kimberley Region**. Canberra, Australia: Department of Linguistics, Research School of Pacific Studies, Australian National University, 1993. 408p. index. bibliog. maps (Pacific Linguistics. Series C, No. 124; ISSN 0078-7558). ISBN 0-85883-418-9.

Thieberger has arranged material in his handbook into 7 sections. Sections 1 through 3 contain an introduction, guide to the handbook, and material on general work on the languages of Western Australia, the latter providing a family tree list of southern Western Australian languages. Section 4 is the heart of the book with information on individual languages grouped arbitrarily into various geographic regions, each accompanied by a map showing geographical distribution. A wealth of detail is provided for each language in a standardized format including: location, names of the language and different spellings, classification, dialects, number and distribution of speakers, researchers in the language, practical spelling system, word lists, texts, grammars, language programs, language learning material, literature in the language, and material available about the language. Section 5 gathers all the references on material available into one alphabetically arranged bibliography and provides annotations as to place where available and a brief description of the language-related content of the work. Section 6 is an index to all the alternative language spellings and names from section 4 while section 7 is an index to many of the researchers listed in section 4 who have conducted fieldwork in Western Australia with page references back to the main citations.

939. Tryon, Darrell T., ed. **Comparative Austronesian Dictionary: An Introduction to Austronesian Studies**. Berlin: Mouton de Gruyter, 1995. 4 v. in 5. maps. (Trends in Linguistics. Documentation, 10). LC 94-20164. ISBN 3-11-012729-6.

Members of the Austronesian, or Malayo-Polynesian, language family account for at least 20 percent of the world's languages today. They range from Madagascar just off the east coast of Africa throughout Southeast Asia and across the Pacific to Easter Island. This comparative dictionary is an annotated dictionary of synonyms for some 1,200 lexical items in 80 different Austronesian languages. In assembling this impressive, comprehensive work, Tryon had the assistance of many experts in the field. The lexicon found in volumes or parts 2-4 follows that used by Buch for Indo-European with a few deletions of some items inappropriate to the Austronesian world (Carl Darling Buch, *Dictionary of Indo-European Synonyms*, University of Chicago Press, 1949). All materials used in the dictionary were collected between 1986 and 1989.

Volume or part 1 (itself in two physical volumes or fascicles) begins with an introduction in chapter 1, followed by chapters 2-5 that treat the Austronesian language family. Chapter 2 describes the membership and geographical distribution with family tree diagrams. Chapter 3 deals with some of the theoretical problems in terms of subgroupings and also with Proto-Austronesian phonology. Chapter 4 lists all known Austronesian languages and provides details such as alternative names, dialects, location, and current number of speakers. Chapter 5 provides a series of 80 language sketches with demographic and linguistic details along with a locator map and includes a phonological statement and the principal morphosyntactic characteristics of the language. Each sketch has its own bibliography. References from all the introductory chapters are gathered together following the language sketches. A glossary of Austronesian reconstructions concludes part 1.

Atlases

940.   McFarland, Curtis D., comp. **A Linguistic Atlas of the Philippines**. Tokyo, Japan: Institute for the Study of Languages and Cultures of Asia and Africa, Tokyo University of Foreign Studies, 1980. 130p. index. illus. bibliog. maps. (Study of Languages and Cultures of Asia & Africa. Monograph Series, No. 15). LC 81-213111.

This atlas supplies a wealth of information on the languages of the Philippines. The introduction provides an overview of the country's complex linguistic situation and establishes a framework for the data and maps that follow. A section on census data and maps begins with a table listing the total number of speakers for the various languages as shown in the Philippine national census of 1970 and 1975. It is followed by maps showing the distribution of the 4 most widely spoken languages (Sebuano, Tagalog, Ilokano, and Hiligaynon) and then by maps showing language distribution within the 12 administrative regions.

A section on language groups follows. It begins with a language tree illustrating the possible subgrouping of Philippine languages. A map for each group follows, locating the speakers of individual languages for each group. The text accompanying each of the language group maps provides census data and notes on genetic relationships. An appendix contains various comparative tables for some 20 vocabulary words in an effort to illustrate how different the Philippine languages are from one another. The volume concludes with a bibliography and an index of languages.

941.   Salzner, Richard. **Sprachenatlas des Indopazifischen Raumes**. Wiesbaden: Otto Harrassowitz, 1960. 2v. bibliog. maps. LC 62-58447.

This atlas covers languages of the Indo-Pacific region: Austroasiatic, Indonesian, Melanesian, and Polynesian. The 64 colored maps are in one volume, the accompanying material in another. The material includes a classified list of some 4,000 languages/dialects; the numbers assigned to each are the same ones used on the maps to indicate where spoken. This list is complemented by another list of almost 5,200 language/dialect names and variants arranged in alphabetical order; it is keyed to the classification scheme. A bibliography of the reference sources used by the author follows. Other useful materials include a key to the numbers used on the maps for geographical names and a list of the maps with a legend.

942.   Wurm, S. A., and Shirô Hattori, eds. **Language Atlas of the Pacific Area**. Cartography, Theo Baumann. Canberra: Published by the Australian Academy of the Humanities in collaboration with the Japan Academy; distr., Stuttgart: Geo-Center, Internationales Landkartenhaus, 1981-1983. 2 pts. index. bibliog. maps. (Pacific Linguistics, Series C, No. 66-67). ISBN 0-85883-239-9 and 0-85883-240-2(pt.1); 0-8583-239-9 and 0-85883-290-9(pt.2).

Part I of this atlas consists of 24 colored maps of the New Guinea area, Oceania, and Australia. Part II contains maps numbered 25 through 47 of the Japan area, Philippines and Formosa, and mainland and insular Southeast Asia. The maps accompanied by text and bibliographies in some cases, show the distribution of languages. Indexes of language names found in the maps are included for some areas.

Cumulative Bibliographies

943.   Asuncion-Landé, Nobleza C. **A Bibliography of Philippine Linguistics**. Athens, OH: Ohio University, Center for International Studies, 1971. 147p. index. (Papers in International Studies. Southeast Asia Series, No. 20). LC 76-183389.

In this unannotated bibliography the author lists materials from the 1560s to 1970. The main part is an alphabetical arrangement of 1,977 references to books, dissertation, theses, research reports, reviews, seminar papers, and articles from magazines and newspapers. Nearly half of the entries deal with Tagalog. All materials regardless of their scholarly contribution are included since this work is intended for the use not only of linguists, educators, and students, but also laypersons. The author provides language and topical indexes.

944.   Carrington, Lois. **A Linguistic Bibliography of the New Guinea Area**. Canberra, A.C.T., Australia: Department of Linguistics, Research School of Pacific and Asian Studies, the Australian National University, 1996. index. illus. map. (Pacific Linguistics. Series D, No. 90; ISSN 0078-7566). ISBN 0-85883-449-9.

The New Guinea area as used in this bibliography includes all of Papua New Guinea, the Solomon Islands with their outliers, Irian Jaya, and Eastern Indonesia. The time frame covered reaches back to pre-World War II, with an occasional earlier entry, some even from the late 19th century, and up to 1995; though is most complete through 1990. Each entry is coded on a five-point assessment scale ranging from maximum linguistic interest for works of total linguistic concern to micro linguistic interest for a work perhaps containing only a few vocabulary items, or a brief translated song, or a group of local terms. Entries are arranged alphabetically by author and then by year. Most of the works cited are in New Guinea languages or modern European languages. Often there is a brief biographical note following the author's name and occasionally an annotation at the end of the entry, mainly descriptive of the item such as the language under examination, especially if not readily apparent from the title. Languages along with their geographic location are indexed, but the author cautions that the index only serves as a guide to the main languages mentioned. The index is also complicated by changes in names and locations over time.

945.   Carrington, Lois, and Miriam Curnow. **Twenty Years of Pacific Linguistics: An Index of Contributions to Pacific Linguistic Studies, 1961-1981**. Canberra, A.C.T., Australia: Department of Linguistics, Research School of Pacific Studies, the Australian National University, 1981. 161p. index. (Pacific Linguistics. Series D, No. 40). ISBN 0-85883-249-6.

946.   Carrington, Lois. **Six More Years of Pacific Linguistics: An Index of Contributions to Pacific Linguistic Studies, 1981-1987**. Canberra, A.C.T., Australia; Department of Linguistics, Research School of Pacific Studies, the Australian National University, 1987. 209p. index. (Pacific Linguistics. Series D, No. 80). ISBN 0-85883-362-X

The two works cited above index Pacific Linguistics publications which were issued through the Linguistic Circle of Canberra. Through these 26 years many of the distinguished scholars of linguistics and language study in this area of the world contributed as authors to Pacific Linguistics. The publications appear in four series: series A, occasional papers; series B, monographs; series C, books; and series D, special publications (bulletins, archival materials, textbooks, maps, and more). Series A has a number of subseries devoted to: New Guinea linguistics, Philippine linguistics, South-East Asian linguistics, Australian linguistics, linguistics of Melanesia, Borneo linguistics and pidgin and Creole linguistics. Both the 20-year and 6-year index have an author/title index, language index, topic index, regional index, and a map index. Entries in each of these five indexes are accompanied by a notation referring the user to the detailed catalogue of publications in series number order which gives complete publication information.

947.   Cense, A. A., and E. M. Uhlenbeck. **Critical Survey of Studies on the Languages of Borneo**. 's-Gravenhage: Martinus Nijhoff, 1958. 82p. index. illus. bibliog. (Koninklijk Instituut voor Taal-, Land- en Volkenkunde. Bibliographical Series, 2). LC 74-151154.

Publications on the languages and dialects, with the exception of Chinese, of the island of Borneo and Indonesia are discussed here in bibliographic essays. The authors have attempted to be as exhaustive as possible, even including ethnographic and missionary texts with little linguistic value. Full bibliographic information for the 323 works in the text is given in the appended cumulative bibliography. There is also an index of languages and dialects.

948.   Coppell, W. G. **Austronesian and Other Languages of the Pacific and South-East Asia: An Annotated Catalogue of Theses and Dissertations**. Canberra: Dept. of Linguistics, Research School of Pacific Studies, Australian National University, 1981. 521p. index. bibliog. (Pacific Linguistics. Series C, Books, No. 64). LC 82-134593. ISBN 0-85883-238-0.

Though dissertations and theses related to Austronesian and related languages make up the bulk of this catalogue, entries relating to non-Austronesian languages are well-represented. The cut-off date for inclusion is 1979 with most material dated 1951 or later. Theses from all over the world in many languages are gathered here. Substantial abstracts usually obtained from the documents themselves or from *Dissertation Abstracts International* (DAI) nearly always accompany the entries. References to DAI or information relating to works which have been published elsewhere is appended to the relevant entries. A good subject (including language and dialect) index follows the bibliography. The author also includes a useful outline of languages and dialects by country for this area of the world.

949.   Hendrickson, Gail R., and Leonard F. Newell, comps. **A Bibliography of Philippine Language Dictionaries and Vocabularies**. With a foreword by Andrew B. Gonzalez. Manila: Linguistic Society of the Philippines, 1991. 163p. index. bibliog. (Linguistic Society of the Philippines. Special Monograph Issue, No. 30). ISBN 971-1059-17-7.

The compilers have cast a wide net in this compilation covering both manuscripts and published works—wordlists, vocabularies, and dictionaries— from the 16th century to 1990 on the Malayo-Polynesian language within the political boundaries of the Republic of the Philippines. With the exception of pre-twentieth century publications, they have restricted inclusion to lexicons estimated at 1,500 or more entries. The introduction and a separate reference section list the many sources from which the compilers obtained information. Very detailed information is given about variant editions of each title and, in the case of manuscripts, location is noted when such information is available. Listing of entries is alphabetical by compiler with an index by language; both are then further arranged in chronological order. One could quibble about some of the headings in the language index, for example, the separate listing of Tagalog and Pilipino—the legislated name for Tagalog—which is really one language. But, in fact it makes sense to separate them since the compilers make this distinction in the titles of their dictionaries. There are also problems with distinctions between languages and dialects. The user of this specialized work in all likelihood will be aware of the complex language situation in the Philippines and be able to sort it out.

950.   Herbert, Patricia, and Anthony Milner, eds. **South-East Asia Languages and Literatures: A Select Guide**. Honolulu: University of Hawaii Press, 1989. 182p. illus. bibliog. ISBN 0-8248-1267-0.

The purpose of this guide is to provide for newcomers "a concise introduction to the history, major languages, scripts, dating systems, manuscripts, printing and publishing histories, and literary genres of South-East Asia" (p. vii) and for librarians and scholars a quick reference source. As such, it is not meant to be, nor is it as comprehensive as the guide by Kratz (see entry 953). A nice layout and the occasional illustration to break up the text make it an appealing book to read and browse. Scholars and librarians at academic institutions in Southeast Asia as well as Britain, France, the Netherlands, and Australia all made contributions to the chapters on Burma, Thailand, Cambodia, Laos, Vietnam, Malaysia, Indonesia, Philippines, and overseas Chinese. Despite a variety of authors, the editors have standardized the length, content, and format such that even the headings within each chapter are the same. Short references are provided in the text with full bibliographies at the ends of chapters.

951.   Huffman, Franklin E. **Bibliography and Index of Mainland Southeast Asian Languages and Linguistics**. New Haven, CT: Yale University Press, 1986. 640p. index. (Yale Language Series). LC 85-52119. ISBN 0-300-036795.

This is a relatively exhaustive bibliography of some 10,000 works on mainland Southeast Asian languages and linguistics. It incorporates material from two standard bibliographies in this field published more than 20 years ago that covered Mon-Khmer, Tai and Sino-Tibetan (see entries 931 and 921). Coverage here is for five linguistic groups: Austroasiatic (including Viet-Múong and Munda), Tibeto-Burman (but without Sinitic), Tai-Kadai (including Kam-Sui), Miao-Yao, and mainland Austronesian (Chamic). Huffman provides in the introduction a concise and up-to-date summary of the debate on linguistic affiliations in the area.

In the bibliography he gathers a wide variety of published and unpublished materials: monographs, articles, theses, manuscripts, conference papers, and even forthcoming works. The arrangement of entries is alphabetical by author and then chronological under each author. Titles are given in the original language, or a transliteration thereof, followed by an English translation except for the common European languages. An entry may be followed by a list of reviews and/or a descriptive annotation when the content is not clear from the title. To illustrate the level of detail provided, Grierson's monumental *Linguistic Survey of India* is accompanied by more than 3 pages of content notes.

The language and subject index, the key to using the bibliography, is organized by language/dialect name. Each name heading is followed by alternative names in parentheses, and then followed by an indication of membership in one of the 5 major language groups. This whole language/dialect heading is then followed by abbreviations for subject categories which are then keyed not to item or page numbers but to relevant authors' names and dates of publication. With this system a user of the index can get a quick overview of who has written on a particular language and subject. Moreover, the index functions as a compendium of some 2,500 to 3,000 language and dialect names since each alternative name is separately listed. This important scholarly work is likely to remain the standard reference in this field for some time.

952.   Klieneberger, H. R., comp. **Bibliography of Oceanic Linguistics**. London: Oxford University Press, 1957. 143p. index. (London Oriental Bibliographies, Vol. 1). LC 57-59123.

Klieneberger cites more than 2,000 books and periodical articles concerning the languages of Oceania (Polynesian, Micronesian, Melanesian, and Papuan). The arrangement is by some 13 geographic areas and then by language with an additional section for bibliographies and also a pidgin English and Beach-la-mar language section. Some entries include references to reviews and have codes indicating the libraries where material can be located. A few entries have brief annotations. A language index covers more than 600 languages. There is an author index as well.

953.   Kratz, E. Ulrich, ed. **Southeast Asian Languages and Literatures: A Bibliographical Guide to Burmese, Cambodian, Indonesian, Javanese, Malay, Minangkabau, Thai and Vietnamese**. London: I. B. Tauris, 1996. 455p. (Tauris Academic Studies). ISBN 1-86064-114-8.

The subtitle of this work accurately describes the contents except that Khmer was omitted. It is intended to be a study guide "to facilitate [for teachers and researchers] bibliographical access to relevant reference materials, source texts and translations . . . and to provide students with a historical introduction to the study of South-east Asian languages and literatures" (p. 3). Chapters written by contributors who are members of the Department of the Languages and Cultures of South-east Asia and the Islands of the School of Oriental and African Studies (SOAS) in London cover either a particular language or literature, or may cover both at once. Style and format differ from chapter to chapter, but each is signed and ends with a substantial bibliography. References are to works in English, European languages, and the vernacular. In comparison to Herbert and Milner's 1989 guide (see entry 950), it is more comprehensive and cites more recent works. To use Burmese as an example, the chapter in Kratz on just language—there is another on literature—is longer than the single chapter on Burma in Herbert and Milner, moreover, the bibliography in Kratz is more comprehensive and brings references current through 1994.

954. Kunz, E. F., comp. **An Annotated Bibliography of the Languages of the Gilbert Islands, Ellice Islands, and Nauru**. Sydney: Published by the Trustees of the Public Library of New South Wales, 1959. 202p.

This book contains 3 separate bibliographies on the languages of the areas indicated in its title. Background and historical information introduce each bibliography. Each is divided into sections under the following headings: bibliographies, dictionaries and vocabularies, linguistic works, periodicals written in the native language, and works (books, pamphlets, etc.) written in the native language. Within a heading entries are arranged chronologically. Brief content notes accompany most entries. Indexes for subjects and authors/translators follow each of the 3 bibliographies.

955. Makarenko, Vladimir. **A Preliminary Annotated Bibliography of Pilipino Linguistics, (1604-1976)**. Edited by Andrew Gonzalez and Carolina Nemenzo Sacris. Manila: De La Salle University Libraries and Linguistic Society of the Philippines, 1981. 257p. index. (De La Salle University Libraries. Bibliography Series, No. 3).

The author includes nearly 1,800 linguistic works on Pilipino, also known as Tagalog. Works on the other Philippine languages are beyond its scope. Because of the importance of Pilipino as the national language of the Philippines from 1936 to 1973, sociolinguistic material and popular articles on language issues are also listed. Sources consulted by the author are noted in a preliminary section. The main bibliography is separated into 2 sections, each arranged alphabetically by author. The first lists works in Russian (entries are transliterated). The second and largest section contains material in Western European, English, and Tagalog languages. Descriptive notes and references to reviews occasionally accompany an entry. A subject index is appended.

956. Nemenzo, Catalina A., comp. **Southeast Asian Languages and Literature in English: An Annotated Bibliography**. Quezon City: University of the Philippines, 1969. 984p. index. (Philippine Social Sciences and Humanities Review, Vol. 34, Nos. 1-4).

All types of materials, both published and unpublished, written in English from 1624 to 1966 on the languages and literatures of Southeast Asia are included in this annotated bibliography with nearly 7,500 entries. Besides sections on Indochina and Southeast Asia in general, the compiler covers the following countries in separate sections: Borneo, Burma, Cambodia, Laos, Vietnam, Indonesia, Malaysia, Philippines, Singapore, and Thailand. In each section she lists entries under the subdivisions of bibliography, languages (further arranged by subject) and literature. For each entry she indicates by means of symbols the location of that work in libraries in the Philippines. Subject, corporate author, and author indexes are appended.

957. Noorduyn, J. **A Critical Survey of Studies on the Languages of Sulawesi**. Leiden: KITLV Press, 1991. 245p. index. bibliog. map. (Koninklijk Instituut voor Taal-, Land- en Volkenkunde. Bibliographical Series, 18; ISSN 0074-0462). ISBN 90-6718-028-9.

Some 60 to 80 indigenous languages, depending on how one draws the line between language and dialect, are found on the island of Sulawesi—formerly known as the Celebes—together with some of the offshore islands. The introduction provides a nice overview of the study of these languages and, in particular, has a good discussion of the various language maps for the area. Just two languages, Buginese and Makasarese, account for more than half of the population with the remaining having few speakers. In cases where languages have been little studied and reliable publications are scarce, the criteria for including publications or unpublished works in this survey have been kept broad so as to include other types of materials, e.g. anthropological works if they contain any lexical or textual material. There are chapters on the Sangiric, Minahasan, Gorontalo-Mongondic, Tomini, Kaili-Pamona, Saluan, Bungku-Mori, Muna-Buton, and south Sulawesi language groups. Chapters, or variously language sections within the chapters, have brief surveys ending with a bibliographical listing of all the works discussed in that chapter or section. The work concludes with an index of languages and dialects and an index of personal names.

958.   Teeuw, Andries. **A Critical Survey of Studies on Malay and Bahasa Indonesia**. With the assistance of H. W. Emanuels. 's-Gravenhage: Martinus Nijhoff, 1961. 176p. index. bibliog. (Koninklijk Instituut voor Taal-, Land- en Volkenkunde. Bibliographical Series, 5).

The first 90 pages of this book contain a long bibliographic essay surveying the Malay and Bahasa Indonesian languages. The essay's 36 sections incorporate publications devoted to, or important for, the study of these languages, including the fields of general linguistics, literature, ethnography, history, translations of the Bible and of the Koran, or concerned with language policy. A complete author-arranged bibliography follows. An appendix lists practical manuals and textbooks not mentioned in the essay.

959.   Uhlenbeck, Eugenius Marius. **A Critical Survey of Studies on the Languages of Java and Madura**. 's-Gravenhage: Martinus Nijhoff, 1964. 207p. index. illus. bibliog. map. (Koninklijk Instituut voor Taal-, Land- en Volkenkunde. Bibliographical Series, 7).

A wide variety of linguistic and language materials are included in this survey on the Sundanese, Javanese, and Madurese languages of Java and Madura. Each language (and Old Javanese) is dealt with in a separate chapter followed by an author-arranged bibliography. At the end is a cumulative index for authors, reviewers, and subjects.

960.   Voorhoeve, P. **Critical Survey of Studies on the Languages of Sumatra**. 's-Gravenhage: Martinus Nijhoff, 1955. 55p. illus. bibliog. map. (Koninklijk Instituut voor Taal-, Land- en Volkenkunde. Bibliographical Series, 1). LC 58-21593.

Though dated, this is the first volume in a series of critical bibliographies compiled under the direction of the Royal Institute of Linguistics, Geography, and Ethnology. The present work covers the languages spoken on the island of Sumatra and on the islands to the east and to the west closely related to the main island. Chapters deal with the various languages island by island and sometimes by archipelago. The works the author mentions in the text of the chapters are followed by numbers that correspond to the numbers in a selected bibliography following the text. Since references in this bibliography are not in any particular order, an author index would have been useful. A linguistic map of Sumatra locates the languages and by means of codes indicates the presence of a wordlist, dictionary, grammar, grammatical sketch or studies, or texts for that language in the bibliography.

961.   Ward, Jack H. **A Bibliography of Philippine Linguistics and Minor Languages: With Annotations and Indices Based on Works in the Library of Cornell University**. Ithaca, NY: Southeast Asia Program, Cornell University, 1971. 549p. (Linguistics Series, 5). (Cornell University. Southeast Asia Program, Data Paper, No. 83). LC 73-161419.

Ward limits this bibliography to linguistic works (and some ethnolinguistic, sociolinguistic, and psycholinguistic works) on the Austronesian and pidgin and Creole languages of the Philippines. He also includes textual material in any of the major languages of the Philippines up to a date of 1700. Preceding the main body of the bibliography (published works, pamphlets, theses, and manuscripts) are lists of serials/periodicals and sources consulted. Each entry is accompanied by content codes and often a short narrative description. An index is organized first by language and then by the content codes.

962.   Zainab Awang Ngah. **Perkamusan Melayu/Indonesia: satu bibliografi/Malay/Indonesian Dictionaries: A Bibliography**. Kuala Lumpur: Perpustakaan Universiti Malaya, 1990. 411p. index. illus. ISBN 967-943-030-8.

Introductory and reference materials in this annotated bibliography of Malay/Indonesian vocabularies and dictionaries are in both Malay and English, but the annotations are only in Malay. With the exception of manuscripts and a few bilingual and polyglot dictionaries, all works cited are physically located in three collections in Indonesia: the University of Malaya Library, the National Library of Malaysia, and the Dewan Bahasa dan Pustaka library. Sections 1-4 comprise the bibliography itself. Sections 5 is a bibliography of studies in books, theses, periodical articles, and conference papers about Malay dictionaries and vocabularies. Similarly, section 6 is a bibliography of newspaper articles. Section 7 is an addendum, while section 8 provides a chronological listing of all the materials listed in sections 1-4. In addition there are three indexes for authors, titles, and subjects.

26

Paleosiberian

963.   Jakobson, Roman, Gerta Huttl-Worth, and John Fred Beebe. **Paleosiberian Peoples and Languages: A Bibliographical Guide**. New Haven, CT: HRAF Press, 1957. 222p. (Behavior Science Bibliographies). LC 57-14764. (Reprinted Westport, CT: Greenwood Press, 1981; LC 81-1993; ISBN 0-313-22804-3).

Some of the languages in Siberia which do not belong to the Uralic, Altaic, Indo-European, Sino-Tibetan, or Eskimo families are often grouped under the name Paleosiberian. Other labels sometimes used are: Paleoasiatic, Hyperborean, Arctic, Marginal, or Americanoid. This is the first attempt at a bibliography of the widely scattered studies, both published and unpublished, on these languages which have been written in many languages. Besides sections for bibliographies and works concerning several or all Paleosiberian peoples, there are sections for the Gilyak language, the Chukchee group, the Yukaghir group, and the Yeniseian group. In all, the authors list about 1,900 works. Cyrillic script entries are transliterated and all titles not in English are translated. Short descriptive notes accompany many entries.

27

African

Manuals and Atlases

964. Conseil international de la langue française. **Inventaire des études linguistiques sur les pays d'Afrique noire d'expression française et sur Madagascar**. Établi sous la direction de Daniel Barreteau. Paris: Conseil international de la langue française, 1978. 624p. index. illus. bibliog. maps. LC 79-371995. ISBN 2-85319-052-8.

There are two main parts to this book. One part is a linguistic inventory arranged by sections for language family or group. Each section provides considerable background information, including number of speakers and a historical sketch of the classification, lists the languages in that family or group, summarizes research, and cites further references.

The second part is concerned with sociolinguistics and has sections devoted to individual countries. Each section discusses the linguistic situation in that country and provides bibliographies. There is a classificatory index of languages and dialects as well as an index of the numerous maps scattered throughout the text.

An appendix contains a short, separate bibliography by Suzanne Lafage, "La langue française en Afrique noire et à Madagascar: Éléments pour une bibliographie."

965. Dalby, David. **Language Map of Africa and the Adjacent Islands**. Provisional ed. London: International African Institute, 1977. 63p. index. map. ISBN 0-85302-062-0.

The provisional edition of this language map of Africa consists of 1 large folded black and white map accompanied by a handbook. Dalby explains that the map is designed to show the approximate modern geographical distribution of home languages in Africa, based on majority first language usage in the home, and to show second, a revised classification of African languages, based on known levels of historical relationship. The handbook contains a checklist which is a classified index to the language and dialect names on the map and contains the numerical codes used on the map. There is also an alphabetical index of the language and dialect names. The author promises a revised edition with colored maps. Mann and Dalby's thesaurus is a companion volume to this map and handbook (see entry 973).

966. Fivaz, Derek, and Patricia E. Scott. **African Languages: A Genetic and Decimalised Classification for Bibliographic and General Reference**. Boston: G. K. Hall, 1977. 332p. illus. bibliog. maps. (Bibliographies and Guides in African Studies). LC 77-10111. ISBN 0-8161-8026-1.

The authors largely base the classification scheme for African languages which they present in this guide on the work of Joseph H. Greenberg (see entry 967). The motivation for devising the scheme was the need in library science to provide additional levels of classification for language/language group/language family and subject within the single, totally inadequate number of 496 allocated within the Dewey decimal classification scheme for the more than 1,000 African languages and even larger number of dialects.

The classification schedules are arranged by language families. A language index follows with all the entries from the classification schedules arranged in alphabetical order. A reference and sources section contains for each language family footnotes on areas of uncertainty and disagreement as to language relationships and references to sources cited and consulted. Appended language family charts summarize language relationships in diagrammatic form.

967. Greenberg, Joseph Harold. **The Languages of Africa**. 3rd ed. Bloomington, IN: Indiana University, 1970. 180p. index. maps. LC 62-63505. ISBN 0-87750-115-7.

Greenberg presents here a complete genetic classification of the languages of Africa. It is an expanded and extensively revised version of his *Studies in African Linguistic Classification* (New Haven, CT: Compass, 1955). He devotes a chapter each to the Niger-Congo, Afroasiatic, Khoisan, Chari-Nile, Nilo-Saharan, and Niger-Kordofanian languages, providing evidence, including comparative word lists, for the classification. There is an index to language classification which consists of a key to the classification and a classificatory index of languages. A language in this index is followed by two sets of letters and numbers. The first set is its classification according to the key. The second set is an indication of its position on one of the maps accompanying the work. The maps are quite generalized; the author refers the reader to the *Handbook of African Languages* (see entry 968) for further details.

968. International African Institute. **Handbook of African Languages**. London, New York: Published for the International African Institute by the Oxford University Press, 1952-1959. 4 pts.

969. Part 1: **La langue berbère**, by André Basset. 1952. 72p. illus. bibliog. maps. LC 52-04595.

970. Part 2: **The Languages of West Africa**, by Diedrich Westermann. 1952. 215p. maps. LC 53-23791. (New edition by Diedrich Westermann and M. A. Bryan. With a supplementary bibliography compiled by D. W. Arnott. Folkestone: Published for the Institute by Dawsons, 1970. 277p. index. bibliog. map. LC 76-25958. ISBN 0-7129-0462-X).

971. Part 3: **The Non-Bantu Languages of North-Eastern Africa**, by A. N. Tucker and M. A. Bryan. With a supplement on the Non-Bantu Languages of Southern Africa by E. O. J. Westphal. 1956. 228p. bibliog. maps. LC 57-1706.

972. Part 4: **The Bantu Languages of Africa**, compiled by Margaret Arminel Bryan. 1959. 170p. index. map. LC 60-1171.

Although parts of the Handbook differ somewhat in content and arrangement, in general they survey the indicated languages, providing information on phonetics, morphology, syntax, vocabulary, and writing, and thus laying the groundwork for the classification which is presented along with dialect information. Usually there are indications of where the various languages and dialects are spoken, who spoken by, and number of speakers. Some include an index of language and dialect names plus a bibliography. All contain one or more maps showing language distribution.

973. Mann, Michael, and David Dalby. **A Thesaurus of African Languages: A Classified and Annotated Inventory of the Spoken Languages of Africa: With an Appendix on Their Written Representation**. With Philip Baker, et al. London: Hans Zell, 1987. 325p. index. LC 88-100139. ISBN 0-90-5450-24-8.

This thesaurus, an important, scholarly work, is a companion volume to Dalby's *Language Map of Africa and the Adjacent Islands* (see entry 965). That work maps the languages of the continent; this work provides the documentation and indexing for it. With only a few revisions Dalby's classification of languages with some 120 language sets is followed in Mann and Dalby's language inventory, the main part of this thesaurus.

The inventory provides notes on the individual languages, their variant names, and immediate classification as well as references to sources consulted. Another part, arranged according to political units, provides a listing of languages spoken as home languages together with details on languages used for inter-group communication, officially recognized languages, and languages used in education or the media. The authors append a comprehensive bibliography and a language index to the whole work. This is a rather difficult tool to use, but because of the wealth of information it contains well worth the effort for the scholarly researcher.

Cumulative Bibliographies

974. Adewọle, Lawrence Olufemi. **The Yoruba Language: Published Works and Doctoral Dissertations, 1843-1986**. Hamburg: Helmut Buske, 1987. 182p. (African Linguistic Bibliographies, Vol. 3; ISSN 0721-2488). ISBN 3-87118-842-5.

Yoruba, a language belonging to the Kwa family, is a major language of Nigeria and is also spoken in Togo, Benin, and elsewhere. This bibliography covers both published and unpublished language and linguistic studies. Some of the 1,339 entries have short annotations. A name index contains co-authors, editors, and persons cited in annotations, in titles, etc. as well as authors. The latter, however, only clutters the index since the bibliography is alphabetically arranged by author. A subject index is helpful though some headings are poorly constructed.

975. Akinṣlure, Millicent O., comp. **Languages and Language Problems in Sierra Leone: An Annotated Bibliography**. Freetown, Sierra Leone: Njala University College Library, 1979. 241p. index. (Njala University College Library, Occasional Paper, No. 5). LC 82-207071.

This bibliography deals mainly with indigenous Sierra Leonean languages and language problems. It lists not only books, theses and articles, but also journals, pamphlets, published and unpublished reports, works in progress, workshops, conferences, and public lectures. Part I with 799 entries has a general section and individual sections for each of 15 languages. Part II, with nearly 200 more entries, deals with language problems. Brief annotations accompany most entries. The compiler provides author and general indexes.

976.   Baldi, Sergio. **Systematic Hausa Bibliography**. Rome: Pioda, 1977. 145p. index. (Istituto Italo-Africano. Collana di studi africani, 3). LC 79-348579.

In this bibliography the compiler lists books, articles, and other materials published about the Hausa language in English, French, German, Hausa, Russian, and a few other languages. Citations are arranged chronologically under various subheadings in five chapters: 1) generalities; 2) linguistics (grammars, instruction books, phrase books, linguistic studies, dictionaries, and vocabulary studies); 3) literature; 4) religious subjects; and 5) Hausa spoken outside Nigeria. Various indexes provide the following: an index of authors; list of governmental and missionary organizations, publishers and journals which have printed anonymous works; a list of titles of anonymous works; and a list of Hausa works printed in Arabic characters.

977.   Barreteau, Daniel, Évelyne Ngantchui, and Terry Scruggs. **Bibliographie des langues camerounaises**. Paris: Éditions de l'ORSTOM, Agence de la coopération culturelle et technique, 1993. 269p. index. bibliog.

The nearly 2,400 entries in this alphabetically arranged bibliography are for works published mainly in French, English, German, and the various languages of Cameroon. Occasionally a title is translated into French or English. Some works have descriptive annotations (in English or French) and all are accompanied by language codes and subject keywords (in French). The authors provide a list of the codes and an index for the keywords as well as for authors.

978.   Bastin, Y. **Bibliographie bantoue sélective**. Tervuren: Musée royal de l'Afrique centrale, 1975. 56p. index. bibliog. (Archives d'anthropologie, No. 24). LC 76-473806.

Works in this selective unannotated bibliography on the Bantu languages are divided into two chapters. The first chapter dealing with descriptive studies has a classified arrangement; the key to this arrangement is provided in an alphabetical list of languages. The second chapter contains comparative studies arranged by author.

979.   Bourdin, Jean-François, Jean-Pierre Caprile, and Michel Lafon. **Bibliographie analytique des langues parlées en Afrique subsaharienne, 1970-1980**. Paris: Association d'études linguistiques interculturelles africaines, 1983. 556p. index. (Les Langues parlées en Afrique, études, documents et bibliographies). (Bulletin bibliographique de CIRELFA). LC 84-149731. ISBN 2-7359-0011-8.

The language section with 1,523 entries is the largest of the three sections which make up this analytical bibliography. The other two sections deal with ethnology and education. Within each section entries are organized by year, but within each year are arranged in no particular order. In addition to providing the usual bibliographic information, the compilers assign subject key words to each entry and often include analytical notes. The indexes of authors, language and ethnic groups, geographical names, and concepts are important for accessing the bibliography because of its erratic organization.

980. Der-Houssikian, Haig, comp. **A Bibliography of African Linguistics**. Edmonton, Canada: Linguistic Research, Inc., 1972. 96p. index. (Current Inquiry Into Language & Linguistics, 7). LC 73-177482.

A more descriptive title for this bibliography might specify that it is a selected bibliography of comparative and historical African linguistics; with only a few exceptions language-specific studies are excluded. Preceding the bibliography the compiler provides an introduction to classificatory literature from Bleek to Greenberg. The 714 entries for books and articles are arranged chronologically from the first entry published in 1811-12 to the last entry dated 1971. The appended author and subject index is very useful given the arrangement of the entries.

981. Dugas, André. **Bibliographie analytique des travaux de linguistique africaine émanant d'institutions nord-américaines, 1955-1987**. Paris: Agence de coopération culturelle et technique, Université du Québec à Montréal, 1989. 352p. index. ISBN 2-9800835-3-4.

Dugas picked 1955 for a beginning to his bibliography of works produced by North American institutions as that is the year Greenberg published his first genetic classification of African languages (for a reference to this work see entry 967). Some 1,570 entries are alphabetically arranged by author from Aaron to Zwicky. They include references to books, chapters, journal articles, theses, and ERIC documents. The introduction is written in French, but the subject and language keywords accompanying entries are all in English. The index of authors picks up co-authors. There is also a language index, but without subheadings such languages as Bantu and Swahili have several hundred entries listed without any further guidance to the user. A subject index would have made this a more useful work.

982. Hendrix, Melvin K. **An International Bibliography of African Lexicons**. Metuchen, NJ: Scarecrow, 1982. 348p. index. bibliog. LC 81-16533. ISBN 0-8108-1478-1.

The term lexicon is used here to refer to any stock of words or word elements. It therefore includes dictionaries, vocabularies, wordlists, glossaries, conversation and phrase books, and polyglotta, as well as semantic, etymological, technical, scientific, and classified studies. The term African is used to designate not only the continent itself, but also the adjacent islands. The bibliography contains more than 2,600 entries covering some 350 years, while representing about 600 languages and approximately 200 dialects. Nearly all entries are annotated with an indication of the languages in each work and, in the case of bilingual or multilingual works, the direction of language translation. There is both a language and dialect index and an author and name index. This is a valuable source for both published works and unpublished manuscripts, many produced outside the Western world.

983. Hintze, Ursula. **Bibliographie der KWA-Sprachen und der Sprachen der Togo-Restvölker**. Berlin: Akademie-Verlag, 1959. 102p. maps. (Deutsche Akademie der Wissenschaften zu Berlin. Institut für Orientforschung. Veröffentlichung, Nr.42). LC 61-21935.

This bibliography lists over 1,000 studies dealing with the Kwa languages and other languages of Togo in West Africa. Within the introductory general bibliography and the 11 sections of the main bibliography, entries are arranged chronologically. Much of the material cited here is from the 1800s and early 1900s with the earliest work dated 1658. An author index is appended. In a pocket there are 11 colored maps showing the geographic distribution of the various languages.

984. Ita, Nduntuei O. **Bibliography of Nigeria: A Survey of Anthropological and Linguistic Writings from the Earliest Times to 1966**. London: Frank Cass, 1971. 271p. index. LC 79-169811. ISBN 0-7146-2458-6.

Entries in this classified bibliography are arranged in 2 main sections. One section contains studies dealing with Nigeria as a whole or with several ethnic divisions. Another section contains works for the individual main ethnic groups within the country. In addition to linguistic studies proper there are entries for dictionaries, vocabularies, phrase books and grammars. The compiler adds both an author and an ethnic index.

985. Jakobi, Angelika, and Tanja Kümmerle, comps. **The Nubian Languages: An Annotated Bibliography**. With a foreword by Peter L. Shinnie. Köln: Rüdiger Köppe, 1993. 135p. index. illus. bibliog. map. (African Linguistic Bibliographies, Vol. 5; ISSN 0721-2488). ISBN 3-927620-35-1.

The languages of the Nubian language group are, or were, spoken in four areas of the Sudan and Egypt: Nile Nubian, Darfur Nubian, Kordofan Nubian, and Haraza. Though their external affiliation was controversial at one time, Nubian languages are now assigned to the Eastern Sudanic subgroup of the Chari-Nile branch of Nilo-Saharan. Old Nubian, the language of the medieval Christian kingdoms, is one of the few ancient African non-Afroasiatic language with a written literature. In addition to language and linguistic materials on these languages, the compilers have included associated anthropological, historical, and philological works in their bibliography. Entries are simply listed alphabetically by author, but each annotated entry has at least two keywords, one referring to the subject—there are 17 such subject terms—the other to the language or language group. There is then an index of these keywords.

986. Jones, Ruth, comp. **West Africa: General, Ethnography/Sociology, Linguistics**. With the assistance of a panel of consultants. London: The International African Institute, 1958. 116p. index. (Africa Bibliography Series: Ethnography, Sociology, Linguistics and Related Subjects).

987. Jones, Ruth, comp. **North-East Africa: General, Ethnography, Sociology, Linguistics**. With the assistance of a panel of consultants. London: The International African Institute, 1959. 51p. index. (Africa Bibliography Series: Ethnography, Sociology, Linguistics and Related Subjects). LC 60-34932.

988.   Jones, Ruth, comp. **East Africa: General, Ethnography/Sociology, Linguistics**. With the assistance of a panel of consultants. London: The International African Institute, 1960. 62p. index. (Africa Bibliography Series: Ethnography, Sociology, Linguistics and Related Subjects). LC 60-44644.

989.   Jones, Ruth, comp. **South-East Central Africa and Madagascar: General, Ethnography/Sociology, Linguistics**. With the assistance of a panel of consultants. London: The International African Institute, 1961. 53p. index. (Africa Bibliography Series: Ethnography, Sociology, Linguistics and Related Subjects). LC 61-65578.

Though this series covers a number of subjects it is still a rich source of linguistic material. It is based on the bibliographical card index in the Library of the International African Institute and thus has no annotations. It aims to list all significant works for the time period covered. The organization of each volume is first by geographical division, then subdivided by subject. The linguistic subject section is further subdivided by language. Some ethnographic texts of interest to linguists may also be found in the ethnography section. Each volume in the series has two indexes: one for authors, another for ethnic and language names.

990.   Kastenholz, Raimund, comp. **Mande Languages and Linguistics**. With a foreword by Karim Traoré. Hamburg: Helmut Buske, 1988. 274p. index. bibliog. (African Linguistic Bibliographies, Vol. 4; ISSN 0721-2488). ISBN 3-87118-887-5.

The Mande languages found in West Africa form a group within the Niger-Kordofanian language family. Kastenholz' bibliography on these languages gathers a wide variety of both published and unpublished materials on comparative and general linguistics; dictionaries, glossaries, and word lists; texts in Mande languages; other materials containing original data from Manda languages; and works dealing with distribution and number of speakers. Researchers will have to work hard to locate some of the unpublished materials and works dating to the early 1800s. The classification system is organized first by broad geographical area, then by language. Most entries are for works in English and French with the titles of non-English works translated. Short comments accompany many entries, particularly those whose titles do not convey their relevance for the languages or dialects in question. There is an index of languages and dialects, and another for authors.

991.   Kraehe, Mary Alice, Cristina W. Sharretts, and Christine H. Guyonneau. **African Languages: A Guide to the Library Collection of the University of Virginia**. Charlottesville, VA: Collection Development Department, University of Virginia library, 1986. 169p. index. maps.

The authors compiled this bibliography of more than 1,200 works as a guide to the dictionaries, grammars, and teaching materials of African languages held by the Library at the University of Virginia. In addition to materials for the Khoisan, Nilo-Saharan, Congo-Kordofanian, and Afro-Asiatic families they list works for Afrikaans, Malagasy, and pidgins and Creoles. Some general works and a selective list of serials are also included. The unannotated entries are arranged alphabetically by author under each language heading. An index includes author, editor, and compiler names. Half a dozen maps show the general areas where languages are spoken.

992.   Lamberti, Marcello, comp. **Somali Language and Literature**. With a foreword by B. W. Andrzejewski. Hamburg: Helmut Buske, 1986. 106p. index. (African Linguistic Bibliographies, Vol. 2; ISSN 0721-2488). LC 86-222444. ISBN 3-87118-707-0.

This bibliography on the Somali language gathers together material written in Somali, English, and half a dozen other languages on such topics as: language classification, grammar, historical linguistics, lexicology, morphology, orthography, phonology, and syntax. It also includes related materials from the fields of applied linguistics, language policy, and sociolinguistics. Coverage is intended to be complete through 1980 with some titles added through 1984. A subject index provides access to the author arranged entries.

993.   Mann, Michael, and Valerie Sanders, comps. **A Bibliography of African Language Texts in the Collections of the School of Oriental and African Studies, University of London, to 1963**. London: Hans Zell, 1994. 429p. index. (Documentary Research in African Literatures, No. 3). ISBN 1-873836-31-7.

Altogether this bibliography inventories some 8,138 works—7,770 African language texts in the main listing covering over 300 African languages (excluding Arabic, Afrikaans, and Classical Ethiopic), plus another 368 works in a supplementary listing of works in non-African languages representing the original sources of translations, or in a few cases, translations of African language originals into Western languages. It is more than just an inventory of the main collection at the School of Oriental and African Studies (SOAS) as the title would seem to indicate; rather it represents the collecting efforts of the International African Institute (IAI) and that of the International Committee on Christian Literature for Africa (ICCLA) which transferred many of its holdings to SOAS, just as the IAI has earlier transferred some of its titles to the ICCLA.

The bibliography's scope is limited to texts that were principally intended for local readers. Works of linguistic description such as grammars, dictionaries, and manuals are excluded, as are texts that have appeared in academic journals, and texts intended for the use of Western language learners. These excluded materials can be found in Meier's complementary work (see entry 994). The cut-off date is 1963, the year corresponding roughly to the end of significant additions to the archive collection and the original printed SOAS library catalogue. Despite the richness of the collection, it is representative (within its stated scope) rather than exhaustive, as the compilers found in a check with a number of more local bibliographies. Entry numbers are used in cross-references and a series of indexes: short title, author, and language (by country, by classification, alphabetic). Within entries extensive use is made of abbreviations and symbols, so much so, that a reader is obliged to keep a marker at the table in which they are interpreted for constant referral.

994.   Meier, Wilma, ed. **Bibliography of African Languages/Bibliographie afrikanischer Sprachen/Bibliographie des langues africaines/Bibliografiya Afrikanskikh yazikov**. Wiesbaden: Otto Harrassowtiz, 1984. 888p. index. LC 84-174201. ISBN 3-447-02415-1.

This comprehensive bibliography of more than 14,000 entries covers material from the early 16th century through 1980. Thus it includes the early works of missionaries and missionary societies and civil servants and doctors serving colonial administrations. For more modern works the editor has made a particular effort to secure literature published by Eastern European authors. Works cited deal with the structure of individual languages as well as with the history, classification and geographical spread of linguistic phenomena, and the development of national and standard languages.

The main section of the bibliography, with full bibliographic information, lists works alphabetically by author and then chronologically. Both monographs and journal articles are included. Two particularly useful language indexes each list languages in alphabetical order with the language names and code numbers of the genetic classification following that of Fivaz and Scott (see entry 966) or that of David Dalby (see entry 965) for such languages as Afrikaans and the Creoles and pidgins. One language index then arranges entries under each language by author, also giving years of publication and subject headings; the other language index arranges entries in chronological order, giving names of authors and subject headings. For African linguistics this is the most comprehensive and up-to-date cumulative bibliography.

995.   Murphy, John D., and Harry Goff, comps. **A Bibliography of African Languages and Linguistics**. Washington, DC: Catholic University of America Press, 1969. 147p. index. LC 71-98990. ISBN 0-8132-0496-8.

The majority of the 1,218 entries in this selective, unannotated bibliography deal with the indigenous languages of Africa south of the Sahara. A lesser percentage deal with the African varieties of Arabic, the Hamitic languages, Malagasy, Afrikaans, and various Creoles. It is selective in that the compilers only include those works which they regard as useful. They provide indexes of languages and authors.

996.   Newman, Paul, comp. **Hausa and the Chadic Language Family: A Bibliography**. Köln: Rüdiger Köppe, 1996. 152p. index. (African Linguistic Bibliographies, Vol. 6; ISSN 0721-2488). ISBN3-927620-36-X.

Newman divided his bibliography on the Chadic languages and Hausa, the most widely spoken of the 125 or so Chadic languages, into 3 parts. The first part is a short listing of collections on Hausa and Chadic. The second part contains works on Hausa and Gwandara, a creolized offshoot of Hausa, while the third part on the Chadic languages, contains works on individual Chadic languages as well as comparative works. Some works are double-listed in both parts 2 and 3 so there are fewer unique works than the 1,821 numbered entries would seem to indicate. A few entries have short descriptive annotations or note of a review.

997.   Spaandonck, Marcel van, comp. **Practical and Systematical Swahili Bibliography; Linguistics 1850-1963**. Leiden: E. J. Brill, 1965. 61p. index. LC 67-3728.

This bibliography on Swahili language and literature contains about 800 references. The linguistic chapter covers selected grammars, instruction books, phrase books, exercises, vocabularies, dictionaries, and linguistic articles published since 1850. Swahili literature is dealt with in a separate chapter as is Congo

Swahili. The latter, a special form of Swahili also called Ngwana, or Up-Country Swahili, is so different linguistically from the Coast dialects that the compiler felt justified in separating it out. Each chapter is subdivided by form, language, and subject headings. An index lists authors, languages, dialects, and names other than those of authors.

998.   University of Rhodesia Library. **Catalogue of the C. M. Doke Collection on African Languages in the Library of the University of Rhodesia**. Boston: G. K. Hall, 1972. 546p. (University of Rhodesia Library Bibliographical Series, No. 2). LC 72-2074. ISBN 0-8161-0997-4.

This catalog reproduces approximately 7,000 cards for the 3,000 books, pamphlets, and manuscripts which make up the Doke collection. The collection contains works on more than 200 African languages and dialects. The bibliography is organized into separate author and subject sections preceded by a biographical essay on Doke and his scholarly activities.

999.   Unseth, Peter. **Linguistic Bibliography of the Non-Semitic Languages of Ethiopia**. East Lansing, MI: African Studies Center, Michigan State University, 1990. 113p. index. illus. bibliog. (Ethiopian Series. Monograph, No. 20). LC 90-623170.

All the languages of Ethiopia except Somali and the Semitic languages are represented in this bibliography of works dealing with linguistic description, classification, or geographical location. The reason for the two exclusions is that other bibliographies have already been published for these languages (see entries 1007 and 992). All published works up through the beginning months of 1987 and unpublished manuscripts with a record of location are included. Most works listed are written in English, Italian, German, and French. Unseth helpfully provides lists of Ethiopian language names and charts of language classification as well as a language index. What is termed an author index is really the bibliography proper. The only annotations are for reviews.

1000.   Warren, Dennis M. **Bibliography and Vocabulary of the Akan (Twi-Fante) Language of Ghana**. Bloomington, IN: Indiana University, 1976. 266p. (Indiana University Publication. African Series, Vol. 6). LC 74-30739. ISBN 87750-184-X.

The two main parts of this work are an Akan bibliography and an Akan vocabulary. The bibliography itself includes more than 1,500 works dealing with or utilizing Akan, including texts and textbooks. More than 10 appendixes as well as several indexes are appended. The second part, the vocabulary, consists of nearly 5,000 words from the arts, religion, and the sciences accompanied by definitions in a classified arrangement.

1001.   Whiteley, Wilfred Howell, and A. E. Gutkind, comps. **A Linguistic Bibliography of East Africa**. rev. ed. Kampala: East African Swahili Committee and East African Institute of Social Research, 1958. 1v.

In this revised edition the compilers bring together listings for books, articles, and manuscripts on the languages of Tanganyika, Kenya, and Uganda. In chapters for each country they list entries by language or in a general section. Works on Swahili are in a separate chapter.

1002.   Zocli, Ernest, comp. **Bibliographie de la langue swahili. Abidjan, Côte d'Ivoire: Institut africain pour le développement économique et social, 1974(?). 41p. (INADES-Documentation). LC 80-124918.**

This selective bibliography consists of 344 references to books and articles concerning the Swahili language. It cites linguistic studies, grammars, dictionaries, vocabularies, and textbooks in Swahili and other languages. Since entries are arranged by author, a subject index would have been useful.

28

Afro-Asiatic (Berber and Semitic)

1003.   Al-Ani, Salman H., and Dilworth B. Parkinson. **Arabic Linguistics Bibliography: 1979-1995**. Bloomington, IN: Indiana University Linguistics Club Publications, 1996. 104p.

Though the intent of this selective, unannotated bibliography is to update Bakalla's 1983 bibliography which covered materials published up to 1979 (see entry 1004), it does not quite measure up. It covers works written in fewer languages and has no subject indexing. For the years 1979-1995 this work covers books, journal articles, and dissertations written in English, Arabic, French, and German on historical approaches and phonetics, phonology, morphology, syntax, semantics, pragmatics, discourse, sociolinguistics, bilingualism, second language acquisition, and research on different varieties of Arabic. Citations to works in Arabic are transliterated.

1004.   Bakalla, M. H. **Arabic Linguistics: An Introduction and Bibliography**. 2nd rev. ed. London: Mansell; distr. in the U.S. and Canada, New York: H. W. Wilson, 1983. 741p. index. illus. LC 83-240527. ISBN 0-7201-1583-3.

This revised edition of the author's *Bibliography of Arabic Linguistics* (1975) listing 5,360 monographs, articles, and dissertations in some 20 languages is indispensable to the researcher in this field. In the introduction, Dr. Bakalla, a well-known scholar, surveys the field of Arabic linguistics in its various periods and across all its branches. Forewords by four other leading scholars provide additional background information. Prefatory materials are in both English and Arabic.

References are listed in 3 sections: general works (including bibliographies); works written in Occidental languages or using Latin script; and works written in Oriental languages or scripts, especially Arabic. Within sections the arrangement is alphabetical by author and then chronological. Entries provide complete bibliographic information as well as references to reviews and review articles. Some entries also contain brief annotations. For material in non-Latin scripts bibliographic information is transliterated. In addition an English translation is provided for materials in Arabic. A detailed analytical index provides excellent subject access. There are also indexes for editors and translators, co-authors and co-editors, reviewers, and Arab authors.

1005.   Galand, Lionel. **Langue et litterature berbères: vingt cinq ans d'études: chroniques de l'Annuaire de l'Afrique du Nord**. Paris: Éditions du Centre national de la recherche scientifique, 1979. 205p. index. bibliog. LC 79-122901. ISBN 2-222-02401-3.

The bibliographic essays in this volume cover a 25-year time period, 1954 through 1975. Each essay essentially summarizes material on the Berber language from an issue (or two) of the *Annuaire de l'Afrique du Nord* (Tome I through Tome XII-XIII). Some 1,512 references are consecutively numbered throughout the text. Preceding each chapter is a subject outline with corresponding reference numbers. Subject and author indexes also make use of these numbers.

1006.   Hospers, J. H., ed. **A Basic Bibliography for the Study of the Semitic Languages**. Leiden: E. J. Brill, 1973-74. 2v. LC 73-181086. ISBN 90-04-03623-7(v.1); 90-04-03870-1(v.2).

This 2-volume set contains signed, scholarly bibliographies on the Semitic languages. Volume 1 has sections for Akkadian, Sumerian, the Anatolian languages, Hurrian, Urartian, Elamitic, Ancient Persian, Ugaritic, Phoenician-Punic, Amarna-Canaanite, Hebrew, Syriac and Aramaic, Epigraphic South Arabian, the Ethiopian languages, and a concluding section dealing with studies on comparative Semitics. Volume 2 deals with Arabic; pre-classical, classical, and modern literary Arabic are in one section, modern Arabic dialects in another section. Entries in all sections of both volumes are classified under numerous subject, language/dialect, and form headings. There are no indexes.

1007.   Leslau, Wolf. **An Annotated Bibliography of the Semitic Languages of Ethiopia**. The Hague: Mouton, 1965. 336p. index. (Bibliographies on the Near East, 1). LC 65-27399.

This work is a revised and expanded version of the author's *Bibliography of the Semitic Languages of Ethiopia* (New York Public Library, 1946). It covers books and periodical articles on both North Ethiopic (Geez, Tigre, and Tigrinya) and South Ethiopic languages (Amharic, Argobba, Gafat, Gurage, and Harari). Chapters for general works on Semitic languages and Ethiopian languages precede the individual language chapters. Analytical tables at the beginning of each language chapter list grammars and dictionaries in chronological order and according to the languages in which they were written. Short descriptive annotations accompany the entries with occasional critical evaluations for grammars and dictionaries. A good subject index and indexes of authors and reviewers conclude the volume.

1008.   Sobelman, Harvey, ed. **Arabic Dialect Studies, a Selected Bibliography**. Washington, DC: Center for Applied Linguistics of the Modern Language Association and the Middle East Institute, 1962. 100p. LC 62-51838.

Charles A. Ferguson provides an introduction to the 6 signed bibliographic essays in this volume. Each essay is devoted to a particular Arabic dialect: Syrian Arabic, by Charles A. Ferguson; Egyptian Arabic, by Richard S. Harrell; Arabian Peninsula Arabic, by R. A. C. Goodison; Iraqi Arabic, by Haim Blanc; North African Arabic, by T. B. Irving; and Maltese Arabic, by P. P. Saydon. The essays provide evaluations of the significant scholarly work published on these dialects. A list of the publications mentioned in the text accompanies each essay.

1009.   Waldman, Nahum M. **The Recent Study of Hebrew: A Survey of the Literature with Selected Bibliography**. Cincinnati, OH: Hebrew Union College Press, 1989. 464p. index. bibliog. (Bibliographica Judaica, 10: ISSN 0067-6853). LC 89-19885. ISBN 0-87820-908-5.

The first half or so of this book is a thematic survey of linguistic studies of the Hebrew language mainly during the period from World War II to the mid-1980s which was rich in events that influenced the study of Hebrew. Among these events which Waldman mentions in the preface are the availability of Ugaritic materials in the 1930s, the discovery of the Dead Sea Scrolls, the emergence of the State of Israel with the influx of Jews speaking different dialects, Weiman's pioneering study in 1950 on Hebrew structuralism, Chomsky's transformational grammar, and the appearance of the Aleppo Codex. The survey itself is divided into six chapters devoted to Biblical Hebrew, the Second Commonwealth and Rabbinic Hebrew, the Masoretes, communal traditions and Jewish languages, medieval grammarians and poets, and modern and contemporary Hebrew. The second half of the book is a bibliography on pages 267-448 and an author index to that research. Some 3,700 items by about 1,350 authors are listed in a single alphabetic author listing. Waldman cites books, chapters, journal articles, conference proceedings, Festschriften, and dissertations. The survey itself provides subject access to the bibliography.

29

Native American (Eskimo-Aleut and Other North, Central, and South American Indian)

See also the *Bibliography of Native North Americans* (entry 355).

1010. Booker, Karen M. **Languages of the Aboriginal Southeast: An Annotated Bibliography**. Metuchen, NJ: Scarecrow Press, 1991. 241p. index. LC 90-28779. ISBN 0-8108-2401-9.

Booker intends for her bibliography to update through 1989, for the languages of the aboriginal southeast, Pilling's work (see entry 1021). These are the language families of Muskogean, Algonquian, Caddoan, Iroquoian, Siouan, and a number of isolates. For these languages she includes all types of published materials including conference proceedings and theses, their linguistic analysis, and works on other areas of culture that are language-connected. Nearly all of the 1,912 alphabetically arranged entries have a one- or two-sentence descriptive annotation. An index contains both language and topic headings.

1011. Bright, William. **Bibliography of the Languages of Native California: Including Closely Related Languages of Adjacent Areas**. Metuchen, NJ: Scarecrow Press, 1982. 220p. index. (Native American Bibliography Series, No. 3). LC 82-3331. ISBN 0-8108-1547-8.

In this bibliography Bright updates and expands his earlier work, *Studies in California Linguistics* (University of California Press, 1964). The emphasis, as was previously, is on substantive works about the native languages of California, plus the Yuman languages found in Baja California and Arizona as well as the Numic branch of Uto-Aztecan found in the Great Basin. Bright includes dissertations and theses in this revision. The 1,077 entries, alphabetically arranged, date from the 1800s to 1981. An index lists dialects, languages, language groupings, and such subject terms as borrowing, color terms, general, glottochronology, kin terms, and place names.

1012. Campbell, Lyle. **American Indian Languages: The Historical Linguistics of Native America**. New York: Oxford University Press, 1997. 512p. index. illus. bibliog. maps. (Oxford Studies in Anthropological Linguistics, Vol. 4). LC 95-31905. ISBN 0-19-509427-1.

Native American languages of North, Middle, and South America are covered in this survey of what is currently known about the history of these languages. The book is chock-full of valuable reference materials. A table of phonetic symbols used in the many numerous examples of the languages found throughout the survey precedes the introduction. The introduction and general history chapters themselves have appendixes on Native American pidgins and trade languages and a comparison, in table format, of the major classifications of North American languages. Lists in chapters 4-6 present the classification of languages in the various language families of North, Middle, and South America. These chapters also refer to a set of 27 black and white maps showing language distribution found at the back of the book which precede notes to the chapters and a list of references more than 50 pages in length. Three indexes for authors, subjects, and languages, language families, and proposed genetic relationships complete this excellent, authoritative work by Campbell, himself a scholar with a long list of publications in the field.

1013.   Evans, G. Edward, and Jeffrey Clark. **North American Indian Language Materials, 1890-1965: An Annotated Bibliography of Monographic Works**. Los Angeles, CA: American Indian Studies Center, University of California, 1980. 154p. index. bibliog. (American Indian Bibliographic Series, No. 3).

Evans and Clark's main purpose in compiling this bibliography is to provide an update to Pilling's bibliographies which cover the 19th century and were published between 1887 and 1894 (see entry 1021). It includes, for those North American Indian languages north of the Mexico border, all dictionaries, grammars, orthographies, primers, readers, and the like. The compilers list works alphabetically by author under the language the work treats exclusively or principally. They provide cross-references from any dialects and other languages dealt with in an item. Descriptive, frequently lengthy, annotations accompany the 187 entries. An author/title index is included.

Several related Evans' bibliographies (numbers 1 and 2 in this same series) are more narrowly focused on materials for study and teaching and thus not included here.

1014.   **Handbook of North American Indians. Volume 17. Languages**. Volume editor: Ives Goddard. Washington, DC: Smithsonian Institution, 1996. 957p. index. illus. bibliog. maps (in pocket at end of volume).

Volume 17 on languages is "the tenth volume to be published of a 20-volume set planned to give an encyclopedic summary of what is known about the prehistory, history, and cultures of the aboriginal peoples of North America who lived north of the urban civilizations of central Mexico" (p. xi). In this volume a number of contributors are responsible for the individual chapters surveying the native languages spoken by American Indians (including those of Baja California), Eskimos, and Aleuts. There are 15 chapters on general topics and 12 grammatical sketches of individual languages selected to provide a diversity of language types and geographical coverage. Another valuable chapter on "Sources" attempts to cite, if possible, a printed grammar, dictionary, and collection of texts for each native language of North American. Figures, illustrations, photographs, and photographic reproductions (for example, of pages from primers and syllabaries) are found distributed throughout the volume. In the introduction Goddard supplies a table displaying a consensus classification of the languages which can also be found on the volume map. This well-executed, fold-out map tucked into an end pocket shows the distribution of language families by means of colors and numbers with a map index for other linguistic units. Another smaller map also in color is a reproduction of John Wesley Powell's original 1891 map showing the linguistic stocks of American Indians north of Mexico. A bibliography at the volume's end gathers all references cited by the chapter contributors.

1015.   Loukotka, Čestmír. **Classification of South American Indian Languages**. Johannes Wilbert, editor. Los Angeles, CA: Latin American Center, University of California, Los Angeles, 1968. 453p. index. illus. bibliog. maps. (Latin American Center, University of California, Los Angeles. Reference Series, Vol. 7). LC 67-65490.

The main part of this volume is a classification of South American Indian languages. Loukotka groups some 117 language stocks and languages into 3 main categories: languages of Paleo-American tribes, languages of Tropical Forest tribes, and languages of the Andean tribes. For each of the languages he records, when possible, the most frequent synonyms, geographic location, degree of mixture, citation to a reference (author, date, and page number), and notes on availability of material for less well-documented languages. Some 750 vocabulary lists are interspersed throughout the catalog. The comprehensive bibliography that follows cites 2,201 works, including 346 unpublished manuscripts, up through 1964. There is an ethno-linguistic index of tribal names and synonyms as well as an index of authors. A colored map with its own index registers a total of 1,492 languages.

1016.   Marino Flores, Anselmo. **Bibliografía lingüística de la República Mexicana**. Prólogo de Manuel Gamio. México: Instituto Indigenista Interamericano, 1957. 95p. illus. maps. (Ediciones especiales del Instituto Indigenista Interamericano). LC 59-37910.

Two maps in the first part of this book show the distribution and density for 33 of the indigenous languages in Mexico. A table also indicates, based on 1950 census materials, the number of people, by state, who are monolingual and bilingual. The unannotated bibliography in the second part lists studies under sections for more than 40 indigenous languages from Amuzgo to Zoque. The sections on Maya, Nahuatl, and Otomi have the most entries. A final section lists general language studies of Mexico. A significant number of works date back to the 1800s and early 1900s.

1017.   Marken, Jack W., comp. **The American Indian Language and Literature**. Arlington Heights, IL: AHM Pub. Corp., 1978. 204p. index. (Goldentree Bibliographies in Language and Literature). LC 76-4624. ISBN 0-88295-569-1(cloth); 0-88295-553-5(paper).

The author limits this bibliography to studies on the Indians of North America, excluding Indians of Mexico and South and Central America. Nearly 3,700 unannotated entries are classified in some 15 sections. Four general sections (bibliography, autobiography, general literature, and general language) are followed by geographical sections which are then further subdivided into general literature and general language subsections. The general language subsections are then organized along tribal lines.

1018.   Parodi, Claudia. **La investigacion linguistica en México (1970-1980)**. 1a ed. México: Universidad Nacional Autonoma de México, Instituto de

Investigaciones Filologicas, 1981. 205p. index. (Cuadernos del Instituto de Investigaciones Filologicas). LC 81-215036. ISBN 968-58-0103-7.

A nearly 80-page essay introduces this unannotated bibliography covering studies on both the Indian languages and the Spanish language in Mexico. It includes journals, books, conference proceedings, and Festschriften published from 1970 to 1980. Items concerning the Indian languages are mainly grouped by language family and then by language. Items concerning the Spanish language are grouped under such headings as phonetics and phonology, semantics, grammar, linguistics, psycholinguistics, sociolinguistics, and applied linguistics. Indexes for authors, languages, and subjects conclude the work.

1019.   Parr, Richard T. **A Bibliography of the Athapaskan Languages**. Ottawa: National Museums of Canada, 1974. 333p. maps. (National Museum of Man, Ethnology Division, Paper No. 14). (Mercury Series). LC 75-312128.

In this bibliography Parr brings together materials in linguistics (and in anthropology, archeology, folklore, and ethnomusicology) for the Athapaskan languages. The cutoff date is December 1972. About 5,000 entries are arranged by some 55 languages and include published materials as well as theses and the archive holdings of the Smithsonian, the National Museum of Canada, and other depositories. About one-fourth of the titles are annotated. The author includes five maps showing language group distribution.

1020.   Pentland, David H., and H. Christoph Wolfart. **Bibliography of Algonquian Linguistics**. Winnipeg, Canada: University of Manitoba Press, 1982. 333p. index. LC 83-164492. ISBN 0-88755-128-9(cloth); 0-88755-611-6(paper).

Listing printed works and theses from 1891 through 1981, this bibliography updates Pilling's Algonquian language bibliography published in 1891 (see entry 1021). It also replaces an earlier one by Pentland, et al. (1974). Some earlier titles left out of Pilling and reprints or new editions of works originally published before 1891 are included here. The authors have, unlike Pilling, chosen to include materials on Wiyot, Yurok, and Beothuk. Entries, often with short content notes and references to reviews, are arranged by author. Co-authors, editors, and the like are cross-referenced. An index arranged first by language and then by subject identifies entries by author, date and short title.

1021.   Pilling, James Constantine. **Bibliographies of the Languages of the North American Indians**. New York: AMS Press, 1973. 3v. LC 76-174200. ISBN 0-404-07390-5.

This 3-volume set is a reprint of the nine annotated bibliographies originally published from 1887 to 1894 as Nos. 1, 5-6, 9, 13-16, and 19 of the Bulletin issued by the Bureau of Ethnology of the Smithsonian Institution. The languages covered are: Eskimo, Siouan, Iroquoian, Muskhogean, Algonquian, Athapascan, Chinookan, Salishan, and Wakashan. They are the most comprehensive works available for the 19th century. Evans and Clarks's bibliography updates this work from 1890 through 1965 (see entry 1013); for the languages of the southeast Booker's bibliography updates it through 1989 (see entry 1010); while Pentland's work updates it from 1891 through 1981 for the Algonquian language (see entry 1020).

1022. Pottier, Bernard. **Bibliographie américaniste, linguistique amérindienne.** Société des américanistes. Paris: Musée de l'Homme, 1967-1982. 9v. index. LC 75-378226.

This voluminous bibliography covers linguistic works written mainly in English and Spanish published from 1965 to 1982 that deal with the Indian languages of North, Central, and South America. Entries are accompanied by complex geographic, language, and subject codes. Each volume has indexes utilizing these codes. Volumes have various co-editors.

1023. Singerman, Robert. **Indigenous Languages of the Americas: A Bibliography of Dissertations and Theses.** Lanham, MD: Scarecrow Press, 1996. 311p. index. (Native American Bibliographical Series, No. 19). LC 95-35046. ISBN 0-8108-3032-9.

Singerman's bibliography with 1,679 entries attempts to list for 1892-1992 all Ph.D. dissertations and the more-difficult-to-locate Master's theses and essays (also designated Master's papers, projects, or reports) issued by universities and other institutions of higher learning in the United States including Puerto Rico, Canada, and the United Kingdom which deal with the languages of all tribal groups in the Western Hemisphere. Most such works were written in English, but some in French and Spanish are also cited. The entries are arranged in a classification system which first lists general works in a section further subdivided by topic (for example, biography, loan-words, discourse, phonology, and sign language). Other sections are devoted to language families (such as Eskimo-Aleut, Haida, Keresan, isolates, and pidgins and Creoles) further subdivided by language/dialect and two more sections on Mesoamerica, and South America and the Caribbean. For each work, the author, title, degree, institution, and date are supplied along with a citation to such publications as *Dissertation Abstracts International, Masters Abstracts International,* and other sources as available. If the work was subsequently published, Singerman also includes a citation to that publication. About half of the entries have a brief descriptive annotation. He supplies an index of authors and an index of languages, dialects, and tribes.

1024. Tovar, Antonio, and Consuelo Larrucea de Tovar. **Catálogo de las lenguas de América del Sur: con clasificaciones, indicaciones tipológicas, bibliografía y mapas.** Nueva ed. refundida. Madrid: Gredos, 1984. 632p. index. bibliog. maps. LC 86-210170. ISBN 84-249-0958-5(cloth); 84-249-0957-7(paper).

While this newly revised edition of Tovar presents the latest research in classifying the Indian languages of South America, it does not entirely replace Loukotka's earlier work with its wealth of information, particularly the vocabulary lists (see entry 1015). The two works complement each other and should be used together. Typological evidence for Tovar's classification, accompanied by references to specific relevant research, is contained in the first 27 short chapters. A long, exhaustive bibliography of these accompanying references arranged by author follows. Six maps illustrate the geographical distribution of some of the languages. A comprehensive index of more than 2,300 language and dialect names completes this excellent reference work.

1025.   Voegelin, Charles Frederick, and Z. S. Harris. **Index to the Franz Boas Collection of Materials for American Linguistics**. Baltimore, MD: Linguistic Society of America, 1945. 43p. index. (Language Monograph, No. 22). LC 46-1739.

This is the index to a collection of manuscripts, now housed in the Library of the American Philosophical Society, gathered by Franz Boas as authors submitted their papers to him for the *International Journal of American Linguistics* and for *Publications of the American Ethnological Society*. Some have been published in whole, in part, or used as a basis for subsequent publication. The main part of the index lists linguistic items alphabetically arranged by the language under study. A short description of the physical item is given; most entries are also accompanied by a short description of the contents and in some cases references are given to the publications resulting from the manuscript. There are 2 cross-reference lists, one by manuscript number, the other by author. This is an important tool for access to a lot of original research on American Indian languages.

1026.   Weeks, John M., comp. **Mesoamerican Ethnohistory in United States Libraries: Reconstruction of the William E. Gates Collection of Historical and Linguistic Manuscripts**. Culver City, CA: Labyrinthos, 1990. 247p. index. bibliog. illus. map. LC 89-84021. ISBN 0-911437-37-1.

Gates, an Ohio businessman and enigmatic figure in the history of Mesoamerican anthropology and ethnohistory, assembled an extensive collection of manuscript materials and rare imprints relating to Mesoamerian ethnohistory, particularly linguistics. The introduction provides valuable background information on Gates' collecting activities, disposition of the collection, and his relations with various individuals and universities. Weeks' catalogue of the Gates collection provides a descriptive guide to the manuscripts and the various depositories which received portions of the original collection during its dispersion between 1924 and 1946. Tulane, Princeton, and the Brigham Young Universities received rare imprints and original manuscripts. The guide also identifies the photographic, transcript, and typewritten copies made by Gates and given to other institutions such as the Library of Congress, Newberry Library, Tozzer Library, John Carter Brown Library, and the National Anthropological Archives.

"The bibliography contains almost 800 entries, covering about 350 years of linguistic literature, and representing about 30 indigenous languages" (p. 19). The phrase historical and linguistic in the subtitle of this work is broadly interpreted to include "Bibles, catechisms, confessionaries, conversation and phrase books, devotinaries, doctrinaries, grammars, hymnals, sacramentals, sermonaries, and vocabularies as well as pictorial manuscripts, historical narratives, and other material of predominantly historical or nonlinguistic interest" (p. 19). Entries are arranged by author or main entry and include title, date of publication or compilation, and pagination. For published works, place of publication and publisher are given. Additional information provided may include information such as the location of original manuscripts or published work; location of photographic, typescript, or transcript copies; citation in sale or other catalogues; and references to bibliographies and other guides to the literature. Most entries indicate the indigenous language subject of the work and other descriptive information including linguistic and historical data. There are indexes for personal names, place names, and subjects. The guide is a treasure trove of primary source materials from the 16th to the 19th century for Mesoamerica.

30

Artificial Languages

1027. Dulichenko, A. D. **Mezhdunarodnye vspomogatelnye yazyki**. Tallinn: "Valgus," 1990. 447p. index. bibliog.

Although the introductory materials and headings are in Russian, the works listed in this bibliography of international auxiliary languages are cited in the original language of publication, many of which are in English and other Western European languages. The main bibliography cites 780 works arranged by date, then by language. It begins with a work by Claudius Galenus from the 1st century A.D. and ends with a1973 work on Popido. Appendixes contain various indexes: chronology, language, personal name, and country.

1028. Harrison, Richard K. **Bibliography of Planned Languages (Excluding Esperanto): A Guide to Books and Brochures Pertaining to Planned Languages (Also Known as "Universal" Languages, "Constructed" Languages, and "International" Languages)**. Orlando, FL: R. K. Harrison, 1992. 60p. LC 92-90270. ISBN 0-9633073-0-4. Available: http://www.webcom. com/~donh/biblio.html. (Accessed February 21, 1999).

Harrison excludes Esperanto from his bibliography since it is much easier to obtain information about it than other planned languages. Entries include author, title, imprint with pagination, and Library of Congress call number. These are alphabetically arranged under a general heading of interlinguistics, then by language name: Volapük, Ido, Ro, Occidental-Interlingue, Novial, Interlingua (here it refers to the language invented by Dr. Alexander Gode), Glasa, modified English, Latin and modified Latin, parsigraphy and similar plans (symbol and number languages), a posteriori languages (derived from existing languages), a priori and mixed languages, and fictitious languages. Brief notes or samples from a particular language sometimes accompany entries. The bibliography is not meant to be comprehensive; it only contains items readily available, well-known, or historically important. An expanded, revised (?) bibliography is maintained by the author on the Web (copyright 1991-1995). Its organization is the same except that fictitious languages have been integrated into the a priori list.

1029. Tonkin, Humphrey. **Esperanto and International Language Problems: A Research Bibliography**. 4th ed., rev. Washington, DC: Esperantic Studies Foundation, 1977. 45p. index. LC 77-156043.

This bibliography dealing with international language problems, particularly as these relate to the international language Esperanto, is organized into 2 parts. Part I deals with the problem and the search for a solution. Part II focuses on Esperanto with chapters on Esperanto as a language, as a social phenomenon, as a literary language, and in society. Inside each chapter the text is arranged in numbered paragraphs within which the author may refer to one or more works. An index of authors refers the user back to these numbered paragraphs.

31

Pidgin and Creole Languages

1030. Baird, Keith E. **A Critical Annotated Bibliography of African Linguistic Continuities in the Spanish-Speaking Americas**. Thesis (Ph.D.) Union of Experimenting Colleges and Universities, Cincinnati, 1982. 130p.

A lengthy introduction with valuable background information precedes this selective annotated bibliography. Baird arranges the entries under headings for Africa, Spain, Americas-General, and then the Spanish-speaking countries of Central and South America, the latter in alphabetical order. Critical annotations ranging in length from a short sentence to 3 paragraphs accompany the entries.

1031. Hazaël-Massieux, Marie-Christine. **Bibliographie des études créoles: langues, cultures, sociétés**. Québec: CIRELFA; ACCT; Institut d'études créoles et francophones; distr. Diffusion Didier érudition, 1991. 254p. index. ISBN 2-86460-167-2.

Annotations accompany approximately a third of the more than 1,000 entries in this bibliography of studies on French Creoles and colonial varieties of French as well as new varieties such as Senegalese French. In addition to the annotation, an average of four to six descriptors (geographic terms, language names, subjects) are assigned to each work. The compiler has deliberately excluded works which are virtually inaccessible, documents shorter than five pages in length, Creole texts not considered to be literary or significant, works reiterating positions of the same author in a more representative study already included in the bibliography, works on the history of colonization, and finally, literary works in French in which creole texts of varying lengths are cited. There are subject and author indexes. Subject categories with many listings—some with as many as 200-300, and no subheadings are quite tedious and time-consuming to use. All cited materials may be obtained through interlibrary loan from the Institut d'Études Créoles et Francophones de l'Université de Provence.

1032. Hughes, H. G. A. **Papiamentu: A Bibliography**. Afonwen, Clwyd: Gwasg Gwenffrwd, 1993. 21p. (1 microfiche).

Papiamento, variously spelled Papiamentu or Papyamentu, is a Spanish-based creole spoken in Aruba, Bonaire, and Curaçao, Caribbean islands of the Lesser Antilles north of Venezuela. It has the longest literary tradition of any creole language based on the publication of a short catechism in 1825. A list of references consulted by the author precedes the bibliography itself. Entries for works written in English, French, Spanish, and German provide a bare minimum of bibliographic information. It is meant to be a short, introductory bibliography only.

1033.   Oukada, Larbi, comp. **Louisiana French: An Annotated, Linguistic Bibliography**. Lafayette, LA: Center for Louisiana Studies, University of Southwestern Louisiana, 1979. 133p. index. LC 79-56146.

The term Louisiana French as used in this bibliography with its diachronic perspective, encompasses three varieties of French in the state: Colonial French, the speech of the descendants of the first settlers from Europe; Acadian French spoken in southwest Louisiana by settlers from Nova Scotia; and, the creole spoken mainly by blacks.

The 924 entries for works published from 1807 through 1976 are arranged in sections according to form: master's theses, dissertations, articles, books, French periodicals printed in Louisiana, and newspaper and magazine articles. Except for a final section listing studies on the sociocultural characteristics of French-speaking Louisianians, all works listed deal with linguistic aspects of Louisiana French. Within each section the arrangement is chronological. The compiler provides descriptive annotations varying in length and detail depending on the importance of the work. A combined author/main entry/subject index is not very effective in providing subject access.

1034.   Primus, Wilma J. **Creole and Pidgin Languages in the Caribbean; a Select Bibliography**. St. Augustine, Trinidad: University of the West Indies, Library, 1972. 80p. index. (Bibliographic Series/University of the West Indies, St. Augustine, Trinidad, Library, No. 5).

Though a few works written prior to 1930 are included here, its focus is on works written after this date. Material on language teaching has been included for areas in which the creole language exists side by side with the standard language from which it was derived. The bibliography is divided into five main sections: bibliographies, general works, English-based creoles and pidgins, French-based creoles and pidgins, and Spanish/Portuguese-based creoles and pidgins. Because of Reinecke's anticipated bibliography (see entry 1035), the author was highly selective in the general works section. Other sections are meant to be extensive, if not fully comprehensive. There are nearly 600 unannotated entries for both monographs and journal articles. There is an index of authors.

1035.   Reinecke, John E., et al., comps. **A Bibliography of Pidgin and Creole Languages**. Honolulu, HI: University Press of Hawaii, 1975. 804p. index. (Oceanic Linguistics Special Publication, No. 14). LC 73-91459. ISBN 0-8248-0306-X.

Numerous people collaborated on this comprehensive annotated bibliography of pidgin and creole languages. All types of material in many languages published up through 1971, with the exception of newspaper articles, audio materials, and background works, are included. It has more than 10,000 entries arranged under 117 headings for single languages or language families, and 3 more for bibliographies, collective works, and general and miscellaneous. Some headings are followed by a short introduction detailing the types of work included in that section. Short descriptive, and sometimes evaluative, annotations accompany most entries. An index divided into 4 parts lists names of authors, translations of the Christian scriptures, titles of anonymous publications, and periodicals printed wholly or partially in pidgin/creole languages.

1036. Tomás, Maria Isabel. **Os crioulos portugueses do Oriente: Uma bibliografia**. Macau: Instituto Cultural de Macau, 1992. 247p. index. maps. (Documentos & ensaios, 2). ISBN 972-35-0112-0.

More than 900 items are listed in this classified bibliography of Asian Creole Portuguese. It covers Portuguese-based Creoles from Diu to Macau, the endogenous creoles of the former Portuguese Orient which share sociohistorical and structural characteristics. Chapter 1 lists bibliographies while chapter 2 lists general works followed by five chapters devoted to India, Sri Lanka, Malacca and Singapore, Indonesia, and Macau and Hong Kong. A final chapter, chapter 8, deals with the influence of Portuguese on certain languages of the Asian region. Thirteen maps illustrate language distribution. There are three indexes: authors/compilers, anonymous titles, and maps.

1037. **Tsuzaki Reinecke Pidgin Creole Collection: List of Cataloged Publications**. Honolulu, HI: University of Hawaii Library, University of Hawaii at Manoa, 1990. 271p., 23p (indexes). index.

During their years of work on pidgin and creole linguistics, Drs. John Reinecke and Stanley Tsuzaki collected large numbers of books, periodicals, theses, papers, tracts, conference proceedings, and other miscellaneous items. They donated these materials to the Hamilton Library Special Collections at the University of Hawaii at Manoa in the early 1980s. Though the collection continues to have additions, this list includes only holdings current through November 1989. The list is organized for the most part alphabetically according to language subject headings devised by Dr. Reinecke, then alphabetically by author or main entry. Each of the 2,151 entries is numbered and may include a full cataloging record or a reprint record which only has author, title, and subject citations without necessarily complete information about the publication of the larger piece from which it is taken. The latter citations are potentially aggravating to the researcher who finds a work of interest, but cannot locate it other than by visiting the collection itself. There is an index of names (personal, uniform title, corporate, conference) and an index to journals.

1038. Valdman, Albert, et al., eds. **Bibliographie des études créoles: langues et littératures**. Préparée par le Comité international des études créoles. Paris: Agence de coopération culturelle et technique/Bloomington, IN: Indiana University Creole Institute, 1983. 152p. index. (Publication CIRELFA. Bulletins signalétiques). LC 86-220902.

The purpose of this bibliography is to update for French-based pidgins and creoles Reinecke's general bibliography (see entry 1035). Nearly all of the 948 entries, arranged according to language and geographic area, are provided with a series of major and minor descriptors. The most important works are indicated by an asterisk and many of these have annotations. The editors provide an index of authors.

1039. Voorhoeve, Jan, and Antoon Donicie. **Bibliographie du négro-anglais du Surinam: avec une appendice sur les langues créoles parlées à l'intérieur du pays**. 's-Gravenhage: Martinus Nijhoff, 1963. 115p. index. (Koninklijk Instituut voor Taal-, Land- en Volkenkunde. Bibliographical Series, 6). LC 81-187623.

This is a bibliography of both works about and written in the Sranan language. Much of the latter is religious literature. Some 113 of the 467 entries are concerned with studies of the language. These range in date from 1765 to 1961 and are for books and periodical articles in Dutch, German, French, or English. An appendix provides about 40 references on the creole dialects spoken in the interior of Surinam. The index is for authors and subjects.

Author Index

Title Index

Diacritical marks that appear in the main body of the text may not appear in this index. Reference is to entry numbers.

Subject Index